The Economic Way of Thinking

SECOND EDITION

Paul Heyne
University of Washington

SCIENCE RESEARCH ASSOCIATES, INC.
Chicago, Palo Alto, Toronto
Henley-on-Thames, Sydney, Paris, Stuttgart

A Subsidiary of IBM

With gratitude to my joint authors,
Wallie and Ruth

Library of Congress Cataloging in Publication Data

Heyne, Paul T
 The economic way of thinking.

 Includes index.
 1. Economics. I. Title.
HB171.5.H46 1976   330   76–21665
ISBN 0–574–19250–6

Preface

Introductory economics has long been an easy subject to teach. It's been a hard subject to *take*, but that's another matter. Moreover, the amount of learning that comes out of principles courses bears no reasonable relationship to the amount of teaching that goes in.

Principles of economics has been an easy course to teach because we have used it largely to regurgitate the bits of technique acquired during our own training in economics. There are so many such bits and pieces, and they are so hard for students to grasp, that the principles teacher need never worry about what to do today. He can always introduce a new complication or spend the hour clarifying the complication introduced yesterday. And he doesn't even have to prepare his complications. A single phrase—elasticity, total-average-marginal revenue, long-run competitive equilibrium, marginal-value-product, IS-LM, the multiplier—will serve as an adequate text for an entire class session.

What Are We After?

What should be the learning goal in the beginning economics course? It is clear from what has already been said that the present author has little use for what he takes to be the usual learning goal: the introducing the student to bits and pieces of technique. Why should we want a beginning student to be familiar with the concepts of average variable, average total, and marginal cost, their downward-then-upward shapes, the necessary intersection of marginal cost at the low point of average cost, and everything else contributing to the demonstration that in the long run, under perfectly competitive conditions, price will be equal to average total and marginal cost for all firms after quasi-rents have been capitalized? To ask the question is to answer it. We have no good reason for wanting a beginning student to know all this. Then why have we continued to teach it?

Part of the explanation is our commendable concern to teach *theory*. It is economic theory that gives to economics almost all its predictive or clarifying power. Without theory, we must grope our way blindly through economic problems, conflicting opinions, and opposing policy proposals.

But economic theory has proved itself unusually difficult to communicate. So those responsible for teaching undergraduate economics, struck by the apparent failure of theory-oriented principles courses, have sometimes opted instead for a problems-and-issues course. In such a course, students typically read and discuss statements by labor leaders, industry representatives, agricultural lobbyists, politicians, and a few domestic radicals or foreign socialists. They look at figures on income distribution, gross national product, employment, prices, and rates of economic growth. They read and discuss the arguments for guaranteed incomes and against planned obsolescence, for free enterprise and against unregulated competition, for business social responsibility and against the welfare state. And when it is all over, what have they learned? They have learned that opinions abound, with data to support every one of them, that "it's all relative," that every American is entitled to his opinion, and that economics is not a science and probably a waste of time.

The insistence upon teaching theory is correct insofar as it is a denial of the significance of facts without theories. Theory is essential! But what theory? Economic theory, of course. But that begs the real question. What *kind* of economic theory? And in what *context*? Before we can answer we must know what we're after.

Concepts and Applications

The author of this book wants beginning students to master a set of concepts that will help them think more coherently and consistently about the wide range of social problems that economic theory illuminates. The principles of economics makes sense out of buzzing confusion. They clarify, systematize, and correct the daily assertions of newspapers, political figures, ax grinders, and barroom pontiffs. And the applicability of the economist's thought tools is practically unlimited. Students should come to appreciate all of this in a beginning course.

But they won't unless we, the teachers and textbook writers, persuade them. And we can only persuade them by showing them. *The principles of economics must therefore be taught as tools of analysis.* The teaching of a concept must take place in the context of application. Better, the potential application should be taught first, then the tool. There is so much evidence from pedagogy to support this approach that it's hard at first to understand how any other approach could ever have conquered the field.

"Here is a problem. You recognize it as a problem. What can we say about it?" That's step one.

"Here is how economists think about the problem. They employ the concept of such-and-such." Step two entails the exposition of some concept of economic theory.

After the applicability of the concept to the original problem has been demonstrated and some of the implications examined, the concept should be applied to additional problems. That's step three.

It isn't as easy as one-two-three, of course, and we don't mean to imply that it is. The teaching of economic principles requires imagination, insight, a knowledge of current events, and a sense of perspective, as well as familiarity with the formal techniques of economic analysis. Those are all scarce goods. And it presupposes a conviction on the part of the teacher that economic theory really is useful for something more than answering artificial questions and passing equally artificial examinations.

The Virtue of Restraint

Perhaps no one would disagree in principle with any of the above. If so, our practice has been far out of step with our precept. One reason is undoubtedly the obsession with formal technique that characterizes so much teaching of economic theory at all levels. The disciple will very rarely rise above the master. And if the masters in our profession are more concerned with form than content, the effects will be felt at the principles level. We need not debate here the question of how much of the material taught in intermediate and advanced theory texts really belongs there, or what balance should be struck in graduate theory courses between the logic-mathematics and the economics of theory. For the question of what should go into a beginning course can be answered without resolving the other questions. And that answer is: *Very little*.

For very little indeed of what might go into a Compleat and Current Compendium of Economic Theory is actually useful in enabling us to make sense of the real world and to evaluate policy proposals. Almost all the genuinely important things that economics has to teach are elementary concepts of relationship that people could almost figure out for themselves if they were willing to think carefully.[1]

The challenge is getting people to *appreciate* these few, simple concepts. To do that, we must practice the virtue of restraint. We must attempt less and thereby accomplish more. An introductory course should distinguish itself as much by what it excludes as by what it incorporates. Unless it is our aim to impress students with the esoteric quality of economists' knowledge, we should teach no theory in the introductory course that cannot be put to work immediately. Otherwise we drown the beginning student; he is made to thrash about so desperately that he doesn't learn to swim a single stroke. Our aim should be to get him swimming and to instill in him the confidence that through practice he can learn to swim better.

Every introductory economics teacher ought to read a short essay by Noel McInnis entitled "Teaching More with Less." Here are three excerpts:

> I dare say that all of us who teach have been guilty of telling our students much more than they cared—or needed—to know. In fact, I would theorize that we have probably been

1. The best argument for this view that I have heard is provided by Ely Devons in the first two of his *Essays in Economics* (London: George Allen and Unwin, 1961), pp. 13–46.

telling them more about our subjects than *we* care to know. That is one reason why we feel compelled to rely on notes to deliver lectures.

Our present methods of communicating often obscure meaning rather than reveal it. . . . We often see the tragic results of this in our "best" students, who can repeat what we have told them but cannot apply it in a new context so that it means something. Their learning may have been comprehensive, but it has not been comprehend*ing*.

Survey courses in almost all disciplines are becoming increasingly impractical because of their compulsive attempt to cover all relevant information. They could be made highly practical once again—or perhaps for the first time—if they were organized to convey the five or six most fundamental organizing and conceptual principles of the discipline, utilizing only the most immediately relevant information to bring the principles of life.[2]

The author of this book agrees wholeheartedly with McInnis. Our implementation of this vision will undoubtedly be found far from perfect. But the teacher who wonders why this or that topic is not treated in the book, or why there is no complete exposition of some familiar portion of theory, should remember that knowledge is imparted by what is left out as well as by what is included. Judgments on relevance and relative importance will, of course, vary. But the argument of McInnis should be faced every time we are tempted to add another jot or tittle to the corpus of what we teach in beginning principles courses.

One Semester or Two?

Every economics teacher, whether of graduates or undergraduates, knows how disconcertingly little most students bring with them from principles courses into subsequent studies. Sometimes they don't seem to remember anything except that they've "heard of it." Is the solution more credit hours of introduction? In our judgment the solution lies rather in the direction of fewer hours spent in the introductory course.

What is true and relevant tends to get lost when a beginning course is extended over two semesters. The student gets many fuzzy ideas of what the subject is *about*, but little grasp of what it *is*.

Moreover, there are too many pedagogical and administrative problems associated with the truncated unity of a two-semester single course. Teachers change, textbooks change, micro comes before macro and then macro is put before micro, students drop out after the first semester and return two years later for the second semester. Why have we nonetheless persisted? It sometimes seems as if we're afraid to teach it all in one semester for fear that we'll cut our demand in half. If we can persuade the curriculum makers, especially in the business schools, that six hours is the absolute minimum, we can better maintain the demand for our services.

But they're beginning to find out what happens in introductory economics courses. Or is it that they're only now beginning to talk about it openly? The handwriting is on the wall for required but onerous and useless courses. Perhaps we should change our tactics before it's too late.

2. *Change: The Magazine of Higher Education* (January–February 1971), pp. 49, 50, 51.

One worthwhile semester can leave the beginning student eager for more. And economic education doesn't have to end with the introductory course. It won't, at least for many of the students whom we want to continue, if we do a better job of getting them started. The demand for economic principles may even prove to be elastic: if we cut the hourly cost in half, the number of customers may more than double.

Some economists have argued in discussions with the author that although a one-semester course may be adequate for the general student, two semesters are the essential minimum for economics or business majors. We haven't been convinced. We maintain that a brief and lively introduction to economics is the best start for everyone, whether he or she plans never to take another course or to go on to graduate school in economics. After all, a one-semester principles course does not preclude subsequent courses in theory, courses that could be required or strongly recommended for majors. And more students might enroll in the theory courses if the introductory course managed to persuade them that economic theory is a worthwhile and occasionally even an exciting study.

Anyone who teaches introductory economics for fifteen or twenty years has numerous opportunities to borrow good ideas from others and time enough to forget from whom they were borrowed. This is pleasant because it nourishes an illusion of originality, but it is embarrassing when acknowledgments should be made. I am genuinely grateful to more people than I can remember, and I hope they'll remind me the next time I see them. Those who are familiar with Alchian and Allen's *University Economics* will know how much I have learned fron that source. Armen A. Alchian and William R. Allen pioneered with their demonstration that introductory economics could be a useful and even exciting course. I want to acknowledge my debt to them while absolving them from all responsibility for any misguided "improvements" of my own.

The second edition of this book has been improved in many ways through the comments of W. H. Hutt (University of Dallas), Ronald A. Krieger (Goucher College), Donald A. Wells (University of Arizona), John B. Egger (Southern Methodist University), Richard A. King (North Carolina State University), Howard Miller (Northwest Nazarene College), James G. Witte (Indiana University), Peter L. Danner (Marquette University), Kenneth D. Goldin (California State University, Fullerton), Alan Randall (University of Kentucky), and Edward B. Bell (The Cleveland State University).

Thomas Johnson of North Carolina State University has been such a valuable source of ideas, criticism, and encouragement since this book was first conceived that he cannot be entirely absolved, as can the others, from all blame for its remaining errors and shortcomings. And Marjorie Edens and Juliana Heyne have been notorious accessories before the fact.

Paul Heyne

Contents

The Theory of Economics does not furnish a
body of settled conclusions immediately applicable to policy. It is a method rather than a
doctrine, an apparatus of the mind, a technique
of thinking which helps its possessor to draw
correct conclusions.

John Maynard Keynes

The Economic
Way of Thinking

"*Non-economists* tend to be too academic. They abstract too much from the real world."

That isn't the way you usually hear it. People in business and college students who have sampled the writings or the courses of professional economists have often gone away with the suspicion that what they learned was "purely theoretical." Interesting intellectual exercise, perhaps, but not very helpful to anyone who wants to understand how an economy actually works. If you have heard comments to that effect, and are more than half-convinced of their truth, there is little chance we will persuade you otherwise in a short introductory chapter. The author has found economics exciting and important for anyone who wants to understand the problems and possibilities of our society, but your own experience with this course will have to provide the test of that judgment.

It might be helpful, though, if you reflect for a moment on the quotation with which we began. People who sneer at "fancy theories" and prefer to rely on common sense and everyday experience are often in fact the victims of extremely vague and sweeping hypotheses. This morning's newspaper contains a letter from a young person in Pennsylvania who was once "one of a group of teen-age pot smokers. Then a girl in the crowd got pregnant. Her baby was premature and deformed and needed two operations." The newpaper's adviser to the teen-age lovelorn printed that letter approvingly, as evidence that the price of smoking marijuana is high.

Perhaps it is. But suppose the writer of that letter had written: "Then the Pittsburgh Steelers won the Super Bowl and the Philadelphia Flyers took the Stanley Cup." Everyone would object that those events had nothing to do with the group's pot smoking. But how do we know that? If the mere fact that the young girl's misfortunes followed her pot smoking is evidence of a causal relationship, why can't we also infer a causal relationship in the case of the Steelers and the Flyers?

The point is a simple but important one. We cannot discover, prove, or even suspect any kind of causal relationship without having a theory in mind. Our observations of the world are in fact drenched with theory, which is why we usually can make sense out of the buzzing confusion that assaults our eyes and ears. We actually observe only a small fraction of what we "know," a hint here and a suggestion there; the rest we fill in from the theories we hold, small ones and broad ones, vague and precise ones, well tested and poorly tested, widely held and sometimes peculiar, carefully reasoned and dimly recognized.

I. M. D. Little is a distinguished British economist who wrote the sentences with which this chapter began, in an article describing his experiences as an adviser to the British Treasury. Here is the paragraph from which they were taken.

> Economic theory teaches one how economic magnitudes are related, and how very complex and involved these relationships are. Non-economists tend to be too academic. They abstract too much from the real world. No one can think about economic issues without some theory, for the facts and relationships are too involved to organize themselves: they do not simply fall into place. But if the theorist is untutored, he is apt to construct a very partial theory which blinds him to some of the possibilities. Or he falls back on some old and over-simple theory, picked up from somewhere or other. He is also, I believe, apt to interpret the past naively. *Post hoc ergo propter hoc*[1] is seldom an adequate economic explanation. I was sometimes shocked by the naive sureness with which very questionable bits of economic analysis were advanced in Whitehall. Of course, economists may be too academic in another sense: they may not appreciate administrative difficulties, or may lack a sense of political possibility. But, then, there is no danger of these things being overlooked.[2]

Thinking Like an Economist

Economics is basically a way of thinking. The theories of economists, with surprisingly few exceptions, are simply extensions of the assumption that individuals choose those options which seem to them most likely to secure their largest net advantage. Everyone, it is assumed, acts in accordance with that rule: miser or spendthrift, saint or sinner, consumer or seller, politician or business executive, cautious calculator or spontaneous improviser.

Economic theory, we said, is simply an extension of that assumption. But *simply* is a treacherous word. Did you ever have a math instructor who began: "To solve this kind of problem, we simply . . ."—when it wasn't simple to you at all? The economic way of thinking is somewhat like that. The basic assumption resembles a magician's top hat: It seems to be empty; but in practiced hands it produces a fascinating array of surprises. And once you've seen for yourself how it's done, you can go back home and astonish all your friends.

The simile of the magician's top hat is apt in another way. Economics has a reputation for being mysterious and incomprehensible. And because the subject utterly baffles so many who study it, economics has also acquired a reputation for being diffi-

"People's incomes rise on average when they move from rural to urban areas. They also become more likely to commit a crime. Why not reduce the crime rate by taxing the income of those who migrate from the country to the city?"

---

1. Literally, "After this, therefore because of this"; the logical fallacy of assuming that A must have caused B if A preceded B in time. The argument of the penitent Pennsylvania pot smoker is an example.
2. I. M. D. Little, "The Economist in Whitehall," *Lloyds Bank Review* (April 1957).

cult, dull, and irrelevant. This book developed out of a growing suspicion that students have found economic theory to be mystifying and tedious largely because we economists have tried to teach too much. We have dazzled our students with complex theorems and exercises in pure logic instead of helping them to see how economic theory can illuminate their world. This book will try to achieve more by attempting less.

The text is organized around a set of concepts that collectively make up the economist's basic kit of intellectual tools. The tools are all related to the fundamental assumption stated above and are surprisingly few in number. But they are extraordinarily versatile. They unlock such mysteries as foreign exchange rates, business firms that make profits by accepting losses, the nature of money, and different prices charged for "identical" goods—mysteries that are generally conceded to be in the economist's province. But they also shed light on a wide range of issues that are not ordinarily thought of as economic at all: traffic congestion, environmental pollution, the workings of government, and the behavior of college administrators, to mention just a few which you will encounter in the chapters ahead.

The primary goal of this book is to start you thinking the way economists think, in the belief that once you start you will never stop. Economic thinking is addictive. Once you get inside some principle of economic reasoning and make it your own, opportunities to employ it pop up everywhere. You begin to notice that much of what is said or written about economic and social issues is a mixture of sense and nonsense. You get in the habit of sorting the sense from the nonsense by applying the basic concepts of economic analysis. You may even, unfortunately, acquire the reputation of being a cynic, for people who habitually talk nonsense like to cry "cynic" at anyone who points out what they are doing.

But long introductions are seldom either interesting or persuasive. The best way to find out about the economic way of thinking is to do some for yourself. Just one word of caution before you begin.

The economic way of thinking provides a valuable but limited perspective on human behavior and social relationships. A person who knows no economics will probably fail to understand many of the most interesting, important, and sharply contested social issues of our time. But a knowledge of economic theory is not an adequate substitute for a sense of history, a capacity for empathy, and that basic humility which is the hallmark of all good scientists. Alfred North Whitehead has said it most eloquently:

> The duty of tolerance is our finite homage to the abundance of inexhaustible novelty which is awaiting the future, and to the complexity of accomplished fact which exceeds our stretch of insight.[3]

---

3. *Adventures of Ideas* (New York: The Free Press, 1967), p. 52.

Substitutes Everywhere:
The Concept of Demand

Chapter 2

You must have read or heard statements like these many times in your life:

1. Fire safety requires that there be two exits from each apartment unit.

2. We need a new car.

3. Our state will need large amounts of additional water in the coming decade.

4. Traffic surveys have established the need for a new expressway.

5. Every citizen should be able to obtain the medical care he or she needs regardless of ability to pay.

6. There is no substitute for victory.

Fire safety, water, the smooth and rapid movement of traffic, medical care, victory, and even automobiles are all "goods." We say "even" automobiles because some doubts have begun to be expressed about the goodness of automobiles in our congested cities. But you can ask the man who owns one, and a lot of young people who don't. They will assure you that a new car is very much a good. Then what's wrong with those statements?

The element common to all six is the notion of *necessity*. And that is what makes each statement seriously misleading.

Take the first one. Will apartment dwellers who live in units with only one exit all be injured or killed by fires? Of course not. It's just that the risk is greater with one exit than with two. But then why not three exits? Or four? Why not go the whole route and make the outside walls nothing but doors? The answer is that, while fire safety is a good, it isn't the only good apartment dwellers are interested in. Low rental costs and low heating and cooling costs are also goods, to say nothing of protection from burglars who notice that multiple exits are also multiple entrances. Moreover, there are other and perhaps better ways to increase fire safety. Extinguishers, alarm sprinklers, and large ashtrays also reduce the risk to apartment dwellers of injury or death from fire. If more than one exit is required, why not also require a fire extinguisher on every wall?

That sensible-sounding statement about apartment exits overlooks three interrelated facts: (1) Most goods are not free but can be obtained only by sacrificing something else that is also a good. (2) There are substitutes for anything. (3) Intelligent choice among substitutes requires a balancing of additional costs against additional benefits.

Costs and Substitutes

Now go back and look at the other five statements. "We need a new car." Who "needs" a new car? Obviously only those who value a new car more than what they must sacrifice to obtain one. That might be a vacation trip this year, new clothes, a lot of movies, and a stereo set. Is it worth it? There are, after all, plenty of substitutes for a new car: an overhaul of the present one, a used car, a bicycle, a car pool, public transportation, moving closer to work, or staying home more. The intelligent consumer tries to determine his preferences after he has considered these various costs and benefits. Of course, once he has made up his mind he might still want to say "We *need* a new car" in the hope that the definitive tone of his statement will dissuade his wife from making her own comparison of the costs and benefits of a new one.

Consider statement 3: "Our state will need large amounts of additional water in the coming decade." Does any state really need large amounts of additional water? Dams and reservoirs, pipelines, and desalinization plants are ways of obtaining more water. But they have costs. Do the benefits justify the costs? If you think there are no substitutes for water, then you are thinking too academically. You have abstracted unrealistically from the real world. Probably you are assuming that water is used primarily for drinking, whereas in fact the overwhelming bulk of the water consumed in the United States goes for other uses. Since we shall use the case of water a bit later as an extended working exercise, we can pass this problem by for now. You might want to begin thinking, though, about the substitutes for water in such places of chronic scarcity as Arizona and Southern California.

You will be able to make much more sense out of the water problem and the expressway issue we take up next if you keep in mind that entities like *states* or *cities* never really want anything. Wants and goals are always attached ultimately to individuals. What does the person who says "The people want . . ." really mean? That all the people want it? A majority? Those who count? It is usually a good rule in analyzing statements like those above to ask: Who wants more water, or more expressways, or more fire safety?

It's amazing what people will want --- if they think they won't have to pay for it.

> Things are seldom what they seem
> Skim milk masquerades as cream.

The fourth of our misleading propositions—"Traffic surveys have established the need for a new expressway"—leads into one of the vexing issues in city planning. Perhaps it would never have become such a troublesome issue had we realized that expressways have costs as well as benefits, that there are excellent substitutes for more expressways, and that intelligent city planning calls for the weighing of additional benefits against additional costs. Those who hope to derive most of the benefits from a new expressway while paying only a small percentage of the costs will not want others to notice the full costs of the expressway or how many substitutes there really are. That is why they pretend that a traffic survey can establish "needs." But a traffic survey only shows how many cars travel given routes *at existing costs to the drivers*, including such nonmonetary costs as delay, danger, and ulcers. Suppose that the cost of downtown parking increased 500 percent. What do you think would happen to rush-hour traffic? Commuters would form car pools and begin using public transportation. If the cost *to drivers* of commuting were made high enough, through parking charges, toll fees, or some other device, the need for a new expressway could turn overnight into a "need" for a rapid transit system. It's a strange kind of need that can vanish so quickly in the face of a price change.

The fifth statement sounds humanitarian and liberal. "Every citizen should be able to obtain the medical care he or she needs regardless of ability to pay." But how much medical care does any person need? We might all agree that a woman with an inflamed appendix and no money should have an appendectomy completely at the taxpayers' expense if she is unable to meet any of the costs herself. But what of the man with a splinter in his finger? The services of physicians are not free goods, and they would not become free goods even if every physician treated his patients without charging a fee. There just would not be enough physicians to go around if everyone consulted a doctor for every minor ill. The lower the price of visiting a physician, the more frequently will people substitute a trip to the doctor for such other remedies as going to bed, taking it easy, or waiting and hoping. One could rather confidently predict that lower monetary fees would result in higher fees of other sorts, like waiting in line for many hours.

What about the sixth statement: "There is no substitute for victory"? It just isn't so. That may be a good battle cry, but it's unrealistic political analysis. Victory is usually obtained by making sacrifices. If the sacrifices reach a certain intensity, people choose compromise or even defeat, although they are then inclined to *say* that they have "no choice." Once again we notice that the intelligent formulation of policy, including foreign policy, flows from a careful balancing of additional expected costs and additional expected benefits.

The word *expected* should be stressed. We live in a world of uncertainty, forced to make choices that will affect our future without knowing for sure just how they will do so. A common mistake in reasoning about economic problems is to assume that there is no uncertainty or that economic decision makers are omniscient. At last report, omniscience was still a virtue denied to mortal man. Condemned as we are to living with uncertainty, we can at least keep from making matters worse by pretending otherwise. Be alert for statements, in this book and elsewhere, which assume that completely adequate information is always available. You might even notice that information, too, is a good which has costs of acquisition and for which there are substitutes available.

The Concept of Demand

"Needs" turn out to be mere "wants" when we inspect them closely. That's an important difference, for in the case of wants we may ask: "How *urgently* are they wanted?" Economists get at this question through the concept of *demand*. Demand is a concept that *relates amounts that are purchased to the sacrifices that must be made to obtain these amounts.*

Ask yourself the following questions: How many records do you want to own? How many times do you want to go out to dinner in a year? What grade do you want from this course?

If you can answer any of those questions, it is because you have assumed some cost in each case. Suppose you said you want an A from this course and plan to get one. What difference would it make if the price of an A went up? The teacher isn't taking bribes; the price of an A *to you* (that's what counts) is the sacrifice you must make to obtain it. Would you still want an A if it required twenty hours of study a week, whereas a B could be had for just one hour a week? You might still want it, but you would probably not be willing to buy it at such a high price when a fairly good substitute, a B, is so much cheaper. And that is what counts. Human wants seem to be insatiable. But when a want can only be satisfied at some cost—that is to say, by giving up the satisfying of some other wants to obtain it—we all moderate our desires and accept less than we would like to have.

The phenomenon of which we're speaking is so pervasive and so fundamental that some economists have been willing to assign it the status of a law: *the law of demand*. This law asserts that there is a negative relation between the amount of anything that people will purchase and the price (sacrifice) they must pay to obtain it. At higher prices, less will be purchased; at lower prices, more will be purchased.

Would you agree that this generalization can be called a law? Or can you think of exceptions? Genuine exceptions, if they exist at all, are rare. Why would anyone be indifferent to the sacrifices he must make? Or prefer more sacrifice to less? That is what a person would be doing if he took more of something as the cost of obtaining it increased.

Alleged exceptions to the law of demand are usually based on a misinterpretation of the evidence. A masochist, for example, would not provide an exception, because pain is for him a good and not a sacrifice. But what of the familiar case where the price of something rises and people increase their purchases in anticipation of further price rises? If you think about it carefully you will see that this is not an exception to the law of demand. The expectation of higher prices in the future, created by the initial price rise, has increased people's

Let's stock up now before the price goes even higher!

current demand for the item. It is not the higher price but the changed *expectations* that have caused people to buy more. We would observe something quite different if the initial price increase did *not* create those changed expectations.

Another possibility is that changes in the price of substitutes or in available income have not been considered. When the price of beans goes up, but the price of hamburger goes up even farther, people may buy more beans because they are now relatively cheaper. And if people's incomes rise, they may also buy more beans or hamburger despite their higher price.

It has sometimes been argued that certain prestige goods are exceptions to the law of demand. For example, people supposedly buy mink coats because their price is high, not low. No doubt there are people who buy some items largely to impress others with how much they can afford to pay. And people sometimes, in the absence of better information, judge quality by price, so that over a limited range, at least, their willingness to purchase may be positively rather than negatively related to price.

Even these seeming exceptions can be explained in a way consistent with the law of demand. People may be purchasing prestige rather than mere mink, or judging quality by price because they have no better information. But we are not interested in rare curiosities. Whether or not you are willing to call it a law, the fact is undeniable and extremely important: increases in the price of goods will characteristically be accompanied by decreases in the total amount purchased, and decreases in price will characteristically be accompanied by increases in the amount purchased. It is a serious mistake to overlook this relationship.

Money Costs and Other Costs

The price in money that must be paid for something is not a complete measure of its cost to the purchaser. Sometimes, indeed, it is a very inadequate measure, as in the case of the student who wanted an A. Economists know this at least as well as anyone else. The concept of demand definitely does not suggest that money is the only thing that matters to people. Confusion about this point has done so much to create misunderstanding that we might profitably take a moment to clarify the matter.

Consider the case of a man buying soft drinks. Assume that he can purchase them in either returnable bottles or throwaway bottles, and that a six-pack of throwaway bottles is priced at 90 cents, whereas a six-pack of returnable bottles is priced at 80 cents plus an 18-cent deposit. Which will he buy? Which is cheaper?

It depends on the cost to him, of which the retailer's price is only one element. If he doesn't mind saving and returning bottles—that is, if the cost to him of doing so is low—he will probably find the returnable bottles cheaper and will buy them. On the other hand, if he lives in an apartment with very limited storage space, gets to the store rarely, consumes large quantities of soft drinks, and has a waste-disposal chute a few steps from his door, he may well find the throwaway bottles cheaper and will purchase them in preference to returnable bottles.

Now suppose that our hypothetical apartment dweller with a passion for pop attends an ecology conference and comes away convinced that we must recycle to survive. The cost to him of using throwaway bottles suddenly jumps, for now he suffers pangs of guilt every time he tosses a bottle in the waste-disposal chute. The added cost in moral regret may be sufficient to induce him to switch to returnable bottles.

Or it may not. Suppose that he is going on a camping trip and wants to take along a dozen bottles of pop. He must backpack them in to his camp site, and backpack the empties out again if he returns the bottles. The added cost of carrying a dozen empties may be enough to overcome the added cost of an uneasy conscience, so that, in this case at least, he reverts to throwaway bottles. (Of course, he will throw them in a trash can.)

But let's change the last situation. Suppose the price of throwaway bottles is not 90 cents but $1.00, $1.20, or $1.80. At *some* price we may confidently expect that the cost of transporting empties will become less than the combined cost of buying throwaway bottles and living with guilt. (Of course, the deposit on returnable bottles will have to rise at the same time, or he may just buy and discard returnable bottles.)

There are several lessons to be drawn from this tale of the pop bottles. To assert that people purchase less of anything as the cost to them increases does *not* imply that people pay attention only to money, or that people are selfish, or that concern for social welfare does not influence economic behavior. It *does* imply that people respond to changes in cost and—a crucial implication—that a sufficiently large change in price can be counted on to tip almost any balance. When someone says that Americans won't give up the convenience of throwaway bottles and cans unless the government outlaws them, he overlooks several possibilities. A widespread change in attitude toward the environment could overcome the cost of being inconvenienced. And a sufficiently large tax on throwaway containers (call it a deposit if you wish) would make convenience a luxury too expensive to enjoy very frequently.

The essential point in all this is that the money price of obtaining something is only one part, and occasionally even a very small part, of its cost. What the law of demand asserts is that people will do less of what they want to do as the cost to them of doing it increases, and do more as the cost decreases.

Who Needs Water?

People are creatures of habit, in what they think as well as what they do. Perhaps this explains why so many have trouble recognizing the significance of substitutes and hence such difficulty in appreciating the law of demand. Water provides an excellent example.

Just a few years ago there was much concern over a serious water shortage in New York City. Several years of less than normal rainfall had depleted the city's reservoirs, and there was great fear that New York would run short of water during the summer unless consumption could be sharply reduced. A few brave souls suggested that the city should install more water meters and raise the price of water. The suggestion was not taken very seriously because, as everyone supposedly knows, water is a necessity. "People won't go thirsty just because the price of water goes up a little, or even a lot," said the critics. And so New York launched a massive campaign of education plus legal threat to try to get its citizens to be more sparing in their use of water.

Lawn sprinkling and car washing were condemned. Restaurants were told not to give customers a glass of water with their meals unless they specifically asked for it. The ornamental fountains of the city were turned off—largely as a symbolic gesture, since the water in the fountains is recirculated. Citizens were asked to refrain from keeping their beer cool by letting the shower drip on it. One of the more amusing aspects of the campaign was a set of ads for a particular Scotch whiskey that urged people to drink their Scotch with water. The word *water* was crossed out in the advertisement and *soda* was written above it, with an appended admonition to save water by drinking soda.

The water shortage was not relieved by any of these measures but by a providential end to the drought. "Man proposes but God disposes." Even man might have disposed, however, had he proposed more intelligently. The basic error lay in the assumption that water is a necessity. The truth is that there are many substitutes for water, a fact which becomes glaringly obvious as soon as we break loose from the habit of assuming that people do nothing with water except drink it.

Here are just a few of the substitutes for water in New York City: dirty automobiles, brown lawns, plumbers, migration, deodorant, larger refrigerators (to hold the beer that would otherwise be cooled in the shower), plus a host of small inconveniences. The trick is to persuade people to *use* these substitutes: to call the plumber, for example, and have that leaky toilet repaired rather than allow it to continue wasting fifty gallons of water a day. To spend money on a larger refrigerator. To tolerate a dirty automobile. To put an ice cube in their glass of drinking water rather than let the tap run for several minutes to cool the water. In the case of industries using huge quantities of water, to sacrifice the advantages of a New York location in favor of locating near more plentiful water supplies. Or to install recyling equipment.

But what is the best way to induce the use of substitutes? Educational campaigns and moral exhortation can help. But how much? Most people are expert rationalizers when their own interest is involved, and it is all too easy to put off calling the plumber until the end of the month, or next month, or the month after that. Always fully intending, of course, to do one's civic duty and get that leak repaired.

What about criminal penalties for wasting water? Enforcement becomes a problem here. Are the police to stage surprise raids to catch people cooling their beer in the shower? Shall we fine a man for rinsing his tumbler too many times before taking a drink? What constitutes *criminal* waste?

A quite different approach is available. Is there any way to enlist almost everyone in a conscientious effort to seek out and use substitutes for water? A sizable increase in the price of water just might do the job. Wouldn't the careless householder call the plumber more quickly if that leaky toilet cost more per month than the plumber would charge to fix it? Wouldn't people accept dirty automobiles more readily, or at least not let the hose run the whole time they were washing the family car, if water became very expensive? There is some price for water at which it becomes cheaper to buy a new refrigerator than to use the shower as a cooler. Industries that use large quantities of water will tend to locate elsewhere if the price of water is high in their area of first choice.

And so it goes. There are substitutes for anything. A higher money price will induce some people to find and use some of those substitutes. And the higher the price, the more will substitutes be used.

A Useful Device

Many of the most useful concepts in economics can be conveniently expressed by means of graphs.

Suppose that we somehow obtained the following data on the relation between the price per gallon of water and the number of gallons that would be consumed (not swallowed!) per day in New York City at each of these different prices:

Price Charged the Consumer per Gallon	Millions of Gallons Consumed per Day
$.0035	60
.0028	80
.0021	120
.0016	160
.0012	200
.0009	240
.0003	360
.0001	450
.0000	510

We graphed these values in Figure 2A. The dots express graphically the data from the demand schedule above. If you are not

PLUMBERS BILL

$ 26.⁰⁰

WATER BILL

$ 42.⁰⁰

P (PRICE OF WATER PER GALLON)

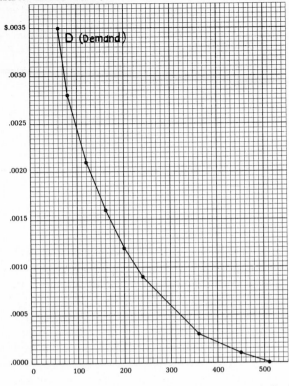

Q (QUANTITY OF WATER PER DAY, in millions of gallons)

Figure 2A   Demand curve for water

accustomed to working with graphs, study Figure 2A until you understand exactly how it was constructed from the demand schedule.

The graph of Figure 2A also *adds* something to the information contained in the schedule. We have connected the dots by means of straight lines. The assumption underlying this procedure is that the price can be changed by very small amounts and that, as a result, there will be small continuous changes in the daily consumption of water. When dealing with the total demand of a large number of consumers, it will be easy to find an individual who makes no response to a small price increase. But you can also find important changes, such as the man who gets his leaky toilet fixed.

Now use the demand curve in thinking through the following questions. (By the way, it is called a demand *curve* even though it is composed exclusively of straight lines. A straight line is simply a curve that, like a baseball pitcher's curve, failed to "break.")

1.   How much water do New Yorkers "need"? How much will they consume per day if the price of water is zero? Is there an important difference between the two questions?

2.   If the price of water has been set for many years at $.0008 per gallon, how much water will the city authorities say that New

Yorkers need per day? What are they assuming when they say this?

3. Suppose that New York's reservoirs are being rapidly depleted, and experts predict that the supply will become critically low before fall unless daily consumption is reduced to 180 million gallons. How could the city's water managers obtain this desired reduction in consumption?

4. Notice by how much water consumption would increase if the price were originally $.0035 and were then decreased to $.0003. Do you think that residents of the city would increase their *drinking* by this amount? How might the additional 300 million gallons per day be used?

Time Is on Our Side

If you are at all the suspicious sort of person, you will have wondered whether water consumption really would or could change in response to price changes by as much as the demand curve indicates. Changes take time. And that is an important observation. Changes in the amount purchased will be greater for any given price change the longer the time period allowed for adjustment.

Check this out for yourself with a mental experiment. Suppose the price of water has been $.0003 a gallon for twenty years and it is raised overnight to $.0028. What substitutions for water will be made *right away*? What substitutions would you expect to observe after a month or two had passed? What substitutions would you expect to observe over the next ten years—assuming that everyone expects the price to remain at the higher level?

Try a similar mental experiment with the price of gasoline. Suppose that the federal government levied an additional tax on gasoline of 50 cents per gallon. How do you think this would affect the amount purchased in the subsequent week? In the subsequent six months? After four years had elapsed?

By taking our examples almost entirely from the area of household decisions, we may have obscured the important fact that customers include producers as well as consumers. Business firms use water and gasoline, too, and they sometimes use so much that they are exceptionally sensitive to price changes. You'll be neglecting some of the major factors that cause demand curves to slope downward if you overlook the contribution producers make to the demand for many goods. In the case of water, location decisions are often made on the basis of the expected price of water, and those decisions then affect the quantities demanded in different geographic areas.

But it takes time for customers to find and begin to use substitutes. It also takes time for producers to devise, produce, and publicize substitutes. As a result, the amount by which people increase or decrease their purchases when prices change depends very much on the time period over which we are observing the adjustment. Occa-

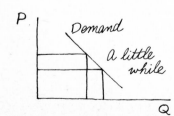

sionally even a rather large price increase (or decrease) will lead to no significant decrease (or increase) in consumption—*at first*. And this sometimes causes people to conclude that price has no effect on consumption. A very mistaken conclusion! Nothing in this world happens instantaneously. People, creatures of habit that they are, must be allowed time to prove that there are substitutes for anything.

Once Over Lightly

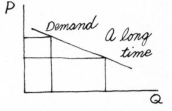

Every good has substitutes: other goods which will be used in its stead when the cost of using the original good rises, goods for which the original good will become a substitute when their cost rises. Pork replaces beef when the price of beef goes up, and a restaurant beef-steak takes the place of a movie when theater tickets become more expensive.

By talking about "needs," we can sometimes win arguments we might otherwise lose. Needs are actually wants of many different urgencies.

People want more or less of a good as the cost those people must pay decreases or increases.

The concept of *demand* is preferable to the concept of *need* because demand relates the amounts that are purchased to the sacrifices that must be made to obtain these amounts.

The "law of demand" asserts that more will be purchased at lower prices, less at higher prices—assuming that something in addition to the price has not changed to offset this consequence.

The money cost of a good is only one part of the cost that affects people's decisions.

A sufficiently large change in money cost (price) can usually over-come the effects that nonmoney costs exert on people's decisions.

A change in price will usually induce a larger change in amounts purchased when more time is allowed for consumers and producers to learn about and invent new substitutes.

QUESTIONS FOR DISCUSSION

1. Assume that Congress has decided to reduce consumption of nonreusable containers in order to preserve Spaceship Earth. Evaluate the following arguments that might be used in the discussion of how to go about achieving this goal.

    a. "We know we cannot survive unless we stop using things and then discarding them. The only sensible approach, therefore, is a legal ban on all nonreu-sable containers of any kind."

    b. "People will do the right thing once they understand the problem. I don't think we should start passing laws. We should assume that the American peo-ple are public-spirited and we should educate them to the facts."

    c. "It has been proposed by some that we place a tax on the manufacture of dis-posable containers to encourage the use of deposit-and-return. This would not work because people just would not care about the tax. Moreover, a tax says in effect that it's all right to pollute if you're rich, but not if you're poor."

2. Most systems of hospitalization insurance substantially reduce the cost to the patient of hospitalization, sometimes to zero. How does this affect hospital use? Why? Evaluate the argument that it does not affect hospital use since "no one gets sick just because hospitals are cheap, or avoids getting sick because they're expensive."

3. In 1967 the president of the American Medical Association was quoted as saying that medical care was a privilege and not a right. Today the AMA officially proclaims that "health care is the right of everyone." What quantity and quality of health care do you suppose they're talking about?

4. In 1973 the average home in the Pacific Northwest consumed 15,000 kilowatts of electricity annually, compared with a national average of about half that, 7700 kilowatts per year. What principles discussed in the text do you suppose this illustrates?

5. Here is a classroom exercise that might be fun and also sharpen your ability to recognize substitution possibilities. Let one person come up with two goods that seem to have no connection and challenge others to construct a plausible set of circumstances in which one would be a substitute for the other. (Avoid the easy, though correct, answer that all goods are in the last analysis substitutes inasmuch as the acquisition of each uses up scarce time or income.)

6. If a prestigious store (Neiman-Marcus in Dallas, for example) were to put its Chanel Number 5 perfume on sale for one-fourth the current price, do you think customers would purchase more? What do you think would happen if a drugstore in a modest-income neighborhood did the same thing? Suppose that each store sold Chanel Number 5 under another label, one that customers had never heard of, and offered it successively at each of the two prices. At which price do you think each store would sell more perfume?

7. If the government forbids motorists to drive more than 55 miles per hour, does everyone stay within the 55-mile limit? What are the costs of going faster? What are some of the costs of going faster that do not fall on the speeding motorist? Do these latter costs affect motorists' decisions? Why might the fact that faster driving uses up more of the nation's scarce petroleum reduce the speed of some drivers but not others?

8. Why do people live in New York City if the costs of doing so—high rents, noise, dirt, congestion, the risks of being robbed or assaulted—are so high? Is it true that most of them "have no choice"? What do you think would happen if the costs listed above were significantly reduced?

Prices, Income, and Demand

Americans are traveling a lot more today than they used to. That familiar statistic the Average American traveled about 75 percent more interurban miles in 1970 than in 1950. What has made us so mobile? Technology and restlessness? They surely played a role. But why was it that in 1970 we traveled 30 percent less by bus, 75 percent less by train, 75 percent more by automobile, and flew nine times as many passenger miles?

These changes were not inevitable. In large part they were a response to higher incomes and shifts in relative prices, reflecting what the economist calls *elasticities of demand*.

Price Elasticity of Demand

It is extremely cumbersome to talk about "the amount by which people increase or decrease their purchases when the price changes." But this is an important relationship with many useful applications. So economists have invented a special phrase that summarizes the relationship. The formal title of the concept is *price elasticity of demand*.

That's an appropriate name. Elasticity means responsiveness. If the amount of any good that people purchase changes substantially in response to a small change in price, demand is said to be elastic. If even a very large price change results in little change in the amount purchased, demand is said to be inelastic.

Price elasticity of demand is defined precisely as *the percentage change in quantity demanded divided by the percentage change in price*. Thus, if a 10 percent increase in the price of eggs leads to a 5 percent reduction in the number of eggs sold, the elasticity of demand is 5 percent divided by 10 percent, or .5. To be completely accurate, it is *minus .5*, since price and amount purchased vary inversely. But for simplicity we shall ignore the minus sign and treat all coefficients of elasticity as if they were positive.

Whenever the coefficient of elasticity is greater than one (ignoring the sign)—that is to say, whenever the percentage change in quantity purchased is *greater* than the percentage change in price—demand is said to be elastic. Whenever the coefficient of elasticity is less than one, which means whenever the percentage change in quantity purchased is *less* than the percentage change in price, demand is said to be inelastic. Compulsive learners will want to know what is said when the percentage change in quantity is exactly equal to the percen-

$$\frac{\% \ change \ in \ Q}{\% \ change \ in \ P}$$

tage change in price, so that the coefficient of demand elasticity is exactly one. You may file away the information that demand is then *unit elastic*. (Economics is a very systematic discipline.)

You can begin to familiarize yourself with the uses of this concept by asking whether demand is elastic or inelastic in each case below. In some instances you will have to supply information from your own experience. But you have all presumably had some experience with salt and gasoline. Each case is discussed in the subsequent paragraphs.

1. "People aren't going to buy much more no matter how far we cut the price."
2. "This is a competitive business. We would lose half our customers if we raised our prices by as little as 2 percent."
3. The demand for salt.
4. The demand for Morton's salt.
5. The demand for Morton's salt at the Kroger store at Fifth and Main.
6. The demand for gasoline.
7. The demand for Shell gasoline.
8. The demand for gasoline at Friendly Bob's Shell service station.
9. "The university's total receipts from tuition would actually increase if tuition rates were cut by 20 percent."
10. "It's odd but true. Wheat farmers would gross more money if they all got together and burned one-quarter of this year's crop."
11. If the statement in 10 is true, does it follow that they could gross even more money by burning one-half of the crop?

Thinking about Elasticity

1. "People aren't going to buy much more no matter how far we cut the price." If a businessman doubts that even a very large price decrease will do much to increase his sales, he believes that his demand is highly inelastic. He will obviously not want to lower his price under such circumstances, for he will lose more through the lower price than he will gain through the larger volume. But if people don't respond very much to a price cut, will they also be relatively insensitive to a price hike? If they are, a businessman out to increase his income will want to raise his price. Businessmen typically complain that prices are too low. Then why don't they raise their prices? It's a free country, isn't it? The answer, of course, is that they would usually lose too many customers if they did so. It is the elasticity of demand that determines whether or not a businessman can add to his money receipts by raising his prices.

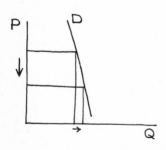

2. "This is a competitive business. We would lose half our customers if we raised our prices by as little as 2 percent." The businesswoman making this statement is saying in effect that she faces a highly elastic demand: a 50 percent decline in quantity demanded would follow a mere 2 percent increase in price. The coefficient of elasticity is 25. The demand is very elastic indeed. Another way of putting it would be to say that her customers are extremely sensitive to any price change. And that makes it difficult for her to raise her prices, however eager she might be to do so.

3. The demand for salt. What makes demand curves elastic or inelastic? The availability of good substitutes is clearly an important factor. Another is the importance of the item in the budget of purchasers. If the expenditure on some good is large relative to the income or wealth of the purchaser, he will be more sensitive to any change in its price. Isn't that true from your own experience? Suppose you smoke and also attend movies twice a week. A book of matches costs a penny and movies $2.50. It is not likely that a 200 percent increase in match prices will have much effect on your smoking. But a 50 percent increase in the price of movie tickets would substantially affect your movie going if you have a typical student's income.

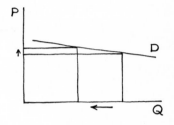

Apply this to table salt. One pound of salt lasts a long time and costs less than 20 cents. So who cares? Housewives will be relatively insensitive to any change in the price of salt. Moreover, salt has few good substitutes. You would not be inclined to put sugar on your eggs if the price of salt rose dramatically, just as you would not cut the pepper and double the salt if the price of salt fell substantially.

Adam Smith, often called the founder of modern economics, observed in *The Wealth of Nations* (1776) that "salt is a very ancient and very universal subject of taxation. . . . The quantity annually consumed by any individual is so small, and may be purchased so gradually, that nobody, it seems to have been thought, could feel very sensibly even a pretty heavy tax upon it." Moreover, salt was one of "the necessaries of life" in Smith's terminology. We can object to the term *necessary* and express Smith's meaning more accurately: salt has few good substitutes. The result is a highly inelastic demand and an apparently irresistible temptation to governments in ancient times to levy taxes on salt.

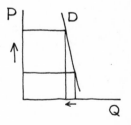

But it's possible to exaggerate the inelasticity of even the demand for salt. Householders in wintry regions sometimes sprinkle table salt on their sidewalks or porch steps to melt the ice. If salt were ten times as expensive, many would substitute chopping and scraping for salt.

4. The demand for Morton's salt. Why would the demand for Morton's salt be less inelastic than the demand for salt? Because there are substitutes—namely, other brands of salt. The Morton Salt Company is not in the privileged position of ancient governments, which could raise the price of *all* salt. If someone in the marketing department at Morton chanced to read Adam Smith

and was inspired by him to double the price, the grocery stores that are Morton's customers would tend to make their purchases from other salt manufacturers.

5. The demand for Morton's salt at the Kroger store at Fifth and Main. If there are more good substitutes for Morton's salt than for salt, there are even more good substitutes for the Morton's salt sold at the local Kroger store. We have moved from a very inelastic to what is probably a highly elastic demand for the same quantity. And that is why you aren't victimized when you purchase salt. You might be willing to pay $2 a pound if salt was not available at a lower price. But fortunately for you, there are many options. A seller who tried to take advantage of that fact that the total demand for salt is highly inelastic would lose his customers. The demand for *the salt he sells* will be quite elastic.

People often make the mistake of assuming that those who sell "vital necessities" can get away with charging almost any price they choose. We have learned to be suspicious of the phrase *vital necessities*. Now we see again the grounds for this suspicion. Food has as good a claim as anything to the title "vital necessity." But the relevant fact is that *no one buys food*. Housewives do not purchase a pound of "food"; they buy a pound of hamburger, or bacon, or calf's liver. And there are many sellers selling many kinds of food. All of which means that there are excellent substitutes for specific food commodities, and hence demand curves are highly elastic. So sellers are for the most part closely constrained in the prices they can charge.

6, 7, 8. The demand for gasoline, for Shell gasoline, and for gasoline at Friendly Bob's Shell service station. Much of what has just been said about salt can also be applied to the demand for gasoline. Because gasoline is a more significant item than salt in the consumer's budget, we should expect the demand for gasoline to be less inelastic than the demand for salt. Once again, however, no one buys mere gasoline. There are many options, so that the proprietor of Friendly Bob's Shell service station cannot afford to raise his price even when he's complaining that he makes almost nothing on a tankful of gasoline. The demand curve with which he must live is very elastic.

Remember also what was said in the last chapter about the importance of time: greater substitution will occur in response to a price change as time passes. We can now express the same thought another way: demand curves are more elastic over longer time periods than they are over shorter time periods. Gasoline provides an excellent example. If the federal government pushed up the price of gasoline across the board by imposing a large additional tax, motorists would at first grumble but pay. Then they would begin to form car pools and investigate public transportation. Still later some would move in order to be closer to work. When they replaced their present cars, many would switch from eight cylinders to four. Automobile manufacturers would meanwhile be shifting toward greater production of economy cars and reduced production of gas-guzzlers. Some technological changes to reduce gasoline consumption that were not economical at the former price of gasoline would become economical at the higher price. These are the kinds of factors that make demand curves more elastic in the long run.

9. "The university's total receipts from tuition would actually increase if tuition rates were cut by 20 percent." The university's total receipts from tuition are the product of the tuition rate and the number of students who enroll. If a 20 percent decrease in the tuition rate results in an increase in tuition receipts, then there must have been a more than 20 percent increase in enrollment. The percentage change in quantity demanded is greater than the percentage change in price, so demand is elastic.

This suggests a simple way of thinking about elasticity. Keep in mind that the quantity demanded will always move in the opposite direction from the price. *If a price change causes total receipts to move in the* opposite *direction from the price change, demand must be elastic.* The change in the quantity purchased has to be larger in percentage terms than the price change, because total receipts are nothing but the product of price and quantity. And that is the definition of an elastic demand. *If a price change causes total receipts to move in the* same *direction as the price change, demand must be inelastic.* The change in amount purchased was not large enough to outweigh the change in price. And that is the meaning of an inelastic demand. You can satisfy yourself that this relationship holds by running through a numerical example.

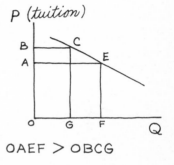

$$OAEF > OBCG$$

Assume that 1000 students will enroll if the tuition is $500 per year, but only 900 will enroll if the tuition is $600 per year. Is the demand elastic or inelastic within this range of tuition charges? We notice that the university's total receipts change *in the same direction* as the price change: 1000 × 500 is less than 900 × 600. So the demand is inelastic by the rule given above. We can confirm this with a little arithmetic. The percentage change in quantity demanded is 100 enrollments divided by 950. (A percentage change is the change divided by the base: we chose 950, the average of 1000 and 900, as the base because we want to get the same answer whether we raise the price from $500 to $600 or lower it from $600 to $500). The percentage change in price is $100 divided by $550—where we again use the average of the two values between which we're moving as the base. The coefficient of elasticity is $^{11}/_{19}$, or .58.

$$\frac{100}{950}$$

$$\frac{100}{550}$$

Now assume instead that enrollment falls from 1000 to 800 as a result of the tuition increase from $500 to $600. In this case total receipts and price are moving *in opposite directions*: 1000 × 500 is greater than 800 × 600. So the demand must be elastic. A few calculations will verify this conclusion. The percentage change in

$$\frac{200}{900}$$

$$\frac{100}{550}$$

quantity is now 200 divided by 900; the percentage change in price is again 100 divided by 550. (The units don't matter; they cancel out.) The coefficient of elasticity is $^{11}/_9$, or 1.22.

Do not jump to the conclusion that the university will always be in a better financial position, given an elastic demand, if it lowers its tuition. True, lower tuition charges will mean larger receipts whenever demand is elastic; but a larger enrollment probably also means larger costs. The university must decide in such a case whether the addition to total receipts will be larger than the addition to total costs. But problems of pricing strategy must be deferred until we reach Chapters 10 and 11.

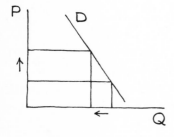

10. "It's odd but true. Wheat farmers would gross more money if they all got together and burned one-quarter of this year's crop." The logic of number 9 applies also here. Farmers can only gross more money while selling less wheat if the percentage change in price is greater than the percentage change in the amount sold. Demand would have to be inelastic. The only difference is that we have reversed the causal relationship assumed up till now. We have been tacitly assuming that sellers set the price and buyers respond. This is not always the best way to look at the price-quantity relationship. In some industries, such as agriculture for the most part, it is more useful to assume that the quantity available for sale will determine the price. We'll be talking a lot about this in Chapters 10 and 11. For now it is only important to notice that the relationship between changes in total sales and changes in price depends on the elasticity of demand.

Farmers may never have heard about elastic or inelastic demands. But when they lobby for government controls on production, they are usually very much aware of the relation between price and the amount that is sold. You can, like Molière's famous M. Jourdain, who spoke prose for forty years without knowing it, make good use of demand elasticities without ever having heard the term.

11. Could wheat farmers do even better by burning one-half of the crop? The elasticity of demand will almost certainly not be the same at all points along a demand schedule or curve. As a general rule, demand will be more elastic at higher prices (and smaller quantities) than at lower prices (and larger quantities). Why? Basically because people tend to be more sensitive to price changes when the price in question is large (relative to their incomes) than when it is small. Consequently, if farmers somehow agreed upon a scheme for destroying wheat in order to raise its price, at some point they would run into an elastic demand. And as soon as the demand turned from inelastic to elastic, total receipts would go down as a consequence of further price increases.

This relationship may become clearer to you if you examine a straight-line demand curve. Along the upper left portion of the demand curve, any price change of a given amount will be a *smaller percentage change* than it will be along the lower right portion of the curve. At the same time, the *percentage change* in quantity demanded will be getting *larger* as we move from the lower right portion of the curve to the upper left. Since elasticity of demand is the ratio of these percentage changes, the coefficient of elasticity must be increasing continuously as we move up and back along a straight-line demand curve.

The Myth of Vertical Demand

But enough of such technicalities. In the six statements with which we began Chapter 2, what was implicitly assumed about the elasticity of demand? Our objection to each statement, you recall, was that it ignored the fact that all goods have substitutes and that substitution does occur when prices change. In other words, demand curves are *not* completely inelastic. A completely inelastic demand curve would graph as a vertical line. You would be wise not to look for such demand curves in the real world.

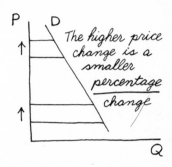

The higher price change is a smaller percentage change

You would also be wise to look out for people who argue as if completely inelastic demand curves are the rule. Here are some additional examples to give you practice in being wary.

"The Mona Lisa is a priceless painting."

Don't believe it. If the French government decided to sell the Mona Lisa at auction, it would be bought at a finite price. No doubt wealthy collectors would be eager to buy it, and might even carelessly say something like "I'd give *anything* to get it." The inaccuracy of their speech would be demonstrated as the bidding proceeded, and the collectors, one by one, dropped out of the auction.

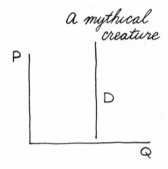

a mythical creature

"National security requires four million men in uniform."

That sounds like a Pentagon statement. We might put the Pentagon to a hypothetical test by asking the chairman of the Joint Chiefs of Staff whether he would still insist on four million servicemen if the cost of maintaining a military establishment of this size rose to $100 billion annually. If he refused to budge and kept insisting that the Pentagon demand is completely inelastic at four million men, we could shrug our shoulders and recall what the law of demand does and does not assert. It asserts that people find substitutes for anything when the cost *to them* increases. It does not assert that people become willing to reduce their purchases when *someone else* must pay a higher price. If the salaries of generals were made to vary inversely with the total number of men in the army, the military demand for personnel would prove to be far more elastic than the Pentagon is now willing to admit.

"Cleaning up air pollution will be costly. But we cannot weigh money against clean air."

The assumption once again is that the demand for some good, in this case clean air, is completely inelastic. But it obviously is not to anyone who thinks about it for a moment. There are degrees of clean air. How clean do we want the air to be? "As clean as possible" is no answer because we can always make the air cleaner. We could get rid of all factories, all cars, and all home heating systems. If we wanted still more cleanliness in our air, we could start getting rid of people who perspire excessively. But long before this point we would all have noticed that the demand for clean air is not perfectly inelastic. Clean air is a good. But there are costs involved in obtaining it. Intelligent pollution-control programs seek to balance the benefits of additional clean air against the additional costs that must be incurred to get it.

Once Again with Emphasis

The law of demand can be expressed in the language of elasticity: *There is no such thing as a completely inelastic demand* over the entire range of possible prices. Most purchasers will respond at least a little to changes in the cost to them, and all purchasers will respond to a sufficiently large change. If this seems too obvious to bother mentioning, consult your daily newspaper for evidence that it is by no means obvious to everyone. Well-intentioned people and some not so well-intentioned talk constantly of basic needs, minimum requirements, and absolute necessities.

Demand curves are rarely as inelastic as orators suppose. That does not imply, of course, that they are always elastic. That is a more difficult question to be answered by looking at each case. But as we shall subsequently discover, it is a very important question for anyone who wants to decide how well our economic system functions.

Income and Demand

One of the reasons for the low price elasticity of demand for gasoline in the United States is that its price *relative to income* fell steadily until 1973. The average price of gasoline was about 29 cents a gallon in 1955 when per capita disposable income was $1666. This means that it took $145 or 8.7 percent of per capita disposable income to buy 500 gallons of gasoline in 1955. For 500 gallons of gasoline to use up 8.7 percent of income in 1973, its price would have had to have been 73 cents a gallon. So it's not surprising that the driving habits of Americans did not change drastically in 1974 when the price of gasoline rose to about 60 cents a gallon.

In using the concepts of demand and elasticity it's important to keep an eye on other factors that may be changing along with the price. Elasticity measures the responsiveness of the quantity demanded to changes in the price on the assumption that nothing has occurred to change the demand curve itself. From the beginning of the book, whenever we've talked about a change in the price of some good we've meant a change in its *relative price: its price in relation to other goods.* For the last decade or so the United States has experienced a general rise in prices. The average of all prices, including wages and other income sources, has been going up. Now if all prices rise by the same percentage, then relative prices do not change at all. Since we're trying to understand the way in which relative prices guide consumer and producer decisions, we have to separate the change in a good's price that was caused by general inflation from the change caused by an alteration in the scarcity of that particular good.

Take the case of gasoline prices. An increase from 36 cents per gallon for regular at the beginning of 1972 to 58 cents at the end of 1974 was a 61 percent increase (using the original price as the base). But the average of all prices paid by consumers rose 26 percent over this period. The increase in the relative price of gasoline was therefore only about 35 percent. That is equivalent in its effects to an increase from 36 to about $48^1/_2$ cents.

Or take the price changes from 1955 to 1974. The average price of gasoline in 1955 was 29 cents. From 29 to 58 cents is a 100 percent increase. When we deduct the rate of increase in the general price level between 1955 and 1974, however, the change in the relative price of gasoline was only about 6 percent. In short, gasoline was not actually much more expensive in 1975 at 58 cents than it had been in 1955 at 29 cents a gallon. And it's the relative price that matters.

Demand and Quantity Demanded

You can avoid a very common confusion by carefully observing the distinction between *demand* and the *quantity demanded*. Demand is a relation between quantity demanded and price. The demand for gasoline is expressed by a series of prices and a series of corresponding quantities that would be demanded (or amounts that would be purchased) at those prices, expressed either in a schedule or a curve. A movement from one row of the schedule to another, or from one point on the curve to another, should always be called a change in the *quantity demanded*, not a change in the *demand*. The latter would be a change in the schedule itself, a shift in the curve caused by a change in tastes and preferences, incomes, or the perceived properties of substitutes. The relative prices of substitutes are among their most important properties.

If this seems a terribly pedantic distinction, try your hand at locating the error in the following argument. It arises from a failure to observe the distinction.

> If the government puts a large new tax on gasoline so that its price goes up, the demand will fall. But when the demand for anything falls, its price tends to fall. So we can't be sure that the tax will actually raise the price of gasoline.

Can you spot the error? It's in the main clause of the first sentence.

The *demand* will not fall. Only the *quantity demanded* will fall. So the next two sentences are mistaken conclusions. When the quantity demanded falls in response to the price increase, that's the end of the matter. Of course, the higher price may over time call forth new substitutes, and the appearance of new substitutes is capable of causing the demand curve to shift—a true change in demand.

If a combination of rising incomes, environmental concern, and new interest in outdoor exercise induces more people to want bicycles, the demand for bicycles will increase. And both the price and quantity demanded may well increase as a consequence. This actually occurred in 1971. You have grasped the distinction between demand and quantity demanded if you see clearly why this in no way contradicts the law of demand. An increase in demand, or a shift upward and to the right in the demand curve, will pull up both price and quantity demanded. But it was still true with the high demand of 1971, as it had been with the low demand of 1969, that a smaller quantity of bicycles was demanded at higher than at lower prices. And this is what the law of demand asserts.

Income Elasticity of Demand

Price elasticity of demand is the oldest child in a rather large family of elasticity concepts. The size of the family should not surprise you. Economics is useful because change occurs; it attempts to predict or understand the consequences of changes. Elasticity concepts provide a way of focusing on particular change relationships and of discussing them in quantitative terms. And so new children are born regularly into the elasticity family as economists pursue their varied investigations. We won't try to introduce you to the whole family (an impossible task anyway given the birth rate), but one more is worth meeting at this time.

Income elasticity of demand is a close companion to price elasticity of demand. Its definition is analogous: *the percentage change in quantity demanded divided by the percentage change in income.* If a 20 percent increase in your income leads to a 15 percent increase in your expenditures on housing, the income elasticity of your demand for housing is $^3/_4$ or .75. Notice that the coefficient of elasticity in this case could be greater than unity, between zero and unity, or less than zero (negative). If a 20 percent increase in your income leads to an 80 percent reduction in your margarine consumption (because you're now buying butter), the elasticity coefficient will be minus 4. We cannot ignore the algebraic sign in the case of income elasticity of demand; for while more income permits more consumption, it need not result in more consumption of any particular commodity. Suppose that we put income on the vertical axis as we did with price. Curves expressing the relationship between price and quantity demanded slope downward to the right, expressing the inverse relationship between these two variables and yielding negative coefficients of elasticity. But a curve that shows the relationship between income and the quantity demanded of some good can slope upward to the right or be vertical or slope upward to the left. A single such curve, expressing, say, the responsiveness of Homer Iliad's weekly hamburger purchases to changes in his income, might well resemble a backward C. The income elasticity of Homer's demand for hamburger could thus be shown as positive, zero, or negative, depending on the income range under consideration. Let's reflect on Homer's habits to convince ourselves that this is quite plausible.

When Homer's income was very low, he yearned for meat but could rarely afford it. When he got a 5 percent raise, he doubled his consumption of hamburger, displaying an income elasticity of demand of 20 (100% divided by 5%). Homer's coefficient declined as his income rose further, both because any absolute change in income is a smaller percentage change when income is higher and because at higher income levels Homer could afford more expensive cuts of meat. As Homer's income rose still further he eventually reached a point where more income didn't lead to any more hamburger consumption at all. As his wealth increased, Homer began substituting steaks and roasts for hamburger, something he would have liked to do even when he was poor but couldn't because of the price of these cuts.

You might return now to the opening paragraph of this chapter and think about the ways in which the average American's traveling habits have been affected by changing prices and rising incomes.

The income elasticity of the demand for travel is positive and fairly large in the United States: we like to travel when our income permits it. But why so much more by air and so much less by bus? In large part it's because the price of air travel has decreased considerably relative to the price of interurban bus travel. The fares by themselves won't show that. But remember that money cost is only part of the costs that shape decisions. The commercial jet substantially raised the relative cost of bus travel, at least for everyone who counts the time spent in transit as part of the cost. Those who believe that getting there is half the fun would, of course, appraise the relative costs of bus and air travel somewhat differently. A feeling of dependence, of being limited by someone else's schedule, is also a cost to many people. And that factor has decreased the relative cost of traveling by automobile.

Technology is a powerful force in a culture, and so are the attitudes and values of its people. But they don't determine our patterns of consumption without a powerful assist from prices and incomes. We choose within constraints; but we do choose. And should our patterns of choice generate serious social problems, economics points to some simple levers by which we can mutually persuade one another to choose differently. That is the theme of the next chapter.

Once Over Lightly

Price elasticity of demand is a measure of the percentage change in the quantity of a good demanded relative to the percentage change in its price.

Demand is (price) elastic when the percentage change in quantity demanded is greater than the percentage change in price. Demand is inelastic when the percentage change in quantity demanded is smaller than the percentage change in price.

Price elasticity of demand depends upon the importance of the price relative to one's income, but even more upon the quality and price of available substitutes.

More separate sources of supply for a good imply better substitutes for any particular good and hence a more elastic demand.

Total receipts or expenditures move in the opposite direction from price when demand is elastic and in the same direction as price when it is inelastic.

The concept of "needs" implies a perfectly inelastic demand curve—an extremely rare phenomenon.

Changes in income cause demand curves to shift. The income elasticity of demand for a good is the percentage change in the quantity demanded divided by the percentage change in income. It can vary over a wide range of negative or positive values.

The demand for a good refers to the *schedule of relationships* between price and quantity demanded and must be distinguished from the quantity or amount that is demanded. The quantity of a good demanded changes with its price. But a true change in demand will alter both price and quantity demanded.

QUESTIONS FOR DISCUSSION

1. John loves butter and thinks that margarine tastes like soap. George can't tell the difference. Whose demand for butter is likely to be more elastic?

2. Would the elasticity of a crowd's demand for cold lemonade be affected by the proximity of a drinking fountain?

3. How do you think the development of other copying machines affected the elasticity of demand for Xerox machines?

4. Is the demand for prescription drugs elastic or inelastic? Why? Do you agree with the statement sometimes made that the prices charged for prescription drugs can be freely set by the manufacturers, since people must buy whatever the doctor prescribes?

5. How does ignorance affect elasticities of demand?

6. How might the development of science and technology affect demand elasticities?

7. Does a society's transportation system in any way affect elasticities of demand? How?

8. What is the elasticity of demand for water in New York City, according to Figure 2A? (Be careful: the elasticity varies.)

9. The demand for aspirin at currently pre-vailing prices seems to be highly inelastic. What do you think would happen to the elasticity of demand if the price of aspirin relative to everything else were five times as high? Fifty times as high? Why?

10. Figure 3A shows a hypothetical demand curve for strawberries.

   a. What price per case would maximize the gross receipts of strawberry growers? (Peek at part *d* of this question rather than waste too much time trying all sorts of different prices. The price that maximizes gross receipts will be found at the midpoint of a straight-line demand curve when the curve is extended to the axes. If you see why, good. If not, it's a bit of knowledge with only academic useful-ness anyway.)

   b. If the price of strawberries is deter-mined by the total quantity harvested in conjunction with the demand, what size crop will result in the price quoted in part *d*?

   c. What would the gross receipts of strawberry growers be if the crop turned out to be 30,000 cases?

   d. Can you prove that the demand for strawberries is elastic above a price of $24 per case and inelastic below that price?

   e. If strawberry growers can make more money by selling fewer than 30,000 cases, why would they ever market that much? Why wouldn't they destroy some of the crop rather than "spoil the market"?

11. Higher prices for beef, automobiles, or television sets will lead to a reduction in the *amount of each demanded*. Think of some specific changes (such as in tastes,

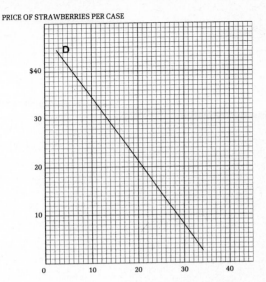

PRICE OF STRAWBERRIES PER CASE

CASES OF STRAWBERRIES PER HARVEST
(in thousands)

Figure 3A Demand curve for strawberries

prices of substitutes, quality of comple-mentary goods) that would cause the *de-mand* for each to increase so that more might actually be demanded at higher prices. Why is this completely consistent with the law of demand?

12. A change in expectations can cause a change in demand. Explain how this could lead to a situation where a price decline was followed by a decrease in the amount pur-chased.

13. What would you say is the price elasticity of demand for the rewards of criminal ac-tivity? Would increasing the price of crime (that is, raising its cost to the criminal) sig-nificantly reduce the crime rate? What would you estimate is the income elasticity of demand for the rewards of criminal ac-tivity? Is either of these a useful applica-tion of elasticity concepts?

Scarcity and
the Price System

A chapter should not begin with definitions, for definitions are boring and put students off. So don't read these definitions. Skip immediately to the next paragraph. But remember, if you get confused for a moment, that the three key terms of this chapter have been defined in the initial paragraph. A good is *scarce* whenever there is not enough available for everyone to have all he wants without having to sacrifice something else he wants in order to obtain it. A *shortage* exists when the quantity demanded at the prevailing price is greater than the quantity available. A *surplus* exists when the quantity demanded at the prevailing price is less than the quantity available.

But don't stop to memorize this. Go right on to learn about lobster, copper, sugar, house rents near army bases, and the problem of becoming president.

No one blames the thermometer for low temperatures or seriously proposes to warm up the house on a cold day by holding a candle under the furnace thermostat. People do, however, often blame high prices for the scarcity of certain goods and act as if scarcity could be eliminated by pushing down prices through legislation or by moralizing.

To the lover of lobster, its high price does indeed look like the cause of its scarcity. Lobster rarely appears in our house because its price is high. But what would happen if the lobster lovers' lobby pushed a bill through Congress which placed a ceiling price on lobster well below the currently prevailing price? Would lobster be any less scarce? Lobster fans would now *want* to buy more lobster. But would they succeed? The low ceiling price might in fact cause lobster to disappear from most of the stores in the country.

Contrary to the doctrine now being propounded by some who are impressed with the enormous wealth of the United States, even we, the wealthiest people in the world, have not ended scarcity. Nor is it likely that we ever shall. We may learn to be more content with fewer material goods, or we may manage to produce and distribute material goods in such abundance that no one any longer gives much thought to acquiring more. But even then we would not have abolished scarcity. For the present and in the foreseeable future, we shall have to live with the fact that the means of satisfying our wants fall far short of the wants themselves.

So we must economize. We must allocate our resources intelligently, trying to obtain from what we have as much as possible of what we want. We must learn to manage scarcity, since we cannot hope to abolish it. The management of scarcity does include scaling down or otherwise altering wants as well as expanding production. It's often possible to loosen the pinch of scarcity merely by reevaluating one's objectives and discovering that a particular goal really isn't worth the cost of attaining it, or that the want behind the desire for some good can actually be satisfied in another and less difficult way. But the management of scarcity, especially in an economy as large and diversified as ours, with so many different resources and varied preferences, will remain an enormously complex social task. In this chapter we want to enlarge our understanding of those complexities by exploring some of the implications of scarcity. We shall notice that scarcity is quite different from shortage, and that something can be scarce even when a surplus of it exists.

The Meaning of Scarcity

The climate of Gazebo, a fictitious South Sea island, is perfect for growing both oranges and pineapples. But since there are far more pineapple plants than orange trees on the island, 50,000 pineapples are harvested each month and only 5000 oranges. Which is more scarce?

We cannot tell from the information given. Scarcity is a *relationship*. If the people of Gazebo love pineapples and hate oranges, pineapples could be more scarce despite their greater abundance. Scarcity is a relationship between availability and desirability, or between supply and demand. If pineapples in Gazebo were considered unfit for human consumption, and there was no way to sell them to others, they would not be scarce at all. No one speaks of the scarcity of garbage—except perhaps hog farmers, for whom garbage is not garbage.

If everyone can have all that he wants of some good without being required to sacrifice anything else that is also wanted, that good is not *scarce.* It is a *free good.* There are obviously not many free goods available in our society, despite the song that says the best things in life are free. Perhaps the best things in life cannot be purchased with money; but that does not make them free goods.

Scarcity makes rationing unavoidable

If anything is scarce, it must be rationed. That means that a criterion of some kind must be established for discriminating among claimants to determine who will get how much. The criterion could be age, eloquence, swiftness, public esteem, willingness to pay money, or almost anything else. We characteristically ration scarce goods in our society on the basis of willingness to pay money. But sometimes we use other criteria in order to discriminate.

Harvard College each year has many more applicants than it can place in the freshman class, so Harvard must ration the scarce places. It discriminates on the basis of high school grades, test scores, recommendations, and other criteria.

Only one person at a time can be president of the United States. Since many more people than that want the position, we have evolved an elaborate system of discrimination in the form of conventions and elections. Although there is considerable doubt about just what the criteria for discrimination are, the system does discriminate. We end up every fourth year with only one satisfied candidate.

Joe College is the most popular man on campus and has coeds clamoring for his favor. He must therefore ration his attentions. Whether he employs the criterion of beauty, intelligence, geniality, or something else, he must and will discriminate in some fashion.

But the other side of discrimination is competition. Once Harvard announces its criteria for discrimination, freshman applicants will compete to meet them. The criteria for selecting a president are studied carefully by the hopefuls who begin competing to satisfy those criteria long before the election year. If the coeds eager to go with Joe College believe that beauty is his main criterion, they will compete with one another to seem more beautiful.

Competition is obviously not peculiar to capitalist societies or to societies that use money. The point is of fundamental importance: *competition results from scarcity* and can only be eliminated with the elimination of scarcity. Whenever there is scarcity, there must be rationing. Rationing is allocation in accord with some criteria for discrimination. Competition is merely what occurs when people strive to meet the criteria that are being employed.

Rationing results in competition

Of course, the criteria employed do make a difference. If a society rations on the basis of willingness to pay money, members of that society will strive to make money. If it uses physical strength as a primary criterion, members of the society will do body-building exercises. And if the better colleges and universities use high school grades as an important criterion for selection, high school students will compete for grades. They might be competing for grades to acquire other goods as well (status among classmates, compliments from teachers, use of the family car); but it is odd for colleges to complain of grade grubbers when their own rationing criteria promote grade grubbing.

Scarcity and Prices

Monetary prices are the most common rationing device in our society. The high price of lobster both reflects the fact that lobster is scarce *and* rations to eager gourmets the limited quantity available. What happens when the price of lobster is not allowed to rise to the level that reflects its actual scarcity? Suppose that our lobster lovers' lobby managed to get a law through Congress setting $1 a pound as the maximum price that could be charged for lobster.

The quantity demanded would immediately increase. Lobster

lovers would race to the grocery stores in anticipation of inexpensive epicurean delights. But many would find only frustration. Someone else would have gotten there first. The lower price does nothing to increase the number of lobsters available, and, in the long run, it will reduce the amount of lobster that reaches the grocery stores and fish markets as lobstermen find it more profitable to do something other than trap lobsters. The lobster lovers' lobby did nothing to make lobster less scarce. They only suppressed the rationing device. They put ice cubes on the thermometer, so to speak; they did not turn on the air conditioning. They mistook a symptom (the high price) for the cause of their discontent (the scarcity of lobster).

But since lobster is still scarce, it must still be rationed. When price was prevented from serving as the discriminatory criterion, swiftness took its place. Those who were first to the stores took home the lobster, and the rest had none. Later on we might expect friendship with the butcher or fishmonger to become an important discriminatory criterion. And if this happens we would expect the social popularity of these tradesmen to increase as lobster lovers start competing to satisfy the new rationing system. Fishmongers will be seen at all the more glittering social events, and party givers will call months in advance to be sure of their butcher's presence. Proximity to Maine will be another rationing device. Why pay the cost of shipping lobster any farther if New Englanders are willing to buy all that is available? When the lobsters no longer come to the people, the people will have to go to the lobsters.

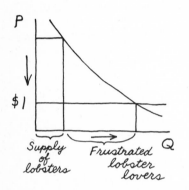

Copper in Klutz

Scarcity is an inescapable fact of life, but shortages are avoidable. *A shortage is defined by economists as a situation in which the quantity demanded is greater than the quantity supplied.* Since the quantity demanded depends on the price (later we shall see that the quantity supplied also depends on price), it is possible to eliminate any shortage merely by allowing the price to rise.

We can see what this means and gain further practice in working with graphs by using Figure 4A. The line labeled OD is the original demand for copper in the hypothetical country of Klutz. It shows the number of pounds of copper that will be purchased each month in Klutz at prices between roughly $1.35 and $.25 per pound. The line labeled LD is the demand for copper in Klutz at some later date. It is the demand after a major change (an expansion, let us say, in the country's electrical supply network) causes copper users to be willing to pay more to obtain any given quantity of copper. Another way of describing the difference between OD and LD is to say that, with LD, copper users want to buy more copper than before at each and every price.

We might begin by asking how much copper was needed in

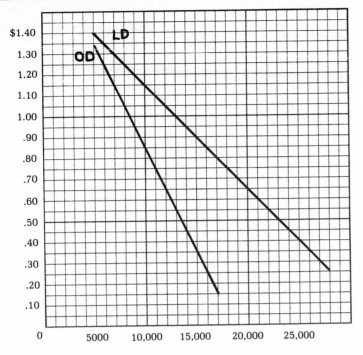

Figure 4A   Copper in Klutz

Klutz at OD. The question is meaningless, of course. Klutz has a
highly developed economy and every industrialized economy uses
large amounts of copper. But it is still misleading to say that Klutz
needs any particular amount of copper per month. As the graph
indicates, more or less will be demanded as the price is lower or
higher.

Suppose now that exactly 10,000 pounds of copper become
available to Klutz users each month. Will this be enough? Will
there be a shortage of copper? Not if the price is 85 cents per
pound. At this price copper users will want to buy 10,000 pounds
per month, exactly the amount available.

What would happen if the monthly supply fell for some reason
to 8000 pounds? If the price did not rise, some prospective purchasers of copper would be unable to obtain as much as they want.
In order to get more, some would offer to pay a slight premium,
and the price would rise. It would tend to continue rising as long as
anyone who was willing to pay a higher price (if necessary) could
not obtain all the copper he wanted at the existing price. But as the
price rises, some prospective purchasers alter their plans. They
decide they now want less copper than they originally planned to
purchase. The price is bid up by the competition of those who

want more than is available to them. And as it rises, the amount demanded declines. At a price of $1.05 per pound, the quantity demanded equals the quantity supplied. Therefore $1.05 is the *equilibrium price* for the new situation of reduced supply. It is the price that "clears the market." This means that all purchases that people want to make *at the prevailing price* can be made, while purchases that people are willing to make only at some lower price cannot be made.

Do prices really change in the way described above, or is this just part of the mythology of economists? The picture we have given is a simplified one. It describes quite accurately the way some prices change, but not others. We shall examine later what happens in the very common situation where sellers have some power to set prices. But we can pass by for now the question of whether this process is "typical" in order to focus on our principal concern at the moment: the relation between scarcity and shortage or surplus.

What would have occurred if the government of Klutz had decided that copper was an essential commodity, and therefore its price could not be allowed to rise? When the supply fell from 10,000 pounds per month to 8000 pounds, a shortage would have appeared: the quantity demanded at the legally fixed ceiling price would exceed by 2000 pounds per month the quantity supplied. The shortage is a clear consequence of the ceiling price and can be eliminated by removing the ceiling.

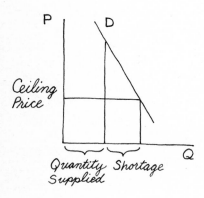

Ceiling Price

Quantity Supplied — *Shortage*

Suppose that with the supply at the lower level of 8000 pounds and the price effectively fixed at 85 cents a pound, the demand shifts from OD to LD. How large will the shortage now be? Purchasers will want to buy 16,000 pounds. The shortage will therefore be 8000 pounds per month.

Would you like to see a shortage turn into a surplus before your very eyes? Let the demand continue at LD and the monthly supply at 8000 pounds. And let the government of Klutz now decide that since copper is an essential commodity its price must be supported at $1.30 a pound. If you wonder how a government can argue first for a low maximum price and then for a high minimum price, both on the grounds that copper is an essential commodity, remind yourself once again that those who talk about "essential" commodities are often not much interested in logical conclusions.

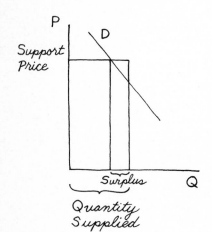

Support Price

Surplus

Quantity Supplied

If the government supports the price of copper at $1.30 a pound by offering to buy for stockpiling all the supply which cannot be sold at that price, then 1000 pounds will have to be added each month to the government's stockpile. *Voilà!* A surplus. It's easy once you learn the trick, as many governments other than that of Klutz have often demonstrated. *A surplus*, in case you are still looking for the formal definition, *is a situation in which the quantity supplied exceeds the quantity demanded.*

Notice that copper is still scarce despite the surplus. Surpluses do not necessarily mean that scarcity has been overcome. They may only mean that prices are not being allowed to decline. It's tempting to assert that just as any shortage can be eliminated by a large enough increase in price, so any surplus can be eliminated by a large enough decrease in price. But that could be misleading unless you realize that the price decrease might have to be so large as to make the equilibrium price negative. Suppliers might have to pay demanders to take the commodity away. If that sounds silly, how do you think we eliminate surpluses of trash?

Supply Curves: A Brief Introduction

We've been assuming in the copper case that the problem is to allocate a *fixed monthly output* of copper among competing demanders. That assumption simplifies the exposition. But you know very well that the output of goods like lobster or copper is not fixed and unalterable. We mentioned, at the beginning of the discussion of copper in Klutz, that the quantity supplied also depends upon the price. In other words, there are supply curves as well as demand curves. In Chapter 5 we will reflect on the nature of costs and the relationship between costs and supply curves. But a little anticipation at this point will be helpful.

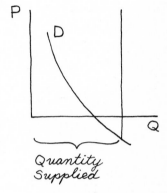

Figure 4B adds a supply curve (S) to Figure 4A. It's a relatively inelastic supply curve: throughout the range of quantities and prices shown, a change in price will be accompanied by a smaller percentage change in the quantity supplied.

Price ceilings and price supports will lead to even larger shortages and surpluses when the quantities supplied as well as those demanded are responsive to price changes. Look at Figure 4B. With demand at LD, the market clearing price will be 95 cents per pound. An effective price ceiling of 80 cents would create a monthly shortage of 4000 pounds, by inducing demanders to want an extra 3000 pounds each month while prompting suppliers to reduce their offerings by 1000 pounds per month.

Price Rationing and Non-Price Rationing

Shortages and surpluses that persist for any extended period of time will almost always be found to be a consequence of failure to allow prices to perform their rationing function. Since rationing is a necessary consequence of scarcity, some other method of rationing will come into play when a price is set at a level that does not reflect actual scarcity. A few years ago the United States government tried to hold down the price of copper in the face of rising demand and a diminished supply. New discriminatory criteria came into operation, such as willingness to stand in line, ability to influence sellers, and dishonesty (thefts of copper increased significantly). Are these rationing devices any better than price?

It is hard to see in what way they might be better. One important consequence of rationing by means of price is that it allocates the scarce commodity to those who are willing to pay more. If you

PRICE OF COPPER PER POUND

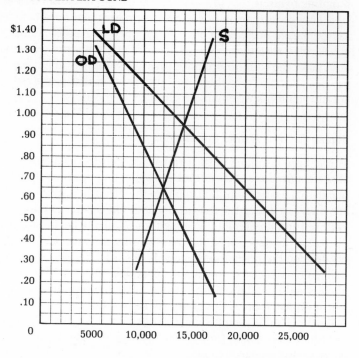

POUNDS OF COPPER PER MONTH

Figure 4B Supply and demand for copper

assume that some prospective buyers are willing to pay more than others because they plan to use the copper in products for which consumers are willing to pay more, rationing by means of price has a tendency to allocate scarce commodities toward those uses for which consumer demand is greatest. And that makes sense.

Remember the law of demand and the phenomenon of substitutability on which it ultimately rests. At a low, fixed price, copper users have little incentive to economize by finding copper substitutes. When the price of copper is allowed to rise, a long chain of substitutions is set in motion. Home builders may cut down on the number of bathrooms, for example, in order to hold down the cost of the houses they are constructing. New home buyers may look at the cost of an additional bathroom and decide, all things considered, that three aren't really much better than two. Scarcity calls for economizing. Higher prices for copper encourage everyone who uses it to do exactly that.

Allocating Housing Space

You will get a better sense of what happens when prices are not allowed to ration scarce goods if we run through an example closer to student experience. Suppose that the army suddenly reactivates a large military base that is far from any large population center. Small towns in the vicinity of the base will experience a large increase in the demand for housing from military personnel and their dependents who prefer to live off the base. Housing will become more scarce and rental prices will begin to rise.

If rental prices are allowed to rise, people will want to purchase less housing space. Renters will lease smaller apartments or double up with friends. Some personnel will change their minds and elect to live on the base. Some dependents will decide to locate farther from the area of the base. Some military families will settle for being together just on weekends. Moreover, owners of living space will economize, too. People who own large houses will open up their basements and spare bedrooms to renters. This means, in effect, that they will be demanding less housing space for their own use. All these economizing activities will alleviate the shortage and, if rental prices rise high enough, eliminate it completely. The scarcity will still exist; there is no way to eliminate it, and few ways even to reduce it substantially in the short run. But the challenge is to live with scarcity by economizing effectively. Higher prices stimulate a more effective coping with the problem of scarcity by inducing people to substitute other goods for housing space in an area of acute scarcity.

It has been argued in cases just like this that rent controls should be imposed to keep greedy landlords from exploiting the situation. But if legal rent ceilings are imposed, the price of housing will be prevented from performing its rationing function. A shortage will appear. The quantity demanded (at prevailing and legally fixed rentals) will exceed the quantity available. Some way will have to be found to ration the short supply. We can easily predict some of the rationing devices that will appear.

Families with children will be discriminated against. Why rent to people with children, who are more likely to damage property, when at the same price you can find plenty of renters without children?

People who are noisy or have other habits offensive to landlords will be discriminated against. Why tolerate unpleasant tenants when there are plenty of pleasant ones around?

Members of minority races will be discriminated against for the same reason, if landlords tend to harbor racial prejudices.

Discrimination will occur also on the basis of personal influence, friendship with someone who has an apartment he plans to vacate, and all sorts of bribes, legal or illegal.

There will be a decline in the quality of accommodations from the tenants' standpoint. Landlords will provide minimum heat. They will refuse to paint. They will insist on large deposits and extract large breakage fees from tenants.

Moreover, with rent controls, we would have less reason to

expect that housing would go to those most desirous of obtaining it. At $75 a month the single soldier who wouldn't much mind living on the base might wind up nonetheless with an apartment in town, thus depriving the newly married army couple of an apartment for which they would be willing to pay $125. If rents are allowed to rise, those who care less buy less, leaving more for those who care more. That at least makes more sense than rationing without regard to intensity of desire.

It is quite true that poor people tend to get less than rich people when rationing occurs by means of price. That, in fact, is the very meaning of "rich" and "poor" when used in an economic context. But this is not the whole picture. Price rationing accommodates divergent preferences as well as differences in wealth. In any event, this is an objection to the existing distribution of wealth, not to price rationing.

One may object for many reasons to rationing by means of price. The advantages and disadvantages of particular rationing procedures must finally be considered on a case-by-case basis. Few of us, for example, would be satisfied with a system that rations justice by means of price, and so we don't allow competitive bribing of judges by litigants (though we do tolerate competitive hiring of legal counsel). But rationing by *some* set of discriminatory criteria is inevitable as long as there is scarcity.

Once Over Lightly

Scarcity is a relationship between availability and desirability. A good is scarce when there is not enough available for everyone to have all that he wants at no cost.

Scarce goods must be rationed in some way.

Every rationing system must employ discriminatory criteria of some kind.

Competition is the attempt to satisfy whatever discriminatory criteria are being used to ration the desired goods.

Rationing by the criterion of monetary price encourages people to acquire money. The social consequences of this will depend largely on the discriminatory criteria that must be satisfied in a society in order to obtain monetary income.

A shortage of a good exists when the quantity demanded is greater than the quantity supplied. A shortage can always be eliminated by a sufficiently large price increase.

A surplus of a good exists when the quantity supplied is greater than the quantity demanded. If a surplus still existed when the price of a good was zero, that good would not be scarce.

Rationing a good by means of monetary price discriminates in favor of those who receive high monetary incomes, whether through diligence, luck, genius, or knavery. But it also discriminates in favor of those who want the good more strongly and are therefore willing to give up a larger portion of their monetary income to obtain it.

QUESTIONS FOR DISCUSSION

1. Many ceiling prices were fixed by law in World War II. How were scarce goods rationed?

2. New York has a system of rent controls covering many of the apartments in the city. How are scarce apartments rationed? (New York began to abandon rent controls in 1971.)

3. State colleges and universities usually set a very low tuition. How do they ration scarce facilities? Who do you think gains from this system? Why might professors and administrators of state schools prefer *not* to have scarce facilities rationed by means of higher price (tuition)?

4. There are no toll charges for driving on many urban expressways during the rush hour. How is the scarce space rationed?

5. Parking space is often sold on college campuses at a zero price. How is the scarce space rationed? If all students who bring cars onto the campus are charged $10 a year by the college as an automobile registration fee, is the fee a rationing device?

6. If the supply of turkeys in a particular November turned out to be unusually small, do you think a turkey shortage would result? Why or why not?

7. a. There is currently much concern about a growing surplus of college teachers. How could the surplus be reduced or eliminated? Do you think this will happen? Why or why not?
   b. Notice that a surplus of college teachers can be viewed as a shortage of college teaching positions. How will the scarce supply of positions be rationed if price (salary of teachers) is not allowed to perform this function?

8. How do you account for the fact that so many people were concerned about world food shortages in 1974 when only five years earlier the governments of Austral-ia, Canada, and the United States had been worrying about surpluses?

9. If you travel through the Western states in the summer, you are much more likely to encounter a shortage of camping spaces than of motel rooms. Why?

10. When motels raise their rates "during the season" and reduce them "off season," are they exploiting customers or promoting a better allocation of resources?

11. The government did not impose controls on sugar prices in 1974, and the price per pound rose about 600 percent. Did the high price cause any more sugar to be available in 1974 than would have been available at a lower, controlled price? Do you think there would have been any refined sugar available on grocers' shelves if the government had frozen the price near its original level? Where would it have gone?

12. Would scheduled airline flights continue to be bunched at the popular hours if airports based landing fees on the time of day as well as weight? What are the costs created by the present system with its alternating shortages and surpluses of landing and takeoff times?

13. Here are data on total energy consumption in the United States in selected years (measured in trillions of British thermal units). Project energy consumption for 1975 and 1980 by making a rough extrapolation. Compare your projection for 1975 with the data for actual energy consumption. (Try looking in the most recent *Statistical Abstract of the United States*, which has a comprehensive index.)

1955	39,956
1960	44,816
1965	53,969
1970	67,143
1975	_____
1980	_____

14. In 1972, to celebrate an anniversary, a Chicago bank offered to sell $100 bills for $80 cash to each of the first 35 customers who appeared at opening time (9 A.M.) on its birthday.

    How do you suppose the bills were rationed? What kind of people do you think managed to buy the cut-rate $100 bills?

15. Think about a registration scheme under which students would have to pay more tuition for 10 o'clock classes and receive discounts for taking 8 o'clock classes. Would you favor such a plan? Why do colleges *not* charge higher prices for the hours in greater demand? A student willing to pay a friend $5 to stand in line for him and grab a 10 o'clock section might protest vigorously if he were charged an extra $3 to take a 10 o'clock class—even though the $3 fee gets rid of the line which he was willing to pay $5 to avoid. If you think these apparently inconsistent responses are plausible, how would you explain the contradiction?

16. If a ceiling price of $1 per pound was placed on lobster sold at retail, where could you go to eat a lobster?

17. If the distribution of income were completely equalized, would everyone purchase the same quality automobile? Against whom do automobile prices discriminate?

18. Are dragons that eat people scarce today?

Opportunity Cost
and the Supply of Goods

Until now most of our attention has been focused on demand. We've been looking at the way in which prices ration available supplies by persuading people to substitute alternative goods. But what determines the available supplies, or the amount of each good offered for sale?

The answer is *cost*. But this reply raises as many questions as it answers. What do we mean by cost? We shall try to convince you in this chapter that it makes sense to think of *cost as the value of sacrificed opportunities*. Economists call this concept *opportunity cost*, and it ties together, as we shall see, the law of demand and the principles governing supply.

Opportunity Cost: Concept and Applications

The following exchange occurs in a college dormitory on a Monday night in the fall.

"Hey, Jack, do you want to go see the new Bergman movie? It closes after tonight."

"Golly, I'd love to but I can't. We've got a Russian test tomorrow and I'll flunk if I don't cram some vocabulary."

"Forget it. You can borrow my vocabulary cards in your free period tomorrow. An hour with the cards right before class is a B for sure."

"Well—trouble is the Redskins and Miami are on TV tonight and I'd rather watch the game if I don't have to study."

"We'll go at six and be back for the kickoff."

"All right. Just let me see how much money I've got—five, six, seven, eight dollars—to last until I get paid on Thursday. And I'm out of meal tickets!"

"Eat peanut butter sandwiches! I thought you wanted to see the movie."

"I do. O.K. I'll let my stomach shrink until Thursday. Should we leave at quarter to six?"

The real cost of any action (going to a movie, buying a pair of jeans, manufacturing a lawnmower, moving to Halifax, raising beef cattle, building a hardware store, taking out an insurance policy) is the value of the alternative opportunity that must be sacrificed in order to take the action. The cost for Jack of going to the movie was at first calculated as a passing grade (given up!) in Russian. When his friend showed him how to reduce that cost, Jack looked at the next most valuable opportunity he would have to sacrifice if he went to the movie: watching the Monday night football game, a game he particularly wanted to see. His friend eliminated that cost for him and

Jack turned to the money cost. But money wasn't the real cost. The real costs that dollars and cents represent are the opportunities given up when the money is spent in one way rather than another. The two dollars Jack will spend for the movie represent some meals he would have liked to eat but is willing to sacrifice in order to see the film.

The theory of supply in economics is not essentially different from the theory of demand. Both assume that decision makers face alternatives and choose among them, and that their choices reflect a comparison of the benefits anticipated from the alternatives. The logic of the economizing process is the same for producers as it is for consumers.

Producers' Costs as Opportunity Costs

When we think about producers' costs, asking ourselves for example why it costs more to manufacture a ten-speed bicycle than a redwood picnic table, we tend to think first of what goes into the production of each. We think of the raw materials, of the labor time required, perhaps also of the machinery or tools that must be used. We express the value of the inputs in monetary terms and assume that the cost of the bicycle or the table is the sum of these values. That isn't wrong. But it leaves unanswered the question of why the inputs had those particular monetary values. The concept of opportunity cost asserts that those values reflect the value of the inputs in their next best uses, or the value of the opportunities forgone by using the inputs in the production of bicycles and picnic tables.

The manufacturer's cost of producing a bicycle will be determined by what he must pay to obtain the appropriate resources. And, because these resources have other opportunities for employment, he must pay a price that matches the "best opportunity" value. The value of forgone opportunities thus becomes the cost of manufacturing a bicycle. This makes excellent sense, for the meaningful cost of obtaining one more bicycle is the value of what must be given up or sacrificed or foregone in order to obtain that bicycle.

Consider the case of the picnic table. Part of its cost of production is the price of redwood. Assume that the demand for new housing has increased recently, and that building contractors have consequently been purchasing a lot more redwood lumber. If this causes the price of lumber to rise, the cost of manufacturing a picnic table will go up. Nothing has happened to affect the physical inputs that go into the table, but its cost of production has risen. Because houses containing redwood lumber are now more valuable than formerly, the table manufacturer must pay a higher opportunity cost for the lumber he wants to put into his picnic tables.

The concept of opportunity cost explains also how labor enters into production costs. A worker must receive from his employer a wage that persuades him to turn down all other opportunities. A skilled worker will be paid more than an unskilled worker because and only insofar as those skills make him more valuable somewhere else. A worker who can install wheel spokes while standing on his head and whistling "Dixie" is marvelously skilled. But our bicycle manufacturer will not have to pay him additional compensation for that skill unless his unusual talent makes him more valuable somewhere else. That could happen. A circus might bid for his talents. If the circus offers him more than he can obtain as a bicycle producer, his opportunity cost to the manufacturer rises. In that case the manufacturer will probably wish him goodbye and good luck and replace him with another worker whose opportunity cost is lower.

If the National Basketball Association and the American Basketball Association merge into one league, what happens to the opportunity cost of physically coordinated seven-footers? With two leagues, each player has two teams bidding for his services. What either team must pay to get him is determined by what the other team is willing to pay, and both will be willing to pay a lot if they think he will make a big difference in ticket sales. If the leagues merge, however, the right to hire a particular player is assigned to a single team, and the opportunity cost of a well-coordinated seven-footer will fall to the presumably much lower level of his value in other lines of work. It's not surprising that owners of professional basketball teams prefer one league to two.

Let's take a less unusual case. If a large firm employing many people moves into a small town, the cost of hiring grocery clerks, bank tellers, secretaries, and gasoline station attendants in the town will tend to go up. Why? Because grocery stores, banks, offices, and gasoline stations must all pay the opportunity cost of the people they employ, and these people may now find better opportunities for employment in the new firm. Suppose the new firm is interested in hiring women exclusively; only the opportunity cost of hiring women will increase at first. But that will pull women out of some jobs, thereby creating additional opportunities for men and causing the opportunity cost of male workers to rise.

The resource that most clearly illustrates the opportunity-cost concept is probably land. Suppose you want to purchase an acre of land to build a house. What will you have to pay for the land? It will depend on the value of that land in alternative uses. Do other people view the acre as a choice residential site? Does it have commercial or industrial potentialities? Would it be used for pasture if you did not purchase it? The cost you pay for the land will be determined by the alternative opportunities that people perceive for its use.

Case Studies in Opportunity Cost

Let's examine some other cases of varying costs to see how the concept of opportunity cost explains familiar but often misunderstood phenomena.

Why, in the last 40 years, has the cost of a haircut gone up so much more than the cost of goods generally? It's because potential barbers have alternative opportunities. If people want their hair cut by professionals, they must be willing to pay enough to bid barbers away from these alternative employments. As wage rates increase elsewhere in the economy, the opportunity cost of being a barber, and hence the opportunity cost of using his services, rises.

Why is it often so much harder to find a teen-age babysitter in a wealthy residential area than in a low-income area? The frustrated couple unable to find a babysitter may complain that all the girls in the neighborhood are lazy. But that is a needlessly harsh explanation. Teen-age babysitters can be found by any couple willing to pay the opportunity cost. That means bidding the babysitters away from their otherwise most valued opportunity. If the demand for babysitters in the area is large because wealthy people go out more often, and if the local girls receive such generous allowances that they value a date or leisure more than the ordinary income from babysitting, why be surprised to find that the opportunity cost of a babysitter is high?

Why did the cost of a college education rise so steeply during the 1960s? A very large part of the explanation lies in sharply increased instructional costs, made up partly of higher faculty salaries and partly of reduced teaching loads. But how did these developments come about? Ask your friendly neighborhood professor and he will probably tell you about the long years that must be spent getting a Ph.D. and the impossibility of doing research while teaching twelve hours. Any good member of the professorial guild will assent to the virtues of those arguments. But no good economics professor will be much impressed with their cogency as an explanation of why professors earned more and taught less at the end of the decade than at the beginning. The rapidly rising demand for professors provides the explanation. State legislatures poured money into building new colleges and expanding old ones; the federal government responded to the Sputnik scare by appropriating vast sums for higher education and for research, which gave teachers new opportunities; the World War II baby boom became a college-student boom in the 1960s; and a larger percentage of the population became persuaded that a college degree was the passport to the good life. The government and private industry meanwhile increased their demand for the services of highly trained persons, widening the range of opportunities for people with extensive education. The net result was a vastly increased demand for the services of college professors. College professors, too, are scarce resources with opportunity costs. A larger number of them were obtained by bidding them away from alternative employments with the offer of higher salaries and reduced teaching loads. (Every college professor knows that it is easier to raise his income by finding a better opportunity elsewhere than by reciting his virtues to his current dean. Deans are more attentive to the recitals of professors with alternative opportunities.)

Why does the high school dropout rate decrease during a recession? The opportunity cost of remaining in high school varies with the job market for teen-agers. A decline in job opportunities reduces the opportunity cost of remaining in school for some young people; therefore fewer drop out.

Why are poor people more likely to travel between cities by bus and wealthy people more likely to travel by air? A simple answer would be that the bus is cheaper. But it isn't. It's a very expensive mode of transportation for people for whom the opportunity cost of time is high; and the opportunity cost of time is typically much lower for poor people than for those with a high income from working.

Do you have the idea? Figure out for yourself the cost of going to college. If you include in your calculations the value to yourself of whatever you would be doing if you were not in college, you have grasped the principle of opportunity cost.

A final example. Consider the case of a woman who runs a small grocery store all by herself. She says that she does pretty well because she has no labor costs. Is she right? The cost of her own labor is not a monetary outlay, but it certainly is a cost. And that cost can be measured by the value of the opportunities she forgoes by working for herself.

A Note on Alternative Systems

The concept of opportunity cost is as applicable to a socialist society, where resources are allocated by government planning, as it is to a market economy in which relative prices guide decentralized decisions. For economic planners in the Soviet Union, the cost of building a railway from point A to point B is the value of whatever would have been done with the resources had they not been allocated to the railroad. Opportunity costs will be calculated by different means and different decision makers in a socialist society. But the concept of opportunity cost is an important aid to clear thinking for any person and any society interested in getting the most out of available resources.

But government officials often have the power to obtain scarce resources without bidding for them. And thereby they can sometimes conceal the real costs of a policy. There is no good reason to go abroad for an example: we have an excellent illustration in our own historical experience with the military draft.

The Cost of a Volunteer Military Force

Selective service, as it is euphemistically called, has been around for a long time. While almost everyone regards it as an evil, most

Americans still seem to think of it as the only way to obtain military personnel in wartime. "The country needs 3 million men in uniform, and a draft is the only way to get them."

We objected in Chapters 2 and 3 to all such notions as "The country *needs* 3 million men in uniform." But we'll let it pass this time in order to ask, "Why is a draft the only way to get them?" Isn't there some wage rate for military service that would induce 3 million men to volunteer? Even in time of war? We don't draft policemen, firemen, steeplejacks, or others who do dangerous or disagreeable work. Why must we draft military personnel?

There may be good arguments for the draft, but the familiar argument that a volunteer army would cost too much is not one of them. The Department of Defense and others who worry about the relative costs of a conscripted and a volunteer military are conveniently overlooking the concept of opportunity cost. The true employment cost of creating a military force of 3 million men is *not* the wages paid to them, especially not when most of them have been conscripted against their will. It is rather the sum of the values of the opportunities forgone when these 3 million men entered the military.

What does it cost when a young man becomes a soldier? The best way to find out would be to offer him a bribe, and to keep raising the bribe until he accepted it. If Marshall would enlist for $5000 per year, Basil for $8000, and Philip for no less than $60,000, those represent the opportunity costs of Marshall, Basil, and Philip. The social cost of drafting all three would then be $73,000, even though the government can conceal this fact by offering far less in wages and then compelling each to serve.

The opportunity cost, or the genuine cost, is a function of forgone alternative employment opportunities and all sorts of other values: preferences with respect to life-style, attitude toward war, degrees of cowardice or bravery, and so on. When the government bids for military personnel, raising its offer until it can attract just the desired number of enlistments, the government in an important sense actually minimizes the cost of its program. For it pulls in those with the lowest opportunity costs of service —everyone like Marshall but no one like Philip. Under a draft this could occur only through the most unlikely of coincidences. Figure 5A provides a simple way to grasp the argument we're attempting to make.

Opportunity Costs and Budget Costs

There *is* a supply curve of military volunteers, and whatever its precise nature, it will certainly slope upward to the right. Some people (those who assign low value to their available alternatives) will volunteer at a very low wage. But 3 million volunteers can be secured, on our assumptions, only if the wage offer is at least $8000

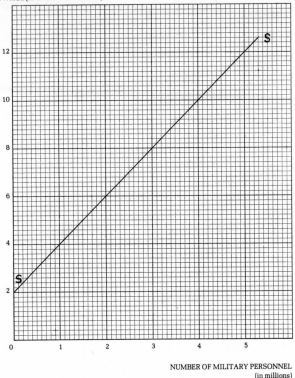

Figure 5A Supply curve of military volunteers

per year. That would mean a wage bill of $24 billion annually. But because taxpayers don't like to have their taxes raised, Congress is reluctant to approve such a huge appropriation. And the people in the Department of Defense care very much about the likes and dislikes of the people in Congress. They can cut that upsetting bill in half by offering only $4000 and compelling enlistments. The published cost will now be only $12 billion. Hurrah for cost savings!

But what of the genuine costs? The cost of the *volunteer* army under our assumptions would be $15 billion. That is the value of the area under the supply curve up to 3 million men, or the sum of the values of the opportunities forgone by those who enlisted. The other $9 billion paid out by the government is not a true cost to society as a whole. It is rather a transfer of wealth from taxpayers to members of the military who would have enlisted at a lower wage but who nonetheless receive the higher wage that is required to induce the enlistment of the 3 millionth volunteer. You should note in passing that this required wage will be lower in periods of high unemployment in the economy, when the value of alternative opportunities for volunteers decreases.

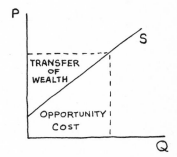

What will be the actual cost of a *conscripted* army? We can't say, except that it will certainly be larger. Only if the draft happened to hit exactly those and only those men who would have enlisted under a volunteer system would the cost be as low as $15 billion. But that is most unlikely. The more draftees who are grabbed from the upper rather than lower end of the supply curve, the higher will be the true cost of a conscripted army. For example, a man who would have volunteered at a wage of $4500 is offered $4000. He rejects the offer, and he is subsequently not drafted. Instead, a man who would only have volunteered at $12,000 is drafted. There was a "budget saving" of $500 annually and an actual loss of $7500.

The military draft fails to minimize the cost of obtaining military personnel. That may in your judgment be one of the least of its faults; or it may be outweighed in your mind by presumed advantages. But at least it's a flaw that economists can point out.

Do Costs Determine Prices?

When sellers announce a price increase to the public, they like to point out that the increase was compelled by rising costs. The *Wall Street Journal* publishes frequent announcements of this kind, and it's rare indeed when the announcement fails to include an expression of regret that higher costs made this unfortunate step necessary. In Chapter 10 we'll explore more fully the principles that guide sellers when they're setting prices. All we want to do now is use the concept of opportunity cost to examine critically the basic notion that prices are determined by costs. We want to show you that it makes as much sense to assert that costs are determined by prices. More accurately, we shall argue here that costs are always determined in part by demand. They are not something independent of demand as so many people carelessly assume.

Demand and Cost

We can begin with an example discussed earlier in this chapter. Does it make sense to claim that the price of haircuts has gone up because barbers' wages have risen? If people weren't willing to pay high prices for haircuts, how could barbers' wages rise? The price people are willing to pay to have their hair cut professionally is one important factor that causes costs, that is, wages, to be what they are.

Plastic surgeons receive high wages for their services. Is this why it costs so much to have a face lift? Not exactly. The causal relationship also runs in the opposite direction. It's the fact that people are willing to pay a high price for cosmetic surgery that makes the cost of hiring a plastic surgeon so high. Few people have the requisite skills, of course, and their acquisition is difficult and time-consuming. That's why the demand for cosmetic surgery raises the income of the surgeons rather than merely increasing the number of people willing and able to provide the service. But the cost of a plastic surgeon is obviously not independent of the demand for plastic surgery.

When the owners of professional football teams announce in the summer that ticket prices will be raised in the fall, they like to blame the increase on rising costs, especially the high wages that must be paid to the players. But why do the players receive such high wages? It can't be that their work is so dangerous and grueling because it was just as dangerous and grueling in the days when players received only a few hundred dollars for the season. It's the demand, the willingness of many people to pay high prices to watch, that has made football players such valuable resources. Soccer players in the United States receive far less, not because they work less hard, but because soccer isn't that popular in this country.

The Case of Land Prices

One of the most interesting cases of the relationship we're stressing is found in agriculture. The value of the real estate owned by farmers in this country rose more than 800 percent from 1940 to 1974, according to data published by the Department of Agriculture. Anyone who decides to go into farming today will find that he has to pay a high price to obtain productive land. It would clearly be misleading to assert that the high cost of land is a cause of high food prices. It was the demand for land, determined in large part by the demand for agricultural products, that pulled up the cost of farming land. When farmers argue for higher government support prices for their crops because land costs so much, they are ignoring the fact that higher support prices will tend to pull up the price or cost of the land on which those crops can be grown.

The most dramatic case of misleading reasoning is the argument of a farmer whose land lies near a large city. As the suburbs expand, residential developers offer to buy the land for a price that is three or four times higher than the price it can command as agricultural property. If the farmer refuses to sell because he wants to stay in farming, it is very unlikely that he will complain about the rising cost of land. But farmers who rent land near large cities often do just that. The landowner will understandably want to sell the land to developers unless the tenant farmer is willing to pay three or four times more rent. We can certainly sympathize with the tenant farmer dispossessed by the growth of the suburbs. But it's important that we see why he's being asked to pay a rent so much higher than before: it is the demand for land that is raising its cost.

Consumer Prices as Opportunity Costs

In all these examples we've tried to show that the costs of productive resources like labor and land are prices determined by demand. That, in fact, is what's meant by calling them opportunity costs. We can just as easily argue that the prices of consumer goods are, in reality, costs—opportunity costs that measure the value of the goods in alternative uses. Take, for example, the case of our old friend the lobster.

Lobsters are, unfortunately, scarce. More lobsters will be brought to market as higher prices offer larger incentives to lobster fishermen; but the demand in recent years has increased considerably faster than the supply, and the price has consequently risen sharply.

PRICE PER LOBSTER

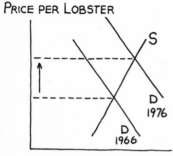

QUANTITY OF LOBSTER
PER MONTH

The higher price can be viewed as the opportunity cost of the resources engaged in bringing lobsters to market. But when the lobsters have all been brought to market on a given day, so that the supply is, for that day at least, completely inelastic, then the price can be viewed as the opportunity cost of the last potential purchaser who was persuaded by the high price to do without lobster. Think of it as follows: lobsters have many alternative uses, at least as many as there are potential lobster eaters. Lobsters have only one function, it is true, from the aggregate point of view. (We're notorious for ignoring the values and preferences of the lobster.) But the consumption of a lobster by one gourmet prevents its consumption by another. Lobster lovers in effect bid against one another for the limited supply. As the price rises, more and more potential consumers are reluctantly persuaded to do without. The price that clears the market, that makes the quantity demanded equal to the quantity supplied, will be the price that just barely persuades the most reluctant of the disappointed lobster lovers to go home from the seafood market with ocean perch or flounder fillets. It is *that person's* opportunity cost that is expressed by the market clearing price.

The point of all this is that people don't pay what lobster is worth to them but rather what lobster is worth in its most valued alternative use: as food for the consumer who was just barely deterred by the price from making a purchase. It's the opportunity cost of this disappointed lobster lover that the price reflects, as well as the opportunity costs of the resources that might have been used to bring additional lobsters to market.

How many people realized in late 1974 when they were paying 75 cents per pound for sugar that the price was equal to the cost? Not the growers' cost, of course, but the opportunity cost of those sugar and candy-bar lovers who were finally persuaded by the rising price to sacrifice the sweets they craved.

Once Over Lightly

The real cost of any good is the value of what must be sacrificed in order to obtain it. Economists call this its opportunity cost.

Insofar as the resources employed in producing goods can be obtained only through competitive bidding, costs of production will reflect the value of the alternative uses of the resources. This implies that producers will want to suppress competitive bidding for the resources they use if they can find an effective way to do so.

The value of a human being may be infinite; but the wages of human beings in any task will be much closer to the value of their services in alternative employments than to infinity.

Budget costs are not always real costs because they sometimes overlook or conceal opportunity costs. People in business for themselves often overlook the opportunity costs of the resources they themselves own. And governments may be able to employ coercion in place of bidding to obtain resources at less than opportunity cost.

The law of demand and opportunity cost are opposite sides of the same coin. The monetary price of a good expresses the value of other goods the purchaser could have obtained with that sum if he had not purchased this particular good. The price that must be bid to obtain it also expresses the value of that good to the last bidder who gave up his opportunity to have the good when the price rose too high. Because prices express forsaken opportunities, less will be purchased at higher prices and more at lower prices.

Demand determines costs. Costs determine prices. Prices for alternative goods determine the demand for particular goods. Everything depends upon everything else in the opportunity cost way of thinking.

QUESTIONS FOR DISCUSSION

1. What effect would the expectation of a continuing high price for soybeans have on the price of field corn? How does the concept of opportunity cost aid us in seeing the relationship?

2. What is the cost per ticket to a professional baseball club that offers 50 "free" tickets to an orphanage? Does it matter for what game the tickets are offered?

3. Why did the cost of hiring domestic servants increase dramatically during World War II? What would you have replied to people who said that servants "just weren't available"?

4. Some people contend that the ending of the military draft reduced college enrollments. Use the concept of opportunity cost to defend this argument. How did organized draft resistance and mounting public hostility to the Vietnam war affect Congressional perceptions of the relative cost of a conscripted and a volunteer army?

5. Jim Teen, a high school junior, can caddy at the local country club for as many hours as he chooses each weekend. His father insists, however, that Jim mow the lawn each week. It takes Jim one hour to mow the lawn; it takes his younger brother Bill two hours. Can you explain why it might be more efficient for Jim to pay Bill to take over his lawn chore even though Bill is a far less skilled yardman? What sense does it make, if any, to say that it costs more when Jim mows the lawn than when Bill mows it?

6. If the federal government and private foundations allocate large sums for research, will this tend to benefit or harm a small college whose faculty either does no research or cannot land any research grants? Why?

7. By taking an airplane one can go from D to H in one hour. The same trip takes five hours by bus. If the air fare is $30 and the bus fare is $10, which would be the cheaper mode of transportation for someone who could earn $2 an hour during this time? For someone who could earn $10 an hour? Five dollars an hour?

8. When that Chicago bank (mentioned in question 14, Chapter 4) offered to sell $100 bills for $80 cash to the first 35 people who entered the bank at 9 A.M., 4 young men started the queue 17 hours prior to opening time. What was their cost of waiting? How do you know?

9. Why might a multinational corporation with identical plants in different countries pay different wage rates to workers in the two countries even though their skill levels were the same? Does this strike you as unjust? Why might the higher-paid workers object?

10. Think about the cost of television commericals. What enters into the cost of a 30-second commercial plugging Friendly Fred's Ford Dealership? How do you explain the fact that the same commercial will cost $90 on Wednesday morning but $1600 right before "All in the Family"? Local television stations are often asked to donate time for public service spots. Does this cost the station anything? Do you think that station owners' religious beliefs make them more willing to donate time on Sunday morning than on weekday mornings?

11. a. It has been argued that a volunteer army would discriminate against blacks and poor people, because they tend to have the lowest-value alternatives to military service and hence would dominate the ranks of volunteers. Do you agree with the analysis and the objection?

   b. Some critics have argued that if the military relied exclusively on volunteers, the armed forces would be filled with people of such low intelligence and skills that they could not operate sophisticated weapons such as the ABM. International Business Machines relies exclusively on volunteers, and *its* employees are not predominantly people of low intelligence and skills. What's the difference between ABM and IBM? How would you reply to the argument of these critics?

   c. Another frequent criticism of a volunteer military is that we don't want "an army of mercenaries." How high does the military wage have to be before the recipient becomes a mercenary? Are officers compelled to remain in the armed services? Why do they stay in? Are they mercenaries? Is your teacher a mercenary? Your physician? Your minister?

   d. The army has a well-deserved reputation for inefficiency in manpower use. What do you think causes this? Are generals and colonels less competent managers than corporate presidents and plant superintendents? Assume that they're not, and ask yourself what different incentive systems are operating in military and civilian personnel management. What is the cost to a private employer of misusing an employee's talents? What is the cost to a commanding officer of misusing a conscript's talents?

Sunk Costs, Marginal Costs, and Economic Decisions

Chapter 6

"Tuition covers only 43 percent of the cost of educating your son or daughter. We're counting on your annual gift to sustain operations that are fundamental to the kind of education for which our university is noted." Those sentences are from a letter sent to parents by a prestigious university whose tuition at the time was over $3500. Do you think that a student paying $3500 per year in tuition is paying only 43 percent of the cost of her education? Would the university really save $4640 annually if she dropped out?

How do you explain the fact that people choose to drive their own cars to a business convention rather than go with someone else even though they complain that the reimbursement of 10 cents per mile doesn't cover their costs?

Can a business firm make money by selling "below cost"?

To answer these questions you must learn to distinguish between the costs that are relevant to decision making and the monetary outlays that are irrelevant and not really costs at all.

The Irrelevance of Sunk Costs

If the quantity of a good that is supplied depends on opportunity costs, as we stated at the beginning of Chapter 5, then costs that are not opportunities forgone will not determine the quantity supplied and hence will have no way of affecting price. This is summed up in the economist's dictum: *Sunk costs are irrelevant.* It is a simple but important principle in economic analysis as well as a valuable guide to decision making for both businessmen and consumers. But what exactly is a sunk cost?

When you go into a restaurant and order the 16-ounce steak for $6, you incur a cost: the value of whatever you would have done with the $6 had you not ordered that steak. Now suppose that after eating awhile you realize you overestimated your appetite. You eat half the steak and find that you just don't want any more. You wish that you had ordered the 8-ounce steak listed on the menu at $4. What is the cost of leaving the restaurant with half the steak still on your plate?

It is *not*, as many would erroneously suppose, the difference between the price of the 16-ounce and the 8-ounce entree, or $2. You do not give up $2 in the value of forgone opportunities by leaving half the steak on your plate. You incurred the full cost of the larger steak when you ordered it; you committed yourself at that time to pay the price of the large steak and in that moment you incurred all your costs. The opportunity to spend your money on something else disappeared at that moment.

Then what is the opportunity cost of leaving half your dinner behind? That depends. What opportunity do you thereby forgo? If you have a dog, it might be the price of half a pound of dog food, which is the value of the opportunity forgone when you chose not to ask for a doggie bag.

Bygones are bygones, sunk costs are sunk.

> The Moving Finger writes; and, having writ,
> Moves on: nor all your Piety nor Wit
> Shall lure it back to cancel half a Line,
> Nor all your Tears wash out a Word of it.

Of course, we must be certain that a cost is really sunk, or fully sunk, before we decide to regard it as irrelevant to decision making. If you were to purchase a new motorcycle and immediately afterward regret your decision, what would be the cost to you of continuing to own the motorcycle? Clearly, you would not be forced to say, "I did it and now I'm stuck." You could resell the motorcycle. By not doing so you would incur a cost (a benefit forgone) equal to its resale value. The genuine sunk cost would therefore be only the difference between what you paid for it and what you can get by selling it. That is the irrelevant part of your cost. *In the economist's way of thinking it is no cost at all, for it represents no opportunity for choice.* It may be cause for bitter regret and the occasion of some education in the dangers of impulse buying, but it is no longer a cost in any sense relevant to the economics of present decisions.

Yet we all know that people do not consistently reason things out in this way. Many a person who made such a purchase and then regretted it would be tempted to retain possession of the motorcycle rather than sell it for substantially less than the original price. He might justify this action by saying "I can't afford to take the loss." But he already took the loss! He made a mistake, and his full loss occurred when he made it. If he nonetheless chooses to keep the motorcycle, he is probably practicing self-deception. He persuades himself that a motorcycle gathering cobwebs in the garage has the same value as the money he paid to put it there, and more value than the opportunities forgone by keeping it there. But the only relevant cost now is the opportunity forgone *by not selling*.

The Case of the Las Vegas Caper

Let's take another example more closely related to the business world. You own a television retail store, and one of your suppliers is sponsoring a gigantic Dealers Contest. For every television set you buy (no returns allowed), you receive one day in Las Vegas with all expenses paid. You gleefully order 28 sets, and your wife starts planning your two-week holiday together.

Upon your return from Las Vegas you begin wondering how you

will sell all those television sets. One month later you're still wondering. It seems that none of your customers is interested in that brand or model. You are about ready to give up and store the whole lot in the back workroom.

Then you get an offer from an orphanage in some distant city to take all those sets off your hands for $1000. You know that a businessman can't make money by selling below cost, so you sit down to figure out the cost of the sets. You paid $35 apiece to the supplier. Moreover, you have had them in your store for a month tying up valuable floor space. You borrowed the money to buy them from the bank at 12 percent annual interest. You also had various handling costs that you estimate at $100. And you spent $40 on advertising in a vain effort to move the sets. By estimating $70 as the opportunity cost of display space tied up for a month, you arrive at a figure of $1200. You write back to the orphanage that you would be willing to sell the lot at cost for $1200, forgoing any profit on the transaction in the interest of charity. The orphanage replies that $1000 is their top price since they can get the sets they want somewhere else for that price. But you are a good businessman, you know that losses don't make profits, and you refuse.

You were actually a rather poor businessman. Every one of the "costs" you enumerated in arriving at your total of $1200 was a sunk cost and hence no cost at all. *The proper stance for making cost calculations is not looking back to the past, but forward to the future.* Your costs, if you sell, will be the opportunities thereby forgone, or what you can get for the sets if you do not sell to the orphanage. You know the market fairly well and you can estimate you could get $280 by selling them for junk. The relevant cost of the sets is therefore $280. Your gain from selling to the orphanage is $720. Any loss that you're worrying about should be assigned to experience and the glorious memories of Las Vegas. It is irrelevant for decision-making purposes.

$ 980.00 Wholesale cost
9.80 interest
100.00 handling
40.00 advertising
70.00 store space
$1199.80

$ 1000
−280
720

Building Bridges

This way of looking at matters is important enough for us to spend time on one further example. Fred Ballistics is an enterprising engineer who decides to build a bridge across the river. He owns both the access land and the bridge-building rights over the river, so he is free to build his own bridge and charge whatever tolls he pleases. After the bridge has been constructed, at a cost of $10,000, Fred starts to think about the tolls he should charge. How should he calculate the proper toll, assuming that he is interested in the bridge exclusively as a profit-making enterprise? How does the cost of constructing the bridge enter into his pricing calculations?

The answer is *not at all.* Sunk costs are sunk and therefore irrelevant. The questions Fred should now ask are future-oriented questions: What will people be willing to pay to use the bridge? What will it cost him to collect the tolls? What will he have to pay

Annual net
revenue from
operation: $ 75.00

Scrap value
of bridge: $1800.00

Earning rate
at S and L: 5 %

Annual loss
from continued
operation: $ 15.00

for bridge maintenance? What will he get if he sells the bridge for scrap metal? If it turns out that the demand for crossing the bridge is so small that no schedule of rates will yield revenue greater than the costs of toll collection plus maintenance or that the annual net revenue is less than Fred could get by selling the bridge for scrap and putting the proceeds in the local savings and loan bank, Fred should scrap the bridge (assuming, remember, that he is interested exclusively in monetary income).

If it should turn out that bridge crossings are in great demand, so that Fred's enterprising venture promises to be a huge success, he should still ignore sunk costs in calculating his schedule of tolls. Sunk costs are of concern to historians, but not to economic decision makers.

Marginal Effects Guide Decisions

One of the economist's favorite words is *marginal*. It means in economics exactly what it means in everyday speech: situated on the border or edge. The concept is of fundamental importance in economic thinking, because economic decisions, like all effective decisions, always involve *marginal* comparisons. That is to say, they always have to do with movements at the border, with positive or negative *additions*. A synonym for marginal, in fact, is *additional*. What will be the *additional*, or *marginal*, cost that results from this decision? And how does it compare with the marginal cost of alternative decisions?

If you think about it for a moment, you will discover that opportunity costs are always marginal costs. The term *marginal cost* does no more than bring into strong relief an aspect of opportunity-cost thinking. That aspect is so important, however, that we shall want to make frequent use of the term. Later on we shall talk about marginal other things.

Marginal Does <u>Not</u> Mean Average

A student will have no difficulty with the marginal concept if only he does not get it mixed up with the notion of *average*. You may have no intention of confusing marginal with average; if so, what follows may only plant in your head the seeds of a bad idea. Let's hope it doesn't. A simple production schedule of a hypothetical zerc manufacturer will illustrate the distinction.

Number of Zercs Produced	Total Cost of Producing Zercs
42	$4200
43	4257
44	4312
45	4365

A little long division reveals that 42 zercs can be produced at an average cost (total cost per unit) of $100; the average cost is $99 for 43 zercs, $98 for 44, and $97 for 45. A little subtraction reveals, however, that the cost of producing the 43d zerc is not $99 but $57. The incremental expenditure, or the extra cost, incurred by producing the 43d zerc, is its marginal cost. The marginal costs of the 44th and 45th zercs are $55 and $53, respectively. It is clear that marginal cost can be more or less than average cost and can even differ substantially from average cost. It should also be clear that for a zerc manufacturer trying to make production decisions, it is the marginal costs that should guide him. Shall we produce more? Or less? Marginal cost is the consequence of action; it should therefore be the guide to action.

Is a businessman then not interested in average costs? Unless a businessman can cover all his costs from revenue, he will sustain a loss. He won't willingly commit himself to any course of action unless he anticipates being able to cover his total costs. He might therefore set up the problem in terms of anticipated production cost per unit against anticipated selling price per unit. But notice that the *anticipated* costs of any decision are really *marginal* costs. Marginal cost need not refer to the additional cost of a single unit of output. It could also refer to the additional cost of a batch of output, or the addition to cost expected from a decision regarding an entire process. Decisions are often made in this "lumpy" way. Fred Ballistics, for example, would decide whether to keep the bridge in operation for another week or month, not for one more minute.

Similarly, no one plans to build a soda-bottling factory expecting to bottle only one case of soda. There are important economies of size in most business operations, so that unless a businessman sees his way clear to producing a large number of units, he will not produce any. He won't enter the business. He won't build the bottling factory at all. The entire decision—build or don't build, build this size plant or that, build in this way or some other way—is a marginal decision at the time it is made. Remember that additions can be very large as well as very small.

Whether or not the businessman casts his thinking in terms of averages, it is marginal costs that guide his decisions. Averages can be looked at after the fact to see how well or poorly things went, and maybe even to learn something about the future if the future can be expected to resemble the past. But this is history again— admittedly an instructive study—while economic decisions are always made in the present with an eye to the future.

$$\frac{\$4200}{42} = \$100 \qquad \frac{\$4257}{43} = \$99$$

$$\frac{\$4312}{44} = \$98 \qquad \frac{4365}{45} = \$97$$

$$\begin{array}{r} \$4257 \\ -4200 \\ \hline \$57 \end{array} \qquad \begin{array}{r} \$4312 \\ -4257 \\ \hline \$55 \end{array}$$

$$\begin{array}{r} \$4365 \\ -4312 \\ \hline \$53 \end{array}$$

The Cost of Operating an Automobile

"It costs about 12 cents a mile to own and operate an automobile." This statement makes little sense no matter how often it is re- peated. By examining a case with which everyone is familiar, we can tie together much of what has been said in these last two Chapters and see more of the implications.

Suppose that you have been asked by your college to drive your car to an intercollegiate student-government conference. You plan to attend the conference whether you drive your own car or not. The college offers you 8 cents a mile. Will it pay you to drive, or should you say no and hitch a ride with someone else? If you go about deciding by trying to calculate whether the cost to you of owning and operating a car is less than 8 cents a mile, you are being foolish. It makes no more sense to speak of the cost per mile of owning a car than to speak of the cost per mile of owning a house.

(For just the same reason it makes no sense to compute the cost per ton of owning a steel mill, or the cost per student of having a college library, or the cost per prescription of having a cash register in the pharmacy. All such attempts suggest that someone is treating costs that cannot be affected by particular decisions as if they were relevant to the making of those decisions.)

Costs of purchase, license, insurance, and depreciation not due to operation are all unrelated to your decision whether or not to drive. That is why they are irrelevant. The relevant cost is the marginal cost: How much extra will you be out of pocket if you drive? Be sure to include not only the cost of gas but the costs of oil, tire wear, and mileage-induced repairs. Insofar as cost can be expected to vary proportionately with mileage driven, it can properly be expressed as so many cents per mile. If it is less than 8 cents, as it probably would be, you make money by driving your car. As long as the marginal cost remains less than the price paid by the college, you gain from every additional mile "produced" and "sold."

Are the costs of purchase, license, insurance, and time-related depreciation *completely* irrelevant? Shouldn't you be allowed to cover these costs, too? After all, you have to pay them even if they are not related to the trip you've been asked to undertake.

You are certainly free to ask the college for as high a mileage rate as you choose. And if you have no scruples, you are even free to trot out all your sunk costs and wave them righteously. There is ample precedent for such action. But the one person you don't want to confuse is yourself. Only marginal costs are relevant to your decision, whatever price the college finally agrees to pay you.

Perhaps you've begun to suspect that it's our example that is irrelevant. We're interested, after all, in ordinary business decisions, and whatever may be true of the student driver as entrepreneur, businesses surely have to cover *all* their costs, not just marginal costs. It would seem so. But it isn't so. There is no more necessity to cover sunk costs in the business world than there is in our case study.

The plain fact is that each year many businesses fail to cover sunk costs. But most of them do not stop operating. We can illustrate the dilemma by supposing that you bought your car with the

intention of driving it for the college. When you made up your
mind to become a sort of taxi operator, you hoped to make enough
money to pay your way through college. So you purchased a car,
the license, and insurance. You probably would not have done so if
you expected the college to pay only 8 cents a mile. Maybe you had
reason to believe they would pay you 15 cents. Your calculations in
these circumstances might have run as follows:

Purchase price:	$3000.00
License:	20.00
Insurance:	150.00
Gas and oil:	.04 per mile
Wear and tear:	.02 per mile
Chauffeur service:	2.00 per hour

Your problem now is the familiar one of adding apples and oranges. Or even worse, adding apples and velocity. How can you add
$3000 to 4 cents per mile and $2 per hour? Obviously you can't.

You could, however, turn all these figures into costs per year.
The license and insurance are annual costs. The purchase price
could be converted into an annual figure by estimating annual
depreciation and adding the annual interest charge on your initial
outlay of $3000. But you can't state the other costs on an annual
basis without knowing how far and how long you'll be driving. You
must anticipate. Remember what we said earlier: the significant
costs and benefits in economics are *expected* costs and benefits.
That means they are uncertain. But uncertainty is a fact of life, and
if you want to be a student entrepreneur, you will have to live with
it. So you estimate that you will obtain so many miles and so many
hours of business per year. You can plug in your estimate and
obtain numbers for gas and oil, wear and tear, and chauffeur
services per year.

Now you can do your addition and come up with a figure for the
annual cost of doing business. You can then take your estimate of
miles used in calculating gas and oil plus wear-and-tear charges,
multiply by the rate you expect to be paid, and thereby calculate
prospective revenue per year. If the anticipated annual revenue
exceeds the anticipated annual cost, you take the plunge and buy a
car. If it doesn't, you don't.

So sunk costs are relevant? Of course not. Until you take the
plunge they aren't sunk. They are marginal. They are additions to
cost which you are thinking about incurring. That's the essence of
being marginal. And as long as they're marginal, they are relevant.
But only that long! When you have yet to commit yourself in any
way to a business operation, *all* your costs are marginal. Once you
have committed yourself, the situation has obviously changed. If
you want to maximize your profits (or minimize your losses, which
comes to the same thing), you must produce and sell all those units
of output whose anticipated marginal cost is less than the anticipated price to be set by the college.

The parable of the student entrepreneur is applicable to any kind of decision-making situation, in business or elsewhere.

Another Note on Alternative Systems

All of this is just as applicable in a communist or socialist society as it is in a capitalist society. Resources will be differently allocated, and income and power differently distributed, depending on who owns the means of production. But the principles we have described are the general principles of economizing, applicable wherever resources are scarce. The central planners in a socialist state also operate within the constraints imposed by scarcity: the resources available to them have alternative uses; substitution possibilities are pervasive; one good can usually be achieved only by giving up some other good. The planners should therefore calculate the opportunity cost of contemplated actions, treating sunk costs as irrelevant and paying attention only to marginal costs.

Suppose that the minister of coal production in a socialist state is trying to decide how much coal should be mined this month. He can increase coal production by using more workers or employing them for longer hours, or by using more machinery or better machinery. The relevant cost to the society of doing so is the value of whatever is given up through his decision, or the marginal (opportunity) cost. If he obtains new machinery in order to increase coal output, society loses what could otherwise have been produced with the aid of that machinery, or what could have been produced with the resources employed in the construction of the new machinery. The real cost of increased coal production is therefore decreased production of locomotives, or cement, or farm tractors.

If the minister can expand coal production by using machinery already in place that would otherwise stand idle, the opportunity cost is much lower and may even be zero. The sunk cost of the equipment is irrelevant. Notice, though, that the marginal cost will be greater than zero if the machinery has any alternative use, including use as scrap metal.

We see the fundamental importance of evaluations in determining opportunity costs when we contemplate the costs, in such a situation, of expanding output by working the existing labor force longer hours. In a society where workers must be induced through monetary bribes (wages) to work in particular ways, the wage measures the opportunity cost. The wage must be sufficient to attract them from their (subjectively) next best alternative. But if workers can be compelled to do what the state dictates, the wage need not bear any relation to the opportunity cost as determined by the workers. (We saw in Chapter 5 how that occurs under a military draft.) In moving from an eight- to a ten-hour day, the miners might be sacrificing two hours of leisure. Whether this is worthwhile would depend upon the *planners'* valuation of the extra coal produced in relation to the *planners'* valuation of the leisure forgone.

In any event, it would be clearly wrong to suppose that the cost of producing the extra coal can be determined from the *average* cost of coal production. This is worth mentioning because some socialists have argued in the past that marginal cost considerations were only relevant in an economy guided by the pursuit of private profit. It is true that in a capitalist society businessmen will not choose to produce anything whose marginal cost of production exceeds its value to the consumer as measured by its price. But it is just as true that in a socialist society the central planners and enterprise directors should produce nothing whose marginal cost exceeds its value.

The major difference lies in the different social-political rules and procedures by means of which opportunity costs and prices are calculated: for workers, consumers, government officials, or any other resource managers. One of the distinct advantages of a capitalist system, characterized by substantial private ownership and control of resources, is its pricing mechanism. In a capitalist system, competitive offers to buy and sell resources interact to establish scarcity prices and opportunity costs expressed in monetary units. An enormous quantity of information summarizing a vast range of alternatives is distilled into the prices that in turn guide the choices of decision makers.

In no capitalist system past or present have prices ever summarized perfectly the available range of opportunities. And under certain circumstances, as we shall see later, they may do so in a fashion so inadequate as to be politically unacceptable. The relevance of all this for making a choice between alternative economic systems is a very complex issue that cannot be resolved exclusively by economic arguments.

In any economic system, however, the following general principles will be applicable:

Real costs are opportunity costs, the value of opportunities forgone.

Sunk costs are irrelevant, because they are costs that the decision cannot affect.

Opportunity costs are always additional or marginal costs, the costs entailed by the decision under consideration.

Some method of assigning indices of value to alternative opportunities must be used in any economic system, or decision makers will be operating blindly.

Supply and demand, or the market process of competing bids and offers, creates indices of value for decision makers by placing price tags on available resources.

If supply and demand are not allowed to set prices in a centrally planned economy, the planners will still want to know what prices supply and demand would have set if they hope to use the society's scarce resources efficiently.

Costs and Output in Agriculture

We can assemble all these principles into one example by looking at the case of Lawrence Riley, a Kansas farmer who intends to plant his 640 acres in wheat this year. We'll assume that he has weighed the opportunity cost of planting wheat rather than sorghum or some other crop (in whole or in part), so the only question he faces is that of the intensity of cultivation. How much wheat should Riley try to grow on his land?

The actual harvest is going to depend in part on factors like weather over which Riley has no control. But he can control such factors as the quality of seed, closeness of planting, and amount of fertilizer used. By varying these expenditures, he can cause the probable yield to vary enormously. Table 6A shows Riley's calculation of the relationship between total operating expenditures and the yield per acre. Operating expenditures do not, of course, include those costs which are sunk or otherwise unrelated to production decisions, such as interest payments, taxes, or depreciation on equipment. They do, however, include an implicit wage for the work Riley performs in growing wheat.

TABLE 6A

I Operating Costs per Acre	II Total Operating Costs (640 × expenditure per acre)	III Bushels of Wheat Expected per Acre	IV Total Bushels of Wheat Expected (640 × expected yield per acre)	V Marginal Cost per Bushel (additional cost ÷ additional yield)
$ 27.00	$17,280	18	11,520	
33.00	21,120	22	14,080	$1.50
39.20	25,088	26	16,640	1.55
45.80	29,312	30	19,200	1.65
53.20	34,048	34	21,760	1.85
62.00	39,680	38	24,320	2.20
73.00	46,720	42	26,880	2.75
87.20	55,808	46	29,440	3.55
105.80	67,712	50	32,000	4.65

How intensively should Riley cultivate? At what yield per acre should he aim? The answer will depend upon the costs of production shown in the table plus the expected price of wheat. The decisive cost is the marginal cost, the additional cost that Riley incurs in trying to increase his per acre yield. Column 5 was calculated by dividing the *changes* from row to row in column 3 (or 4) into the *changes* of column 1 (or 2). Marginal cost increases at an increasing rate in column 5 because more intensive cultivation yields progressively diminishing returns; there are technological limitations on any farmer's ability to increase the yield from an acre of land. The marginal costs are *in between* the rows because they express the cost of moving from one position to another.

The situation Riley faces can also be shown on a graph. In Figure 6A, *the marginal cost curve is his supply curve.* Do you see why?

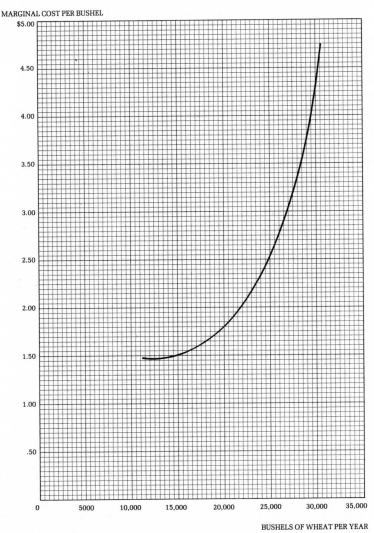

MARGINAL COST PER BUSHEL

BUSHELS OF WHEAT PER YEAR

Figure 6A   Riley's marginal cost curve

If Riley expects the price of wheat to be $2.00 per bushel, he will not want to grow any bushels which cost him more than that to raise. He'll be content with a yield of approximately 34 bushels per acre (21,760 bushels altogether), because additional wheat beyond that costs more to grow than he expects to receive for it. Read across from the price of $2.00 on the marginal cost curve; each extra bushel up to 21,760 costs less than $2.00 to produce. Beyond that output, extra

PRICE PER BUSHEL

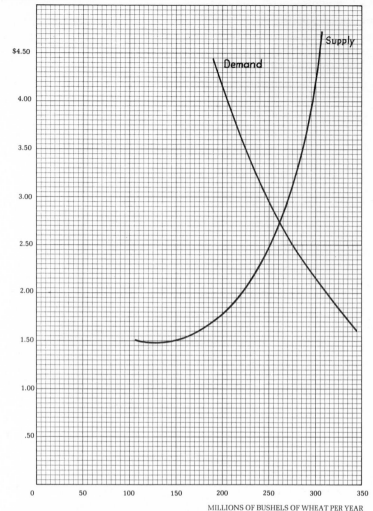

Figure 6B Market Demand and Supply

bushels add more to Riley's costs than to his receipts. So he won't produce more than that if the expected price is $2.00. If he expects the price to be $2.75 per bushel, it will be worth his while to increase production to about 40 bushels per acre or 25,600 bushels altogether.

Will Riley's marketing receipts exceed his total expenses at either or both of these prices? We don't know from the data given because only his operating expenses are presented. But costs that are unaffected by decisions should not be allowed to influence decisions. Riley's supply curve depends exclusively upon his marginal costs.

Notice that if the expected price of wheat is $2.00 so that Riley aims at a yield of 34 bushels per acre and a total harvest of 21,760 bushels, his average operating expenses will be about $1.565 per bushel ($34,048 ÷ 21,760). If his annual nonoperating expenses are $10,000, his total expenses per bushel will be slightly more than $2.02. But neither average is relevant to his production decisions!

The price at which Riley will be able to sell his wheat is going to be determined through the interaction of the market demand with the sum of the supply curves of all wheat farmers. If we adopt the simplifying assumption that there are 10,000 wheat farmers altogether, each with costs exactly like Riley's, then the market supply curve would be the marginal cost curve in Figure 6A with the quantities on the horizontal axis multiplied by 10,000. With the market demand as shown in Figure 6B, the equilibrium price is $2.75. We cannot predict that the actual price will be $2.75, because the farmers' production decisions are based on *expected* prices. If the farmers expected a price of $3.00, and weather or other unanticipated circumstances did not create a divergence between planned and actual output, they would produce about 265 million bushels. And the actual price would turn out to be only $2.60. Keep in mind that economic decisions are always based on *expected* values that may turn out to be mistaken.

We can also use this example to illustrate the point made a few paragraphs back in discussing alternative ways of organizing an economic system. Follow the argument on the graph of Figure 6B. Suppose all farms are state owned and that state planners both set wheat prices and instruct farm managers on how much wheat to grow. Suppose further that the planners order 300 million bushels to be produced and set the price of wheat at the market clearing level of $2.15. Since marginal cost with production at 300 million bushels is close to $4.50, a $2.15 price would result in an enormous shortage under a system of production for private profit; farmers would hold production below 230 million bushels. But *average* operating cost is only around $1.90 per bushel with production at 300 million bushels. Doesn't it make more sense from the overall social point of view for the planners to ignore marginal costs? Isn't society better off with more wheat—especially since the $2.15 price more than covers operating costs?

More wheat is presumably better than less wheat. But more wheat entails less of other goods. The objection is that the 300 millionth bushel costs society $4.50 worth of alternative goods. It is the area under the marginal cost curve, not average cost, which represents what a society loses in other goods by expanding the production of any one good. Average costs are not opportunity costs and are therefore no more appropriate as a guide for socialist central planners than they are for capitalist decision makers. If the planners nonetheless want 300 million bushels produced and consumed, they should at least be aware of the cost to society of their decisions. And that is shown by the *marginal* cost curve.

Once Over Lightly

Costs that are not affected by a decision are irrelevant to that decision. Costs that have already been incurred cannot be affected by present decisions: they are sunk costs and hence irrelevant to decision making.

The cost of a decision is the value of the opportunities forgone if that decision is made.

Opportunity costs are marginal costs, not average costs; they are the additional costs the decision entails.

Cost calculations, like all economizing decisions, must be made by looking to the future, not to the past.

If costs per unit are to be used in economic calculations, the units must be related to decisions. The cost per mile of owning a car or the cost per bushel of owning a farm are both meaningless because "owning" is not a decision that produces either miles or bushels (though it may be a precondition for such decisions).

Because economic decisions are based on future or expected costs and benefits, they always entail some degree of uncertainty.

Where the price of a good is set by market demand and market supply, the marginal cost curve of a producer is that producer's supply curve of the good. The market supply is the sum of all the producers' marginal cost curves.

Producers do pay attention to marginal costs when production decisions are guided by the desire for profit. But marginal costs are equally relevant to efficient decisions when production is not undertaken for profit.

QUESTIONS FOR DISCUSSION

1. A recent news report from London stated that British doctors, while dissatisfied with some aspects of their country's National Health Service, generally appreciated the fact that they could treat patients under this system "without regard to cost." Comment.

2. Physicians in the United States must typically go through four or more years of training after college before they can practice. Does this cost affect the prices doctors receive for their services? Explain.

3. A study of the New York City housing situation revealed that many landlords are abandoning apartment buildings they own because, under rent controls, they cannot get enough revenue to cover their costs. What costs are relevant to such a decision?

4. An official of the National Association of Letter Carriers recently complained that postal service was deteriorating because "management has as its objective delivering mail at less expense." He argued that the postal system should not be expected to break even because "it's a service for the people, not a profit-making organization." Comment.

5. An airline is thinking about adding a daily flight from Denver to Billings. It has estimates of the number of passengers who would use the flight. What costs should and should not be considered in deciding whether the anticipated revenue is sufficient to make the flight profitable?

6. If you were the television dealer introduced in this chapter and you were trying to decide whether to display the sets in your showroom, how would you go about estimating the cost of the display space? Why would you *not* be interested in the cost per square foot of construction as you tried to decide? Under what circumstances

would data on construction costs become relevant to your decision making?

7. The economist's rule "sunk costs are irrelevant" is like a string around your finger. It reminds you to consider only marginal costs, but it cannot identify the marginal costs. That requires informed judgment. You could sharpen your judgment by trying to enumerate and assess the marginal costs of retaining or not retaining your college apartment over the summer vacation. Try to calculate the minimum rental from subleasing that would persuade you to retain it for fall reoccupancy.

8. Your boss tells you in an angry voice, "I don't care what you learned in economics. If you don't include all our sunk costs in your report and recommendation, I'll fire you." Are the sunk costs now irrelevant to your decision making?

9. Should the casualties already incurred in a war be taken into account by a government in deciding whether it is in the national interest to continue the war? This is obviously not a trivial question. And it is a much more difficult question than you might at first suppose, especially for a government dependent on popular support.

10. In order to decide whether or not to drop intercollegiate football, your school undertakes a study of the program's cost. To what extent do you think the following budget items represent genuine costs?
    a. tuition scholarships to players
    b. payments on the stadium mortgage
    c. free tickets to all full-time students
    d. salaries of the athletic director, ticket manager, and trainer

11. The board chairman of the Tennessee Valley Authority complained in November 1974 that "prices charged for coal in today's market bear no reasonable relationship to the cost of producing it."
    a. What do you think he meant by cost of production?
    b. He also complained that TVA got no response when it asked for competitive bids from coal producers: "They don't need to compete because they can sell all the coal they want at their prices." If that's true, is the price of coal above its opportunity cost? What opportunities were determining the price TVA had to pay for coal?
    c. He also commented: "This country cannot afford to let something as vital to our well-being as coal be used to maximize profits." Do you think the prices charged for coal were harmful to the national well-being? What price structure for coal is most in the national interest?
    d. If the federal government, under these circumstances, had compelled coal mine operators to deliver to TVA the quantities of coal it wanted at the average cost per ton, what would have been the *real cost* of the coal burned in TVA generating stations?

12. In its 1973 annual report Phelps Dodge Corporation said it would exhaust the copper in Lavender Pit (Arizona) by mid-1974 and close the mine at that time. But the June price of copper was 25 percent higher than the January price, and the mine kept on operating.
    a. Did the higher price put additional copper in the pit?
    b. What would a geologist mean by the statement, "I can't tell you how much ore is in that mountain until I know the price of copper"?

13. The American Petroleum Institute estimated that proved U.S. oil reserves at the beginning of 1975 were 34.25 billion barrels. Petroleum geologists have estimated that 300 billion barrels of oil lie beneath the ground in fairly well-known locations within the United States.
    a. How would you reconcile these two vastly different estimates?
    b. The API defines "proved reserves" as the amount of oil likely to be recoverable from known reservoirs *under current economic conditions*. Can you suggest an easy way to increase the nation's "proved reserves"?

Efficiency and Comparative Advantage

Efficiency is something almost everyone favors. But what is it? In earlier chapters we talked a great deal about efficiency even when we didn't use the word. It is time now to haul the concept into the open for scrutiny. Efficiency is another of the central concepts in the economist's way of thinking.

Is a diesel locomotive more efficient than a steam locomotive? Most people would say yes. But what reasons would they give for their answer?

If efficiency is to have any precise meaning, it must be understood as a ratio of one thing to another. Engineers use a definition of efficiency that seems to satisfy this test. They define efficiency as the ratio of the work done by a machine to the energy supplied to it, and that ratio is usually expressed as a percentage. From the engineering standpoint, the diesel locomotive is therefore more efficient than the steam locomotive because, per unit of potential energy contained in its fuel, the diesel does more work.

This definition is somewhat unsatisfactory, however, when we think about it more critically. Efficiency cannot be simply the measure of energy output to energy input because, by the laws of thermodynamics, that ratio is always unity for any process. It is rather a measure of *work done* in relation to energy input. But what constitutes "work done"? Doesn't that depend on what is wanted? What qualifies as "work"? Engineers actually call a steam engine less efficient than a diesel because with a steam engine a higher percentage of the energy input is wasted. Strictly speaking, however, even wasted energy does work. It just doesn't do any *useful* work. That means it doesn't do work that anybody wants done. All of which implies that efficiency is not a purely objective or technological matter, but depends inevitably upon valuations.

It is sometimes said that our society places too high a value on efficiency. That's almost like saying that we place too high a value on what we value, which doesn't make much sense. We may be excessively infatuated with technology, but that is quite another matter. A mindless obsession with technology is very different indeed from a concern for efficiency.

The Meaning of Efficiency

Efficiency is inescapably an evaluative term. It always has to do with the ratio of the value of output to the value of input. Efficiency will always have an objective component, of course;

our likes and dislikes don't determine the potential heat in a pound of fuel. But physical facts by themselves can never determine efficiency. It follows that the efficiency of any process can change with changes in valuations, and because everything depends upon everything else, any change at all in any subjective preference is in principle capable of altering the efficiency of any process.

Let's go back to the question of the relative efficiency of diesel and steam locomotives. Each can be put into operation only with the use of a large number of inputs: not only coal or oil and locomotive operators but also all the inputs used in manufacturing the locomotives, the inputs that went into the fabrication of these inputs, the inputs that went into the fabrication of the products that were inputs in the process of producing the products that were inputs in the manufacture of the locomotives, and so on, without any discernible limit. Anything that changes the value of anything that contributes to a locomotive's operation can in principle alter its efficiency.

We don't need any farfetched illustrations to make the essential point. An increase in the price of oil relative to coal, if it is large enough, can by itself transform their relative efficiencies so that a coal-fired steam locomotive becomes more efficient than a diesel. It follows that these relative efficiencies depend on the demand for and supply of oil and coal, and hence on such factors as the motoring habits of the general public, the political situation in oil-producing countries, United States policy on import quotas, and the value placed on the environmental effects of strip-mining coal. Perhaps it never occurred to you that the relative efficiency of the old steam locomotive was affected by the efforts of the United Mine Workers!

To test your grasp of the principle at work here, examine each of the statements below. Ask yourself what kind of change would be capable of creating or reversing the situation. The possibilities are limited only by your imagination.

1. Math can be taught more efficiently with programed textbooks than with teachers.

2. It is more efficient to cultivate corn with a tractor than by hand.

3. It is inefficient to use trained lawyers as court stenographers.

4. It is more efficient to cut down trees with a chain saw than with an ax.

If you thought through these statements, you should have noticed the possibility that changes in printing costs or teachers' salaries, tractor prices or farm labor wages, alternative opportunities available to people trained in law and in shorthand, and even, in the fourth case, changes in attitudes toward noise in the forests are capable of altering relative efficiencies. If you failed to notice these things and more, try again at the conclusion of this chapter.

79

Efficiency and
Comparative Advantage

Some Myths concerning Wealth

Trading has long had an unsavory reputation in the Western world. This may reflect the enormous influence of Aristotle and his medieval followers, who thought there was something unnatural about exchange for monetary gain; but it is more likely the result of a deep-seated human conviction that nothing can *really* be gained through mere exchange. Agriculture and manufacturing are believed to be genuinely productive: they seem to create something genuinely new, something additional. But trade only exchanges one thing for another. It follows that the merchant, who profits from trading, must be imposing some kind of tax on the community. The wages or other profit of the farmer and artisan can be obtained from the alleged real product of their efforts, so that they are entitled in some sense to their income; they reap what they have sown. But the merchant seems to reap without sowing; his activity does not appear to create anything and yet he is rewarded for his efforts. Trading, some have thought, is social waste, the epitome of inefficiency.

This line of argument strikes a deeply responsive chord in many people who still retain the old hostility toward the merchant in the form of a distrust of the "middleman." Everybody wants to bypass the middleman, who is pictured as a kind of legal bandit on the highways of trade, authorized to exact his percentage from everyone foolish or unlucky enough to come his way.

However ancient or deep-seated this conviction of the unproductiveness of trade, it is completely erroneous. There is no defensible sense of the word *productive* that can be applied to agriculture or manufacturing but not to trading. Exchange is productive! It is productive because it promotes greater efficiency in resource use.

Many have taken a fatal wrong turn at the very beginning in considering this question by assuming that exchange, unless it is fraudulent or coerced, is always the exchange of *equal values*. It just isn't so. The exact reverse is true: Exchange is never an exchange of equal values. *If it were it would not occur.* In an informed and uncoerced exchange (and that is the kind we want to consider), both parties gain by giving up something of lesser for something of greater value. If Jack swaps his basketball for Jim's baseball glove, Jack values the glove more than the ball and Jim values the ball more than the glove. Viewed from either side, the exchange was unequal. And that is precisely the source of its productivity. Jack now has greater wealth than he had before, and so does Jim. The exchange was productive because it increased the wealth of both parties involved.

"Not really," comes a voice from the rear. "There was no real increase in wealth. Jack and Jim feel better off, it's true; they may be happier and all that. But the exchange didn't really produce anything. There is still just one baseball glove and one basketball."

We must be respectful but wary toward that small voice. What does wealth consist of? What constitutes production? Many people have drifted into the habit of supposing that an economic system produces "material wealth," like cars, houses, basketballs, breakfast cereals, and ball-point pens. But none of these things is wealth unless it is available to someone who values it. Additional water is additional wealth to a farmer who wants to irrigate; it is not wealth to a farmer caught in a Mississippi River flood. A food freezer may be wealth to an American housewife but not to an Eskimo. The crate in which the freezer was delivered is trash to the housewife but a treasure to her small son, who sees it as a playhouse.

Economic growth consists not in increasing the production of *things* but in the production of *wealth*. Material things can contribute to wealth, obviously, and are in some sense essential to the production of wealth. (Even such "nonmaterial" goods as love and peace of mind do, after all, have some material embodiment.) But there is no necessary relation between the growth of wealth and an increase in the volume or weight or quantity of material objects. The indefensible identification of wealth with only material objects must be rejected at root. It makes no sense. And it blocks understanding of many aspects of economic life.

So the small voice from the rear was confused. Both Jack and Jim do have greater wealth after their exchange. Recall what we concluded earlier about efficiency: it is measured by the ratio of one *value* to another, not by physical ratios of any sort. You can think of Jack and Jim's exchange as an act of production. Jack used the basketball as an input to obtain the output of a baseball glove. For Jim the glove was the input and the ball the output. The result of the productive process (the exchange) was an output value greater than input value for both parties. Nothing further is required to make an activity productive. The exchange expanded real output.

Efficiency and the Gains from Trade

The preliminary work has been done. We're ready now to introduce you to the principle of *comparative advantage*, a concept that sums up almost everything we've been talking about thus far. We'll allow Smith and Brown to make the introduction. They are suburban neighbors, each with a large lawn and a sizable flower garden. Every Saturday afternoon during the summer, Smith and Brown reluctantly go out to mow their lawns and weed their gardens.

Smith always finishes earlier despite the fact that the lawns and

gardens are identical in size. He is a strong and agile man who can
mow his lawn in 40 minutes and weed his garden in 80 minutes.
Brown takes two hours to mow his lawn and another two hours to
weed his garden, so he is still toiling while Smith is sipping lemonade. You should have these data clearly before you as you proceed,
so we'll summarize them in a little table:

Smith		Brown	
Lawn:	40 minutes	Lawn:	120 minutes
Garden:	80 minutes	Garden:	120 minutes

We're ready for the question: Is it possible for either or both to get
to the lemonade sooner on Saturday by engaging in a little trade?
(We shall assume that neither Smith nor Brown has a preference for
one kind of chore over the other and that the use of different tools is
not a factor in the problem. Dropping these assumptions would add
complexity without affecting the underlying principles.) We're all
familiar with the advantages of specialization. If the mason builds
the carpenter's chimney and the carpenter builds the mason's garage,
they each gain by taking advantage of their own and the other party's
special skills. That's familiar enough.

But it doesn't seem to fit the case of Smith and Brown. For Brown
appears to have no special skills, to be less efficient than Smith in
both mowing and weeding. So it would appear, but appearances are
misleading.

Suppose that Smith gave up all weeding and instead confined his
yardwork to mowing first his own lawn, then Brown's. He could then
finish his yard work in just 80 minutes, a gain of 40 minutes for Smith.
If Brown meanwhile weeded both gardens, he would still be working
240 minutes, for no gain or loss. Smith has gained from trade with
Brown and without inflicting any loss on Brown.

The Principle of Comparative Advantage

What happened? Nothing very unusual. Smith just happens to be a
more efficient mower than Brown, and Brown a more efficient
weeder than Smith. Like the mason and the carpenter. So each
specialized in that activity in which he was more efficient; that is,
each pursued his comparative advantage. It is a *comparative* advantage, because each is more efficient in one activity than the other
activity only *in comparison* with his neighbor. But that is what matters.

Whoa! The small voice from the rear is stirring again. "But
Brown is *not* a more efficient weeder than Smith. The clumsy slob
is less efficient than Smith in both activities." That small but
helpful voice has erred again. It just is not true that Brown is less
efficient than Smith in both activities. He really is more efficient
than Smith in weeding.

Proof is provided by the arithmetic calculation which shows that

Smith added to his wealth (his lemonade sipping time) by specializing in mowing, and then trading with Brown. And he did not do it at Brown's expense, for Brown's wealth was not reduced. No such gain would be possible if Brown were not more efficient than Smith in weeding—which implies, of course, that Smith is less efficient than Brown in weeding.

Nonsense? No—just a momentary paradox. The paradox disappears when we remember to wear the spectacles of opportunity cost. What is the cost to Smith of weeding a garden? It is two lawns left unmowed. And the cost to Smith of mowing a lawn is one-half a garden unweeded. The cost of anything is the opportunity thereby forgone; the cost of weeding is therefore to be expressed in this case in terms of mowing, and the cost of mowing in terms of weeding.

What about Brown? The cost to him of mowing a lawn is one garden left unweeded, and the cost of weeding a garden is consequently one lawn left unmowed. We can now determine who is the more efficient or lower-cost producer of weeded gardens by comparing relative costs.

The cost of a garden weeded by Smith is two lawns unmowed. For Brown it is one lawn unmowed. One is less than two. Brown is therefore the lower-cost or more efficient producer of weeded gardens.

We aren't just playing with words, as demonstrated by the crucial fact that either or both can increase their wealth if Brown specializes in weeding and the two engage in trade. Common sense resists this conclusion only because Brown takes *more time* to weed a garden than does Smith. Suppose, someone objects, that we express the costs in man-hours. Then Brown's cost will be one and one-half times as high as Smith's, and common sense will be salvaged. But only at the expense of everything we have argued for! Such an approach assumes that the real measure and determinant of value is the labor embodied in a commodity. But the assumption fails completely to explain relative prices. The cost of any commodity, in the economist's way of thinking, is not what is embodied in it, but what is given up in order to obtain it. It is the value of what is sacrificed, or of the opportunities forgone.

But could we not take leisure, the third good in our problem, as the measure of cost? Let's examine this possibility. Smith gives up 80 minutes of leisure to weed a garden, Brown gives up 120. By this measure Smith is the more efficient producer of weeded gardens, and common sense is again salvaged.

You may take this route if nothing else will satisfy you. But if you take it too far you will end up in confusion. Since leisure or lemonade-sipping time is a valued opportunity, the cost of mowing a lawn or weeding a garden can legitimately be expressed in terms of the leisure time given up. But the fact that Smith sacrifices less leisure than Brown to do a job does not prove that Smith is more efficient in some absolute sense. For Smith's leisure may be more valuable than Brown's! It makes sense to measure costs ultimately in terms of leisure only if we believe that leisure is "the ultimate good" *and* if we can assume that an hour of leisure is of equal value to everyone. This sort of absolutism does have a psychological appeal. There is a streak of egalitarianism in almost everyone which wants to assert that one person's leisure counts for exactly as much as any other's. And that conviction is remarkably resistant to all sorts of evidence suggesting that it just isn't so. Question 9 at the end of this chapter has been included for everyone who has trouble freeing himself from the presupposition that labor time or its opposite, leisure, is the proper ultimate measure of cost. And it's important to shake loose from that presupposition because opportunity-cost thinking recognizes *no* absolute measures of value: the value of *every* good must finally be expressed in terms of other goods.

The Terms of Trade

We stated a few paragraphs back that Smith or Brown or both can gain from specialization and exchange. In the one case we worked through, Smith appropriated the entire gain. That was a result of the specific terms of trade: the relative prices at which mowing and weeding were exchanged. The terms of trade were one garden for one lawn. At that price, Smith appropriated the entire gain from trade.

Satisfy yourself that you understand what we're doing by calculating the terms of trade that would assign the entire gain to Brown. If Brown weeded his own garden plus only half of Smith's, Brown would be working 180 minutes altogether. Smith would be left with two lawns to mow (80 minutes) plus half of his garden to weed (40 minutes), so he would be no better or worse off. The terms of trade that assign the whole gain to Brown are thus

$$1 \text{ L} = \tfrac{1}{2} \text{ G} \quad \text{or} \quad 1\text{G} = 2\text{L}$$

The argument is consistent with what you know about relative prices. The people who gain from an increase in the price of a good relative to other goods are those who specialize in its production. Brown likes to see the price of a weeded garden rise from one mowed lawn to two for the same reason that any producer likes to see the price of his specialty increase.

Of course, at some intermediate price ratio they could share the gain from trade. If

$$1 \text{ L} = \tfrac{3}{4} \text{ G} \quad \text{or} \quad 1 \text{ G} = 1\tfrac{1}{3} \text{ L}$$

Smith could gain 20 minutes and Brown 30 minutes from specialization and trade. (Don't conclude that Brown gains more! That requires the doubtful assumption that leisure is equally valuable to both. Turn to question 9 for the antidote.)

Comparative Advantage in International Trade

Popular thinking hangs on tenaciously to the notion that some countries may be able to produce almost everything at a lower cost. If wages in Japan or Mexico or Italy are lower than in the United States, won't Japanese, Mexican, and Italian manufacturers be able to produce just about anything more cheaply than U.S. manufacturers can do it? How can the United States compete with countries that tolerate wage rates, even for skilled workers, below our legal minimum? In Japan, Mexico, and Italy, however, you could find workers arguing that they can't compete with America's low-cost techniques of mass production. And the suspicion would properly arise that something is wrong with the argument.

The basic flaw in such arguments is their neglect of opportunity cost. It is *logically* impossible for one country to be more efficient than another in the production of everything. And that becomes apparent as soon as you remember to calculate efficiency as a ratio between what is produced and what is consequently *not* produced. The real cost of producing anything is the value of what is given up in order to produce it. Calculations in dollars, yen, pesos, and francs (or working hours) all too easily obscure these real costs of production.

Suppose that Japan and the United States each produced only three goods: grain, textiles, and radios. Suppose further that competition had moved prices in both countries to levels that reflected the opportunity costs of each good, with these results:

Prices per Unit of Good
(identical quantity and quality)

	United States	Japan
Grain	30 dollars	9,000 yen
Textiles	20	4,500
Radios	50	13,500

Which country is the more efficient or lower-cost producer of these goods? Before we can answer we must find some way of comparing costs. What measure is available?

Dollars and yen clearly won't do. It's obviously absurd to suggest that the United States is more efficient in producing all three goods simply because the dollar prices are lower than the yen prices. That would be true only if a yen had the same value as a dollar. We shall see in the later chapter on international exchange how the relative values of national currencies are established. It's enough for now to note that this is a blind alley because currency exchange rates only reflect, they do not determine, relative costs.

Some people might want to use the labor time invested in the production of these goods as the ultimate measure of their relative costs. To do that we would first have to find some common denominator for labor of different skill and effectiveness plus some way of translating such other inputs as machinery and land into units of labor time. And even if we could find a satisfactory way to do this, we would still be forced to adopt the arbitrary assumption that an hour of labor in Japan is as valuable as an hour of labor in the United States. But is it? Attitudes toward work and leisure are culturally determined, and there is no good reason to assume that an hour of working time is exactly as "costly" in one country as in another.

Then how can we decide which country is the lower-cost producer of these goods? The answer is: *There is no way at all to do so.* All we can do is determine that one country or the other is the more efficient producer of a particular good *relative to some other good or goods.* This is the meaning of comparative advantage.

Take radios, for example. The price ratios show that in the United States, a unit of radios costs either $1\,^2/_3$ units of grain or $2\,^1/_2$ units of textiles. It costs that much because that's what is given up in obtaining one unit of radios. In Japan, a unit of radios costs $1\,^1/_2$ units of grain or 3 units of textiles. Those are the quantities of grain and textiles that are given up in Japan when additional radios are produced. It follows, then, that Japan is more efficient than the United States in producing radios *relative to grain,* but less efficient *relative to textiles.*

Which country is the more efficient textile producer? If you've gotten the idea by now, you will immediately ask: relative to what? A unit of textiles costs $^2/_3$ unit of grain and $^2/_5$ unit of radios in the United States, and $^1/_2$ unit of grain and $^1/_3$ unit of radios in Japan. So Japan is the more efficient (lower cost) producer of textiles relative to both grain and radios.

The United States in turn is the lower-cost producer of grain relative to textiles: $1\,^1/_2$ units of textiles are given up to produce a unit of grain versus 2 units of textiles given up in Japan. The United States is also the lower-cost producer of grain relative to radios: $^3/_5$ unit of radios is the cost of a U.S. unit of grain; $^2/_3$ unit of radios is the Japanese cost.

Don't lose the point in all the fractions. A *nation can become an inefficient producer of good X simply by becoming a fabulously prolific producer of good Y.* When you become extraordinarily good at one thing, it is costly for you to do anything else. If Japan starts to produce radios and TV sets at a lower cost than they can be produced in the United States, that does not imply that U.S. radio and TV manufacturers have failed in some fashion. It could just as well mean that U.S. productivity has been increasing rapidly in other industries.

Comparative Advantage: The Economist's Umbrella

The term with which economists summarize everything we have been discussing in this chapter is *comparative advantage.* It might even be thought of as a term to summarize the entire collection of concepts presented thus far. To pursue comparative advantage means simply to sacrifice that which is less valuable for the sake of something more valuable.

Why do demand curves slope downward to the right? Because people pursue their comparative advantage. A rise in the price of any good means that its users will now be able to obtain the satisfaction it provides at a *relatively lower cost* by using some substitute.

How is the opportunity cost of any resource established? Through the pursuit of comparative advantage. People bid for a resource after estimating the potentiality of that resource relative to other resources for providing whatever it is they're after.

Why are only marginal costs and not sunk costs relevant to decision making? Because marginal costs reflect the *comparative advantages of alternative decisions*, while sunk costs can never do more than reflect the comparative advantages of past decisions. But no one makes decisions with the hope of affecting what happened yesterday.

It is comparative advantage—the advantage resources have over other resources in particular uses relative to other uses—that determines the most efficient way to employ a society's resources. And the pursuit of comparative advantage will lead decision makers to employ resources in the most efficient way if the relative costs decision makers must pay reflect opportunity costs.

The economic way of thinking may at root be nothing more than the ability to think consistently in terms of comparative advantage.

Once Over Lightly

Efficiency depends upon valuations. While physical or technological facts are certainly relevant to the determination of efficiency, they can never by themselves determine the relative efficiency of alternative processes. Efficiency depends upon the ratio of output *value* to input *value*.

Exchange creates wealth, because voluntary exchange always involves the sacrifice of what is less valued (input) for what is more valued (output). Exchange is as much a wealth-creating transformation as is manufacturing or agriculture.

People specialize in order to exchange and thereby increase their wealth. They specialize in activities in which they believe themselves to have a comparative advantage.

Comparative advantage is determined by opportunity costs. No person, no group, no nation can be more efficient than another in every activity, for even the most highly productive agents must have some activities in which they are less highly productive. If you're four times as intelligent, three times as strong, and twice as beautiful as another person, then that person has a comparative advantage in beauty—and you, handsome as you are, have a comparative disadvantage in beauty.

Relative prices help people decide where their comparative advantages lie insofar as relative prices reflect opportunity costs.

Relative prices also determine the distribution of income or the gains from specialization and trade.

Anything that prevents voluntary exchange promotes inefficiency by interfering with wealth-increasing specialization.

QUESTIONS FOR DISCUSSION

1. Is it more efficient to build dams with lots of direct labor and little machinery or with lots of machinery and little labor? Why might the answer vary from one country to another?

2. Which is more efficient: Japanese agriculture with its carefully terraced hillsides or American agriculture with its far more "wasteful" use of land? How have relative prices in the two countries brought about these different methods of farming? How have opportunity costs entered into the formation of these relative prices?

3. Attorney Fudd is the most highly sought-after lawyer in the state. He is also a phenomenal typist who can do 120 words per minute. Should Fudd do his own typing if the fastest secretary he can obtain does only 60 words per minute? Prove that Fudd is *not* twice as efficient as his secretary at typing, that he is in fact *less* efficient at typing, and that he should therefore retain a secretary.

4. The dean knows that Professor Svelte is the most capable administrator in his department, far more capable than Professor Klunk. Can you think of any reasons (related to efficiency rather than nepotism) for nonetheless appointing Klunk over Svelte as department chairman?

5. Have you ever noticed how few gasoline stations are found in the center of large cities? With such heavy traffic one ought to be able to do an excellent business. Why then are there so few?

6. The key to question 5 is the high price of land in the center of large cities. Would it make sense for the city government, which has the right of eminent domain, to take over some of this land in order to provide "vitally needed service stations"?

7. It has often been claimed that under a capitalist system business firms will sometimes continue to use obsolete equipment rather than the new, "most efficient" equipment because they have a lot of money tied up in the old equipment. Does this make sense? What is the relevance to such decisions of "money tied up"? Would an efficient enterprise manager want to behave differently under a socialist system?

8. You own and occupy a large brick house in an old residential neighborhood. The area is being rezoned to allow multiple-family occupancy and apartment buildings. How would you go about deciding whether to (a) continue to occupy the house as a single-family dwelling, (b) divide the house into several apartments, or (c) tear down the house and erect a new apartment complex? If you were to choose (b), could you be accused of retarding the economy by failing to adopt the most up-to-date equipment because of your vested interest in obsolete equipment? Does this differ from problem 7?

9. Here is a problem for those still infatuated with a labor-or-leisure theory of value. Suppose we want to verify the hypothesis that, since "a man's a man for a' that," one hour of Brown's leisure is equal in value to one hour of Smith's leisure. We gather the following evidence:

   a. We ask them. Brown says his leisure is worth more because he is fat and lazy. Smith agrees that Brown's leisure is worth more.

   b. While Smith and Brown are sipping lemonade together, Jones across the street offers them $10 apiece to work for an hour cleaning his garage. Smith accepts with alacrity, but Brown says he won't do it for less than $20.

   c. Smith often walks home from work because he has, as he says, "nothing better to do." Brown would take a cab if his car were in the shop because he is always eager to get home.

   d. Smith daydreams while sipping lemonade. For Brown, this is a time for imaginative creativity; he thinks up all kinds of useful ideas for the employee suggestion box at the office.

   If all this evidence is not sufficient to refute the hypothesis that Smith's leisure and Brown's leisure are of equal value, what possible evidence *could* refute it? If there is no way at all of refuting or confirming a hypothesis, does the hypothesis assert anything? If it asserts nothing, why retain it? You might still want to retain a hypothesis that can be neither proved nor disproved on the basis of existing data if it is useful in some way; we do speak of "useful hypotheses." But of what use is the hypothesis that every person's leisure is equal in value to every other person's leisure? It is seriously misleading for many purposes, and it contains implications that are contrary to a great deal of evidence.

10. Imagine a society with only two goods and three producers. We shall call the goods X and Y, and the producers Abe, Ben, and Cal. In a given period of time, each is capable of producing the following quantities of X and/or Y.

    Abe: 8X or 4Y or any linear combination in between (6X and 1Y, 2X and 3Y, and so on)

    Ben: 3X or 3Y or any linear combination in between

    Cal: 1X or 2Y or any linear combination in between

    Is leisure a good in this society? Only if X or Y happens to be leisure! (We have craftily defined away that stumbling block.) Now answer the questions below.

    a. What is each producer's cost of production for a single X and a single Y?

    b. Who is the lowest-cost producer of X? of Y? Who is the highest-cost producer of X? of Y?

    c. Who is the most efficient and the least efficient producer of X and of Y? If your answer does not agree with your answer to the preceding question, you have not accepted this chapter's explanation of efficiency.

    d. If you were the commissar of production in this society and you decided you wanted only 2Y produced, plus as much X as possible, whom would you order to produce Y? What orders would you issue if you wanted 4Y, plus as much X as possible?

    e. Explain to someone who is completely ignorant of economics exactly why you would not want to call Abe the most efficient producer of Y, even though he can produce more Y during a given time period than can either Ben or Cal.

11. The United States used wood as a fuel in metallurgy long after the British had changed to coal. Was this evidence of technological backwardness in the United States? If the United States was technologically backward, how would you explain the fact that all sorts of machines for woodworking were perfected in the United States in the first half of the nineteenth

century? Fireplaces are often said to be inefficient ways to heat a room. Why then were they so widely used in the United States in the nineteenth century in preference to stoves? (Hint: larger logs can be used in fireplaces.) Why did stoves become more popular as wood prices increased?

12. When important supplies of natural rubber to the United States were cut off by World War II, scientists learned to make synthetic rubber products that eventually proved better than natural rubber products. Did the war increase the intelligence of chemists? Do you think that government price supports for cotton had anything to do with the discovery of synthetic textiles?

Information, Middlemen, and Speculators

Chapter **8**

"How to save about $900 and lose $3000 . . . right on your own home."

That was the headline under which the National Association of Real Estate Boards ran an advertisement urging people to use the services of a realtor in selling their homes. The ad continued:

> Don't laugh. It could happen. For instance, suppose you decide to sell your house. Yourself. You decide it's worth $15,000, and you sell it for $15,000. Great. But how did you arrive at that price? By guesswork. It takes a lot more than that to determine a property's value. It takes a Realtor who knows houses and what they're worth. Suppose he said your house was worth $3000 more. A fair price to buyer and seller. It could happen. Of course, you'd save the Realtor's fee. But at quite a cost.
>
> So when you decide to sell a house, use your Realtor. He's not just anyone in real estate. He's the professional who is pledged to a strict code of ethics. That's good. Especially if you want to make the best sale you can. Or for that matter, the best buy.

That ad is eloquent testimony to something mentioned in Chapter 7: the public's deep-rooted suspicion of middlemen. The fact that the realtors association thought the ad worth running is strong evidence that such a suspicion exists, and the argument employed in the ad is further evidence. For the ad seems designed to obscure the realtors' function while defending it, almost as if the truth is more than the public would tolerate.

Suppose, we might ask, that the realtor said your house was worth $3000 *less*: "A fair price to buyer and seller." Isn't it just as likely that the homeowner selling his own house will guess too high as too low? Or even more likely in view of the hopeful optimism typical of so many homeowners? Then the use of a realtor will cost him twice over. And just what constitutes a "fair price"? Moreover, if realtors obtain higher prices for sellers, how can they simultaneously obtain better buys for purchasers, as the last paragraph asserts? Something is wrong with the argument.

The Cost of Information

Don't criticize the realtors association too harshly. The plight of middlemen forced to explain their function is not an easy one. The most important fact to be noticed at the outset is that *information is a scarce good*. If you want to sell your house for as much as you can get, the appropriate buyer is the one person in the world willing to pay the highest price. That seems obvious. What isn't obvious is how you find him. You are presumably not omniscient, so you will never even discover the existence of many potential purchasers. It is almost a certainty, therefore, that when you finally do sell, you will not have found that one buyer willing to pay the very top price. Does this imply that you should keep searching indefinitely?

Information is a scarce good with its own costs of production. It simply does not pay to go on acquiring information forever before acting. A rational seller will continue acquiring information, therefore, only so long as the anticipated marginal gain from doing so is greater than the anticipated marginal cost of acquiring information. A rational buyer will behave in the same way. The reason that both can gain from using the services of a realtor is that the realtor enables each to obtain additional information at low cost. When you think about it, this seems in fact to be the primary function of middlemen: they promote efficiency and hence increase wealth by acting as low-cost producers of valuable information. Realtors provide sellers and buyers with better opportunities than they would otherwise have, by putting them in possession of additional information. That is a valuable service. (It's true that only the seller actually "hires" the realtor. But the fact that buyers go to them and make use of their multiple-listing services shows that realtors provide a service to buyers, too.)

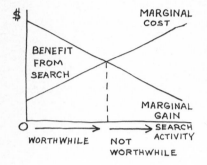

Suppose you own ten shares of General Electric stock and want to sell it. You could go around to your friends and try to peddle it or you could put an ad in the newpaper. But it is very likely that you would obtain a higher price by using the services of a middleman, in this case a stockbroker. No doubt if you advertised long enough you could find a buyer willing to pay the price the stockbroker obtained for you. But it is most improbable that the cost of your search would be less than the broker's fee.

"Getting it wholesale" is a popular pastime for many people who think that they're economizing. Perhaps they are. If they enjoy searching for bargains (and many people do), then they may well gain from their activities. But for most people, retailers are an important low-cost source of valuable information. The retailer's inventory reveals something of the range of opportunities available, information that is often difficult to obtain in any other fashion.

The same is true for job-placement agencies. Many people resent the fee charged by private agencies for finding them a job. But unless they felt that the information obtained through the agency was worth more than the fee, they would presumably not have used the agency's service. Employers are also willing to pay for such services, and for exactly the same reason.

A large part of the middleman's bad press stems from our habit of comparing actual situations with better but nonexistent ones. The exchanges we make are rarely as advantageous as the exchanges we could make if we were omniscient. So we conclude that the middleman takes advantage of our ignorance. But why look at it in that way? Using the same argument, one could say that the doctor takes advantage of your illnesses, and that he should receive no return for his services because he would be unable to obtain a return if you were always healthy. That is both true and irrelevant. We are neither always healthy nor omniscient. Physicians and middlemen are consequently producers of real wealth. Other prestigious persons performing similar services are lawyers, teachers, preachers, and corporation executives.

Markets Create Information

We can return now to an important point first introduced in Chapter 6. There we asserted that supply and demand, or the market process of competing bids and offers, creates indices of value for decision makers by placing price tags on available resources. The capacity of the market to generate high-quality information at low cost is one of its most important but least appreciated virtues. Middlemen are important participants in this process.

But, you may ask, what is "the market"? That's a good question and not an easy one to answer in a few words. The market is clearly not a place, though it may sometimes be closely identified with a particular place. Nor is it anything one can observe in the usual sense of observation. It is finally just a set of interrelationships, or what we called a "process of competing bids and offers." Some markets, like stock markets and commodity markets, are "well organized," which means that the bids and offers of prospective buyers and sellers are rather comprehensively assembled so that a single price tends to be established for all transactions over a wide geographic area. The market for used furniture, on the other hand, is relatively unorganized. Transactions take place at prices that vary greatly because buyers and sellers are not in extensive contact. The market for retail groceries falls somewhere between these extremes. Hamburger prices will consequently vary more over a given area at one time than livestock prices, but less than used furniture prices.

It is sometimes said that stock markets and commodity markets are more nearly "perfect" than retail grocery markets and used furniture markets. This is a misleading way to describe the difference because it implies that the latter markets ought to be changed (perfection is better than imperfection). Remember, however, that such a recommendation makes sense only if the costs of improving the markets are less than the gains from more efficient exchange made possible by the improvement.

In every case, however, the relationships between buyers and sellers, whether constant and extensive or sporadic and scattered, generate prices. Each such price is a piece of potentially valuable information to other people concerning available opportunities. The more such prices there are and the more widely they are known, the wider the range of opportunities available to others.

Opportunity costs consequently decline because markets exist, which is really a way of saying that the range of opportunities available to decision makers expands. And that is a way of saying that wealth increases or that economic growth occurs. And is that not what we finally mean by an increase in wealth? A wider range of available opportunities? The freedom and the power to do more of what one wants to do?

Those who make markets—middlemen, brokers, arbitrageurs—facilitate exchange by specializing in the production of information. They do so presumably because they believe themselves to have a comparative advantage in information production. Anyone who thinks that he "knows better" is free to take advantage of his knowledge—unless, as so often occurs, legal restrictions are imposed on trading. A society that prohibits exchange or suppresses markets, whether from hostility to the trader or for some other reason, denies useful information to its members.

Speculators

All this is rather abstract. To make it more concrete we can examine a type of trading that probably suffers most from public misunderstanding: speculation.

The dictionary defines speculation as "trading in the hope of profit from changes in the market price." That's good enough for our purposes. The most celebrated (or, more accurately, the most execrated) speculator is probably the Wall Street "bear." He "sells short"; that is, he sells shares of stock he does not currently own for future delivery. He believes that the stock will go down in price, so that when the time comes for him to deliver, he can purchase the shares at a low price and sell them at the previously agreed-upon higher price.

A more important speculator is probably the commodity speculator, who may trade in such items as wheat, soybeans, hogs, lumber, sugar, cocoa, or copper. He buys and sells "futures." These are agreements to deliver, at some specified date in the future, amounts of a commodity at a price determined now.

These are the spectacular speculators whose feats make the financial pages. A less publicized speculator is you yourself. You are buying education now, partly in the hope that it will increase the value of the labor services you'll be selling in the future. But the future price of your services could turn out to be too low to justify your present investment.

Another familiar speculator is the housewife who reads that the price of sugar is expected to rise and responds by loading her pantry with a two-year supply. If the price of sugar rises far enough, she gains. If it does not, she loses. She has tied up her wealth in sugar,

thereby cluttering her shelves and depriving herself of the opportunity to purchase more valuable assets—an interest-bearing savings account, for example.

The motorist who fills his tank when he sees a sign advertising
gasoline at two cents a gallon less than he's accustomed to pay is
speculating; the price may be four cents lower two blocks ahead.
And the motorist who drives on an almost empty tank in hope of
lower prices up ahead is a notorious speculator.

But many people overlook the fact that they themselves are
speculators, heaping blame on the "profiteers" who allegedly "take
advantage" of special situations and innocent people in pursuit of
their own unprincipled profit. Is the speculator really the enemy of
the people he is so often alleged to be?

Consequences of Speculation

It is often said that speculators exploit natural disasters by driving
up prices before the disaster occurs. And sometimes the expected
disaster never even materializes. That is true. But it is only one
small and misleading part of the truth. Suppose evidence begins to
accumulate in early summer that the fungus called corn leaf blight
is spreading to major corn-producing areas of the Midwest. A
significant percentage of the year's corn crop could be wiped out as
a result. People who think this is likely to occur will consequently
expect a higher price for corn next year. This expectation will
induce some people to hold some corn out of current consumption
in order to carry it over into the next crop period when, they
believe, the price will be higher. That is speculation.

Notice how many different parties engage in such speculation:
farmers who substitute other livestock feed for corn in order to
maintain their corn stocks at a higher level, either to avoid having
to buy corn next year at a higher price or to sell it then at the higher
price; industrial users who increase their inventories now while the
price is relatively low; and traders who might not know a bushel of
corn from a peck of soybeans but who hope to make a profit from
buying cheap now and selling dear later. There are well-organized
commodity markets to facilitate this kind of transaction. The
effect of all these activities is to reduce the current supply of corn;
the price consequently rises. And just as the critic protested, it rises
before the disaster occurs.

But that is only a part of the picture. These speculative activities
cause corn to be transported *over time* from a period of relative
abundance to one of greater scarcity. The price next year, when the
blight is expected to have its effects, will therefore be lower than it
otherwise would be. Speculators thus even out the flow of commodities into consumption and diminish price fluctuations over
time. Since price fluctuations create risks for those who grow or use
corn, speculators are actually reducing risk to others. More accurately, they are purchasing risk (in hope of a profit) from others

less willing to take risk (and willing to pay something in the form of reduced expected returns to avoid it).

Prophets and Losses

All this assumes, however, that the speculators are correct in their anticipations. What if the expected poor harvest fails to materialize? What if an unusually large crop appears instead? Then the speculators are transporting corn from a period of lesser to a period of greater abundance and thereby magnifying price fluctuation. This is clearly a misallocation of resources, involving as it does the giving up now of some high-priced corn for the sake of obtaining later an equal amount of low-priced corn. That is not socially profitable.

But neither is it profitable for the speculators. They will sustain losses where they had hoped for gains. We should not expect them, consequently, to behave in this fashion *except as a result of ignorance.* Are speculators likely to be ignorant?

No one is omniscient. And speculators make mistakes. (Why would they otherwise be called speculators?) But living as we do in an uncertain world, we have no option but to act in the presence of uncertainty. No one escapes uncertainty and the consequences of ignorance by refusing to act or to think about the future. And if anyone thinks he knows more than the speculators, he can counter them at a profit to himself by betting against them. It is interesting and somewhat revealing to note that those who criticize speculators for misreading the future rarely give effective expression to their own supposedly greater insight by entering the market against them. Hindsight, of course, is always in copious supply—and the price is appropriately low.

As we have repeatedly tried to show, information is a scarce good. Better information means greater efficiency because it provides a wider range of opportunities and hence expanded scope for the exploitation of comparative advantage. Speculators provide information. Their offers to buy and sell express their judgments concerning the future in relation to the present. The prices generated by their activities are, like all prices, indices of value: information for decision makers on present and future opportunity costs. This information is at least as important to conservatives as it is to gamblers. It is true that the information they provide is "bad" information when the speculators are wrong. But harping on this is again a case of comparing one situation with a better but unattainable situation. Anyone who thinks he can read the future better than the speculators is free to express his convictions with money, profit from his insight, and benefit society in the process.

Meanwhile those whose ordinary business activities involve them in the use of commodities that are speculatively traded do make effective use of the information generated by the speculators. Farmers employ the prices predicted in the commodity exchanges, as do industrial users and even housewives shopping for groceries. And those who use goods not ordinarily thought of as speculative commodities also take advantage of the information generated by speculators. For we all use prices as information; and prices reflect competing bids and offers inevitably based to a large extent on a (speculative!) reading of the future.

Once Over Lightly

An opportunity of which you're unaware is not a real opportunity. Information is therefore a valuable resource whose possession enables people to increase their wealth.

Information is a scarce good whose production usually entails costs. The efficient decision maker accumulates additional information only as long as the anticipated marginal benefit is greater than the marginal cost.

A great deal of economic activity is best understood as a response to the fact that information is a scarce good. The much abused "middleman" is in large part a specialist in information production. Just as the real estate broker enables prospective buyers and sellers to locate one another, so the typical retailer provides customers with knowledge of the goods sellers are offering and brings sellers into contact with those who want the sellers' offerings.

The common habit of viewing the middleman as an unproductive bandit on the highway of trade stems from the erroneous assumption that information is a free good.

Everyone who makes a decision in the absence of complete information about the future consequences of all available opportunities is a speculator. So everyone is a speculator.

People who think they know more than others about the relationship between present and future scarcities will want to buy in one time period for sale in the other. If they are correct, they make a profit on their superior insight and also transport goods through time from periods of lesser to greater scarcity. If they're wrong in their predictions, they perversely move goods from periods of greater to lesser scarcity and suffer the penalty of a personal loss on their transactions.

Because prices are summary indicators of scarcity, they are valuable information. Those whose buying and selling activities create prices are generating information that is useful to others.

QUESTIONS FOR DISCUSSION

1. Are you speculating when you buy fire insurance on your home? Could you save money by getting together with your friends to form an insurance cooperative, thereby eliminating the necessity of paying something to a middleman (the insurance company)? What kinds of useful information do insurance companies provide?

2. If you found that you could reduce your bills for new clothing 10 percent by buying exclusively from catalogs, would you do it? Why would some people be unwilling to take advantage of this "saving"?

3. Does advertising provide information? Before answering, think about the various kinds of advertising you're familiar with. What safe generalizations can one make about *all* advertising? Since advertisers sometimes deceive customers, should advertising be put under government regulation to eliminate all deceptive claims? Would you include the claims of political candidates who buy time for advertising themselves on television?

4. A man approaches you in a busy airport terminal, shows you a handsome wristwatch, which he says is worth $135, and offers to let you have it for $25. Would you buy it? Would you be more willing to buy it if you had better information? What do you "know" when you buy a watch from an established local jeweler that you do not know in this situation?

5. Evaluate the following paragraph from a newspaper article:

    One sure way to save money on groceries is to eliminate the middleman by buying directly from farmers and other suppliers. That is what a group of socially motivated and normally hungry people have decided to do by forming a grocery cooperative.

6. You find out in late December that you can probably make $1000 on a business deal if you can gain the goodwill of a client by getting him two tickets to the Super Bowl game. You manage to buy two well-located seats from a scalper for $250. Were you cheated by the scalper? Or are you glad that scalpers exist? Why do so many people dislike scalpers intensely?

7. In February 1972 the price of beef in grocery stores rose rapidly, contributing to an overall increase in the cost of groceries and pushing up the index of consumer prices at a time when the government had announced its determination to stop inflation. The president of the United States publicly blamed the middleman. Why?

8. Students frequently complain about the low prices the campus bookstore pays for used texts. Why then do they sell to the bookstore? Is it true that they cannot find a buyer on their own? Or is it more true that they are unwilling to go to the trouble (incur the cost) of finding a buyer on their own? What useful service does the college bookstore perform in handling used texts? Can you be sure it's a genuine service and not just a "rip-off"?

9. Would you expect prices for goods of similar quality offered in garage sales to vary more than prices for goods offered in regular retail outlets? Why?

10. You decide in May that this summer's corn crop is going to be much larger than people expect. What buying or selling operations could you undertake to wager on your prediction? What kind of effect will your action have on prices? It obviously isn't possible to carry corn backward in time, to make the October harvest available in May. Nonetheless your action will have the effect of increasing May corn consumption and decreasing October consumption. How will this occur?

Price Setting and the Question of Monopoly

The term *administered prices* was first introduced to public discussion in the 1930s in order to make a distinction between prices that were set by supply and demand and prices supposedly established by "administrative action." Since that time the term has been widely used, especially by critics of "big business." Some of these critics have accused professional economists of ignoring the dominant role of "administered prices" in the American economy, and of pretending that prices are all set by supply and demand. According to most of these critics, the American economy is today largely controlled by monopolists and oligopolists, who pay no attention to supply and demand, but instead use their market power to manipulate prices according to their own selfish and narrow interests.

It is impossible to evaluate any of these claims without first obtaining a clearer notion of what is meant by such terms as *administered prices* and *monopolist*. We have consciously steered around these issues as much as we could in the preceding chapters. The tactic that usually enabled us to do so was the implicit assumption that there were so many buyers and sellers in any market at which we were looking that none of them had any power to affect the price by his own individual action. It is now time to look more closely at issues that have been bypassed.

Who Qualifies as a Monopolist?

We begin with the word *monopoly*, the product of two Greek words meaning "sole seller." Are there any monopolists in that strict sense of the word? Try to think of something that is sold exclusively by one seller.

Telephone service is a favorite example. But is it an accurate example? There are many sellers of telephone service in the United States, as a matter of sometimes forgotten fact. Bell may have invented it, but neither regional companies with his name nor their parent, American Telephone and Telegraph, are the only ones who sell it. Still, that may be beside the point. For any given buyer there is typically only one seller, since telephone companies enjoy exclusive selling privileges in particular areas. On the other hand, a buyer doesn't have to live in a given area; he can move to another franchise area if he prefers the product there. Back comes a justifiably impatient snort: "That's irrelevant." But it's not completely irrelevant. Moving your residence may be a prohibitively expensive way to shift your telephone patronage, and it's hard to imagine anyone actually moving just because he resents the local phone company. But that *is* a way of obtaining a substitute product. And by its absurdity, our example calls attention to the crux of the problem: the availability of substitutes.

Suppose we redefine the commodity sold by telephone companies and call it "communication services." There would be nothing intrinsically misleading about that. After all, that is why anyone wants a telephone: to obtain communication services. But if this is the product being sold, the telephone company is clearly *not* a monopolist, but rather a seller in competition with Western Union, the post office, various messenger and delivery services, loud shouting, fast running, and coast-to-coast communication by computer. The point of all this is simply that, if we define the commodity broadly enough, not a single commodity in the country is sold by a monopolist.

Now let's look at the other side of the coin. Suppose we define the commodity very narrowly. If telegrams are not the same thing as telephone calls, neither is a gallon of milk at the little store next door the same thing as a gallon of milk three blocks away at the supermarket. If you have no car, are rocking a screaming baby who won't stop until he gets his bottle, and have no one to leave the baby with, the milk three blocks away is a vividly different commodity from the milk at the store next door. Ask any parent of a small baby. Thus we are forced to conclude that, when the commodity is defined norrowly enough, every seller is a monopolist, since no two sellers will ever be offering completely identical products.

We are trying to convince you that the word *monopoly* is extraordinarily ambiguous. For everyone or no one is a sole seller depending on how we define the commodity being sold. Furthermore, there is no satisfactory way to decide in all cases just how broadly or narrowly the concept of a commodity ought to be defined. The Supreme Court of the United States has sometimes listened to persuasive arguments on both sides of a contested definition and then divided in its decision. Take cellophane, for example. Is it a separate commodity or should it be put in the category "flexible wrapping materials"? The answer given in cases such as this may determine whether a manufacturer is convicted under the antitrust laws.

Alternatives, Elasticity, and Market Power

So let's try another approach. What would be so bad about a sole seller if we found one? The telephone company hints at the answer when it advertises: "We may be the only phone company in town, but we try not to act like it." If we find a case where there really is a sole seller, the customer will have no alternatives. No one wants to be without alternatives. The poorer our alternatives, the weaker our position and the more easily we can be taken advantage of.

But we learned in Chapter 2 that there are always some alternatives. There is a substitute for anything, even the services of the local telephone company. After all, no one "needs" a telephone. On the other hand, a phone is a valued convenience for many families and business firms. The concept from economics that suggests itself is price elasticity of demand.

No seller is a monopolist in the strictest sense of the word because there is no such thing as a *perfectly* inelastic demand. No seller has any buyer totally over the barrel. On the other hand, very few sellers of anything face perfectly elastic demand curves. Anything less than complete elasticity means that the seller will retain some business when he raises his price, which in turn implies that the seller has at least a morsel of market power. Where is the line between a morsel and monopoly?

There is no clear line of demarcation unless we decide to draw one arbitrarily. Elasticities of demand reflect the availability of substitutes; other things remaining equal, the more good substitutes there are for anything, the more elastic will be the demand for it. Market power is thus seen to be a matter of degree, and to be inversely related to elasticity of demand. Defined in this way, the term *market power* has a meaning that we can talk about and use. But we have not yet found a useful definition for the word *monopoly*.

Privileges and Restrictions

Let's try another approach. In the early nineteenth century there was often no distinction made in the United States between a monopoly and a corporation. The reason was that corporations had always been created by special governmental acts. They received, whether from Crown and Parliament prior to the Revolution or from state and national legislatures afterward, special "patents," as they were called: official documents granting rights and privileges not available to others. Corporate charters were therefore called "grants of monopoly," since they gave to one party a power that was withheld from others. The East India Company was such a "monopoly," and the special privilege of selling tea in the Colonies, given to it in 1773, helped bring on the American Revolution.

Here is another and quite different meaning of monopoly, one related to acts of the state. If the state allows some to engage in an activity but prosecutes others for doing so, or if it taxes or restricts some sellers but not others, or if it grants protection or assistance to some while compelling others to make their own way unaided, the state is creating exclusive privileges. This meaning for the word *monopoly* has contemporary relevance as well as historical significance.

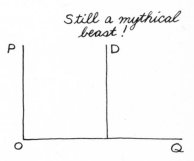

Still a mythical beast!

a less than perfectly elastic demand

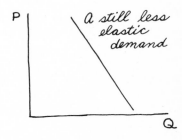

a still less elastic demand

Many business organizations operate with monopoly grants of this kind. In fact, it is becoming increasingly difficult to find one that does not. In the name of all sorts of commendable-sounding goals—public safety, fair competition, stability, national security, efficiency—governments at all levels have imposed restrictions upon entry into various industries or trades. The beneficiaries of these restrictions always include the parties who can escape them. These parties will rarely agree that they enjoy a grant of monopoly power. But the effect of the restrictions nonetheless is to prevent some from competing who would otherwise do so.

We are not saying that restrictions on entry into a market are always to be condemned, or that the businesses which benefit necessarily behave badly afterward, or that society can never be better off as a consequence of restrictions on competition. We are only concerned that the restrictions be noted so that their consequences can be evaluated. They will often turn out to be different from what most people assume. We could, if we wished, use the word *monopolist* to describe any individual or organization operating with the advantage of special privileges granted by the government. The trouble is that most people no longer use the word in this way. By such a definition, the postal service is a monopolist, as are most public utilities, many liquor stores, morticians, and crop-dusters; the American Medical Association, state bar associations, and labor unions; farmers with acreage allotments, licensed barbers, and trucking firms. The list is long indeed.

And so we are going to take the heroic step of dropping the word *monopoly* from our working vocabulary. Its meanings are too many and too vague. " 'When I use a word,' Humpty Dumpty said in a rather scornful tone, 'it means just what I choose it to mean—neither more nor less.' " *Monopoly* is a favorite word of contemporary Humpty Dumpties. And that's why we are not going to employ it. We shall try to use alternate terms that are more likely to communicate the precise situation we have in mind.

Price Takers and Price Searchers

Let's go back now to the phrase with which this chapter began: administered prices. Is there a distinction between administered prices and prices that are set by supply and demand?

It's a free country, as they say, and businesses are usually free to set their own prices. The United States Steel Corporation has substantial discretion when it prints up its price lists, and a wheat farmer from Kansas can feel quite safe from the threat of prosecution if he decides to offer his crop at $5.00 per bushel. But there is obviously an important difference that helps to explain why United States Steel keeps one eye on the government when deciding on its prices and wheat farmers do not. The difference, we shall nonetheless insist, is a difference of degree, not kind.

Take the case of the wheat farmer first. If he consults the financial pages of his newspaper or tunes in for the noonday market reports, he will find that number 2 ordinary hard Kansas City wheat opened at $3.34³/₄ a bushel. That news may disappoint or delight him, but there is almost nothing he can do to change it. If he decides that the price is an excellent one, and sells his entire crop for immediate delivery, the market will feel scarcely a ripple. Even if he is one of the biggest wheat farmers in the state, he is still such a small part of the total number of those offering to buy or sell wheat that he cannot affect the price. The difference between what the closing price will be if he sells all his crop, and what it will be if he sells only half of it, will not be as much as ¹/₄ cent.

Economists therefore call the wheat farmer a *price taker*. He cannot affect the price by his own actions. The price at the local grain elevator is determined by the actions of many buyers and sellers all over the country. If the farmer exercises his legal right to put a price tag on his wheat two cents higher than the market decrees, he will sell no wheat. And since he can sell all the wheat he has at the going price, he has no incentive to offer to sell any wheat at less than the going price. Price takers face perfectly elastic demand curves, or what for all practical purposes amount to perfectly elastic demand curves. The demand curves are horizontal at the going price.

Most businessmen are not in this position. They can raise their prices if they choose, without losing all their sales. And they cannot, as can the farmer, always sell everything they're capable of producing without lowering their prices. At higher prices they will sell less, at lower prices they will be able to sell more. They must choose a price or set of prices. Economists therefore call them *price searchers*. Torn between the desire for higher prices and the desire for larger sales, they must search out the price or set of prices most advantageous to them.

Price searchers include United States Steel, the trustees of a private university weighing a tuition increase, the proprietor of a local grocery store, and the little boy selling lemonade on a hot afternoon. There is a long tradition in economics of referring to all price searchers as monopolists. But this is a technical use of the word *monopolist* that is confusing to everyone except professional economists. Since the little boy selling lemonade does not face a perfectly elastic demand curve, he is not a price taker but a price searcher. It seems silly to anyone not dipped in the history of economics to call him a monpolist. So we shall not do it. The term *price searcher* captures the situation in which we're interested. Price searchers all have some market power. But it is a matter of degree, inversely related to the elasticity of the demand the seller faces.

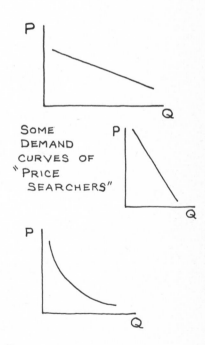

THE DEMAND SCHEDULE FACED BY A SINGLE WHEAT FARMER:

PRICE	QUANTITY HE CAN SELL
$ 3.37	NONE
3.35	ALL HE HAS
3.33	ALL HE HAS

SOME DEMAND CURVES OF "PRICE SEARCHERS"

Price Takers' Markets and Optimal Resource Allocation

Economists applied the disapproving term *monopolist* to what we shall call *price searcher* in large part because they wanted to emphasize the different consequences of these two types of price

PRICE, COST PER BUSHEL

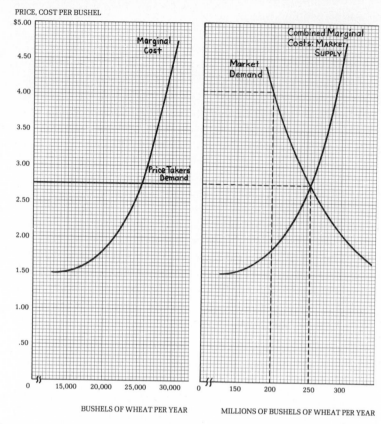

Figure 9A   Single farmer and total market

setting. Markets in which all buyers and sellers were price takers were graced with the approving term *competitive markets*. We want to point up the advantages they saw in price takers' markets without adopting the misleading monopolistic-competitive distinction, a distinction which erroneously implies that price searchers face no competition. To do so we shall use the graph originally presented in Figure 6A.

The graph was used with two different horizontal scales. In the first case it depicted the marginal cost curve or supply curve of a single Kansas wheat farmer. We then multiplied the quantities by 10,000 to let it represent the combined marginal-cost curves of all wheat farmers and to present the market-demand curve for wheat. Figure 9A reproduces both cases.

The market-demand curve interacts with the aggregate marginal-cost curves or supply intentions of wheat farmers to establish a price of $2.75. Since wheat farmers are price takers, each farmer sells his wheat at $2.75 a bushel and total production-consumption is about 256 million bushels: 25,600 bushels from each of the 10,000 farms. That particular price and quantity appeals to economists. No wheat is being produced whose marginal opportunity cost, as represented by the supply curve, exceeds its marginal benefit to consumers, as represented by the demand curve which shows their willingness to purchase wheat in preference to other goods. Moreover, all the bushels whose marginal social benefit is greater than their marginal social cost are being produced. And so resources are optimally allocated to wheat production—neither too few nor too many. The condition of such an optimal allocation is that marginal cost (the marginal value of forgone production opportunities) be equal to price (the marginal value of forgone consumption opportunities). When production takes place at the level where marginal cost is neither less nor more than price, a full quart is being extracted from a quart pot.

While this concept of optimal resource allocation is somewhat abstract and ignores a number of potentially significant qualifications, it does provide a useful first approximation for evaluating the consequences of various market structures. Let's look more closely. With production at 256 million bushels and the price at $2.75, the gross revenue of wheat farmers will be $704 million. But notice that if production were reduced to, say, 200 million bushels, the price would be $4.05 and gross revenue would increase to $810 million. Wheat farmers could do much better for themselves by producing much less! They would do less well for society in the process; but economics does not assume that business decision makers pursue the public interest.

Nonetheless, production will tend to move toward the socially "optimum" level of 256 million bushels with the price at $2.75 *because farmers are price takers*. The crucial element in the situation is the large number of farmers who act independently. While they could all improve their position by acting collectively to reduce production, none has an incentive to do so individually. Each has a private incentive to carry production up to the point at which marginal cost approaches price. And so the outcome of their pursuit of private interests is, in a broad sense, the public interest. But that only occurs because farmers produce and sell in price takers' markets.

Insofar as sellers are price searchers with some power to restrict production and raise the price, the "optimum" allocation of resources will not be achieved. How serious that problem is and whether it can be corrected is the fascinating question that runs through the next two chapters.

Administered Prices Once Again

It would seem then that price searchers set their own prices, whereas price takers accept what the market sets. Is this the distinction between administered prices and those prices which are set by supply and demand? Not if one thinks about it carefully. *Every* seller in the last analysis sets his own price, though some sellers can do so with little or no real searching because they in effect accept the prevailing price (price takers). At the same time, price searchers are by no means free from the constraints imposed by supply and demand. United States Steel is a favorite target of those who decry administered prices, but whatever the faults or failings of the corporation, its decisions are surely conditioned by supply and demand. Supply depends on cost, and cost is taken into account by every price searcher. The supply capabilities and intentions of other steel producers will also be considered. Demand curves are never completely inelastic, so demand must be taken into account if the price searcher hopes to find what he is looking for, which is presumably the most profitable price to set. The current and prospective demands for other products such as aluminum, plywood, plastic, and cement are also relevant information to the searcher for a proper steel price, since any or all of these products may turn out to be substitutes for steel.

So we end up with no usable meaning for the term *administered prices*, either. *All* prices are administered and *all* prices are set by supply and demand. The term *administered prices* will consequently not be used in subsequent chapters. An examination of its history would reveal that it has more often been used as a polite "bad word" than as a concept to aid analysis or critical discussion. Economic problems are sufficiently complex without complicating them further by using terms that generate much heat and no light.

One other term appeared in the introductory paragraph: *oligopolist*. The dictionary suggests that an oligopolist is "one of a few sellers." The Big Three in automobiles and the major cigarette manufacturers are commonly cited as examples of oligopoly situations. But what about the daily newspapers in a large city? Or do they compete with other newspapers that can be trucked or flown in, with news magazines, billboards, television, the yellow pages? What is the commodity that allegedly has only a few sellers? Should it be broadly or narrowly defined? What about gasoline stations? Hardware stores? Automobile dealers? Shops that restring tennis rackets? How few is few? We don't have to multiply examples to discover that all the problems associated with defining a monopolist as a sole seller return to haunt us when we define an oligopolist as one of a few sellers.

There is a special market situation to which many economists have chosen to apply the term *oligopoly*. We'll examine and analyze that situation in Chapter 11. But we shall not use the word *oligopoly*, on the grounds that, like administered prices and monopoly, it creates confusion rather than clarity and understanding.

Once Over Lightly

The word *monopoly* means literally a sole seller. But whether any seller is the sole seller depends upon how narrowly or broadly we define the product. Under a sufficiently broad definition, there are innumerable sellers of every product. Under a sufficiently narrow definition, however, every seller's product differs from every other's and all sellers are monopolists. The word *monopoly* is therefore inherently ambiguous and will not be used in subsequent chapters.

The antisocial connotations of the word *monopoly* stem from the belief that the customers of a sole seller have no alternatives and are therefore at the mercy of the seller. Since there are in fact alternatives to every course of action and substitutes for every good, no seller ever has unlimited power over buyers. Market power is always a matter of degree.

The concept of price elasticity of demand provides a useful way of thinking and talking about the degree of market power. Demand elasticities, which can vary between zero and infinity, reflect the availability of substitutes. The more good alternatives buyers have, the more elastic are the demand curves sellers face and the more limited is the power of sellers to establish terms of sale strongly advantageous to themselves.

In the early years of the United States, a monopoly usually meant an organization to which the government had granted some exclusive privilege. The monopolist was thus the sole legal seller. While this meaning of the term is no longer common, it does have contemporary relevance since federal, state, and local governments are extensively involved in the granting of special privileges that reduce competition.

A useful distinction to make in trying to understand how prices are established is the distinction between *price takers* and *price searchers*. The price taker must accept the price decreed by the market. His buyers have such excellent substitutes for his product that any attempt to raise the price or otherwise shift the terms of sale in his own favor will leave the seller with no customers at all. The price searcher, on the other hand, can sell different quantities at different prices and must therefore search for the most advantageous price.

Competition tends to push production in price takers' markets to the point where price and marginal cost are equal. This equality indicates that resources are being allocated in such a way as to obtain the largest possible *value* of output.

The concept of *administered prices* is misleading inasmuch as almost all prices are "administered" by sellers—within the constraints imposed by their situation. The important question is whether competition imposes adequate constraints in particular circumstances.

The word *oligopoly* is at least as ambiguous as *monopoly*; whether there are just a few or very many sellers depends upon how we choose to define the product. And so the word *oligopoly* will also be discarded in favor of terms that are more precisely descriptive.

QUESTIONS FOR DISCUSSION

1. List some commodities or services that are sold by only one seller. Then list some of the close substitutes for these goods. How much market power is possessed by the sole sellers whom you listed?

2. List some industries, trades, or professions in which government (federal, state, or local) has imposed legal restrictions on entry. Who benefits from these restrictions? Who is harmed by them?

3. There are approximately 11,000 newspapers currently being published in the United States, most of them weeklies. Only about 1800 newspapers publish daily. Of the dailies, there are only 13 published in South Dakota. Only one of these is a morning newspaper. Is a citizen of South Dakota who wants a morning newspaper carrying state and local news therefore at the mercy of a monopolist?

4. Is the college you're attending a price searcher? How much freedom does it have in setting the tuition rate you will pay? Might a just-enrolled freshman answer the above differently from an about-to-graduate senior? Does your college enjoy any special grants of legal privilege?

5. Electric utilities are usually given exclusive franchises by the government to sell electricity in a particular area. Are they in competition with sellers of anything else? Do they compete for sales in any way with electric-utility companies franchised to operate in other areas?

6. Can you think of any cases where price takers have persuaded the government to restrict entry by others into the markets where they sell?

7. Those who use the term *administered prices* do not include in this classification the prices charged by grocery stores. Nonetheless a grocer stamping prices on his products seems clearly to be "administering" his prices. Can you suggest criteria that would enable us to distinguish "administered" from "nonadministered" prices?

8. The number of steel mills in the United States is about the same as the number of paper mills. Does this imply that paper users and steel users have about the same number of alternative supply sources from which to choose?

9. It has been argued that the development of the railroad in the middle of the nineteenth century substantially reduced the market power of many American manufacturing firms. Explain.

10. One often reads that there are "only three firms in the industry" (or five firms, or eight firms), and that this is too few for competition to be effective. How would you define an industry? Do firms in different industries (however defined) compete with one another? Are all the firms within a single industry (however defined) in competition with one another?

11. Do steel girders for bridge construction produced in Utah compete at all with girders produced in Maryland? (The phrase "at all" will usually make a statement true.) Can you think of ways in which wood products compete with steel girders?

Price Searching

How does a price searcher find what he's looking for and what happens when he finds it? We're going to argue in this chapter that price searchers estimate marginal costs and marginal revenues and then try to set prices that will enable them to sell all those units of their product and only those units for which marginal revenue is greater than marginal cost. Does that sound complicated? It's just the logic of the process by which net revenue is maximized. But is it the procedure business firms actually employ? It sounds much too theoretical, like something an economist might dream up but which few real-world sellers would even recognize.

The Popular Theory of Price Setting

It certainly is not the way most people assume that prices get set. The everyday explanation is a simple cost-plus-markup theory: Business firms calculate their unit costs and add on a percentage markup. A large number of price searchers will themselves describe their price-setting practices in terms of the cost-plus-markup theory. Their testimony deserves to be taken seriously; but it isn't conclusive evidence. A lot of people cannot correctly describe a process in which they themselves regularly and successfully engage. Most people who ride bicycles, for example, don't know how they keep the bicycle balanced; and if asked to think about it they'll conclude that they keep the bicycle from tipping by leaning or shifting their weight slightly each time the bicycle inclines in one direction. (Ask some of your friends what they do while riding a bicycle to keep it balanced. Chances are good that they will all give an incorrect answer unless they have been told how they do it.) If that were the way they actually balanced, they wouldn't make the end of the block. In reality they balance by steering, not leaning; they turn the front wheel imperceptibly and allow centrifugal force to counter any tendency to tip. The fact that they don't know what they're doing doesn't keep them from doing it. Although they can only balance successfully by winding along a series of curves whose precise curvature will be inversely proportional to the square of the speed at which they're proceeding, many mathematical illiterates are skillful cyclists.

There are excellent reasons for doubting the cost-plus-markup theory. One is that it tells us nothing about the size of the markup. Why choose a 25 rather than 50 percent markup?

Why do different firms mark up their prices by different percentages? Why will the same firm vary its percentage markup at different times, on different products, and even when selling to different people? Why do sellers sometimes set their prices *below* their average unit cost?

Moreover, if firms can always mark up their prices proportionately when their costs rise, why don't they raise their prices before their costs rise? Why are they satisfied with a smaller net revenue when they could be earning more? That doesn't square with the perennial complaints of many price setters that they aren't making adequate profits. We all know, too, that firms are sometimes forced out of business by rising costs. That couldn't happen if every firm were able to mark up its prices to cover any increase in costs.

The popular cost-plus-markup theory is obviously inadequate. It just doesn't explain the phenomena with which we're all familiar. We'll return to the question of why so many people, including price searchers themselves, nevertheless hold to the theory. But we can't do that until we've gone through the economist's explanation of the price-searching process.

Meet Mr. Artesian

Simple cases are best for illuminating basic principles. The complexities of actual experience can be introduced later. We shall be working for several chapters with the case of Mr. Artesian, who discovers in his front yard a flowing spring of mineral water. Many of his fellow townsmen believe that regular draughts of mineral water promote good health; they are willing to pay for the opportunity to drink from Artesian's spring.

We assume to begin with that Artesian knows precisely the community's demand for his water (an assumption we shall want to relax later). Here it is:

Price per Cup	Cups Demanded per Day
$.40	1
.39	2
.38	3
.37	4
. . .	. . .
.03	38
.02	39
.01	40
.00	40

The demand curve is graphed in Figure 10A. The curve is stepped rather than smooth to enable us to read clearly certain values we'll be interested in.

Artesian wants to sell the water and make as much money as

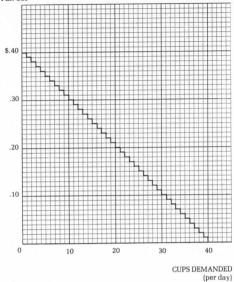

$.40

.30

.20

.10

0

0   10   20   30   40

CUPS DEMANDED
(per day)

Figure 10A Demand curve for mineral water

possible. The spring produces more than 40 cups of water per day, but no more than that amount can be sold at any positive price. The remainder will be allowed to drain back into the ground. But before going into business Artesian must make an investment. He must acquire equipment to capture and dispense the water. While he could hire someone to do this, he estimates that the cost of hiring an attendant would be greater than the cost of renting an automated dispenser. (Don't forget that there would still be a cost for labor if Artesian tended the spring himself: the value of whatever Artesian was unable to do because he was tending the spring.)

So Artesian rents a coin-operated water dispenser for $200 per year plus 4 cents per cup dispensed. The company leasing the machine to him agrees to attach the machine, keep it serviced, provide the paper cups, and also provide an automatic change-maker for customers. Artesian doesn't have to do anything except write a check at the first of each year and hold out his hand each day for the receipts, minus 4 cents per cup of water sold.

What price should Artesian set? Let's follow him as he searches for the price that maximizes his return. He sees at a glance that some prices are too high. At 35 cents per cup, for example, he would sell 6 cups, collect $2.10, surrender 24 cents to the dispenser company, and be left with $1.86 per day. He can do better by cutting his price and increasing his volume.

But he must not cut the price too far. At 10 cents, for example, he would gross $3.10 and net $1.86 again. He can do better at some price in between.

If you were to examine the demand curve for a while, you would discover that Artesian's net receipts reach a maximum of $3.42 at a

Revenue: 35¢ X 6 = $2.10
Cost: 4¢ X 6 =   .24
Net Revenue: $1.86

Revenue: 10¢ X 31 = $3.10
Cost: 4¢ X 31 = 1.24
Net Revenue: $1.86

price of either 23 cents or 22 cents, and decline gradually as he moves the price either up or down from those values. This is because the marginal revenue equals the marginal cost as sales move from 18 (at 23 cents) to 19 (at 22 cents).

What in the world does that mean? And what is *marginal revenue* anyway? If you are already familiar with the concept of marginal cost, you should have no trouble with marginal revenue. *Marginal revenue is the additional revenue* obtained from taking some action under consideration, in this case selling additional cups of water. But if additional cups can be sold only by lowering the price on *all* sales, marginal revenue will be less than price. To see exactly why, and in what way marginal revenue is related to demand, we're going to abandon Artesian momentarily in favor of a digression on marginal revenue.

$$23¢ \times 18 = \$4.14$$
$$4¢ \times 18 = \underline{\quad .72}$$
$$\$3.42$$

$$22¢ \times 19 = \$4.18$$
$$4¢ \times 19 = \underline{\quad .76}$$
$$\$3.42$$

The Meaning of Marginal Revenue

Suppose you are a price taker. The demand curve you face is then, by definition, perfectly elastic at the prevailing price. You can sell all you want to at the going price. The additional revenue you obtain, therefore, from selling one more unit, is always equal to the price per unit. *Marginal revenue equals price for all price takers.*

But suppose you are a price searcher. Your demand curve is now, by definition, less than perfectly elastic. You can sell additional units only by lowering the price. Each time you lower the price enough to sell one more unit, you gain an amount equal to the new price per unit *but you lose an amount equal to the price reduction multiplied by the number of units you could have sold at the higher price.* Gain something, lose something. Your marginal revenue is the first amount minus the second.

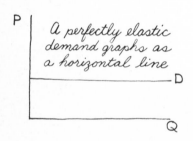

A perfectly elastic demand graphs as a horizontal line

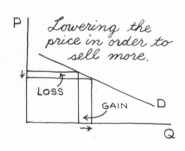

Lowering the price in order to sell more.

Price per Unit	Quantity Demanded	Total Revenue	Marginal Revenue
$6	0	0	
5	1	5	5
4	2	8	3
3	3	9	1
2	4	8	−1
1	5	5	−3

The logic is as simple as the arithmetic. The easiest way to grasp it is to do the calculations. When the price searcher reduces his price from $5 to $4, he sells one additional unit and so gains $4. But he loses $1 on the unit which he could have sold at $5 had he been willing to forgo selling the second unit. $4 minus $1 is $3, the marginal revenue associated with the second unit. We place it *in between* the first and the second unit in the schedule to indicate that $3 is the additional revenue gained *by moving from* sales of one unit (at $5) to two units (at $4).

Marginal revenue is written in between the successive quantities because it's the change in revenue as we go from one quantity to another.

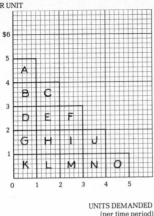

PRICE PER UNIT

UNITS DEMANDED
(per time period)

Figure 10B   Step curve showing marginal revenue

Similarly, cutting the price from $3 to $2 brings him an additional $2 from the extra unit sold at this price, but loses him $1 on each of the 3 units he could have sold at the higher price. $2 minus $3 is a marginal revenue of minus $1.

If you're still awake (it's the tedium that gets you, not the difficulty), you can observe this phenomenon on a graph. Figure 10B shows the same schedule drawn as a step curve built of lettered blocks. Cut the price from $5 to $4, and you gain the blocks C, E, H, and L, but lose block A. The marginal revenue is therefore three blocks or $3.

Cut the price from $3 to $2, and you gain blocks J and N, but sacrifice D, E, and F. The marginal revenue is minus one block.

Marginal revenue is *less* than price for this price searcher because, to put it in common language, he "spoils his market" by expanding his sales. He can expand his sales only by reducing his price. And we're assuming here that the reduced price must be offered to all customers, not just to the customers he attracted through the lower price. (He cannot engage in price discrimination.)

There are questions at the end of the chapter for additional practice on marginal revenue. Be sure you understand what the concept means or you will occasionally be confused by arguments in this and succeeding chapters. Once again: marginal revenue will be *equal* to the price for all price takers. It will be *less* than the price for price searchers, who cannot confine a price reduction to the customers gained by that reduction, but must also offer the reduced price to previous customers. (It would be *more* than the price only for sellers facing upward-sloping demand curves. Upward-sloping demand curves are barred from this course, but figuring out why marginal revenue would be higher than price in such a weird circumstance might be a useful logical exercise.)

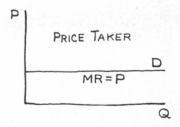

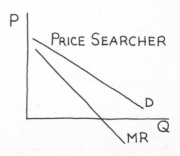

PRICE PER CUP

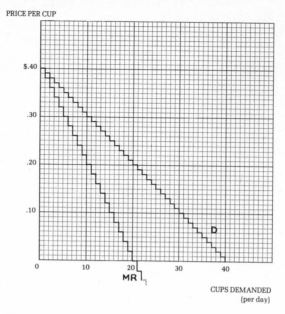

Figure 10C Marginal revenue

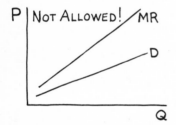

Back to Artesian

Let's return to Artesian's search for the most profitable price. We asserted that a price of either 23 cents or 22 cents maximizes Artesian's net receipts. This can be proved by anyone willing to calculate the consequences of all possible prices. Net receipts grow gradually as the price is lowered from 40 cents, reach a maximum at 23 cents or 22 cents, then decline gradually through successively lower prices.

We also asserted, and thereby launched ourselves on a long digression, that marginal revenue equals marginal cost as sales move from 18 units per day to 19 units, and gave this equality as a reason for maintaining that net receipts were maximized between the prices of 23 cents and 22 cents. Figure 10C shows the same information as Figure 10A, and adds the marginal-revenue curve derived from the demand curve on the assumption that the same price will be charged for each sale.

The marginal revenue is 40 cents from the first unit, 38 cents from the second unit, 4 cents for the nineteenth unit, zero for the twenty-first unit, becoming negative and progressively more negative after the twenty-first unit. You should be able to see now why net receipts are maximized at a price of either 23 cents or 22 cents.

Marginal revenue is the addition to Artesian's receipts as his sales expand. Marginal cost is the addition to his costs as his sales expand. He maximizes his net receipts by selling *every* unit whose marginal revenue exceeds its marginal cost, and selling *no* unit whose marginal revenue is less than its marginal cost. Artesian stops selling, therefore, when marginal revenue equals marginal cost.

Don't allow yourself to be hypnotized by the *equality* between marginal revenue and marginal cost. Obsession with this equality has lost many a beginning economics student a good night's rest. The equality is significant only inasmuch as it demonstrates the absence of an inequality! Think in terms of *inequalities* and you'll rest easily tonight.

Any unit that adds more to revenue (marginal revenue) than it adds to cost (marginal cost) is a profitable unit to sell, no matter whether it adds a lot or a little.

Suppose that Artesian is selling 17 units. Should he cut his price in order to sell 18? Is the 18th unit a profitable one to sell? The marginal cost is 4 cents; the marginal revenue is 6 cents. Sell it, and add 2 cents to the daily profit.

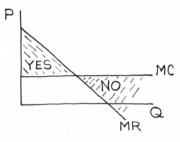

Suppose he is selling 20. Is this a profitable policy? He may well be making a profit, but the question is whether he is maximizing his profit. The marginal cost of the 20th unit is 4 cents. The marginal revenue is 2 cents. Do *not* sell it, and add 2 cents to the daily profit by avoiding a reduction of 2 cents from the daily profit. The principle we're using is common sense itself. Any action that yields more revenue than cost is a profitable action, and should be taken; any action that yields more cost than revenue is an unprofitable action, and should not be taken.

Doing Well and Doing Better

How does Artesian fare? Is he better off as a result of his newly discovered spring? He nets $3.42 per day as a consequence of his price searching, or $1248.30 per year. After writing the check for $200 to cover his remaining annual costs he is left with an increase of $1048.30 in his annual income. Artesian is happy.

But could he possibly fare still better? Artesian consults the demand curve (which he came to know miraculously, you recall) and notices that some cups could be sold at prices higher than 23 cents. There is even one devotee of mineral water in the community who would pay 40 cents to obtain his daily draught. Moreover, water is going to waste in a frustrating fashion. There are people willing to pay more than the marginal cost of 4 cents who are excluded from purchasing by Artesian's price of 23 cents. Wouldn't it be lovely, Artesian muses, if he could sell each cup for the maximum amount the customers are willing to pay. But how?

Artesian decides to place a sign by the fountain: "Please pay whatever the water is worth to you." He sets the machine to dispense a cup of water at 5 cents or more, in order to exclude those who would only be willing to pay the marginal cost or less. If the customers followed instructions, Artesian would sell 36 cups per day at prices ranging from 40 cents to 5 cents, with these results:

Daily gross receipts	$ 8.10
Daily net receipts	6.66
Annual net receipts	2430.90
Annual net income	2230.90

$$36¢ \times 5 = \$1.80 \text{ (receipts)}$$
$$- \underline{1.44 \text{ (cost)}}$$
$$\$ \quad .36 \text{ Net Receipts}$$

There are stories about price searchers who try such tactics. A justice of the peace might ask each groom after the wedding to pay "whatever it's worth to you," hoping that the presence of the bride and the general awe of the occasion will prompt the groom into exuberant generosity. Charitable organizations sometimes conduct sales on this principle, hoping that philanthropic impulses will overcome each purchaser's understandable reluctance to reveal the full value of an item to him. And there exist complicated auction techniques that would accomplish a similar result. But Artesian's customers are not starry-eyed, they do not regard Artesian as a charitable enterprise, and Artesian himself is unwilling to incur the costs of running a complicated auction. So his sign is a dismal failure. His first day's receipts came to only $1.80. Each customer paid the minimum price of 5 cents, and he sold 36 cups.

The College as Price Searcher

We'll come back to Artesian in Chapter 11. The time has arrived for applying some of what we've learned.

College administrators often talk about the high costs of providing an education and the need for charitable contributions to make up that 50 percent or so of the cost not covered by tuition. Have you ever wondered why it is, then, that privately owned colleges grant tuition scholarships to needy students? If colleges are so poor that they must ask for charity, why do they simultaneously *dispense* charity? The answer is that they probably don't. Tuition scholarships for needy students may be a partially successful attempt to do what Artesian failed to do.

Figure 10D is the demand for admission to Ivy College as estimated by the college administration. We shall assume that the marginal cost of enrolling another student is zero. That isn't accurate, but it's realistic enough for our purposes and it doesn't affect the logic of the argument in any event. Ivy College wants to find the tuition rate that will maximize its receipts.

If Ivy restricts itself to a uniform price for all, it will set the tuition at $1000 per year, enroll 2000 students (the enrollment at which marginal revenue equals marginal cost), and gross $2,000,000. But some students whom it would be profitable to enroll are excluded by this tuition rate; and some students who would have been willing to pay more are admitted for only $1000. Ivy's administrators wish they could charge each student what he's willing to pay. If they could find out the maximum each student or his parents would pay rather than be denied admission to Ivy, they could set the annual tuition at $2000 and then give scholarships (price rebates) to each student. The scholarship would equal the difference between $2000 and the maximum each student is willing to pay.

The problem is how to get information on willingness to pay. A student or his parents will not reveal the full value of Ivy to them if

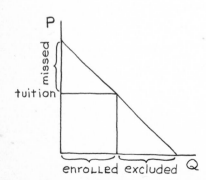

P
missed
tuition
enroLLed   excluded   Q

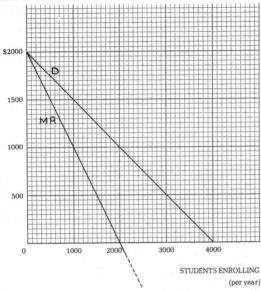

Note: There is a simple gimmick you can use to obtain quickly the marginal-revenue curve corresponding to any straight-line demand curve. Draw perpendiculars to the price axis from the demand curve; bisect the perpendiculars; extend a straight line through these midpoints. The marginal revenue corresponding to any point on the demand curve will then be the point on this line (the marginal-revenue curve) directly below the point on the demand curve in which you're interested. Thus in Figure 10D, the marginal revenue is zero when the price is $1000.

Figure 10D Demand curve for Ivy College

they know that candor will cause them to pay a higher price. But if willingness to pay is correlated with wealth, a solution lies at hand. Ivy announces that scholarships are available to needy students. Need must be established by filling out a statement on family wealth and income. Families will complete the forms in order to qualify for scholarship aid and will thereby provide the college with information it can use to discriminate. If the correlation were perfect between income and willingness to pay, and if families filled out the forms honestly, Ivy could discriminate with precision and increase its gross receipts to $4,000,000 (the area under the entire demand curve). Marginal revenue would be equal to price despite the fact that Ivy is a price searcher.

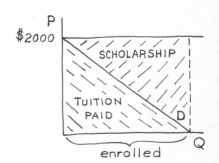

Be careful about condemning Ivy College! Notice some of the consequences of this discriminatory pricing policy. First of all, Ivy earns more income. If you approve of Ivy, why begrudge it a larger income from tuition? Is it better for philanthropists and taxpayers to cover Ivy's annual deficit than for students (or their parents) to do so through being charged the maximum they're willing to pay? Notice, too, that under a perfectly discriminating system of tuition charges, 2000 students who would otherwise be turned away are enabled to enroll at Ivy. They aren't complaining.

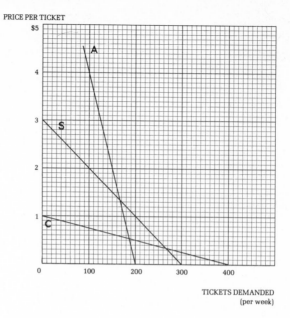

PRICE PER TICKET

TICKETS DEMANDED
(per week)

Figure 10E   Demand curves for theater tickets

Setting Movie Prices

If we assume, as seems reasonable, that price searchers would like to charge each customer the most he will pay, we should expect to observe many instances of price discrimination in our society.

The local movie theater charges $4 for adults, $1.50 for students, and 50 cents for children under 12. Is this because the theater owner likes kids or because it costs him less to show a movie to kids? It is more probable that he is acting like a discriminating price searcher.

Let the demand curves shown in Figure 10E represent the demands of adults, students, and children for tickets to the local movie theater. Children won't come at all if the price is above $1, but will come in droves as the price goes down below $1. Students start attending at prices below $3. Adults attend movies less, but will pay higher prices to do so.

Let the marginal cost of another patron be zero for the theater owner. (Why is this fairly realistic in light of what you know about sunk costs and marginal costs?) If the owner sets one price for everyone, his profit-maximizing price is $2. (The proof is a bit complicated. You could figure it out on the basis of what you know; but the marginal benefit from your efforts is likely to be less than the marginal cost of finding the solution.) He will sell 100 tickets to students and 150 to adults for a total weekly revenue of $500.

By discriminating among these three classes of customers, however, he can do better. He should charge $4 for adults, $1.50 for students, and 50 cents for children and raise his weekly receipts to $725. With this policy he sets marginal revenue equal to marginal cost *for each separate class of potential customers.* In effect, he is cutting the price to gain additional customers without offering equal price reductions to all customers. He is bringing his marginal-revenue curve closer to his demand curve. As a result, fewer adults will go to the movies. But maybe they'll be happier with the teenagers and the little kids out of the house more often. A total evaluation of the discriminatory pricing policy poses a much more complex problem, of course.

$$\$4 \times 100 = \$400$$
$$1.50 \times 150 = 225$$
$$.50 \times 200 = \underline{100}$$
$$\$725$$

Perhaps you've noticed in passing an important prerequisite for successful discrimination of the kind we've been describing. It must not be easy for low-price customers to resell to high-price customers but also by inducing present customers to purchase low-price ones. And that explains why discrimination is usually observed only in situations where the seller has some effective way of identifying purchasers, and where he can make sure that the consumer of his product is the original purchaser.

Another Type of Price Discrimination

Before leaving the topic of the price searcher as a discriminating seller, we want to consider one more possibility. Additional sales are obtained through reduced prices not only by attracting new customers but also by inducing present customers to purchase more.

Horty Kulcher just built a new house and he wants to landscape his lot. He loves roses. But his demand curve is downward sloping. Let us assume he has this schedule:

Price per Bush	Quantity Demanded
$8	1
5	2
3	3
2	4
1	5

Assume that the owner of the garden shop pays $1.25 to obtain rose bushes from his nursery. He would like to sell 4 to Horty. On the other hand, he can only sell 4 if he offers Horty a price of $2, and it's obvious that $2 is not a profit-maximizing price for his transactions with Horty. Marginal revenue falls from $8 to $2 to *minus* $1 as the owner adjusts his price to sell alternatively 1, 2, and 3 bushes. On any sale beyond 2, marginal cost exceeds marginal revenue. Will the owner therefore settle on a price to Horty of $5?

The 1st rose bush is worth $8 to Horty, the 2nd is worth $5, the third worth $3, the 4th worth $2, and the 5th is worth only $1.... less than marginal cost.

Not if he knows Horty's demand and he's searching for the profit-maximizing set of prices! A better option is the following price schedule:

$8 per rose bush
2 for $13
3 for $16
4 for $18

It would now be consistent with Horty's demand schedule for him to purchase 4 rose bushes even though the price is in a sense $4.50 a bush. Horty is caught by the fact that he can only obtain a price that low *if* he buys at least 4 rose bushes. The garden-shop owner is thereby attempting to extract the full value to Horty of each successive rose bush. In other words, he is trying to keep his marginal revenue from falling below the price.

Pity Horty if you wish. On the other hand, you might remember that Horty is paying for nothing he does not want, and that his front yard will be more beautiful as a result of the garden-shop owner's "exploitation."

Cost-Plus-Markup Reconsidered

So how does a price searcher find what he's looking for? By (1) estimating his marginal cost and marginal revenue, (2) determining the level of output that will enable him to sell all those units of output and only those units for which marginal revenue is greater than marginal cost, and (3) setting this price or prices so that he can just manage to sell the output produced. That sounds complicated, and it is. The logic is simple enough. But the estimates of marginal cost and especially the estimates of demand and marginal revenue are hard to make accurately. That's why price searchers are called "searchers." And why they could sometimes be called price "gropers."

The complexity and uncertainty of the price searcher's task helps explain the popularity of the cost-plus-markup theory. Every search has to begin somewhere. Why not begin with the wholesale cost of an item plus a percentage markup adequate to cover overhead costs and yield a reasonable profit? If costs increase, why not assume that competitors' costs have also increased and try passing the higher cost on to customers? Why not begin with the assumption that the future will be like the past and that the procedures which have previously yielded good results will continue to do so? In that case one would try to increase prices roughly in proportion to any cost increases experienced, and one would expect eventually to be forced by competition to lower one's prices roughly in proportion to any lowering of costs.

The cost-plus-markup procedure is in general a rule of thumb for price searchers, offering a place from which to begin looking, a first approximation in the continuing search for an elusive and shifting target. But price searchers only engage in cost-plus-markup pricing as a search technique and only until they discover they are making a mistake. The marginal cost-marginal revenue analysis of this chapter explains how price searchers recognize mistakes and what criteria they use in moving from rules of thumb and first approximations toward the most profitable pricing policy.

Selling below Cost?

Do you agree with the following paragraph?

"In order to preserve our competitive economic system, we need laws that prohibit unfair practices such as sales below cost. Large firms can often afford to sell products below cost until their rivals are driven out of business. If they are not restrained by law, we could easily wind up with an economy dominated by just a few huge corporations."

Most Americans apparently accept this argument. For our laws, at the federal, state, and local level, abound with provisions designed to prevent or inhibit price cutting. Until recently many states enforced resale price maintenance laws, laws that permitted (and in fact assisted) manufacturers and retailers to work together to establish minimum prices and to prosecute retailers who sold below these prices. A special federal law passed in 1937 to exempt such practices from prosecution under the Sherman Act was finally repealed in 1976. But many states still have statutes prohibiting sales below cost, statutes that usually go by some such name as Unfair Practices Act. And regulatory commissions, ostensibly created to hold down the prices that may be charged by public utilities, often wind up enforcing minimum rather than maximum rates. This is true, for example, of the grandfather of all such commissions in the United States, the Interstate Commerce Commission (created by Congress in 1887).

It's fairly obvious why some business firms would approve that kind of legislation: they want protection against competition. But why do consumers and the general public go along? The public seems to have accepted the argument that price cutting can create "monopolies" by driving competitors out of business. And monopolies, of course, are Bad Things.

The paragraph with which this section began states the essential argument. How valid is it? Is it possible to construct a defensible case for laws that prohibit "sales below cost"? A lot of questions should immediately arise in your mind.

What Is the Appropriate Cost?

What is the cost below which prices should not be set? Does anyone actually sell below cost? Why would anyone interested in increasing his wealth ever want to?

Case: Matilda Mudge, proprietor of the Thrifty Supermarket, orders 1000 pounds of ripe bananas. She gets them for 5 cents a pound because the produce distributor is eager to move them before they become too ripe. Mudge advertises a weekend special on bananas: 10 cents a pound. But Monday morning finds her with 500 pounds of bananas, now beginning to turn brown. How low can Mudge cut her price without selling below cost? The answer is *not* 5 cents a pound. That is sunk cost and hence no cost at all. If Mudge will have to pay someone to haul the unsold bananas away on Tuesday morning, her cost on Monday could be less than zero. In that case it might be to her advantage to give the bananas away. If a zero price is to her advantage, how can it be "below cost"? (By the way, did Mudge *buy* the bananas below cost?)

Or suppose Mudge bought a truckload of coffee: 1000 one-pound cans for $300. It was an unknown brand on which a local distributor offered her an attractive price. But it turns out that her customers aren't interested. She cuts the price down to 3 pounds for $1.00, but still can't move it successfully. Four weeks after her purchase she still has 987 cans of coffee cluttering her shelves and storage room. If she now cuts the price below 30 cents, is she selling below cost? She is not. She has no intention of replacing the cans she sells, so that each sale is that many additional cents in the till and one less can in the way. The relevant cost of a pound of coffee could well be zero. The relevant cost is, of course, the marginal cost.

Let's try a different kind of example and then return to Matilda Mudge. It might make sense to estimate the cost of producing a steer, but does it make any sense to estimate separately the cost of producing hindquarters and forequarters? Should the price of steaks, which come from the hindquarter of a beef carcass, cover the cost of producing the hindquarter, leaving it to pot-roast prices to cover the cost of the forequarters from which they derive? The question is nonsensical. Unless it is possible to produce hindquarters separately from forequarters, one cannot speak of the cost of producing one and the cost of producing the other. Hindquarters and forequarters, or steaks and pot roasts, are joint products with joint costs. There is no way to determine the specific costs of joint products or to allocate joint costs "correctly."[1]

Back to Matilda Mudge. Can we legitimately segregate the costs of each item sold in her grocery store? Think of her frozen-food items, for example. How much of the cost of owning and operating the freezer case should be allocated to vegetables, how much to Chinese dinners, and how much to orange juice? It's true that she could not carry frozen cauliflower without a freezer case. But if she finds it profitable to own and operate a freezer case just for the sake of the frozen juices she can sell, and if she then has some extra room in which she decides to display boxes of frozen cauliflower, it might make sense for her to assign none of the freezer cost to the cauliflower.

A successful businesswoman (or businessman) is not concerned with questions of cost allocation that have no relevance to decision making. She knows that production—and a merchant is a producer just as certainly as is a manufacturer—is usually a process with joint products and joint costs. The businesswoman is interested in the additional costs associated with a decision and the additional revenue to be expected from it, not in such meaningless problems as the allocation of joint costs to particular items for sale. If there is room for a magazine rack near the check-out counter, the question

Is free carryout service a service sold at less than cost?

1. If there are techniques for growing steers with relatively larger hindquarters than forequarters, or vice versa, then it may be possible partially to distinguish the costs under appropriate circumstances. Hindquarters can be enlarged at the cost of smaller forequarters, and livestock breeders and feeders do calculate such costs. More advanced economic analysis provides techniques for making these calculations.

is: How much will its installation *add* to total costs and how much will it *add* to total revenue? If the latter is larger, the rack makes sense; and the magazines sold need not have a price that covers utilities, rent, depreciation on cash registers, *or even the wholesale prices of the magazines.*

Mark well the italicized phrase. It may be profitable to sell a magazine for 5 cents even if it costs 10 cents to obtain it from the distributor. Why? Because the magazine display may bring in new customers who add to net revenue through their purchases of other items. Matilda Mudge is not interested in her net revenue on any one item she sells but in the difference between total revenue and total costs. Retailers have often carried cigarettes not for the sake of the profit they make on the sale of cigarettes but for the sake of the profitable sales of other items that are made possible by carrying cigarettes. Similarily, hardware stores that sell odd-lot bolts, screws, and nuts lose money on each sale but (or so their owners hope) more than make it up through the goodwill they thereby create.

"Predators" and Competition

There would be little point in stressing all this were it not for the popular mythology of "selling below cost." Our argument suggests that many allegations of sales below cost are based on an arbitrary assignment of sunk costs or joint costs. Business firms often complain about below-cost sales, of course; but that is because they dislike competition and want government to protect them from its rigors by prohibiting price cutting.

But aren't there dangers to competition in allowing firms to cut prices as low as they wish? It is odd, but not really surprising, how often people identify the protection of competitors with the protection of competition. In reality they are more like opposites. Competitors are usually protected by laws inhibiting competition, laws that benefit privileged producers by restricting consumers and nonprivileged producers. The hobgoblin hauled out to justify this is "predatory price cutting" backed up by a "long purse."

Predatory price cutting means reducing prices below cost in order to drive a rival out of business or prevent new rivals from emerging *with the intention of raising prices afterward to recoup all losses.* It is supposedly a favorite tactic of larger firms who can stand prolonged losses, or temporary losses on some lines, because of their larger financial resources—the so-called "long purse." Economic theory does not deny the possibility of predatory price cutting. But it does raise a long list of skeptical questions, headed by all the questions we have been discussing regarding the proper definition of an item's cost.

How long will it take for such a policy to accomplish its end? The longer it takes, the larger will be the short-run losses accepted by the predator firm and, consequently, the larger must be the long-term benefits if the policy is to justify itself.

What will happen to the physical assets and human resources of the firms forced out of business? That's an important question, because if those assets remain in existence, what is to prevent someone from bringing them back into production when the predator firm raises its prices to reap the rewards of its villainy? And if this occurs, how can the firm hope to benefit from its predatory policy? On the other hand, the human resources may scatter into alternative employments and be costly to reassemble.

Is it likely that the predator firm will be able to destroy enough of its rivals to secure the degree of market power that it must have to make the long-run profits justify the short-run losses? Charges of predatory pricing have most frequently been leveled against large discount houses, drug chains, and grocery supermarkets. But these sellers are not pitted exclusively against small independent competitors: they must tangle with other large discount houses, other drug chains, and other supermarkets. Perhaps A&P could cut its prices far enough and long enough to drive Matilda Mudge out of business; but that wouldn't work on Safeway. And it's Safeway, not Matilda Mudge, that keeps A&P executives awake at night.

We are not denying the possibility of predatory pricing in business. Well-documented examples are hard to find, but it is surely possible. Minimum-price laws, however, offer the *certainty* of higher prices in order to eliminate the *possibility* of higher prices: a case of accepting a known and certain evil as a way of avoiding an uncertain evil of unknown dimensions. That may or may not be a good social bargain. But since it is so often advocated by business firms that clearly stand to gain from it, we should at least approach their arguments skeptically.

Once Over Lightly

Price searchers are looking for pricing structures that will enable them to sell all units for which marginal revenue exceeds marginal cost.

The popularity of the cost-plus-markup theory of pricing rests upon its usefulness as a search technique and the fact that people often cannot correctly explain processes in which they regularly and successfully engage.

A crucial factor for the price searcher is the ability or inability to discriminate: to charge high prices for units that are in high demand and low prices for units that would not otherwise be purchased, without allowing the sales at lower prices to "spoil the market" for high-price sales.

A rule for successful price searching often quoted by economists is: Set marginal revenue equal to marginal cost. This means: Continue selling as long as the additional revenue from a sale exceeds the additional cost. Skillful price searchers are people who know this rule (even when they don't fully realize they're using it) and who also have a knack for distinguishing the relevant marginal possibilities. The possibilities are endless, which helps to make price theory a fascinating exploration for people with a penchant for puzzle-solving.

Firms often charge that their competitors, whether domestic or foreign, are "selling below cost" and call for the government to prevent such "predatory" practices. Most such charges only make sense if they include per-unit cost expenses that are irrelevant to the particular decisions under attack. They make a different kind of sense when we remember that sellers characteristically prefer less competition.

QUESTIONS FOR DISCUSSION

1. If you're still uncertain about the meaning of marginal revenue, here is some additional practice.

Price per Unit	Quantity Demanded
$12	1
11	2
10	3
9	4

   a. Assume that all sales take place at a single price. What is the *addition to total revenue* from selling the second unit, the third, the fourth? Why is marginal revenue less than price?

   b. What set of prices could make marginal revenue *equal* to price as shown by this schedule? (Check the case of Horty and the rose bushes.)

2. "A price searcher should set marginal revenue as far above marginal cost as possible." Explain why this statement is wrong. What is being erroneously assumed by someone who thinks that net receipts will be zero at an output where marginal revenue equals marginal cost?

3. Locate the most profitable uniform price for sellers to set in each of the situations graphed at the top of the next column and the quantity they will want to produce and sell. Then shade the area that represents the net income from that pricing policy. What will happen to net income in each case if the price is rased? If it's lowered?

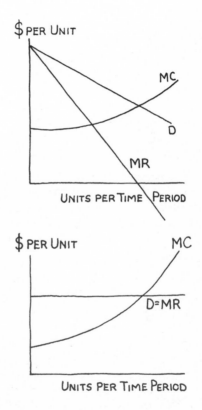

(Caution: What happens if a seller whose marginal revenue curve is the same as his demand curve raises his price?)

4. You want to sell at auction an antique dining-room suite. There are three people who want it, and they're willing to pay $8000, $6000, and $4000, respectively. Your reservation price (the price above which the bidding must go before you'll

sell) is $5000. No one in the room has any information about the value of the suite to anyone else.

    a. At about what price will the suite be sold?

    b. Suppose you run a Dutch auction. The auctioneer announces a price well above what anyone would be willing to pay and then gradually lowers the price until a bid is received. At about what price will the suite be sold?

5. A privately owned university in the Southwest wants to increase the percentage of Mexican-Americans in its student body. Very few of them are willing to pay the university's high tuition rates, however, and the university is reluctant to spend money for scholarships. Outline a system for granting scholarships to Mexican-Americans that would not reduce the university's net income. (You will have to figure out a way of estimating the relevant marginal costs.)

6. List some cases of discriminatory pricing similar to the cases of the college and the movie theater. How do the sellers identify particular customers with the appropriate class of demanders? How do they prevent reselling?

7. You and your fiancée are shopping for wedding rings. After showing you a sample of his wares, the jeweler asks, "About what price did you have in mind?"

    a. Why does he ask this question?

    b. If you tell him you don't plan to spend more than $50 on each ring, are you helping him find the rings to sell you or the price to charge for the rings you prefer?

    c. What might be a good technique for finding out the lowest price at which the jeweler is willing to sell the rings you like?

8. How should Artesian take into account the price he paid for the land on which the spring was discovered in deciding what price to charge for his water?

9. Grocery stores often run newspaper advertisements containing coupons that entitle customers to price discounts. What is the rationale for such a policy? (Hint: Price searchers would like to use lower prices to attract additional customers without being compelled to offer the lower price to customers already secured.)

10. Can hog growers raise the prices at which they sell when their feed costs go up? (Hog growers are typically price takers.) If feed costs are expected to remain at this higher level, what will happen after a time to the number of hogs reaching the market? How will this affect the price of hogs?

11. One store sells Wilson Championship extra-duty felt optic yellow tennis balls at $3.49 for a can of three. Another store in the same shopping center sells Wilson Championship extra-duty felt optic yellow tennis balls at $2.89 for a can of three. How is this possible? Why would anyone buy balls from the first store? Why do you think we repeated the long description in the second sentence instead of just saying "identical tennis balls"?

12. If a surgeon charges $1500 to remove the gall bladder of a wealthy patient and $500 to remove another patient's gall bladder, is she exploiting the first patient or giving a discount to the second? How does she prevent the second patient from buying several operations at the lower price and reselling them for a profit to wealthy patients?

13. Many firms use a technique called "target pricing" in trying to decide what prices to set for new products they're introducing. The target price is a price that enables the firm to recover a certain percentage of the product's development and production costs. What, in addition to costs, must the seller know in order to calculate the return a particular price will yield? If earnings from the sale of the product turn out to fall short of the target, should the firm raise the price? If earnings exceed the firm's expectations, should it lower the price?

14. If it's true that big supermarkets almost always have lower unit costs than small grocery stores, why does anyone ever build a small grocery store?

15. Information is a scarce good and its acquisition has a cost. How does this fact explain the frequent willingness of small firms to charge whatever prices are set by much larger firms?

16. Which of the following products are being sold below cost? With what other products are they competing? Is the competition "unfair"?
    a. Coffee offered by a bank to its customers without charge
    b. As many cups of coffee after dinner as the diner in an expensive restaurant requests, at no extra charge
    c. Commercial television programs
    d. Soft drinks on an airline flight
    e. A roll of film given to each adult customer during the pizza shop's first week of operation

17. There are three elements that must all be present for a firm to be engaged in predatory pricing: pricing (1) below cost, (2) in order to eliminate rivals, and (3) with the intention of raising prices afterward to recoup. What factors would make the last step of the process difficult to complete? Under what kinds of circumstances would it be relatively easy? Can you cite any actual examples?

18. Why did the airlines offer special reduced-rate youth fares until the Civil Aeronautics Board ordered them to stop the practice? What was the CAB's objective?

19. How should the British and French manufacturers of the Concorde supersonic commercial airliner take account of the plane's development costs in determining the prices to charge airline companies? Should they suspend production if they can't obtain a price that will cover development costs?

20. If the railroads, barge lines, and trucking firms of this country were allowed to set their rates free from government regulation, what do you think would follow: "gouging of customers" (higher prices) or "ruinous price cutting" (lower prices)? Does this happen in other areas of the economy where prices are not regulated by commissions, for example, in the grocery or automobile industries?

21. The marginal cost curves of the Anchorage Aardvark Breeding Company and the Houston Aardvark Breeding Company are identical; but the demand curves they face differ, as shown in the graph below.
    a. What price will each firm want to set?
    b. What are their respective percentage markups?
    c. Suppose something happens to raise marginal cost for each firm to $20 while nothing else changes. What price will each now set? What will be their new percentage markups?
    d. What is the relationship between elasticity of demand and the profit-maximizing percentage markup?

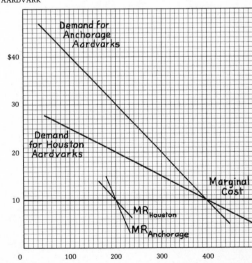

$ PER AARDVARK

AARDVARKS PER MONTH

131

Competition
and Government Policy

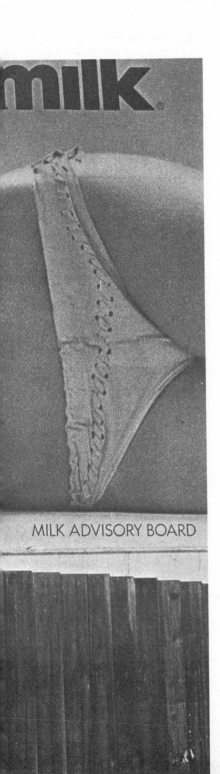

MILK ADVISORY BOARD

Will economic competition disappear unless the government has an active program to preserve it? Or does competition preserve itself, sometimes in the face of diligent efforts by the government to restrict it?

Is the government promoting competition when it prevents larger, more efficient, or more unscrupulous firms from driving other firms out of business? Or does the protection of competitors entail the suppression of competition?

When the government prohibits mergers, is it preventing competitors from eliminating rivals? Or is it barring the development of more competitive and efficient organizational forms?

What do we mean by competition and how are we to decide whether the economy or some sector of it is adequately competitive? Is competition in an industry to be measured by the number of competitors, by the practices in which they engage, or by the behavior of prices, costs, and profits and the industry's record with respect to innovation?

Those questions will not be conclusively answered in this chapter. But we hope that when you've finished thinking through the sources and consequences of competition as well as the origins and effects of government policies you will have a better sense of what the issues are.

Competition Appears

When we last saw Artesian the price searcher, he was ruefully contemplating the consequences of an attempt to extract from his customers the full value to them of a cup of mineral water. As we rejoin him now, he has returned to the price of 23 cents. He is selling 18 cups of water a day and enjoying a daily income of $3.42 from his mineral spring.

Artesian's demand curve reflects the tastes and preferences of people in the community, their income, and the availability of substitutes for Artesian's mineral water. Let's see what might happen if better substitutes became available.

A good substitute for Artesian's mineral water is the mineral water of other suppliers. Perhaps there are no other springs in the community; but mineral water can be bottled and shipped from neighboring towns. Moreover, Artesian's annual income from his spring, if it becomes known, will act as information and incentive to others. The owner of a local grocery store might decide to stock bottled mineral water in the hope of appropriating for himself some of the gains now going to Artesian. Let's assume this occurs.

The grocer can purchase bottled mineral water for $1.40 a gallon. That comes to about 10 cents per cupful of the size which Artesian is selling for 23 cents. The grocer thinks he can undersell Artesian and capture the bulk of his trade. What would be the best price to set?

If we knew the demand curve faced by the grocer, we could use the information we have on marginal cost to determine the profit-maximizing price for which he is searching. We assumed that Artesian knew his demand miraculously, and we could, if we wished, make the same heroic assumption for the grocer. But the assumption would now be considerably more heroic; a larger miracle would be required. For now we would have to know (a) the relative valuations placed on bottled versus fresh water; (b) the proximity of customers to Artesian and the competing grocery and the costs of patronizing one rather than the other; (c) the customers' evaluations of the advantages and disadvantages of buying two weeks' supply at one time; (d) the extent to which information is available to customers regarding these alternative supplies; and other similar factors. Moreover a fundamental uncertainty of a more radical sort is introduced by the probability that the demand facing each supplier is partially dependent on the pricing policy of the other.

Notice what this implies. The price set by Artesian will affect the grocer's demand and hence the most profitable price for the grocer to set. But the price set by the grocer will in turn affect Artesian's demand and thus alter the data with which Artesian determined his original price. What it comes to is that the best price for either one to set depends in part on the price which he himself decides to set. The neat little world of Chapter 10, with its clearly defined curves, becomes blurry. Unfortunately from an analytic standpoint, but perhaps fortunately from an esthetic one, the real world is not as neatly outlined as the pictures in a coloring book.

Perhaps you recall from Chapter 9 the word *oligopoly*, meaning "few sellers." We decided there that the concept of a few sellers shared all the ambiguities of the concept of a sole seller, ambiguities inherent in the problem of deciding just how broadly or narrowly to define the commodity being sold. Some economists have retained the slippery word *oligopoly* and have assigned it a very special meaning: a situation in which the demand curve of one seller depends on the reactions of identifiable other sellers, sometimes called rivals. Whether or not we choose to call this oligopoly—the usage is certainly misleading—situations of that sort, where the demand curves of different sellers are significantly interdependent, are obviously both common and important. As a result, price searchers must often plan their course of action in the manner of chess or poker players.

What can we expect to occur in such a situation? Precise predictions are impossible to make, but a number of possibilities suggest themselves:

1. Each seller will try to make his product more attractive in the hope of capturing and retaining customers. Artesian may install a bench under the shade tree by his dispenser. The grocer may offer to carry the gallon bottle to the customer's car. There are many other ways to differentiate the product, too many even to begin listing them. These actions raise the cost of doing business, but they may also increase the value to the customer of what he obtains for his money.

2. Each seller will try to disseminate information concerning the special virtues of his product. This is usually called advertising, and it has a poor reputation among many observers of the capitalist economic system. It is allegedly a very wasteful activity. Remember, however, that information is a good, a scarce good whose possession enables people to increase their wealth by discovering more profitable exchange opportunities. Much advertising is no doubt wasteful, in the sense that its total cost exceeds the sum of the benefits it provides in the form of better information. But it is not easy to decide just where the line should be drawn. Artesian and the grocer will want to spend more on advertising as long as the anticipated marginal revenue from advertising exceeds the anticipated marginal cost. It would be a lot easier to decide whether this results in an optimum or an excessive amount of advertising if we had better data on what constitutes an optimum amount of information. Meanwhile, we are left with the admittedly unsatisfactory conclusion that advertising sometimes promotes efficiency and sometimes does not.

   As long as the marginal revenue to each seller exceeds his marginal cost, he will want to expand his sales. This is a very significant prediction, because it sheds important light on a third possibility.

3. Artesian and the grocer may meet for lunch and agree to work together. "Why compete," Artesian asks rhetorically, "when all we're doing is wiping out one another's profits? I'll keep my price at 23¢ per cupful, you set a corresponding price of $3.22 per gallon, and we'll just share the market." The grocer agrees and they shake hands. They don't put their agreement in a written contract, because such agreements between competing sellers to maintain prices and share markets are usually unenforceable in court and are, moreover, illegal under the laws of many states and under federal law where it is applicable. In addition, as we shall see, it might be very difficult to write a contract that would cover all the possibilities, and even

more difficult to police it. So Artesian and the grocer content themselves with a "gentleman's agreement."

What might happen now? Suppose that geography, consumer tastes, and other factors are such that exactly half of Artesian's customers switch over to the grocer. Artesian will find his annual profits more than cut in half. He will sell 9 cups daily and net $1.71, or $624.15 annually. After payment of $200 to the dispenser company he is left with only $424.15 (as against $1048.30 previously). Artesian mourns the day the grocer decided to enter the mineral-water business.

Competition Reappears

But agreements of this sort are notoriously unstable. The incentives to change are so persistent that soon one or the other party will seek to circumvent the terms of the agreement. Let's see why.

Fundamentally, the explanation has to do with the inequality of marginal revenue and marginal cost. Artesian would incur only 4 cents in additional costs if he could attract just one of the grocer's customers. And he would add 23 cents to his daily revenue. That is 19 cents worth of inducement to violate the agreement (in a gentlemanly way, of course). Artesian would be willing to pay *up to* 19 cents to attract another customer, if he thought he could do so without inviting retaliation from the grocer or being forced to reduce prices to his existing customers.

He might advertise more, add vitamin C to his water, provide selective delivery service, give trading stamps, or maybe even offer secret price rebates. Meanwhile the grocer's marginal revenue is also well above his marginal cost, and the grocer is contemplating similar actions to "build volume" on mineral water. Maybe the grocer offers a special low price on paper cups to customers who buy a gallon of mineral water, thereby escaping the charge that he has violated the agreement not to reduce the price of mineral water.

Even if the gentlemen were to resist all these temptations, their agreement might still be undermined. For what is to keep some other grocer or the local druggist from doing exactly what the first grocer did? If Artesian and the grocer do not take these new competitors into their cartel,[1] the price of 23 cents will be under-cut. If they do take them in, profits on the mineral-water business will shrink further. And the new and larger agreement would be still harder to enforce effectively, since it now involves more parties and presumably more ways to honor the letter while violating the spirit of the agreement.

The recurring lesson under this third possibility is that a down-

1. A cartel is an agreement among a group of sellers to regulate prices or output. There are also buyers' cartels, such as the owners of professional basketball teams mentioned in Chapter 5 who want a single league to keep down the cost of hiring players.

ward-sloping demand curve is insufficient to guarantee continuing profits. Competition (and every seller faces competition; remember that there is no such thing as a perfectly inelastic demand curve) tends to bring down the price, raise the quality of the product sold, and whittle away the price searcher's net income. That is why price searchers and even price takers yearn so ardently for legal restrictions on competition. Let's turn to this possibility.

Enlisting the Government

Artesian had a good thing going until the grocer found out what a good thing it was. "If people would only be loyal to their local mineral water," Artesian muses one evening, "I'd still be earning over $1000 a year from my spring." The wish becomes father to a thought and the thought inspires a course of action.

Artesian drafts a memorandum to the town council setting forth the following points:

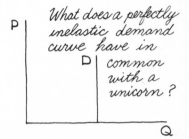

1. Water is a basic necessity of life. Adequate local supplies of high-quality water must therefore be assured.

2. Mineral water is even more basic than regular water, containing as it does vital nutrients.

3. Unrestricted competition, especially from outside the town, can lead to irresponsible price cutting and the destruction of local mineral-water suppliers, thus depriving the town of an important industry, citizens of regular income, and consumers of assured domestic supplies of mineral water.

4. Unrestricted competition will lead to cost-cutting procedures that may threaten the purity of the mineral-water supply and hence the health and safety of the whole community. No price is too high if it guarantees pure water!

5. The town council should therefore pass an ordinance stipulating that every seller of mineral water within the town limits be licensed; that a license be granted only after careful scrutiny by a board of knowledgeable people in the mineral-water industry of the applicant's qualifications and ability to satisfy minimum health and safety standards; and that the board be empowered to revoke the license of any seller who engages in conduct that is unethical or inconsistent with the public interest.

Since legislative bodies at the federal, state, and local level have often adopted just such licensing laws on the basis of very similar arguments, we shall assume that the town fathers grant Artesian's request. Market entry is now restricted and Artesian is in a more fortunate position. If he is doubly fortunate, Artesian will even be appointed chairman of the licensing board. Why not? He is, after all, the local mineral-water expert.

The board will now set high standards of purity and excellence. It will probably not be so crude as to deny licenses outright. It will rather decree that bottled mineral water must be sold only in containers that have been sterilized by being boiled for 24 hours at 120 degrees centigrade (fresh water sold in cups is exempt); that stores selling mineral water must do so in separate areas so that the water does not stand closer than 25 feet to any other food or beverage by which it might be contaminated (businesses selling only mineral water are exempt); and perhaps that a tax of $2 per gallon be levied on all water sold to defray the costs of the inspection and licensing services (mineral water sold from private residences is exempt).

Entry into a market can be prevented without going so far as to prohibit it flatly. Anything that increases the costs of a supplier will restrict his supply, and the imposition of sufficiently large costs will restrict it completely. Licensing can be used to do exactly this, and often is. The prevention of competition is never given, of course, as the reason for licensing. It is always "the public interest" for which sellers profess a fervent concern when they seek to have the government impose controls on potential competitors.

Restricting Competitors

Here are some actual newspaper items with names changed to protect the guilty. Who stands to gain and who to lose in each case?

"Government officials are demanding that hospitals provide registered nurses 24 hours a day or lose their Medicare certifications."

"All plumbers must spend a minimum of 140 hours a year for five years learning higher mathematics, physics, hydraulics, and isometric drawing."

"Woolen makers are arguing that, since woolen worsted fabric is essential to national defense, the government should impose quotas on imports from abroad."

"The prominent owner of a local television sales and service center said today that he welcomed the state's investigation of the television repair business and he demanded regulation of the industry. 'We must eliminate janitors, firemen, milkmen, and similar amateurs who defraud the public by providing poor quality repair service at cut-rate prices,' he argued."

"Automobile dealers are vigorously protesting Sears' application to enter the car-financing business, and are demanding that the state corporations commissioner reject the application."

"The Senate Public Health Committee yesterday rejected a bill to allow use of multiple offices and trade names in the diagnosis of eye problems and fitting of glasses. Single-office optometrists contend that, if an optometrist is in his own office, his boss is his patient. If the optometrist works under a trade name, his boss is his company."

"The owner of the Piney Woods Nursing Home and secretary of

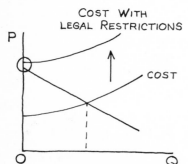

COST WITH
LEGAL RESTRICTIONS

None will be demanded even at the lowest price at which the firm can now afford to sell.

the State Association of Licensed Nursing Homes accused the state health department last night of approving new nursing-home construction without proper investigation of the need for additional facilities or the qualifications of the applicants. 'Unqualified people, including speculators from other parts of the country, are hoping to reap big profits,' he said. 'A great surplus of beds will bring about cutthroat competition, which means nursing homes will have to curtail many needed services, resulting in lower standards detrimental to patients and the community.'"

And once again, the plumbers, who aren't any worse than many others but seem to draw better press coverage:

"Changes proposed in the plumbing section of the city building code would require that a plumber serve as an apprentice for five years, instead of the present three, before becoming a journeyman. In addition, apprentices would have to register annually with the city and could not become apprentices after reaching the age of 25. For a plumber to become a master plumber, that is, one contracting plumbing work, he would have to take an examination. The code now requires only that a plumber seeking master-plumber status furnish bond."

The Ambivalence of Government Policies

An old proverb wisely asserts that the wolf should not be sent to guard the sheep. Should the government be relied upon to preserve competition in the economy? The history of government intervention in economic life reveals a pattern of concern for the special interests of competitors at least as strong as concern for competition. And the two are not identical, even though our rhetoric so often and easily uses them interchangeably.

The real and hypothetical cases described in this chapter show government acting at several levels and in a variety of ways to prevent potential sellers from offering more favorable terms or more attractive opportunities to buyers. They constitute restrictions on competition, regardless of the arguments used to defend such actions. The ultimate effect of a particular restriction on competition may be to preserve competition, by protecting a substantial number of competitors who would otherwise be forced out of business. But whether or not that is the long-term effect in certain cases, it is important to begin any evaluation of government policy toward competition by acknowledging one principle: *A law that restricts competitors restricts competition.*

We aren't going to move from that rule to a recommendation of laissez faire, the historic term for a policy of total noninterference by government in economic life. Complete laissez faire has never been practiced anywhere and, in the author's judgment, would not be desirable even if it turned out to be possible. The laws that define and enforce property rights are economic interventions which establish the basic ground rules for competitive behavior.

Government highway construction is economic intervention. So is the maintenance of a monetary system. There are ways in which government intervenes in economic life that almost no one opposes.

But local and state governments and especially the federal government also have adopted specific policies with regard to competition, policies that are ordinarily justified on the ground that competition is an effective coordinator of economic activity but requires some government maintenance if it is to be adequately preserved. The assessment of these laws, their applications, and their consequences forms an interesting study in history and judicial interpretation as well as economic analysis. All we shall try to do here, however, is raise a few fundamental questions.

The most important such law is the Sherman Act, often called the Sherman Antitrust Act, enacted by Congress with almost no debate or opposition in 1890. (The name reflects the attempts of nineteenth-century businessmen to use legal trusteeships as a device to prevent competition.) Its sweeping language has caused some to call it the constitution of the competitive system. It forbids all contracts, combinations, or conspiracies in restraint of interstate trade and all attempts to monopolize any part of interstate trade. The language is so sweeping, in fact, that it was bound to be qualified in its application. After all, any two partners entering into business together could be deemed to have combined with the intention of making trade more difficult for their competitors and thus gaining an ever larger share of trade for themselves. The federal courts consequently came to hold that combinations or other attempts to monopolize had to be "unreasonable" or major threats to public welfare before they could be prohibited under the Sherman Act.

Interpretations and Applications

To help the courts out in their efforts to apply the policies of the Sherman Act, Congress has passed additional legislation such as the Clayton Act and the Federal Trade Commission Act, both of which became law in 1914. The latter act created the Federal Trade Commission as a supposedly expert body and authorized it to promote competition by prohibiting a wide range of "unfair" practices. A principal provision of the Clayton Act (and subsequent amendments) aims specifically at the question of mergers, prohibiting all mergers that might "substantially" lessen competition. But difficult and important questions remain unresolved.

When does a merger substantially lessen competition? And do mergers ever increase competition? Suppose two steel firms want to merge. This is usually referred to as a *horizontal merger*. At first glance we would be inclined to say that the merger will substantially lessen competition in an industry already made up of a relatively few very large firms. But suppose they sell in different geographic areas? Suppose they each specialize in a different line of steel products? Suppose each is on the edge of failure and that the merger will lead to certain economies which may enable both to survive?

A great deal of dispute has arisen in recent years regarding so-called *conglomerate mergers*: mergers between firms producing widely divergent goods. Does the acquisition of a car-rental firm by an electrical-machinery manufacturer enable the rental firm to compete more effectively against Hertz and Avis? Does it lead to special arrangements between the machinery manufacturer, its suppliers, and the rental firm that tie up a portion of the car-rental business and thus reduce competition? Do conglomerate mergers lead to concentrations of financial power that are dangerous and undesirable regardless of their effects on competition?

What about *vertical mergers*, mergers between firms that previously existed in a supplier-buyer relationship, as when a supermarket chain acquires a food processor? Is this more likely to increase efficiency or to reduce competition by depriving other food processors of opportunities to sell?

What constitutes an illegally unfair trade practice? Is it unfair for a large firm to demand discounts from its suppliers? Is it unfair for suppliers to offer discounts to some purchasers but not to others? What about the whole question of advertising? Do large firms have unfair advantages in advertising, advantages that advertising increases? Must advertising be truthful in order to be fair? Of course it must, almost by definition. But what is the truth, the whole truth, and nothing but the truth? Anyone who thinks about this issue seriously or for very long is forced to admit that the regulation of "deceptive" advertising by the Federal Trade Commission inevitably involves the Commission in complex questions of purpose and effect and in a large number of judgments that appear quite arbitrary.

And always we return to the root problem: restrictions on competitors will reduce their ability to compete. Competition is essentially the offering of additional opportunities, and additional opportunities mean a wider range of choices and hence greater wealth. But the manner in which a firm expands the set of opportunities it offers may diminish, over a short or a longer period, the set of opportunities other firms are able to offer. Under what circumstances do we want the government to restrict one firm's competitive efforts for the sake of the larger or long-run competitive situation? It is important to remember that many of the most effective pressures on government policies stem not from consumer but from producer interests. And those policies will too often be shaped by the desire of producers to protect themselves against the rigors of the competitive life. Many arguments in the name of the public interest are about as honest as Mr. Artesian's moving petition to the town council.

The Range of Opinion

Is the whole body of "antitrust" law perhaps more of a hindrance than a help to competition? There are some who come to that conclusion. There are others, heavily concentrated, it often seems, in the economics profession, who would retain the Sherman Act and the antimerger provisions of the Clayton Act and junk the rest. Some of these defenders claim that the Sherman and Clayton Acts have made important contributions to the maintenance of a competitive economy. Others claim that they could make a much larger contribution if they were seriously enforced. But still others view them at best as harmless rhetoric, at worst as weapons which, in the hands of ignorant political appointees, may do a lot of damage to the economy.

The author is firmly convinced that he doesn't know who is right. "Antitrust" policy is certainly full of contradictions, of cases where the right hand is doing what the left hand is undoing. State laws rarely promote competition; more often they promote the interests of the competitor-protectors rather than the competition-protectors. Federal enforcement of the Sherman Act and the antimerger provisions of the Clayton Act often seems to strain at gnats while swallowing camels. On the other hand, the existence of the Sherman Act, with its ringing denunciation of price-fixing conspiracies, may have retarded the development in this country of the cartel arrangements that have so often appeared in Western Europe and Japan. The economist George Stigler once suggested that "the ghost of Senator Sherman is an ex officio member of the board of directors of every large company." That statement will never meet the minimum criteria for empirical scientific truths; but good history is still a long way from being a pure science.

Toward Evaluation

The conclusions that we shall offer at the end are far more modest than the questions with which we began.

The first modest observation to be made is that price searchers' markets tend to result in reduced output. To avoid spoiling his market, the price searcher forgoes some sales that could be made at prices above marginal cost. He looks at marginal revenue, not at price; and so he sells less and at a higher price than he would if he were a price taker. We introduced the other side of this argument at the end of Chapter 9, when we tried to show the sense in which price takers' markets led to an "optimal" allocation of resources. Figure 11A recapitulates and extends the analysis.

If there were only one wheat farmer, the market demand curve would be the demand curve he faces. And he would be a price searcher. He would calculate his marginal revenue, set it against his marginal cost curve, produce only 200 million bushels of wheat, and hold the price at $3.00 a bushel.

With 10,000 farmers producing wheat, on the other hand, each

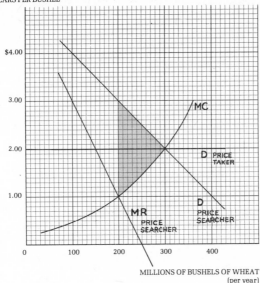

Figure 11A   Price and output comparisons

farmer is a price taker who faces a perfectly elastic demand curve at
the market-determined price. Each farmer maximizes his net return by producing up to the point at which marginal cost equals
price. Competition will reduce the price and expand output until
"equilibrium" has been reached at a price of $2.00 and an output
of 300 million bushels.

Let's review the specific sense in which the reduced output in
price searchers' markets represents a social waste. The marginal-
cost curve shows the opportunity cost of producing each unit of
output. Since opportunity cost measures the value of what is given
up, we can say that the area under the marginal-cost curve between
200 and 300 million bushels shows the gain to society from *not*
producing the last 100 of 300 million bushels, or what it would
have cost society to produce them. The demand curve, on the
other hand, measures what people are willing to pay for wheat, or
the gain to society from obtaining it. Since the area under the
demand curve is greater than the area under the marginal-cost
curve between 200 and 300 million, society gave up more than it
gained by not obtaining 100 million additional bushels. The
shaded area represents this loss of wealth. It is the difference
between the value of additional wheat and the value of the alternative goods that can be produced by sacrificing this additional
wheat.

The argument is admittedly somewhat formal and abstract. But
it is an important argument to understand if you want to evaluate
the effects of market power. In short: price searchers refrain from
providing goods that could be provided at a cost below what

people are willing to pay. This constitutes an inefficient use of resources.

Some further observations and words of caution can now be added.

First of all, price discrimination is capable of reducing this inefficiency. If the price-searching widget producer can find a way to do what Artesian attempted unsuccessfully with his you-set-the-price policy, and what Ivy College did more successfully through tuition scholarships, he improves the allocation of resources. Of course, he also increases his own net income, a fact that will prompt him toward more astute price searching.

Second, the burden of such inefficiency diminishes as price searchers' demand curves become more elastic. Since elasticity depends crucially on the availability of substitutes, legal restrictions on entry will tend to aggravate inefficiency. Restrictions on potential competitors reduce the range and diminish the availability of substitute goods, and allow the price searcher more room to increase his own wealth by allocating resources inefficiently.

Finally, for policy purposes, an inefficient situation must be compared with more efficient situations that are actually attainable. We objected earlier to the frequent error of contrasting a less than ideal situation with an ideal but unattainable situation. There are costs involved in changing market structures, such as the cost of an investigation, prosecution, court order, and compliance under antitrust statutes. Only if these marginal costs are less than the marginal benefits can one maintain that efficiency would be increased by legal action aimed at reducing the market power of price searchers.

Once Over Lightly

A gap between the price of a good and the marginal cost of making it available is a source of potential advantage to someone. Competition occurs in the economy as people locate such differentials and try to exploit them by filling that gap with additional goods.

Competition can take more forms than we can list and usually more forms than a price searcher can anticipate and head off.

Because competition tends to transfer the gains from providing a good to purchasers and other suppliers, firms frequently try to obtain government assistance in excluding competitors, often displaying remarkable ingenuity and stunning sophistry.

The notion that government is the Defender of Competition against Rapacious Monopolists is probably more a hope than a reality. Federal, state, and local governments have created and preserved numerous positions of special privilege whose effect is to restrict competition and reduce the options available to consumers.

An adequate and balanced evaluation of that substantial body of statutes, commission decrees, and judicial holdings which makes up federal antitrust policy has not yet been published.

While price searchers' markets entail a misallocation of resources when compared with price takers' markets, the significance of that misallocation and the cost of correcting it are difficult to determine.

QUESTIONS FOR DISCUSSION

1. How would you account for the fact that while some observers claim competition is declining in the American economy, every business firm insists that it faces strenuous competition?

2. Consult the technical definition of *oligopoly* presented in the text. Are the manufacturers of cigarettes oligopolists by that definition? Are the owners of the gasoline stations in a small town oligopolists? Name some other sellers who are and are not oligopolists by that definition.

3. The attempt by sellers to make their product more attractive to consumers is sometimes called *product differentiation*.
   a. Is product differentiation a wasteful process, imposing costs on sellers that are greater than the benefits conferred on buyers? Think of cases where it probably is wasteful in this sense and other cases where it is not.
   b. Evaluate the following argument: "New practices initiated by sellers to differentiate their products are liable to be wasteful from a social point of view because they are liable to entail high marginal costs and low marginal benefits. But this only means that producers have already made use of the low cost-high benefit techniques of product differentiation; it does not show that the whole process of product differentiation is wasteful."

4. Why must an effective price-fixing agreement between sellers include such restrictions on sales as output limitations or geographic divisions of sales territory?

5. Some states have established legal minimum prices for liquor sold at retail. Do you think this eliminates competition among retail liquor stores? Why do you think retailers in such states often lend glassware without charge to customers planning parties?

6. All the realtors in an area will generally charge the same fee for selling a house, a certain percentage of the sales price established by some realtors association and adhered to by all real estate agents as a matter of "ethical practice."
   a. Why would it be unethical if a realtor offered to accept 5 rather than 6 percent for selling your house? Toward whom would it be unethical?
   b. How do realtors compete with one another?
   c. Is an industry likely to become overcrowded if it's successful in fixing a high minimum price for its product? Is the realtor profession overcrowded in your judgment? What evidence might be used to answer this question? (From 1960 to 1973 the number of employees in the real estate industry increased 44 percent.)

7. A recent survey asked businessmen to describe the unethical practices in their own industry that they would most like to see eliminated. Of those responding 62 percent mentioned "unfair pricing," "dishonest advertising," "unfair competitive practices," or "cheating customers." How would you interpret these responses? How would you define the practices they condemn?

8. Examine the paragraph in the text (page 138) recounting the complaint of the nursing-home operator. How many wrong or

misleading assertions can you locate in that paragraph?

9. The legislature of a large state recently considered a bill that would require all grocery stores and drug stores selling package liquor to provide separate entrances to their liquor departments. It was maintained by supporters of the bill that this was necessary to prevent minors from entering the liquor department. Who do you think lobbied for this bill? Why?

10. A study several years ago pointed out that 73 percent of the professions licensed by a populous Midwestern state required entrants to have "good character." Why? How can good character be determined? Who is best able to determine whether a mortician's character is sufficiently blameless to entitle him to a license?

11. Is the patent granted to an inventor a grant of special privilege? Would you favor abolition of the patent privilege? Why or why not?

12. How might laws prohibiting collusion on pricing encourage mergers? (Hint: Can a firm collude with itself?)

13. What is the difference between reducing prices to attract more customers and reducing prices in order to monopolize?

14. It is often argued that large corporations have undue political influence. It is also argued by some that large corporations are convenient political scapegoats. Which argument is closer to the truth?

15. How important is free entry in promoting efficiency, low prices, and innovation in an industry? What are some of the barriers to free entry in addition to legal restrictions?

16. Evaluate this assertion by the economist M. A. Adelman: "A useful if not very precise index of the strength of competition . . . is the resentment of unsuccessful competitors." How would you evaluate the argument by other firms in their industries that General Motors and International Business Machines ought to be broken up into several separate companies?

Profit

"Perhaps no term or concept in economic discussion is used with a more bewildering variety of well-established meanings than profit." That sentence was written forty years ago by Frank Knight, a distinguished student of the subject, to introduce an encyclopedia article on profit. The situation has not changed greatly since then. A few years ago the *Wall Street Journal* ran a feature article entitled "Some Plain Truth about Profit." The author listed no fewer than seven distinct definitions of the word *profit* that have been employed by "economic experts," decided none of them was very helpful, and then offered his own. A month later the *Journal* published seven letters of response from its readers; their verdicts on the new definition and accompanying exposition ran from excellent through misleading to ridiculous.

So what shall we do? We shall take the coward's course and assert that *there is no correct definition of profit*. The meaning of any word depends, after all, on the way people use it; and it is an incontrovertible fact that people (including economists) use *profit* in many different senses. And we certainly don't want to quibble about mere definitions. But attitudes toward profit and such closely related concepts as cost of production and interest affect economic legislation, and those attitudes depend in large part on what people have in mind when they use the terms. So we're going to expend an unusual amount of effort in this chapter trying to decide what things ought to be called, but only insofar as the names we apply are likely to make a difference in the way we react to the realities they describe.

Profit as "Total Revenue Minus Total Cost"

The most common definition of profit is simply *total revenue minus total cost*. That's almost everyone's intuitive definition of the term and that's how we have used it until now. When a business firm has paid all of its costs, what it has left over is profit. But before we can agree on the size of profits, defined in this way, we must agree on what is to be counted as costs.

What Should Be Included in Costs?

Monetary outlays are not the same as costs from the opportunity-cost perspective. This is clear in the case of an owner-operated business: part of the cost of doing business is the owner's own labor, even though the owner may not figure his salary as part of his regular costs and writes no weekly payroll check to himself. If the owner pays rent for the building he uses, he will count the rental payments as part of his costs; but he may not do so if he himself owns the building. He ought to do so, however, because he is losing the amount that could be obtained from renting the building to someone else, and from the standpoint of society, too, there is a genuine cost in having the building not available for alternative uses.

The business proprietor may also be using equipment that he bought and now owns. If he bought the equipment with a bank loan, he will include his bank payments in his costs. But suppose he bought the equipment out of previously accumulated savings? Then he gave up income that he could have obtained from letting someone else use his savings, and that is certainly part of the opportunity cost of doing business. But he may or may not decide to include this forgone income in his costs. The point is that he should. The income forgone represents a genuine cost both to the business proprietor and to society.

Let's next consider the accounting procedures of corporations. Corporate profits have a legal definition because corporations must pay taxes on their profits. But the legal definition is unsatisfactory from an opportunity-cost point of view. It begins with the commonsense definition of profit as revenue minus costs. But it excludes from cost the dividend payments made to stockholders of the corporation while including the interest payments made to bondholders. Are these payments that different? Both are payments for borrowed funds or for the resources that the corporation was able to purchase with those funds. The principal difference is that payments to bondholders are a contractual obligation of a fixed amount, whereas the dividends paid to stockholders are a kind of residual that may vary from year to year or quarter to quarter. Still, the funds loaned by the stockholders are funds not earning income somewhere else, and the resources purchased by the corporation with these funds are pulled away from alternative opportunities. Surely some portion of the dividends paid by corporations represent genuine opportunity costs, no matter how they are regarded for purposes of taxation.

Profit versus Interest

A persistent difficulty in the measurement of profits is the difficulty of deciding just how much interest a business firm is paying. The legal definition of interest isn't adequate, for payments to banks and bondholders often will not differ functionally from the payments made to shareholders in dividends or even as increases in the market price of their shares attributable to reinvestment of earnings. What we are after in trying to measure the true interest costs of a business firm is the amount the firm must pay in order to obtain the capital it uses.

Capital means goods used to produce future goods: like cash registers in retail stores, typewriters in an office, drill presses in a sheetmetal fabricating shop, or reading skills that are used to produce knowledge. In later chapters we'll take a closer look at the concept of capital and some of the ambiguities associated with its definition. But the simple definition given above is enough to get us into the puzzling phenomenon of interest.

Why Is Interest Paid?

Usury and interest were originally synonyms. Today the word *usurious* carries connotations of overreaching and grasping greed—evidence in our language of popular hostility toward the taking of interest. The hostility seems to be largely rooted in mis-understanding. Interest is not the price of using money, although that is sometimes a convenient way of expressing it. *Interest is the difference in value between present and future goods.* Once you understand why present goods are more valuable than goods in the future, you realize that interest is not something peculiar to capitalist economies, or a consequence of the avarice and monop-oly power of bankers and other moneylenders, or something that could be eliminated just by making more money available. Interest rates are generally talked about as if they were the cost of borrow-ing money, because money is the usual means by which people acquire possession of present goods. But interest would exist in an economy that used no money at all, since it is fundamentally the difference in value between present and future goods.

Why are present goods more highly valued than goods in the future? This is a question that has intrigued a number of the most distinguished minds in the history of economics, and the higher subtleties of the problem still arouse controversy in some quarters. There are, however, two aspects of the question whose significance can be readily grasped.

Time Preference

In the first place individuals have, on the average, *a positive rate of time preference.* That is to say, people tend to place a higher subjective value on consumption in the near future than on con-sumption in the more distant future. Some have interpreted this as evidence of shortsightedness, or of inability to imagine the distant future with as much vividness and force as one contemplates the immediate future, or of an innate human tendency to view the future through rose-tinted glasses. Each of these interpretations casts suspicion on the ultimate "rationality" of time preference. On the other hand, given the facts of human mortality and all the contingencies of life, it is not necessarily irrational or shortsighted to prefer a bird in the hand to two in the bush. Moreover, if people have reason to believe that their income will increase over time, they could very logically conclude that giving up something now entails a larger subjective sacrifice than giving up quite a bit more of the same thing at a future date when one's income is expected to be larger. Whatever the explanation or explanations, however, there can be no doubt that people do display positive rates of time preference. To obtain 100 strawberries today, a person may be willing to give in exchange 115 strawberries one year from now. Conversely, such an individual could be persuaded to give up 100 strawberries now only by the promise of 115 strawberries or more one year hence. He displays a 15 percent rate of time preference. While these subjective rates of time preference vary widely from individual to individual and from one culture to another, they are, on the average, positive in every known society. This by itself would be sufficient to create a premium on present goods over future goods and thus a positive rate of interest.

It may be instructive to consider a case of apparent *negative* time preference. This should help you grasp the principle at work. Consider a person who receives, as a gift, 100 quarts of strawberries. He loves strawberries, and he vastly prefers one quart now to one quart a month from now. But he does not want to eat more than one or two quarts a day, for fairly obvious reasons, so that many of these 100 quarts are without any value to him. They will spoil before he wants to eat them.

Such a person would be willing to give up strawberries now to obtain fewer strawberries in the future! He might go down the block offering each of 45 neighbors two quarts of strawberries apiece in return for one quart at a later date when he will be able to eat them. By this act, which seems to reveal a negative time preference, he clearly increases the value to himself of the gift he received.

Surpluses of this kind are not uncommon. How much pressure do they exert to reduce the average premium on present over future goods, or the rate of interest? Probably very little in an economy with a well-organized system for extensive exchange. If the recipient of the 100 quarts of strawberries can easily sell them (for money), and then use the money (which will not spoil after a few days) to buy strawberries as he wants them, his present surplus will not cause him to reveal a negative rate of time preference. Opportunities to exchange at low cost, which are enlarged by such institutions as money and commodity speculators, keep the rate of interest from falling.

The Productivity of Capital

The second main factor making for positive interest rates in a society—though perhaps it is only another aspect of the factor already discussed—is *the potential productivity of goods*. Suppose that Robinson Crusoe, a familiar figure in economists' arguments, can only keep himself alive from day to day by digging for clams.

Five clams a day will barely enable him to keep body and soul together. And five clams a day is the most he can obtain by digging with his hands during every working hour. If he had a shovel, however, he could increase his daily output to ten clams. But a week's work is required to manufacture a suitable shovel. Since Robinson would starve if he took a week off to make the shovel, he cannot attain this higher income level.

It is clear in such a case that Robinson would be eager to obtain 35 extra clams, and willing to give in return more than 35 clams in the future, for the opportunity to increase his productivity by first making a shovel. The shovel is capital for Robinson. And it is the shovel's value as capital, that is, its potential as a producer of future goods, that causes Robinson to want it and makes him willing to pay a premium to obtain it.

The Risk Factor in Interest Rates

The rates charged by banks to corporate borrowers, by department stores to customers with revolving charge accounts, or by individuals lending to savings and loan institutions, all reflect the society's rates of time preference and the potential productivities of goods. But they also include risk premiums of various sizes plus differences in the cost of negotiating loans. It will ordinarily cost you more per dollar to borrow from a commercial bank than it will cost a large and successful corporation.[1] This does not really mean that you are paying a higher rate of interest, however. You are paying for the costs incurred by the bank in investigating your credit standing and doing the bookkeeping entailed by your loan, as well as a kind of insurance premium that the bank collects from each borrower in anticipation of losses through costs of collection and defaults. If the bank could not charge this premium, it would not find it advantageous to make loans to customers in higher risk categories. So when legislators impose ceilings on the "annual interest" that may legally be charged by lenders, they do not reduce interest rates so much as they exclude certain categories of borrowers from contracting for loans. Since the borrowers would not contract for the loans unless they deemed them advantageous, it is difficult to discover in what way maximum-interest-rate laws benefit borrowers.

This is an important point, and not only because it corrects certain popular but mistaken notions about interest-rate legislation. The return that any lender will demand as a condition of lending depends on the risk he assigns to that particular loan. Commercial lenders aren't unique in that respect. Imagine two

---

1. When the prime rate rose to 12 percent in 1974, it exceeded the maximum legal rate that may be charged in some states for consumer loans. Some banks nonetheless made small consumer loans to their own depositors, below the rate they could get on less risky loans, in order to retain the goodwill and continued patronage of established customers.

corporations, one of them General Motors and the other a shaky corporation teetering on the edge of bankruptcy. Each wants to borrow money. To do so, each issues $1000 bonds maturing in one year. At what price will the bonds be purchased?

Suppose the General Motors issue is all sold at $952. Nine hundred and fifty-two dollars now is worth $1000 at maturity (in one year) at a 5 percent rate of interest. The $952 price would mean, in effect, that people are willing to lend to General Motors for a 5 percent annual return.

But the bonds of the shaky corporation would sell for far less even if they were bought by the same people who purchased the General Motors bonds. The probability of default is so much higher in the second case that lenders could only be persuaded to take the risk if they were offered the possibility of a very high return. If the second issue sold for $714, lenders would be demanding a 40 percent annual return.

If all works out well, they will receive $238 more than they would have earned from a General Motors bond. But that outcome is highly uncertain, and there is also the possibility they will lose most or all of the principal. The higher "interest rate" on the latter bonds should therefore be interpreted as a risk premium rather than as pure interest. Perhaps when legislators contemplate interest-rate ceilings, they should ask themselves whether they have ever purchased bonds at a heavy discount.

Consequences of Uncertainty

When we begin to think about the different rates of return that lenders will demand on risky and relatively riskless loans, we quickly get into the interesting problems raised by uncertainty. Suppose that Joe Jones puts $100 into a savings account on January 1. The bank promises 5 percent interest and Joe is confident that the bank will neither fail nor renege on its commitment. On December 31 he withdraws $105. He earned $5 in interest, a payment for the use of his savings.

Now suppose that he loans the same $100 to a business firm that promises to pay him $5 per year for each year he leaves his funds with the firm and gives him a bond as evidence of its obligation. The firm uses his savings, we may assume, to purchase capital. This doesn't seem to differ in any significant way from the preceding case. Joe has once again received 5 percent per year for the use of his savings. And everyone will in fact call the $5 interest because it is a contractual obligation of a fixed amount.

Let's vary the situation once again. This time Joe loans the firm $100 and receives in return a share of common stock. Now Joe is not entitled to receive any fixed amount. Ownership of the stock entitles him merely to a share of the firm's earnings. The firm may do poorly and pay him only $2 in dividends over the year, or it may do very well and pay him $15 in dividends. That won't be called interest by most people because it was not a fixed contractual obligation. But a good case can be made, from a functional stand-point, for applying the interest label to $5 of the dividends. For if 5 percent is the going rate at which the firm can borrow, and 5 percent is the rate of return that lenders like Joe can fairly confi-dently expect from loaning their funds at little risk, then 5 percent is the opportunity cost of lending funds to firms for capital ac-quisitions. It is what the lender sacrifices by letting any borrower have his savings. It is what he will therefore demand as a condition of making the loan.

Unless he wants to make more than 5 percent and is willing to accept greater risk in the effort to do so! But if the firm subse-quently pays only $2, Joe sustains a loss. He loses the extra $3 he could have obtained pretty much as a matter of course by pur-chasing a bond or putting his money in the bank. If the firm pays $15, Joe makes a profit. The profit is $10, not $15: the amount over and above what is available at a very high degree of certainty. To grasp the point we're making here, you must ask yourself why people loan money at 5 percent when there are opportunities to lend at 15 percent. The answer is that they can't be certain of the 15 percent. It might well be less, perhaps a good deal less. The higher rate of return is reserved for people who are willing to take more risk. But that implies, of course, that the higher return was not generally anticipated. The generally anticipated return, the rate of return that is rather confidently expected, may be thought of as the interest portion of the return. The remainder is profit.

Profit as the Consequence of Uncertainty

This is a different definition of profit from the one with which we began. *Profit* is now being defined as *the difference between the outcome that was generally anticipated when a decision was made and the outcome that was actually realized.* It is not the same as interest, which is the social rate of preference for present over future goods and hence the opportunity cost of obtaining present goods. By this definition, profit as distinct from interest is not a cost at all. It is something that appears because the future is uncertain. If there were no uncertainties in life, there would never be a divergence between anticipation and realization, and there would be, by this definition, no profits at all—and no losses, since a loss is simply a profit with a minus sign, like the $3 Joe lost when the firm paid him only $2 in dividends.

Does all this sound strange to your ears? Unrelated to anything you've previously thought or read about profits? Unrelated even to economics? Stay with us. A series of examples interspersed with commentary will be used to clarify this definition and show its significance. In the process of thinking through the examples, you will discover that however one ultimately chooses to employ the word *profit*, it is useful to have some concept for distinguishing between changes in wealth attributable to uncertainty and returns that are rather confidently anticipated.

Why Do Profits Appear?

Frieda Flyer is a shrewd investor who regularly earns 10 percent a year on the money she invests in careful stock purchases. She purchases $1000 worth of stock on January 1. On December 31 the value of that stock plus dividends accumulated during the year is $1100. Frieda makes a zero profit. The $100 she earned should be called interest because it is the opportunity cost to Frieda of letting someone else have $1000 worth of her power to purchase present goods.

Now Frieda takes a flyer. She puts $1000 into Trustworthy Uranium, Incorporated, and one year later the stock has a market value of $1250. Frieda makes a profit of $150. She might have lost, of course, and she feels very fortunate. If the stock had gone to only $1040, Frieda would have lost $60.

Notice that she expects to be able to earn 10 percent pretty much as a matter of course. Therefore, she would not knowingly invest for a mere 5 percent return, and if she were to receive only 5 percent she would properly call it a loss. It would be 5 percent per year that she did not receive because she chose to gamble on a highly uncertain stock, one that might have gone much higher (and she hoped it would) but actually ended up at only $1040.

Suppose Frieda Flyer buys a Florida lot for $2000 when she receives an advertisement that says that Florida real estate increases in value by 30 percent per year. At the end of the year, the market value of her lot is still $2000. Frieda lost $200, the amount by which her wealth could have been expected to increase had she followed her usual stock-purchase program. We should now begin to have doubts about Frieda's shrewdness as an investor.

If Florida real estate really can be expected to increase in value by 30 percent per year, many people will be eager to buy Florida lots, as long as the alternative rate of return is, let's say, 10 percent per year. Their eagerness to purchase will bid up the price of the lots until the lots are no longer better buys than other available assets. If there happen to be many investors like Frieda who uncritically accept the claims of the advertisement, their eagerness to benefit from the promised appreciation in real estate prices could even bid the present price of lots so high that price decreases rather than increases will occur subsequently. The key point is this: *The price of any marketable asset reflects the present value of generally expected future earnings.* No one can make a profit by putting money into an asset or an operation that is *generally expected* to return more than the going rate of interest. For that would be a "good deal." And the demand for a "good deal" bids up the cost of getting in on it until it's no longer a better deal than other assets or opportunities.

Every investor knows this. The time to buy Xerox or Polaroid was before the word got around. Those who bought stock in these companies after it became widely known that they were going to earn large net revenues from their new products received no profit. The best they could hope for was an interest return on their investment. The market price of Xerox and Polaroid stock was bid up by people eager to share in those companies' future earnings, until the earnings relative to what had to be paid to share in them were no more attractive than earnings generally available in the market.

How to Grow Rich

"The way to accumulate a fortune is to invest in profitable companies." This is a very misleading statement. General Motors is rightly regarded as a highly profitable corporation, because it has consistently earned large returns for many years on its original investment in plant, machinery, and other assets. But the market value of General Motors stock long ago increased to take full account of its expected high future earnings. Consequently General Motors stock is not necessarily a better buy than the stock of many companies with dismal earning records. In fact, it may have been a very poor buy in recent years as stockholders failed to anticipate the effect of higher gasoline prices on the earnings of automobile manufacturers.

The way to accumulate a fortune is to invest in companies that are going to make large earnings that no one else currently knows about. And there's the rub. You must know more than others, or be able to read the uncertain future more accurately, if you hope to make large profits. Or else you rely solely on luck. But you have an equal probability of being unlucky and sustaining a large loss. The significant thing about pure luck is that it's pure.

Let's take an altogether different kind of example to drive home the essential point: that one important source of wealth or income is the successful anticipation of events that are not generally expected. Giuseppe Vibrato attends a conservatory of music for three years, studying for a career in opera. At about the time of Vibrato's graduation, the public abandons all interest in opera. So Vibrato sustains a loss. We mustn't exaggerate the loss, for Vibrato may receive a generous return on his educational investment in the form of many years of listening to himself sing Verdi and Wagner. Education can prepare a person to enjoy life as well as provide him with a marketable skill. But to the extent that Vibrato paid tuition and sacrificed earnings for three years in order to earn an income in opera, the unexpected change in public tastes caused him to sustain a loss.

The very important point to be noted here is that profits and losses can and will appear almost anywhere, for anyone at all, and not just for those who invest in common stocks or real estate.

Aerospace engineers suffer losses when the federal government cuts back on the space program and cancels the SST (supersonic transport). College professors receive profits when the federal government decides to spend huge sums on higher education. Authors make a profit when they hit on a product that captivates the public. Highly trained astrologers took a loss when people abandoned the belief that the stars shape individual destiny—just as some of their intellectual descendants have recently made profits from an unexpected return to older persuasions.

What Function Does Profit Perform?

The core of the argument is that profit is something quite different functionally from other kinds of income. The payment that induces someone to supply labor services is a wage. The payment that induces someone to supply the services of his money, or better, the services of what this money can obtain, is interest. These are necessary payments, in a sense. A manufacturer cannot obtain the services of people or physical property unless he is able to bid them away from alternative employments by paying their opportunity cost. But there is a kind of income that seems *both unnecessary and inevitable:* the income that accrues to people because decisions are always made in the present but only justified in the future, and the future is uncertain. "Unnecessary and inevitable" is a strange combination. But think about it.

When businessmen and others talk about "the necessity for profits," as they often do, they are almost certainly not using the word *profit* in the way that we are now defining it. A business firm will not be able to operate unless it can obtain funds with which to hire services. It can obtain funds only by generating revenue from sales or by borrowing. It will be unable to borrow unless potential lenders believe that future sales will generate sufficient revenue to allow payment of interest on the loans. It will be easy for the firm to obtain funds if people are anticipating very large future net revenues from its operation, but difficult for it to do so if people generally are pessimistic about the firm's prospects. This is all that businessmen mean, or ought to mean, when they speak of the necessity for profits: the need for enough revenue and prospective revenue to enable the firm to pay the opportunity cost of the services required for continued operation. This much is "needed" in the sense that the business firm will not be able to operate indefinitely without it.

We must keep in mind at the same time that the *potential* of profit is an important stimulus to action. If profits could somehow always be confiscated, we would certainly observe less innovation in society and fewer resources devoted to exploration and experiment. But there is a very big difference between a *potential* profit and a profit in the pocket. The potential of a profit prompts people to search for more efficient ways of combining resources, new products for which there might be a social demand, and organizational innovations that promise to increase efficiency. If profit searchers succeed, they benefit society and receive a profit. But they may fail and sustain a loss.

So no business must make a profit. At the same time, profits and losses are inevitable. As long as there is uncertainty about the future, there will be divergencies between anticipated and actual outcomes. This is just as true of a socialist economy as of a capitalist one. Because the central planners in a socialist state are not omniscient, they will sometimes anticipate the future incorrectly. Their mistakes will create profits for some and losses for others. The citizens in a socialist state will also receive profits and incur losses as their actions lead to outcomes different from those that were generally anticipated. Think of the profits that accrued to those who consistently supported Stalin in the 1930s and the losses sustained by those who misread the future. What socialism *can* do is distribute the profits and losses differently from the way they would be distributed under capitalism.

An important task for the student of alternative economic systems is the assessment of the various consequences of different ways of distributing profits and losses. Profits and losses can be attached closely to the individuals who make decisions, or to specific other parties not involved in the decisions, or divided among many different people. Moreover, individuals can be allowed to buy and sell risk freely or they can be prevented from doing so. The efficiency of an economic system, the fairness of its operation, and the degree of freedom it allows the citizens will all be importantly affected by the way a society chooses to distribute profits and losses. But no social system can eliminate profits and losses until it learns how to eliminate uncertainty.

Combining the Two Definitions

We have now examined two different definitions of profit:

Definition 1   Total revenue minus total cost.
Definition 2   The difference between the outcome that was generally anticipated when a decision was made and the outcome that was actually realized.

And here is the question: Will a firm's total revenue ever exceed its total cost in a world with no uncertainty? In other words, can there be a difference between total revenue and total cost that is *not* due to the difference between generally anticipated and actual outcomes? If the answer is no, the definitions are synonymous; the second definition merely explains the source of the difference between total revenue and total cost. But is no a defensible answer?

It's more defensible than you might at first suppose. Total cost is opportunity cost, and so it includes not only a firm's payments to others for commodities and services used, but also the implicit value of any goods—labor, land, capital—that the firm owns. Interest payments are part of the firm's costs, including that portion of its dividends which is about equal to the interest return its shareholders could have received by loaning their money elsewhere. When we include all these opportunity costs in our calculation of total costs, there seems to be no reason why any firm would have to earn revenues in excess of costs. Firms could make zero profits and continue in business. They could even be considered successful firms and be able to borrow new funds for expansion—as long as their revenues were adequate to cover all their costs.

In fact, if there were some way for a firm to get into a line of business that guaranteed more in revenue than it entailed in cost, wouldn't so many people move into that line of business that competition would reduce the difference between revenue and cost to zero? Remember that cost means all costs, including an actual or implicit payment for getting the business organized and keeping it in operation. The certainty of a return greater than this would surely attract new business firms. Their entry would increase output, reduce the price of the product consistently with the law of demand, and thus reduce the gap between total revenue and total cost. The gap might simultaneously be reduced from the other direction as the new entrants increased the demand and raised the cost for the inputs used in turning out the product. Only when the gap between total revenue and total cost had disappeared, or when profits had been reduced to zero, would there no longer be any incentive for new firms to enter.

In the actual and uncertain world, of course, it doesn't work that way. People see profits being made in particular lines of business but they aren't sure how to go about cutting themselves in on the profits. In a world of scarce information, the existence of such profits might not even be widely known. And so profits do exist and continue to exist without being reduced to zero by competition. But this happens *because of uncertainty*, in the absence of which everything relevant to profit making would be generally known, all opportunities for profit making fully exploited, and profits everywhere consequently equal to zero.

Profit as the Consequence of Restricted Competition

But we have left out a very important possibility! What if some profit makers, even in a world without uncertainty, were able to prevent others from entering their line of business and competing away their profits? Then total revenue could exceed total cost and continue to exceed it indefinitely.

We must therefore add a second explanation or cause of profit, something in addition to uncertainty and quite separate from it: *Profit can also arise from restrictions on the ability to compete.*

Such restrictions arise primarily from two sources and can therefore usefully be divided into two kinds: (1) restrictions imposed by the natural scarcity of particular resources; and (2) restrictions imposed by social or political actions. We can see both kinds at work in the case of Mr. Artesian.

One Source of Artesian's Profits: Uncertainty

Recall that Artesian was earning about $1000 per year over and above his total costs when he first got his mineral-water spring into operation. This was clearly a profit by our general definition: total revenue minus total cost. But what was its cause or source?

In the first instance the source of Artesian's profit was uncertainty. If it had been generally known at the time Artesian purchased the property that there was a valuable mineral-water spring on the premises, a spring that could net its owner more than $1000 per year, then Artesian would have had to pay more than he actually did for the land. An asset that can be confidently expected to yield its owner $1000 per year has the same value as $20,000 in a savings account earning 5 percent interest. So if the property had a value, let us say, of $10,000 apart from the spring, its value might be as much as $30,000 with the spring taken into account. Artesian obtained the land for $10,000 rather than $30,000 only because no one knew about the existence of the spring. The difference between the outcome that was generally anticipated when Artesian bought the lot and the outcome actually realized, our first explanation of profit, was $1000 of extra income per year to the owner of the lot. If Artesian had incurred some costs in finding out about the spring, that would have to be subtracted from his profit.

Suppose Artesian decided to sell his land and move to Alaska. He would find people willing to bid the price up well above his own purchase price of $10,000 because they would want to obtain ownership of that $1000 per year stream of income. Of course, they aren't likely to bid the price as high as $30,000 because $1000 of net income from a mineral-water spring will be regarded as a less certain prospect than $1000 in bank interest on a $20,000 savings account. Only if that $1000 could be expected with the same certainty as the bank interest would the sale price approach $30,000. Suppose Artesian is able to sell his land for $22,500. If the spring then earns its new owner $1000 in every subsequent year, the new owner also makes a profit. But his profit is only $375. Do you see why?

We're assuming $10,000 of the purchase price to be the value of the land—for living on, raising radishes, or whatever. This was the value generally anticipated when Artesian made his purchase, and we're just assuming it remains unchanged. (It wouldn't have to. The value of the land for residential purposes could go down because the owner's privacy is destroyed by all the customers of the spring.) So we just ignore $10,000 of the purchase price and all the benefits of ownership not related to the mineral-water spring. We're left with $12,500 paid to obtain the income from the spring. But now $625 of that income has to be considered a cost of doing business ($625 is the annual interest on $12,500, the amount the new owner is giving up by putting his $12,500 into ownership of the land). So if the spring continues to yield him $1000 per year, his profit—total revenue minus total cost—is only $375. On the other hand, if competition appears, as it did in Chapter 11, so that his net revenue falls to $400, the new owner sustains annual losses. For $400 is only 3.2 percent of $12,500, and that's 1.8 percent less than the interest cost of owning the spring.

Another Source of Profits: Restrictions on the Ability of Others to Compete

But will competition necessarily appear? We can see both kinds of restriction at work in the mineral-water case. There may be in the area only one spring whose water has all the invigorating qualities so valued by Artesian's customers. Other sources may be so far away that the water can only be transported into Artesian's market area at a prohibitive cost. In such a situation Artesian could continue indefinitely to earn his $1048.30 annual profit, even though there is no longer any uncertainty about revenues and costs, because he is the owner of a naturally rare resource. Others would like to cut themselves in on Artesian's profit; but they cannot do so without access to mineral water and Artesian has control of the only available supply.

There are many types of unique productive resources. One important type that we might tend to overlook is human skills. Very often firms will continue to earn profits year after year, despite the best efforts of their competitors, because the firms are managed with exceptional skill. Other kinds of rare resources that may restrict the ability of others to diminish a firm's profits are location, reputation, and experience.

But the restrictions imposed on competition by the natural scarcity of resources are seldom enough to satisfy firms that find themselves making profits. For one thing, there are just too many alternative ways of doing things. Even if there is no other mineral water within an economical distance, competitors could sell tomato juice fortified with vitamins and minerals, and claim that it's more healthful and better tasting than Artesian's water. Moreover, unless the profit-earning firm owns the scarce resources that give it a permanent advantage, potential competitors can try to hire those resources away. They can bid for the choice location when the current tenant's lease expires; and even if they don't manage to bid it away, they may force the firm to pay a higher rent to maintain control of the advantageous location. That would erode the firm's profits by raising its costs. If the natural scarcity that is responsible for persistent profits happens to be managerial skills, potential competitors can try to hire away those managers. Again, even if they don't succeed, they may raise the firm's costs by forcing it to pay higher salaries to key employees. So it isn't hard to understand why profit-making firms turn regularly to the government for help in imposing restrictions on competition.

Patents granted to inventors are one important type of political restriction. The purpose of a patent is precisely this: to help the patent owner earn profits over an extended period of time by prohibiting others from making use of the process that is the source of those profits. This can be justified on the grounds that new and more efficient processes would not be developed as often if the developers could not count on earning profits from their innovative efforts. The patent privilege is thus a temporary grant of privilege from the government designed to raise the wealth of successful innovators with the long run aim of raising the wealth of society.

Other forms of government restrictions on competition are usually harder to defend. We discussed this question in Chapter 11 and won't repeat what we said there. All that we're looking for in this chapter is an understanding of the sources and functions of profit. And we're ready now to put it all together.

The Big Picture View

Profit is total revenue minus total cost. That's an acceptable definition from the economist's point of view if cost is calculated as opportunity cost. Some of what is commonly called "business profits" ought to be regarded, from a functional point of view, as implicit payments to factors of production. A substantial portion of corporate profits as well as the net income of unincorporated enterprises, including professional income, is actually a payment for the use of capital and ought therefore to be designated as interest.

What, then, is the source of pure profits? There are two sources, we have argued. One is uncertainty. Because the future cannot be accurately predicted, actual outcomes will often differ from what is generally anticipated at the time decisions are made and hostages are given to fortune. But uncertainty creates losses as well as profits, a very important point to remember in assessing the size and social importance of profits.

The other source of profits is restrictions on competition. These may be due to scarcities maintained by nature or to social and political restrictions of many kinds.

That's the big picture view. If the road toward it was unusually long and tortuous, it's largely because the concept of profit is used in so many different ways and often without much thought. But the perspective one acquires by thinking carefully about the functions of profit makes the trip worth the effort. At least we hope it does.

Once Over Lightly

Profit is a term with many meanings. The meanings must be sorted out if we want to understand the way in which economic systems function.

Profit can be usefully defined as total revenue minus total cost if we include all opportunity costs in our calculation of total cost.

Insofar as interest represents an opportunity cost, it must be distinguished from profit.

Interest is the difference in value between present and future goods. It is usually attached to money simply because money represents general command over present or future goods.

The rate of interest in a society is typically positive because present goods are more valuable than future goods. This reflects positive rates of time preference and the fact that capital is productive (in other words, goods now can often be employed to create more goods later).

Because economic decisions are always made *in anticipation of future costs and benefits*, they are often mistaken. The difference between generally expected and actual outcomes, due to uncertainty, is one source of profit (and loss).

The potentiality of a profit encourages risk taking and innovation on the part of those who hope to appropriate the difference between generally anticipated and actual outcomes. The way in which a society assigns profits and losses will affect people's behavior.

In the absence of uncertainty, any differences between total revenue and total (opportunity) cost would be competed away and profits would become zero—except insofar as restrictions exist on the ability to compete successfully.

Opportunities to compete are restricted by the limited availability of particular resources, which may in turn be due to nature or to social and political contrivance. Such competition-restricting scarcities are an additional source or cause of profit.

Before we decide that any particular profits are excessive or inadequate, it is important that we know what we mean by profit, how it arose, what function it performed, and the consequences of adding to or subtracting from it.

QUESTIONS FOR DISCUSSION

1. You ask your college for permission to set up a lemonade stand at the annual spring commencement, and the college grants permission. After paying your bills for materials (lemons, sugar, cups, and so forth), you clear $250 for an afternoon's work.

    a. Did you make a $250 profit?
    b. Are you likely to be given the lemonade concession again next year? What difference does it make whether or not word gets around about how much you cleared?

c. If the college next year auctions off the franchise, how much would you be willing to bid? Who will then get the profit from the lemonade stand?

2. If a district-court judge enters a $300-million judgment against a corporation for violation of antitrust statutes, do the owners of that corporation sustain a loss? What form will it take? If you believe that the judge was in error and that his decision will eventually be reversed on appeal, how could you profit from your knowledge?

3. You buy shares of common stock in two corporations. Over the next six months, the price of one falls and the price of the other rises. Which was a better buy? Which would be the better one to sell if you want cash?

4. Evaluate the following argument: "General Motors has taken advantage of its dominant position in the automobile industry and made huge profits year after year. It would be perfectly just, therefore, to impose a special tax on General Motors as a way of recovering for society some of the exorbitant profits earned in the past." Who would pay that tax?

5. In July 1971 President Allende of Chile signed a bill authorizing nationalization of the American-owned copper mines in his country. The law called for compensation to be paid to the Anaconda, Kennecott, and Cerro Companies.
   a. Imagine that you are the representative of one of these companies charged with responsibility for negotiating the amount of compensation to be paid. What data and arguments would you use?
   b. What data and arguments would you use if you were the Chilean representative in the negotiations?
   c. Suppose that the nationalization law is repealed, and competitive bidding for the mines is allowed to occur. How will the price of the mines be determined? What difference will it make in the price if prospective owners fear another nationalization law in the future?
   d. Could the owners of such property benefit from nationalization if the compensation they received was *less* than the sum of what they originally paid for the property plus the cost of subsequent improvements? Explain.
   e. "Nationalization of foreign-owned industry cannot benefit a country unless that country pays a confiscatory price." Evaluate.

6. You purchase for $950 a $1000 government bond maturing one year from the date of purchase. Will you make a profit if you hold the bond to maturity? Will you make a profit if there is a sharp, general increase in prevailing interest rates a week after your purchase? What effect will this have on the price you can obtain from selling your bond in the market?

7. Humbert and Ambler are very different personalities. Humbert likes to eat, drink, be merry, and let the future care for itself. He suspects that the world is going to disintegrate in a few years anyway. Ambler is only twenty-one but is already planning conscientiously for his retirement years. What would you predict about their respective rates of time preference? How do people of Humbert's type benefit from the existence of people like Ambler, and vice versa?

8. What effect would you expect the rate of technological innovation in a society to have on the level of interest rates? Why?

9. The Corps of Engineers estimates that a canal between Tussle and Big Stone would save shippers $500,000 per year. The canal would cost $20 million to construct and $200,000 per year to maintain.
   a. Is it correct to say that the canal is a good investment in the long run because it will save society a net $300,000 per year and eventually that will come

to more than the $20 million construction cost?

b. About how low would the interest rate have to be to make the canal a profitable investment. (The canal would not be profitable if the interest payments ate up the saving to shippers minus maintenance costs.)

c. "The advantage of having the government build the canal is that government can do things that are in the public interest while private enterprise is constrained by narrow considerations of profitability." Evaluate that argument.

10. "A wealthy society has little difficulty paying interest. But in a poor country with almost no capital, economic planners cannot afford to take interest charges into account in their calculations." What's wrong with that argument?

11. "When lenders extend credit to high-risk borrowers, they must raise the interest rates they charge low-risk borrowers in order to cover their losses from defaults." Do you agree?

12. What arguments can you offer to support the establishment of legal ceilings on interest rates?

13. Suppose that Congress imposes a 6 percent ceiling on the interest rate that may be charged for federally guaranteed mortgages. Lending institutions, meanwhile, find themselves able to obtain all the mortgage business they want at 8 percent interest. Will they lend at 6 percent? How might the interest ceiling be circumvented? If you wanted to purchase a house and were eligible for a federally guaranteed mortgage, would you want Congress to set an interest-rate ceiling on such loans?

14. Why would an agricultural economist conclude that the benefits of a government price-subsidy plus acreage-restriction program accrue largely to the owners of the land *at the time the program was started?*

15. In the spring of 1963 Fidel Castro announced a sugar-production goal for 1970 of 10 million tons. As the target date approached, and it began to appear that this much publicized target might not be attained, the Cuban government transferred labor and other resources in large amounts from the production of alternative goods into the production of sugar. The goal was still missed by a large margin. How do you suppose the consequent loss was distributed? How would the profit have been distributed had this decision turned out better than anticipated?

16. Why do corporate officers sometimes make illegal election contributions? Does this question have any connection with the topic of the chapter? Are those contributions "investments" subject to profit or loss?

17. When the government takes over privately owned land for a highway and pays compensation to the owners, should that compensation be based on its value in its present use, in the use to which the government will put it, or on the value of adjoining land that will increase (or decrease) in value because of the highway? What is unfair about each option?

18. Does ownership of gold or silver enable a person to protect himself against the hazards of uncertainty?

19. It has been proposed that state and local governments abolish property taxes for homeowners and turn to sales or income taxes for revenue. What effects on home prices would you predict from such a step? Who would be most likely to benefit?

20. In June 1972 the National Coalition for Land Reform asked the Secretary of the Interior to reclaim land given to the Southern Pacific Railroad in the nineteenth century. The Coalition claims the railroad was supposed to sell this land for family-sized plots at $2.50 an acre or less, or forfeit the land. What do you think would

happen if the federal government now required that all such land be sold within the next year in family-sized plots and at prices not to exceed $2.50 an acre? Who would lose and who would gain?

21. A phrase often used in economic discussions is "windfall profits."
    a. What is the difference, if any, between windfall profits and profits that appeared because someone read the future more successfully than others?
    b. Are windfall profits earned income? Are they *deserved* income?
    c. Would you favor a special tax on windfall profits? Would you favor a social subsidy to cover "windfall losses"? How do you think either proposal would work out in practice?

22. The profits of the major oil companies in the United States were a cause of much concern in 1974. Discuss the profits of the oil companies on the basis of the analysis in this chapter.

23. Are the profits of U.S. corporations currently earned more through coercion or through persuasion? (Definitions of terms: *Coercion:* inducing people to cooperate by reducing their options. *Persuasion:* inducing people to cooperate by expanding their options.) If you don't know how to answer the question, try thinking about the adequacy in this context of the proposed definitions for coercion and persuasion.

Productive Resources
and the Distribution of Income

When incomes are rising, that's good; we're getting wealthier. When prices are rising, that's bad; the purchasing power of our income is falling and we're getting poorer. It seems as if we should all cheer for higher incomes and lower prices.

Derived Demand

The catch is that incomes and prices are opposite sides of the same coin. The incomes of physicians are obviously a function of the prices people pay for medical care; the incomes of barbers depend on the price of haircuts. In these cases the connection is obvious because it is relatively direct. But where the connection is less obvious and direct, it is still important. The incomes of construction workers come from the prices people pay for new homes, offices, and factories, as do the incomes of construction contractors and those who supply materials to the building trades. The prices people pay for new automobiles become income for General Motors' assembly-line employees, shareholders, and managers, plus all the employees and shareholders of General Motors' many suppliers.

But don't jump to the conclusion that higher prices for a good necessarily mean larger incomes for its producers. The law of demand asserts that less will be purchased at higher prices. Higher haircut prices, to take the simplest example, might mean less rather than more income for barbers, depending on the elasticity of demand for professional haircuts. That elasticity will in turn depend on how many substitutes there are for barber shops (home clippers, longer hair, a seedy look, and so on).

The concept around which this chapter moves is *derived demand*. The central idea is that people obtain income by selling the services of the productive resources they own. The demand for productive resources is derived, of course, from the demand for the goods these resources are capable of producing. It's quite simple and fairly obvious. But it's also, to judge from the kinds of public policy recommendations one reads and hears, not very widely understood.

How would you evaluate each of the following arguments?

1. "A sizable increase in the legal minimum wage would go a long way toward reducing poverty."

2. "The ominous threat of automation is hanging over our society. We are not far from the time when a majority of the

labor force will be unable to find any work at all, because machines are so much more productive than people."

3. "Without unions to help him compete against large and powerful corporations, the American working man would never have been able to achieve his present economic status."

Minimum Wage Legislation and Marginal Productivity

Let's look at each argument in turn. We are often told that opposition to legal minimum wages is evidence of insensitivity toward poverty. But it's not that simple. A wage is a price, the price of a productive resource. It's also the basis of a human being's income, of course; we're not denying that at all. But from the standpoint of those who hire workers and pay their wages, the wage is a price or cost. The law of demand reminds us that price and quantity purchased tend to move in opposite directions. Won't they do so also in the case of a legally imposed wage increase?

Here is the widely unrecognized consequence of raising wages by law. If the legal minimum is no higher than what employers are already paying, it has no effect. It will have an impact only if some covered employers are paying less than the legal minimum. But when these employers must raise the wage they pay, will they continue to hire as many employees?

Employers hire resources on the basis of some estimate of the probable contribution that resource will make. What will the employment of this resource add to the value of the firm's operation? The phrase economists use is *marginal productivity*, which means the additional value created by a decision to hire the productive resource in question. If the employer wants to increase his wealth, he will only hire resources whose value to his operation is expected to exceed the additional cost he will incur by hiring that resource. It's the simple rule of Chapter 10 once again: Take those actions and only those actions whose expected marginal revenue is greater than their expected marginal cost.

A simple numerical example may help you visualize the relationship between the marginal productivity of a resource and the derived demand for it. A farmer obtains the following yields of corn from the application of fertilizer.

Units of Fertilizer	Bushels of Corn	Marginal Corn Product	Marginal Dollar Product
0	1000		
1	1160	160	$480
2	1240	80	240
3	1280	40	120
4	1300	20	60

Assume that all other inputs and costs remain the same when he

changes the amount of fertilizer used. Note that the marginal
values are *in between* the totals to indicate that they are the effect
of changing from one level of fertilizer use to another. To calculate
the final column we have assumed a price of $3.00 per bushel for
corn.

The marginal revenue to this farmer is $480 from applying one
unit of fertilizer, $240 when he applies a second unit, and so on. The
marginal-revenue product states the value to the farmer of using
various quantities of fertilizer. It is therefore his derived demand
for fertilizer: derived both from the physical productivity of fertilizer and the demand for his corn (a perfectly elastic demand at
$3.00 per bushel).

If we assume that he can use fractional inputs, the curve below
expresses his demand for fertilizer. You can read off the quantities
he would demand at any price (marginal cost) for fertilizer.

Returning now to the original question: An increase in the legal
minimum wage raises the marginal cost of some employees to some
employers. We can predict that some employers will consequently
choose to hire fewer workers. They will lay off or not replace
workers whose estimated marginal productivity is below their now
higher employment cost.

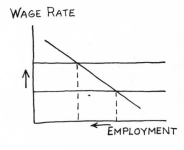

Unskilled workers can consequently be hurt by a high legal
minimum wage. Teen-agers are also hurt by such laws, because
employers often place a low estimate on the value of their contribution. Some workers will be paid the higher wage and retained;
they're better off. But those who are deprived of work opportunities by the legal minimum are clearly worse off. So it is not at all
obvious that increasing the legal minimum wage reduces poverty.

The Fear of Automation

What are we to make of the second argument: that machines are
destroying jobs? The first question to ask is, What does it mean to
say that "machines are more productive than people"? Employers

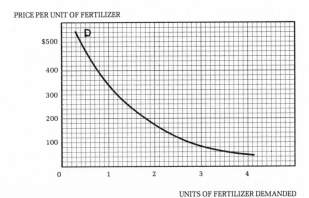

Figure 13A   Demand curve for fertilizer and marginal productivity

aren't interested in mere physical or technical capabilities; they're interested in the relation between marginal revenues and marginal costs. A machine is more efficient than a person, and hence will be substituted for a person only if the *value of the machine's marginal product relative to its marginal cost* is greater than the same ratio for a person. That implies, among other things, that wage rates play an important part in shaping the speed and direction of technological change in the economy.

It would be a serious mistake to suppose, for example, that automatic elevators largely replaced elevator operators in the United States over the last two decades merely because of improvements in technology. Time, money, and energy were spent to develop automatic elevators, and building owners subsequently installed them because of benefit-cost estimates they made, not because automatic elevators were new and shiny. In some other society where the wage rates (opportunity costs) of elevator operators are quite low, elevators run by trained operators may still be more efficient than automatic elevators.

The fear that our society or any society may run out of jobs is an odd kind of fear. A job, after all, represents an obstacle to be overcome. A society that has run out of jobs for people to do has come very close to overcoming scarcity; and that would be something to cheer, not fear. We are not in any such fortunate situation. As technological innovations increase the productive potential of our economy, labor resources are released from some employments and made available for others. The automatic or self-service elevator made it possible for people who were formerly employed in transporting passengers up and down to do something else, to make some other and additional contribution to our total output of commodities and services.

The reallocation of labor in response to changed circumstances, even though it increases the total value of society's output, does lead to a loss of wealth for people. A rising demand for labor attracted some elevator operators into more remunerative employments and pulled up the wages of the rest. Automatic elevators were in part a response to this situation. But as they were introduced, some elevator operators found themselves pushed rather than pulled: deprived of their present jobs and compelled to accept less desirable alternatives, rather than attracted away from their present positions by better opportunities. Such people suffered, at least temporarily, a loss in wealth. They were forced to incur the cost of searching for new employment, and they were not guaranteed that the new job would be better than the old. Resistance to technological change and the fear of automation or cybernation is therefore quite understandable. Even college professors have been known to speak harshly about the introduction of such technological innovations as videotaped lectures and teaching machines.

Keep in mind, however, that prices and wages are important

variables in such processes of adjustment and reallocation. If prices and wages are inflexible or change only very slowly, a larger part of the adjustment burden will be shifted onto something else.

To illustrate: Suppose that a technological breakthrough occurs in automobile production. A manufacturer named Henry Ford finds that he can produce as many automobiles as before, using half as many workers, by employing a moving assembly line. Suppose further that, at existing resource prices, the assembly-line technique cuts the cost of producing these automobiles by 25 percent. There will be fewer employment opportunities in automobile assembly as a result—at least at first. But if the price of the final product is reduced as a consequence of the reduction in cost, and if the demand for automobiles proves sufficiently elastic, there may eventually be more rather than fewer jobs available for automobile-assembly workers. That is exactly what did happen. In addition, a reduction in the wages that must be paid to such workers would diminish the manufacturer's incentive to substitute machinery for direct labor; this, too, could alleviate the disemployment effect of the new technology. That has happened much more rarely.

A decline in the demand for anything results in a lesser decline in the quantity demanded if its price falls. This should be kept in mind whenever you are trying to assess the consequences of any change in technology, organization, or the composition of demand. As a matter of demonstrable fact, many prices and especially wages are "sticky," most notoriously when they are subjected to downward pressure. Such stickiness or inflexibility may have advantages, but it also has obvious disadvantages. In the early 1970s, the demand for many kinds of engineering skills fell to unexpectedly low levels. The more that the wages of engineers decline in response to such a change, the larger will be the number of job opportunities still available for engineers. Wage structures that are relatively rigid in a downward direction will leave employed engineers largely unaffected by the changed circumstances; but more engineers than otherwise will be unemployed.

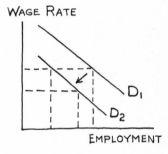

Unions and Wage Rates

What has been the impact of unions on the income of the American worker? The third of the arguments given above asserts that unions help workers to compete more effectively against large corporations, and that they have thereby improved the worker's economic position. A comprehensive evaluation of unions and their impact is beyond the scope of this book. But it is hard to see what insight into their effects can be acquired by someone who starts off with the assumption that workers compete against employers. Workers compete against workers, employers against employers. This is the competition that affects wage rates.

An employer cannot simply pay his workers the lowest wage rate his callous heart suggests because the workers have alternative opportunities, opportunities largely created by the competing offers of other employers. Similarly, no worker can successfully insist on the wage he thinks he deserves if other workers are willing to supply very similar services at lower wage rates. Workers compete against other workers, and unions are in part attempts to control *this* competition.

The implication of this is that unions improve the position of the members they represent by finding ways to restrict competition from those who are not members of the union. They may do this directly, for example, by securing contracts with employers that make union membership a prior condition of employment and then limiting membership. Or they may do it indirectly. Just as a legal minimum wage excludes some people from employment opportunities, so a high wage secured by union contract (perhaps under the threat of a strike, or total withdrawal of labor services) excludes those who would be willing to work for less.

The belief that unions arose in the United States to counter the power of large corporations is unsupported by history. Unions first became powerful in this country in industries characterized by small-scale firms: construction, printing, textiles, mining. The railroads are an exception that supports the rule: it was special legislation that enabled unions to become powerful in the railroad industry. The unions that today bargain with the large corporations in steel, automobiles, and electrical machinery were originally missionary projects of the unions that bargained mostly with small employers.

A good way to guarantee confusion in thinking about all this is to begin with the assertion that labor is not a commodity. A commodity is something bought and sold, of course, and people have supposedly not been bought and sold in this country since the abolition of slavery. If any doubt remained about the status of labor, Congress allegedly cleared it away in 1914 with the ringing declaration of the Clayton Act: "The labor of a human being is not a commodity or article of commerce."

The best that can be said about such declarations is that they have no discernible relevance to any important social question. Labor services *are* offered for sale, and they *are* demanded. There are prices for labor services, and these prices affect the allocation of labor and other resources. The principles that we employed earlier in talking about the pricing and purchase of consumer goods apply also to the pricing and purchase of productive resources. We saw in Chapter 4 how changing prices worked to eliminate shortages and surpluses. Prices play the same kind of role in determining whether there will be shortages or surpluses of productive resources.

Marginal Productivity as a <u>Social</u> Fact

There is nothing in the principles of supply and demand, however, to guarantee that income will be justly distributed. Competition among suppliers and demanders will tend to establish prices for productive resources without regard to the health, family responsibilities, or other personal characteristics of the people who own those resources and derive income from their sale. Moreover, the prices established by supply and demand are only partly responsible for the distribution of income. A more important determinant of income distribution is the initial distribution of wealth. The marginal-productivity theory asserts that the demand for a productive resource depends upon the marginal contribution that resource is thought capable of making to the production of wealth, and that this demand sets a limit to the price the resource can command. It does not explain why resources have their expected marginal productivities or why some people own large amounts of physical and human resources and others own so little.

To some extent people choose whether or not they will own income-producing resources and how much of each kind to acquire. This is done, for example, when people save and invest a portion of their income rather than consume it all; acquiring education or training is one very important form such investment takes. But choices of this sort are never made in lonely isolation by rugged individualists who thereby acquire an unassailable moral right to their subsequent income. Opportunities to invest effectively in human skills or physical capital have been much more readily available to those who were shrewd enough to be born the right color, sex, and nationality, and who carefully selected parents from whom they could inherit an advantageous starting position.

Moreover, productivity itself is a social fact. None of us would be as potentially productive as we are if we had not collectively inherited an enormous stock of scientific and technical knowledge. We all benefit from the complementary resources that others own. And the entire economic system, because it creates opportunities for extensive specialization and trade, increases our wealth by enabling us to concentrate on productive activities in which we may have a considerable comparative advantage. The last two points are especially worth stressing.

Giuseppe Vibrato enjoys a fine income as an opera star because he can use the comparative advantage his voice provides and count on others to grow his food, sew his tuxedos, and build his automobiles. He could not do that, and his income would consequently be much lower, if he lived in a society so small that specialization could not be carried very far.

Giuseppe also benefits from the existence of other specialists in his society: for example, composers, pianists, and sopranos who can play Susanna to his Figaro. How many people would pay, after all, to hear Giuseppe sing, unaccompanied, his own music? It would be absurd for Giuseppe to claim that his income is solely dependent on his voice. Marginal productivity is a *social* product, dependent on the complementary contributions of others.

Economic Rent

We have said that income derives from the ownership of productive resources, and that the value of the resources anyone owns will depend upon such factors as inheritance, luck, natural abilities, earlier choices between present consumption and investment, plus the whole social and technological setting in which that person lives. The price of these resources will be set by the competing offers and bids of all those who own resources and all those who want the goods the resources can produce. Between offers and bids, however, a gulf can appear, a gulf that economists refer to as *economic rent*. Most people use the word *rent* to mean the payment to a landlord for the use of his property. Economists use the word in a broader sense to mean *any return to the owner of a productive resource which is in excess of its opportunity cost*. The concept has enough important and interesting uses to justify the little time that must be spent in mastering it.

Suppose that you want to hire four neighborhood children for eight hours to help you clean your garage on Saturday. (Never mind the implication that you have an unusually large and dirty garage.) It's quite conceivable that each would be willing to work for a different hourly wage. Alice would watch cartoons all day if she weren't working, and since she's getting a little bored with the reruns anyway, she's willing to work for 50 cents an hour. Billy planned to go fishing all day, and he can't be bid away from the lake for less than 75 cents an hour. Chuck has a chance to mow lawns for $1 an hour and won't work for you for any less. Delores just wants to sleep all day; but she is deeply attached to the sack and requires $1.25 an hour to give it up. You will be able to hire all four only if you offer $1.25 an hour, and if you don't discriminate, that means $1.25 an hour for each. Alice, Billy, and Chuck will consequently receive economic rent: 75 cents an hour for Alice, 50 cents for Billy, and 25 cents for Chuck, the amount by which the payment for their services exceeds the opportunity cost.

At the end of the day you will pay $40 in wages. But $12 of this does not represent a real cost from a social point of view. It is actually a mere transfer of wealth from you to Alice, Billy, and Chuck. The payment was necessary to secure the services of all four children; and you must have valued their joint services at $40 or more, since you were willing to pay that amount. But the value of the opportunities forgone as a consequence of your garage-cleaning expedition was only $28.

If you'll check back to Chapter 5 and its examination of the cost of a volunteer army, you'll see the same phenomenon illustrated. The example described in Figure 5A and the accompanying discussion shows an annual budget outlay of $24 billion but a true social cost or opportunity cost of only $15 billion. Put your finger in at page 53 and check: The budget outlay is the rectangular area marked off by 8 thousand dollars times 3 million volunteers. The genuine social cost is the smaller area under the supply curve which represents opportunity costs. The area above the supply curve and within the budget-outlay rectangle, $9 billion, is economic rent.

How Profits Become Rents

Economic rent also appeared in Chapter 12. We asked whether it would be possible for a firm to continue earning revenues in excess of total costs even after every potential competitor had learned how the firm was doing it, or in other words, whether profits could persist in the absence of uncertainty. And our answer was yes, if there were restrictions on the ability of others to compete. An advantageous location or a uniquely talented management team might prevent other firms from competing successfully for a share of the profits, thereby eliminating the revenue-cost gap. But a firm's control of particularly productive resources would not by itself protect the firm's profits against erosion if other firms could bid for control of those resources. Suppose it becomes common knowledge in the industry that the Cagey Crockery Company is earning half a million in profits each year because its two top managers know more about crockery than Woody Hayes and Bear Bryant know about football. Cagey will then have to start raising their salaries to keep them from accepting offers from other crockery makers. Before the word gets around, they will have to be paid only the value of their managerial talents in other industries. But once the word spreads, they can command an economic rent in the crockery industry: up to half a million dollars more than they could earn in any other line of business. To hang on to its profits Cagey might have to pay its superior management team almost the full amount of those profits, since by assumption the profits would disappear if our skillful duo departed. This little tale illustrates the way in which short-term profits for firms can be transformed over time into economic rents for the owners of especially productive resources.

Did we mention Woody Hayes and Bear Bryant, those incredibly successful builders of college football teams that for so many years have packed in the fans and picked off the bowl bids, swelling the revenues of their colleges? Woody and Bear's salaries plus perquisites have no doubt caused many a professor to conclude that the relative salaries of a coach and a professor must reflect the relative value assigned by the university to football versus literature. By no means. They only reflect the relative demands of football fans and literature fans. Any English professor who can find a way for the college to sell 50 thousand tickets at $8 a head to college-sponsored poetry readings will soon discover that universities want him. They will bid energetically for his services, the way they now bid for successful coaches. And he will be able to do what

Woody and the Bear have done: capture as economic rent a portion of the profits created for his employer by his unique abilities.

Rock and Rent

Let's look at another example of economic rent. The Salt Sellers are a popular rock group whose members love to make music together. They give 200 concerts a year, something they would be willing to do for as little as $10,000. At any lower annual wage they would choose to give up the concert tour and find some other kind of work. Thus the opportunity cost of having the Salt Sellers sing is $10,000, or about $50 a concert.

The group may nonetheless receive $5000 for every performance. Each promoter must pay this amount, not to induce the Salt Sellers to sing, but to bid them away from singing for other promoters. The popular demand for tickets to their concerts gives rise to a demand for their services from promoters which in turn creates an economic rent of $4950 for the Salt Sellers.

Do not draw the conclusion that economic rent is an unnecessary payment. In one sense it is; in another sense it is not. The $4950 is unnecessary to induce the Salt Sellers to sing. But it is necessary to induce them to sing *here* rather than *there*. Of course, the promoters might all get together and agree that it's ridiculous to pay the Salt Sellers $5000 when they would willingly work for $50. They might further agree to offer no more than $75 a night for their services. But in the absence of competitive bidding, which is eliminated by the promoter's agreement, how would it be decided where the group is to sing its annual 200 concerts? The quantity of service demanded from the Salt Sellers would far exceed the quantity supplied. If the promoters solved this problem by a lottery, they would appropriate the economic rent for themselves—or for the lucky promoters who won the lottery. Chances are excellent, however, that the unlucky promoters would find ways to violate the agreement; and if they did not, new promoters would probably appear to begin bidding for the now extremely profitable services of the Salt Sellers. And that's why such agreements are notoriously unstable unless the government lends a hand in restricting competition.

Protecting Economic Rents

Let's return for another look at the case of Artesian. When he earned $1048.30 in the first year after discovery of the mineral-water spring, he made a profit: an increase in Artesian's income that arose because the existence of the lucrative mineral-water spring had not been anticipated by others. But after Artesian got his business running successfully, the $1048.30, though still a profit, could also be regarded as economic rent. It was a payment for the use of the resource in excess of its opportunity cost of zero.

Competition, however, began whittling away at Artesian's rent. When he secured legal restrictions on access to the mineral-water market, Artesian was trying to keep competition from reducing or eliminating his economic rent. We very commonly observe economic rents that have been secured by means of legal restrictions on competition. This leads to both a redistribution of wealth and an inefficient allocation of resources.

The restrictions prevent resource owners from transferring their resources out of less highly valued into more highly valued employments. Suppose, for example, that no one is allowed to diagnose and treat illnesses for pay unless he has gone through four years of medical school plus two years of in-service training. This practice increases the wealth of licensed physicians. But it also results in less medical care than would otherwise be provided. Many ailments could be well taken care of by people who have far less training than licensed physicians. These people are denied an opportunity to pursue their comparative advantage, and society in the process is denied the benefits of increased medical care. Most physicians don't see it this way at all. They maintain that licensing is necessary to protect the public against quacks. It is probably true that legal restrictions on the practice of medicine increase the average quality of medical care *sold by physicians.* But it is quite unlikely that they increase the average quality of medical care *received by people who are ill.* That's a very important distinction.

Do you recall from Chapter 11 the owner of the television sales and service center? He wanted to raise the average quality of television repair services by preventing "janitors, firemen, milkmen, and similar amateurs" from competing to provide these services. If he had been successful in securing the state regulation and licensing he wanted, it might have turned out that the average television repair job performed for a fee would have been of higher quality. But he was ignoring the *additional* services that can be provided by "amateurs" who would be prevented by law from employing the skills they possess.

Or look again at the complaint of the nursing-home operator in Chapter 11. He does not tell us, of course, about the protected rent that he obtains from the state system of licensing nursing homes. He directs our attention rather to the "lower standards" that would result from any relaxation of the licensing restrictions. And he is probably correct. Standards of nursing-home care probably would be lower *on average.* But a moment's thought should make it clear that higher average standards are being obtained at the cost of *less overall* nursing-home care. The patient who is effectively denied admission to *any* nursing home by the restrictive practices receives a lower, not a higher, level of care. Presumably, licensing also implies certification of minimum standards, and this can be a way to provide, at low cost, information of value to purchasers. However, certification of quality levels (for example, prime, choice, good, and so on, for beef) does not require a licensing system that restricts the quantity offered. And it does not compel those who prefer less quality (at a lower price) to pay for more quality than they want.

If a union is able to enforce a high wage against an employer, it can thereby prevent him from hiring workers whose marginal productivity in his employment is greater than their opportunity cost. These workers do not "lose their jobs," since they never had the jobs in the first place. This effectively disguises an important consequence of the union's wage-setting practices. But the economic rent of the employed union members is nonetheless being obtained partially at the expense of other workers who are compelled to accept less remunerative employment.

Economic analysis of the pricing of productive resources seems to generate more heat per paragraph than almost any other portion of economic theory. The explanation is not hard to find. People obtain income largely from selling the services of the productive resources they own. Competition has a tendency to push the prices of these resources toward their opportunity cost. Resource owners, however, are eager to secure rents for the resources they own, and they are often quite ingenious at enlisting the aid of the state to restrict competition and thereby protect their economic rents. It is always dressed up, of course, as protection of the public interest. Economic analysis points out the consequences of such efforts, and thereby incurs the ire of those who would prefer not to hear about these consequences. Or is it rather that they don't want others to hear?

WAGE RATE

Employment opportunities are eliminated by enforcement of high wage.

Once Over Lightly

Income is ordinarily obtained by selling the services of productive resources. The price any resource can command will be determined by the demand for the goods it produces and the marginal productivity of the resource. The marginal productivity of a resource is the additional contribution it makes to the production of wealth.

The law of demand applies to productive resources as well as to other goods. The higher the price of a particular resource, the more actively will people look for substitutes.

The common notion that the owners of productive resources compete against the purchasers of these resources is seriously misleading. Employees, for example, do not compete against employers but against other employees and potential employers. Unionization, while it may have other goals as well, is an attempt to restrain competition among workers.

The marginal-productivity theory of the demand for productive resources is not a complete theory of income distribution, much less a theoretical justification for any particular pattern of interpersonal distribution. Its explanation of resource pricing and use must be supplemented with an explanation of why resources are distributed as they are and how the larger social-economic system

contributes to the establishment of particular resource potentialities.

Resources often command prices in excess of their opportunity
cost. That portion of the payment to a resource which exceeds the
amount that would be required to keep the resource from migrat-
ing to its next most valuable opportunity is called *economic rent.*

Economic rent, from the overall social point of view, is a transfer
of wealth rather than a genuine cost. At the same time, it is a
genuine cost to the individual purchaser who must pay the opportunity cost of the next most enthusiastic bidder. In other words,
society did not give up $3 million worth of other goods when
Catfish Hunter decided in 1974 to pitch baseballs for that wage.
But the team that was finally beaten out by the New York Yankee
bid did lose a chance to receive that (expected) value in pitching
services.

The desire to protect economic rents lies behind many successful attempts on the part of resource owners to secure government
assistance in restricting competition.

QUESTIONS FOR DISCUSSION

1. For many years federal minimum-wage
legislation completely excluded workers
in agriculture or domestic service. Yet the
average wages paid to these workers ranked
at the very bottom of the wages paid in the
American economy. How do you explain
the seeming inconsistency in this exclu-
sion?

2. Teachers began encountering serious job
shortages in the early 1970s after many
years of rising demand for their services. An
intensified interest in unionization has
been observed. What can unionization accomplish for teachers in a highly unfavorable job market? Who is it likely to benefit? Who will it harm?

3. "Farmers complaining that they can't get
field hands now that the bracero program
has been curtailed aren't sincere," said an
official of the United Packinghouse
Workers Union. "About one-third of the
unemployed in Los Angeles are former
farm workers, and the farmers could get
them back if they'd make wages and working conditions attractive enough." Do you
think the farmers are insincere? Could they

get enough workers if they tried harder?
Explain.

4. In 1940, according to the Bureau of Labor
Statistics, there were 9,540,000 persons
employed in agriculture. The population
of the United States in 1940 was
132,122,000. In 1970 the corresponding
figures were 3,462,000 farmers in a population of 205,395,000. Thus in 1940 it took
one farmer to provide agricultural produce
for every 14 Americans. Thirty years later
one farmer could take care of almost 60
people.
   a. What made this dramatic change possible?
   b. What happened to the "excess" farmers? Where did they go?
   c. What factors induced people to move
out of agricultural employment?

5. Under a closed-shop arrangement, employers may hire only workers who are already union members. Under a union-shop
arrangement, employers may hire
whomever they please but the employees
must then join the union. What different
effects would you expect these alternative
arrangements to have on wages? On em-

ployment? On discrimination by the union against members of minority races? Why?

6. College professors in the United States have never had an effective union. Then why did their average wage rise spectacularly in the 1960s? How might college professors have used unionization to obtain even larger salary increases over this period? Why might some professors be interested in a law that prohibited anyone without an earned doctorate from teaching in colleges? What consequences would you predict if a few states passed such a law?

7. Do high wage rates in such strongly unionized industries as steel and automobiles pull up the general level of wages in nonunionized, lower-wage industries? If you think they do, what is the process by which this occurs? If contracts that call for high wages reduce employment opportunities in the industries that must pay these wages, where do the excluded workers find employment?

8. What will be the consequences of laws prohibiting discrimination by employers against women? (If you answer quickly, you will almost certainly answer inadequately.)
   a. What will occur if employers are required to pay women equal wages for equal work but are not required to hire women? Assume in answering that employers are male chauvinists who believe women aren't as valuable employees as men.
   b. What will happen if employers are forbidden to discriminate on the basis of sex in hiring, firing, promoting, or paying wages? Assume again that employers are male chauvinists. Would it be illegal under these circumstances to discriminate on the basis of height or physical strength?
   c. There are (or have been until recently) many laws "protecting" women employees by limiting their hours of work, providing for mandatory rest periods, or prescribing special facilities that must be maintained for women

employees. Who do you think these laws protected? Why? Would you say that an employer subject to such laws was practicing sex discrimination when he hired men in preference to women?
   d. Who do you suppose has benefited more from prejudices and resulting employment discrimination against women? Employers or male employees? Why?

9. A plumbers local in Fort Lauderdale, Florida, voluntarily lowered the hourly rate for union workers on low-rise construction projects from $10.70 to $6.90 an hour (in June 1972). The $10.70 rate continued to apply to high-rise construction. The business manager of the union said this was being done to curb inflation and help homeowners. Do you think it might also have been done because nonunion plumbers were available in the area at $4.50 to $5 an hour? Why do you suppose the union did not lower the rate on high-rise construction work?

10. What does baseball's reserve clause have to do with economic rent? Does it keep highly talented players from earning any rent? Why not? Do you think this is its aim? Or is its aim, as the baseball owners say, to prevent the wealthiest teams from corralling all the best players? Why do you suppose the Yankees were able to outbid every other team for Catfish Hunter's services?

11. A television station whose physical facilities could be replaced for $2 million is sold for $22 million. For what was the extra $20 million a payment? What happens when the Federal Communications Commission revokes the license of a station and awards it to another ownership group?

12. If you know that a license to operate a taxicab in New York City can be purchased from an existing license holder for $80,000, what could you infer about the profitability of operating a taxicab in New York City? What actions by the city could raise or lower the market value of a license?

Pollution
and Property Rights

Many people have concluded in recent years that the growing problem of environmental pollution demonstrates the inadequacy of a purely economic point of view. You won't be surprised to find that position vigorously rejected here. Ecology and economics are very closely related, as a matter of fact, and in more than the common Greek stem of the words. Ecology in the narrow sense is a branch of biology that deals with the interrelations between organisms and their environment. In the broader meaning of the word, it is a point of view, an informing conviction that everything ultimately depends upon everything else. Actions prompt reactions; the reactions set the stage for all future actions. And that is also the point of view of economic theory. Economics and ecology are allies, not competitors or antagonists.

The economist maintains that, if pollution is a growing problem in our society, it is because we have systematically encouraged people to neglect certain costs. The problem requires for its solution that we find ways to correct this neglect. If, like Stephen Leacock's Lord Ronald, we fling ourselves upon a horse and ride madly off in all directions, we are not likely to find acceptable solutions.

In looking at the pollution problem through the spectacles of economic theory, we shall discover that voluntary exchange and the market system do not work well under all circumstances. In this chapter and the succeeding one, we shall try to get a clear notion of just what those circumstances are, the consequences of such market failure, and the effectiveness of alternative or supplementary procedures for securing social coordination in the use of scarce resources.

Pollution Is a Cost

A good way to begin is by noticing that pollution is a cost. It is a cost incurred in the production of goods, and it is not essentially different from any other cost. Pollution, like all costs, represents opportunities forgone: opportunities to breathe clean air, fish or swim in sparkling streams, enjoy pleasant vistas, find solace in solitude, listen to birds sing, or eat fish without fear of mercury poisoning. All these activities are goods. They are valued opportunities that many must now forgo because they have been sacrificed for the sake of other goods.

To think about pollution in this way recalls us from Utopia

to the real world where there are many goods, almost all of them scarce, desired with different intensities by different people, with varying marginal costs of production. Pollution cannot be eliminated simply by banning all activities that damage the environment. The opportunity costs of doing that would be far too high to make it politically feasible, or even acceptable to anyone at all who really thought about it. What we actually want is *the optimal amount of environmental damage*. No more. But no less either. We want to reduce such damage as long as the marginal social benefit of doing so exceeds the marginal social cost. And we want to *expand* it—heresy!—whenever the marginal social benefit of doing that exceeds the marginal social cost.

No one lobbies for more environmental damage, of course. But people do want a lot of goods whose production or use entails exactly that. Perhaps they should not want these goods, or would not want them if they fully knew the consequences. Those are difficult and debatable assertions. The economist makes a somewhat different assertion with considerable confidence: People will want less of such goods if they are themselves forced to pay more of the unpleasant consequences of having or using them.

It's just our old friend the law of demand in another set of clothes. The quantity of anything demanded decreases as its price increases. "Not so," comes that voice from the rear which has been silent through several chapters. "We are right now paying a heavy price for pollution in the form of ugliness, discomfort, destruction, and disease. But people go right on polluting in disregard of the consequences."

The voice from the rear has made a point and missed the point. The law of demand does not predict that Rod will drive his car less because Tom, Dick, and Harry must now pay more to let him do so. Rod responds to *his own costs and benefits as he perceives them.* Whether or not we decide that this is selfish and inconsiderate on the part of Rod, we had better not decide to pretend that Rod will behave otherwise or to put all our eggs in the basket of moral restraint.

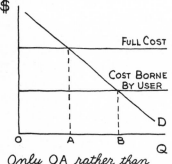

Only OA rather than OB would be demanded if user had to pay the full cost.

Internalizing Costs

The core of the environmental problem is the increasing significance of what the economist calls *externalities*. These are *spillover costs or benefits*: consequences of action that are not taken into account by the actor and which therefore do not influence his decisions.

Individuals engage in activities for the sake of the benefits they expect to receive, after taking into account the associated costs they expect to bear. But the full costs and benefits of many activities are not confined to the actor. They may be spread out over many other people. In some instances they cannot even be traced to the activities of the people who created them. When everyone makes decisions solely on the basis of the costs he himself bears and the benefits he incurs and those decisions entail substantial additional costs or benefits to others, a serious misallocation of resources may result.

Take the case of a Los Angeles commuter. If she is seized by a vision of the public good and so leaves her car in the garage and walks, bikes, or uses public transportation to get to work, she herself bears a sizable cost. For distances are long in Los Angeles, and the public transportation system wins no prizes there. So most people prefer to drive. They thereby reduce their own travel cost substantially (time spent is a cost!) while imposing upon all other inhabitants of the Los Angeles Basin additional pollution—in such forms as engine exhaust and freeway congestion that takes the time of other motorists. Sermonizing about this is not likely to solve anything as long as a great number of Los Angelenos continue to perceive such a large gap between the high subjective cost of "responsible" behavior and the low subjective cost of "irresponsible" behavior—especially when they think that (a) their own sacrifice will make no noticeable difference to the community, and (b) their own sacrifice will not induce others to follow their lead.

The same analysis can be applied to industrial polluters. Suppose that the operation of a particular factory puts smoke and soot in the air. If the cost of installing and operating equipment to eliminate the discharge is substantial, the owner of the factory may very reasonably elect to go on polluting. He pays attention to the costs *he bears*. And he bears only a tiny portion of the total discomfort created by his factory's smoke and soot. With his air-conditioned automobile and office and his home in a distant suburb, he hardly notices it. Why should he go to a lot of expense to get rid of it?

"That's understandable but it's still wrong," says the voice from the rear, grinding out his cigarette on the classroom floor. Why did he use the floor as an ash tray? Because he was behaving in a manner analogous to the automobile driver and the factory owner. The floor is used more frequently as an ashtray as the cost of so using it diminishes *to the smoker*. People do not usually grind butts into floors that they own or must clean. Even if they rent, they will want to preserve the appearance of a floor with which they plan to continue living for a while. But when the cost of using the floor as an ashtray is borne by persons other than the smoker, he is far more likely to minimize or ignore the cost.

You may want to call that selfish behavior. It might be more helpful, however, to think of it as evidence that people have limited conceptions of self-interest. If the smoker takes into account the appearance of the room to those who will use it next; if other people's perceptions of beauty and order are important to him; if ugliness for *anyone* becomes, by an act of imaginative insight, ugliness for *him*, then the smoker has an enlarged conception of self-interest. When such a person acts in his own interest, he takes into account more of the consequences for others than are taken into account by someone with a less inclusive concept of self. The growth of such a capacity for vividly entertaining the feelings of others, or for standing in their shoes, may be the key to the advance of civilization. The late philosopher Alfred North Whitehead argued that the development of this capacity was in fact the meaning of social progress.

We can work and hope for such a world, but we had better in the meantime pay some attention to interim solutions. Every private act has social consequences; the more completely these consequences are internalized, or taken into account by actors, the more satisfactory will be the resulting allocation of resources. The spillover effects of private choices tend to become larger and more significant in an urbanized and highly industrialized society. All of which suggests that we should now give careful attention to more precise ways of assigning responsibility to people for the consequences of their actions.

External Benefits and Free Riders

Externalities can be positive as well as negative. When activities confer benefits on people who cannot be made to pay for the benefits they receive, we encounter the problem of *free riders.*

When Horty Kulcher planted rose bushes in his front lawn, he conferred a benefit upon all his neighbors (except those with rose fever!) for which he charged them nothing. Because he cannot get them to pay something toward the landscaping of his lot and its contribution to neighborhood beautification, his neighbors are free riders. The problem is that Horty consequently doesn't allocate enough resources to landscaping: he fails to produce aesthetic pleasures for which the community would be willing to pay if there were any low-cost way to collect the payments and offer them to Horty as an inducement.

Many goods cannot easily be supplied to those who are willing to pay the price without also being supplied, to some degree at least, to others who refuse to pay the price. A less trivial example than Horty's yard is police protection. If each family had to purchase the police protection it wanted by contracting with private security organizations, the total amount of police protection in any community would tend to be insufficient by the standards of those same people. The value to them of additional police protection would be greater than the cost of obtaining it; and when marginal revenues or benefits exceed marginal costs, output is less than optimal. Why then wouldn't the people of the community expand their purchases? Because they would all be waiting for other families to move first, and hoping to obtain the additional police protection they themselves want as a spillover effect. For when security officers are patrolling the block to protect my neighbor's home, they are simultaneously offering increased security to my home. The problem arises from the fact that it is difficult to exclude nonpayers from obtaining some of the benefits. And when nonpayers can obtain benefits without paying, they try to do just that. They restrict their purchases and hope for a free ride.

Education provides another example. If educated people confer benefits on those around them, then the whole community gains from each person's decision to purchase more education. Conversely, the decision of parents not to purchase education for their children will inflict costs on the whole community. In such a situation people will tend to purchase less education for themselves or their children than the socially optimal amount, as they all pay attention only to the private costs and benefits of their decisions.

Or consider the problem of charity in an urbanized society. Assume that all citizens are charitably disposed and want to see more income made available to impoverished and unfortunate people. While many people derive satisfaction from knowing that they themselves contributed to a charitable cause, most people would also prefer that others assume the burden of contributing. They want to see poor people aided, but they also want to see others do the aiding. And so they will tend to behave like free riders. They will hold back somewhat on their contributions in the hope that other people will "purchase" the quantity of the good —assistance to the poor—that they desire and thus enable them to enjoy the good at a lower cost. That, of course, is why semicoercive techniques are so widely used in successful charity campaigns.

The difficulty in all these cases is simply the mirror image of the difficulty encountered in dealing with environmental damage. Some way must be found to hold people accountable for the costs their activities generate and to make them pay for the benefits they enjoy. And that leads us into the concept of *property*.

The Definition of Property

Most Americans would say that they believe in private property. Many socialists would say that they are opposed to private property. An argument at this level of generality will produce a good deal of heat and little light. For everyone believes in *some* private property, and no one has ever discovered a way to make *all* property private. Moreover, property is often only partially private.

Property comes from the Latin *proprius*, meaning "one's own." When is something one's own and when is it not? That isn't always as clear as you might at first suppose. Ownership usually implies the power to use something, to prevent others from using it, and to appropriate the benefits from using it. If you own an automobile, you may drive it, prosecute people who drive it without your consent, and charge your neighbor $5 a week for the privilege of riding along with you to work. But you may not drive it north on a southbound one-way street; you will not be able to prosecute successfully other drivers who splash mud on your automobile; and under certain circumstances you will be prosecuted yourself if you transport people for hire. Moreover, your right to drive your automobile when you please will be largely fictitious if the police are unable to prevent people from stealing tires, spark plugs, or entire automobiles. And of what value is your right to drive when you please if there are no roads, or the streets that you want to travel are choked with other automobiles, or there are so many drunk and reckless drivers in the community that the probability of your returning alive from a trip to the grocery store is only 80 percent? There are clearly many ambiguities in the concept of private property.

Private property is probably best thought of as a matter of degree. A society based on private property is one in which the power to use resources *tends* to be assigned to particular persons, along with the resulting costs and benefits, and the attendant rights *tend* to be clearly defined and effectively enforced. That is the link between property and what we called the clear assignment of responsibility. The laws and customs of societies differ enormously in their prescriptions regarding property: Which resources may be owned by particular persons? What restrictions are placed on use? How clearly are the privileges and obligations of the owner specified? How effectively are they enforced? Statutory law and prevailing practice may even give quite different answers to these questions, a fact that further complicates our analysis. But the issue is a crucial one for all its ambiguities, uncertainties, and complexities. It is intimately tied up with the problem of externalities.

Property and Pollution

Let's go back to the factory owner who is spewing black smoke into the air. He "owns" the chimney, so he can use it as he pleases. But the smoke leaves his chimney and passes into the atmosphere. Who owns the atmosphere? Our laws and customs have tended to answer that nobody owns the atmosphere. So the factory owner is free to use it as a receptacle for industrial wastes.

Such a situation seems to have been more tolerable fifty or even ten years ago than it is today. At one time we appear to have had a working consensus that the social advantages from allowing the atmosphere to be used as an industrial dump were greater than the disadvantages. People could move away from factories, or purchase residential space near the factories at a low price if they preferred that saving to the delights of clean air. Meanwhile factories held their costs down by discharging wastes into the atmosphere, and this meant a greater availability of the goods that factories produced.

But the situation has changed. The population of the United States has increased substantially. The goods that factories produce are now available in large quantities and many people are beginning to place a lower relative valuation on steel products and a higher relative valuation on attractive scenery. Moreover, a little black smoke may be much more acceptable than a lot of black smoke. When it becomes difficult to breathe, or when people discover that beyond a certain point polluted air causes lung disease, or when new technology reduces the cost of controlling smoke discharges—the possibilities are almost endless—the social consensus may shift rapidly and radically. That seems to be happening now.

What is called for is renewed attention to the rules that define property. It is not accurate to say that we must restrict property rights. One might better argue that an expansion of property rights is in order. When we allowed the factory owner an unrestricted right to discharge soot into the atmosphere, we denied homeowners the right to keep his soot off their windows and curtains. A reassignment of rights in this case should not automatically be viewed as an incursion on private property. In many cases it could more accurately be viewed as a clarification and strengthening of the private-property system.

A lot can be accomplished by levying taxes on activities with substantial social costs in excess of their privately borne costs. The tax in effect turns the social cost into a private cost; it puts the cost on the decision maker. That is one way to *internalize externalities*, a clumsy but descriptive phrase used by economists to mean: induce decision makers to take account of the costs they inflict upon, and the benefits they create for, others.

But the issues are enormously difficult. The property prescriptions of a society are the product of political decisions that in turn grow out of historical experience, notions of justice, predictions about consequences, and conflicting interests. They cannot be easily altered. And not just because interests conflict. There are social costs, which may be substantial, in altering a system of property prescriptions or enforcing new prescriptions. Nor can we always be as certain as we would like to be about the consequences of the changes we contemplate.

What Do People Really Want?

Let's go back to the automobile. Directly or indirectly, the automobile seems to be responsible for a truly astounding part of the environmental deterioration that so many now lament. Our cities have been carved up, cemented over, and stretched out to accommodate mounting masses of automobiles. Automobiles have increased isolation while diminishing solitude. They assault all our senses with fumes, noise, junkyards, collisions, and neon roadways. They gobble up nonrenewable resources. It is largely in their service that oil is spilled on the world's beaches. As a result of their proliferation, national parks during the tourist season are coming to resemble mobile-home sites. But are we willing to pay the cost of having it otherwise? There is no compelling evidence that a majority of Americans is yet willing to alter property definitions and assign to motorists the full cost of their automobile ownership and operation. Freedom to drive might as well be included in the First Amendment. Even toll roads are widely regarded as bordering on unconstitutionality. If someone threw his garbage on your lawn, you would have legal recourse. But you apparently have none when the fumes from his automobile exhaust and the noise of his engine intrude regularly upon the tranquility of your home.

So these will not be easy issues to resolve. If all this sounds terribly pessimistic, it isn't meant to sound that way at all. It is primarily intended as a reminder that perfection is an elusive goal. We are now moving in the direction of rethinking and redefining certain rights of property owners in ways more consistent with the realities of an urbanized and highly industrialized society. There is far more that can be done. But it would be a serious mistake to suppose that all Americans or even a majority of Americans are currently agreed upon just what sacrifices are worth making for the sake of specific kinds of improvement in the environment. If we assume that improvements can be made without sacrifice, or that the requisite sacrifices can be borne by all of "them" and none of "us," we are headed for severe disappointment.

We are also misleading ourselves if we thoughtlessly attribute all evils to the operation of the market system and suppose that our problems would diminish or disappear if we only had more comprehensive planning. Pollution exists in the Soviet Union and the centrally planned economies of Eastern Europe. For them, too, clean air and water are goods but not free goods. Additional quantities of these goods can be secured only by giving up increasing quantities of alternative goods: refrigerators, grain, housing. The central planners in socialist countries must decide which of numerous competing goods to produce without even the assistance of market information: not only information about what is wanted (which they may decide to ignore), but also information on the social-opportunity costs of the various courses they could pursue. There is no evidence that "comprehensive planning" as the solution to problems of the environment is anything more than a beguiling slogan.

Perhaps the most important distinction to make in thinking about these large issues of economic activity and social welfare is the distinction between market processes and property prescriptions. The marketplace is finally a shorthand term for a web of social transactions. It can be used to describe log-rolling by congressmen, the exchange of promises for votes, or the dispensing of governmental favors as a quid for some quo, as well as to describe exchanges involving money. The concept of exchange provides a general model for thinking about social behavior in any kind of political or economic system. Looked at in this way, the difference between economic systems depends not on the extent to which they rely on market processes, for they all do, but on the way in which they assign and enforce responsibility, or on their system of property rights. Who has the power to control what? Who receives the benefits and who bears the costs of what actions? What are the rules? How clearly are they specified? How effectively are they enforced? How susceptible are they to change? These are the crucial questions.

By the way in which we answer them we decide what kind of social consequences will emerge from the operation of market processes.

But when we raise such questions, we clearly move into the realm of political action. Government is the agency to which we usually turn when we believe that the current consequences of market exchange are unsatisfactory. Does the economic way of thinking cease to be useful when government enters the picture? Or can it also aid us here in understanding the social processes of resource allocation? That's the topic for the next chapter.

Once Over Lightly

Pollution is an example of the problems caused by what the economist calls externalities: consequences of action that are not taken into account by decision makers because they are costs or benefits that do not accrue to the decision makers themselves.

The consequences of spillover costs (negative externalities) can be corrected if ways can be found to impose the full costs of actions on those who take them.

Spillover benefits (positive externalities) lead to a misallocation of resources by encouraging "free riders." People purchase too little of the good because they hope to receive it as a spillover benefit from the purchases of others.

A society's system of property rights is its way of assigning the responsibility for actions, both costs and benefits, to particular parties. The responsibilities people will fulfill depend upon the clarity of these assignments and the degree to which they are enforced. When responsibilities are poorly defined, people tend to behave "irresponsibly."

Voluntary exchange through a market system depends upon the clear assignment and effective enforcement of property rights. The presence of substantial externalities will prevent the market system from allocating resources efficiently.

Disagreements about environmental problems are often indicative of deeper disagreements about who should have which property rights. Improved environmental quality is not a free good, and there is a great deal of disagreement about who should bear its costs.

QUESTIONS FOR DISCUSSION

1. Each additional vehicle that enters the freeway during the morning rush hour slows all the other automobiles using the freeway. What are the private costs considered by each motorist as he decides whether or not to use the freeway? What are the full costs or the social costs entailed by his decision? How does the divergence between private and social costs lead to a misallocation of resources in this case? How could this divergence be narrowed?

2. Show that the allocation of resources might be improved by making the freeway into a tollway. Why might you, as a regular user of the expressway, prefer a toll during the rush hour to not paying any toll? When is it more efficient for a limited-access highway to be a freeway, and when is it more efficient for it to be a tollway?

3. You and your family enjoy camping in the national parks. Therefore, in February you urge your congressman to oppose a bill that would increase the fees for such camping during July and August. The following August you enter Teton National Park at 4:00 P.M. on a weekday and find that all the campsites are occupied.
   a. Would you now like to see a higher schedule of camping fees? Why or why not?
   b. Why are fees for the use of privately owned resources more likely to rise when demand increases than fees for the use of government-owned resources?
   c. How do varying ownership systems affect resource allocation? Why?

4. The fine for littering the highway is the same whether the object is a can or a returnable bottle. Why then do you see so many beverage cans along the highway and so few returnable bottles? What would be the effect of requiring a deposit of 5 cents on each container of one quart or smaller capacity?

5. Many informed Americans are beginning to express concern about imminent shortages of electricity, especially in the northeastern United States. Many of the same people have argued in the past against strip-mining of coal, coal-burning electrical power plants, imports of oil (because of the danger of spills), construction of nuclear power plants, and the building of the Alaska pipeline. How should this conflict between competing social concerns be resolved?

6. All these questions involve some degree of incompatibility between alternative goods. How are such conflicts of interest to be resolved?
   a. Do owners of motorcycles have the right to improve the operation of their vehicles by removing the mufflers?
   b. Do zoning laws infringe on property rights or protect property rights?
   c. Do commercial airlines have the right to interfere with your television reception by flying over your house? Should they be compelled to compensate you for the violation of your air space? What would happen if a way were found to compel commercial airlines to compensate everyone adversely affected by their operation?
   d. What would you expect to occur if motorists were required to pay a tax per mile driven approximately equal to the costs their driving imposes upon all others in the society? (Assume we somehow obtained the necessary information on these costs.) Would you favor such a tax? Why or why not?
   e. A large mulberry tree in your neighbor's yard provides you with welcome shade but gives him only a lot of inedible and messy mulberries. He wants to cut the tree down. Does he have the legal right to do so? Does his action affect the value of your property? Is it better from a social point of view that

the tree be felled or remain standing? How might an answer be found and the better result obtained?

f. Do the owners of land along the highways have a right to erect billboards on their own private property? Who owns the view from the highway? If motorists intensely dislike billboards that despoil the countryside, could they get together and bribe farmers to remove them? What would be some of the difficulties in the way of such a solution? What arguments could be used to support this kind of approach?

7. Does an extremely bright student create any externalities for other students in her classes? Can you mention some specific external costs? Some external benefits? How could such a student be persuaded to internalize those externalities? What would that imply?

8. How many instances of significant externalities can you find on your campus? Why do they arise? How might the people who create them be brought to internalize them?

9. You have the right to live in a house and do everything with it and to it that owners usually can do *except sell it*. Is it your property? Are your actions with respect to that house likely to be different from what they would be if your ownership included the right to sell the house? In what ways?

10. You own a car and live in lower Manhattan. In what ways are your property rights in the car limited? What consequences are these limitations likely to have for the decisions Manhattanites make with respect to cars?

11. "I know I ought to buy an umbrella. But I always lose them within two months." In what sense does this person have a weak property right? How is that affecting his decisions? Would you expect to find more

or fewer umbrellas in use in a society where umbrellas are regularly stolen or mislaid than in one where they are rarely lost? Why?

12. No one "owned" the bison that roamed the Great Plains in the nineteenth century. How did this fact contribute to their near extinction?

13. Why are antique stores in large cities so often clustered together in one area? Are the owners looking for competition? Why do the location policies of antique stores differ so markedly from the location policies of grocery stores?

14. In April 1975 a federal jury in Miami ordered the seller of a radial tire to pay $2.3 million in damages to a family because of a fatal accident that followed a blowout of the tire. The tire was under a 40,000 mile warranty and blew out at 31,000 miles. The seller contended that an improper tube had been placed in the tire, that the tire was underinflated, and that the driver (who was the plaintiff in the suit) had handled the car incompetently after the blowout. How did this decision assign property rights? How would you expect such a decision, if allowed to stand, to affect the future allocation of resources? Do you think the decision is likely to promote a more efficient allocation of society's resources?

15. If the present legal owners of such nonrenewable resources as oil and coal suspect that their property will be confiscated in whole or in part within the next ten years, how will their present decisions be affected?

16. Whether or not to develop nuclear power as an energy source is a highly controversial issue in our society. Scores of experts have volunteered their testimony on both sides. Why are the experts in such fundamental disagreement?

Government
and the Market

"Do you believe in letting free enterprise solve our economic problems or should we turn them over to the government?"

Most people have an answer to that question, even if it's the somewhat unsatisfactory answer that each sector should handle those problems with which it's best equipped to deal. But very few people give much systematic thought to the differences and similarities between "free enterprise" and government, or wonder for long exactly why one or the other might be better able to deal with a particular problem.

"Free Enterprise" and Government

Some of the standard contrasts don't hold up very well under close examination. For example, free enterprise is sometimes characterized as the *competitive* system. But there is competition in government, too, as every election year demonstrates. Within any government agency, competition for promotion exists among employees. Competition also occurs between government agencies vying for a larger share of appropriations. The two major political parties are continually competing. The executive branch competes with the legislative, congressmen compete for committee assignments, even district judges compete with one another in the hope of an eventual appointment to a higher court.

Another alleged characteristic of the free enterprise system is its emphasis on "individualism." But very few Americans who participate in the free enterprise system do so as rugged individualists. Many go to work for large corporations right after leaving school and continue as employees until retirement. Is there any significant difference between working in Baltimore as an employee of the Social Security Administration division of Health, Education, and Welfare and working in Flint as an employee of the Buick division of General Motors? When Britain experimented after World War II with nationalizing, denationalizing, and renationalizing its steel industry, most of the employees (and lots of other people, too) had trouble discerning any difference. Some of the characters who frequent the halls of Congress seem far more individualistic, or at least more idiosyncratic, than the people who pass through the corridors of business.

Others would distinguish "free enterprise" from government by reference to the goals or motives that shape policy. But surely this is naïve. The congressman who claims that "the public interest" is his objective will often have his attention riveted on the private interests that can effect his reelection or defeat. The members of the Interstate Commerce Commission are indeed charged by law with regulating the nation's transportation system in accord with the "overall needs" of the economy; but their day-by-day decisions nonetheless reflect the tug of narrower objectives, including each member's desire to maintain and extend the influence of the Commission and his own power, income, and status. The goals and motivations of the people who constitute the government are not demonstrably different from the goals and motivations of those in "free enterprise." Moreover, the rhetoric of "the public interest" has in recent years been adopted by many business firms whose owners and managers are eager to persuade the public that social responsibility and not maximum profit is the ultimate touchstone of their decisions. Rhetoric just cannot be relied upon to give a faithful reflection of reality.

Economic Theory and Government Action

Economic theory attempts to explain the workings of the "free enterprise" system on the assumption that all participants want to advance their own interests and try to do so in a rational way. The marginal cost-marginal revenue rule that we introduced explicitly in Chapter 10, but have in fact been using throughout the book, is merely a formal expression of these assumptions: The way to advance one's interests is to expand each activity whose marginal revenue exceeds its marginal cost and to contract any activity whose marginal cost is greater than its marginal revenue. The economist does not assume, as we have pointed out before, that money or material goods are the only costs and revenues (or benefits) that consumers and producers care about, or that the interests people pursue are narrow and selfish ones. Economic theory can throw light on the social consequences of every kind of human interest.[1] Why shouldn't that apply to the human purposes and the social processes that control the course of government activities?

We aren't trying to expound a political philosophy here or lay out a comprehensive theory of the state. We're only asking why the principles of social interaction that guide production of the *New Yorker* should be so different from those that guide production of the *Federal Reserve Bulletin*. And we're suggesting that they really are not as different as people commonly suppose. Governments as well as privately owned firms produce commodities and services. Governments, too, can only do that by obtaining

1. An interest in chaos might be the one exception. In a society where people did not value rationality, but celebrated instead the rule of caprice, accident, and purposeless action, economic theory would have almost no predictive power. Its predictive power is correspondingly greatest in those areas of social life most marked by foresight and premeditated action.

productive resources whose opportunity cost is the value of what they would have produced in their next most valuable employment. Governments as well as privately owned firms must therefore bid for the resources they want and offer the owners of those resources adequate incentives. You'll want to note that the government can use negative as well as positive incentives: the threat of imprisonment, for example, may be a major incentive as some people decide what portion of their income to offer the Internal Revenue Service each spring. Governments even face the problem of marketing their output and of price searching, though monetary prices do play a much smaller role in the distribution of government products. But there can be no doubt that demand curves exist for government goods and that, since these goods are characteristically scarce, they must be rationed by means of some discriminatory criteria. And the people with a demand for government goods will consequently compete to satisfy those criteria, to pay the established price.

The main advantage of looking at government in this way is that it counters the tendency to think of government as a deus ex machina: a heaven-sent power that can resolve difficulties as magically as a playwright does in the final act of every farce. It makes our expectations of government more realistic. It encourages us to ask about the conditions that enable government to act effectively in any given circumstance and not just to suppose that government always gets what it wants or catches what it chases. This way of looking at government also reminds us that the immediately preceding sentence was misleading in its suggestion that government is an "it"; for government is *many different people interacting*. Finally, this perspective on government encourages us to look for the actual marginal costs and marginal benefits that guide government actions and follow from them.

The term *free enterprise* is probably more useful to orators than to analysts. The distinguishing characteristic of any economic system, we have previously suggested, is the way it assigns responsibilities. Who is allowed to do what? Who is encouraged to do what? Who reaps the consequences, good or bad? A system of private property is one system for assigning responsibilities. Such a system is primarily coordinated through the voluntary exchanges to which people are led by the ratios of exchange (relative prices) they observe, with these prices continually adjusting in response to people's decisions to buy or sell. That's the social process this whole book has tried to describe. But it's far from the answer to everyone's dreams. In Chapter 14 we examined the market system with an eye to the question of what enabled it to work effectively and what contributed to a less satisfactory performance. We're really just continuing that question in this chapter, with a change in emphasis. We're still looking at social exchange and the institutional context within which it occurs. But now we are paying particular attention to government as an entity both operating within the system and operating to change the structure of the system.

Social Exchange and Transaction Costs

There must be rules for the ordering of any society and some procedure for securing their application and enforcement. The Latin word for rule is *regula*; and the government is often thought of as the ultimate regulator or rule maker. The rules can be either few and general or many and detailed. Private property is one such general rule whose enforcement takes the place of many detailed rules. The clear assignment of property rights provides a basis for the ordering of society through voluntary exchange among its members with minimum interference by outside regulators. But that order becomes less satisfactory as the transaction costs of voluntary exchange increase.

Transaction costs is the economist's term for the costs of arranging, concluding, and enforcing voluntary exchanges. It's an important concept for understanding when and why markets fail to yield satisfactory results. Many economists go so far as to suggest that it provides the most comprehensive rationale for government itself: Government is an institutional arrangement for accomplishing people's goals in situations where the transaction costs associated with individual initiative and voluntary exchange are prohibitively high.

That sounds more obscure than it really is. One way to get at the idea is through a mental experiment. Imagine there were no government at all in our society. What would happen? What problems would arise? What important tasks would cease to be performed?

Then ask yourself whether it wouldn't be possible for people to resolve those problems and accomplish those tasks either through individual action or by forming voluntary associations? How might they do so? And what costs would be entailed?

Take the problem of police protection discussed in Chapter 14. Would there be no police if there were no government? Obviously not, since private police forces exist at the present time. But these forces supplement a basic, given level of government police protection, providing additional protection for those who want it and are willing to pay for it. Could we obtain that basic protection in the absence of government?

Why couldn't the people living on one block or the business firms in a particular area get together and agree to contribute toward their own police force? They could, of course. But they would encounter significant costs. Think of all the block meetings, the long discussions, the arguments over the quantity and quality of protection desired, the nuisance of collecting contributions regularly, the negotiations with police-service suppliers. Every block would have to do that. The more that blocks combined, the more difficult would be the task of getting the voluntary association started.

And we haven't even mentioned the cost of free riders. What would we do with the household that refused to contribute because it expected to get the service anyway as a positive externality from the neighbors' efforts? And if one household dropped out, wouldn't some others also refuse to participate? Couldn't the free-rider effect topple our association like a string of dominoes? Perhaps we could meet this dilemma by exerting pressure on the free riders: community disapproval, openly expressed, might bring them in. And if that didn't work, there are other ways to exert pressure. In fact, why not just take a vote and decide that anyone who refuses to cooperate with the association has to move from the block? And then move the antisocial family out by force if necessary? Wouldn't coercion be justified under such circumstances?

Perhaps it would. But then we would have created a government! The distinguishing characteristic of government is precisely its power to secure cooperation through coercion.

Tasks for Government

Political scientists would probably object that this concept of government is much too narrow. And we wouldn't want to dispute the point. We've already said that we aren't trying to provide a complete theory of government; our aim is to call attention to problems of social coordination in which purely voluntary exchange seems to entail prohibitive transaction costs. The point we're trying to make is that government can usefully be viewed as an agency for accomplishing people's purposes in situations where the power to compel cooperation may significantly reduce transaction costs.

The word *may* is important in the last sentence. The list of activities in which government engages in our society is a long and growing one. Government regulates private producers in many ways, not only through rules and directives but also through taxes and subsidies. It also functions as a producer itself. The goods currently produced by government agencies include police and fire protection, national defense, schooling, streets and highways, parks and other recreation facilities, postal service, a judicial system, lending libraries, museums, certification services, public housing, health care for veterans, advice to farmers, a monetary unit and a supply of currency, research activities of many kinds beginning with the official census, electric power, water supplies and sewage systems, navigational aids on the water, and traffic lights on the land.

We have no intention of trying to assess the costs and benefits of even a substantial fraction of these activities. But perhaps we can offer some suggestions on the usefulness of the economic way of thinking in the evaluation of government activities by looking briefly at three issues: government regulation of public utilities, government production of schooling, and government as an agent for handling environmental problems. Each issue deserves at least a chapter in itself. So we'll be forced to offer more quesions than answers.

Utility Regulation

Why does the government regulate the prices and terms of service of electric-power companies? The standard answer is that they are "natural monopolies." To have more than one electric utility serving a community would entail a wasteful duplication of services. But with only one, competition cannot do an effective job of regulation. So the government assumes the responsibility for ensuring adequate service at fair prices.

What constitutes a fair price? The standard answer is a price that enables the utility to cover its costs and earn a reasonable return on investment. But how are costs to be measured? And if the utility is guaranteed a revenue adequate to cover costs, what happens to the incentive to keep costs down? What constitutes a reasonable return on investment? What happens to the incentive to innovate when a minimum profit is guaranteed and no more may be earned?

All these difficulties compel regulatory officials who wish to be effective to involve themselves more intimately in managerial decisions than simple notions of the regulatory task assume. The regulators must acquire detailed knowledge of particular decisions, alternative courses, and market forecasts. Where will they get that kind of information? Probably from the utilities' managers, for no better source is likely to be available. But how reliable will the information be? How certain can anyone be about information regarding the future? Should the regulators adopt a skeptical, adversary relationship in order to make sure that the utility does not exploit its position at the public's expense? Or does an adversary relationship lead to harassment and prevent the utilities' managers from taking courses of action that will, in the long run, be in the public interest? Consolidated Edison of New York has been treated as a villain for so long that its ability to supply continuing electric service to New York City may by now have been irreparably impaired.

Or is the opposite danger the more pressing one? That regulators will cozy up to the industries they're supposed to control and end up protecting the regulated firms instead of the customer? Recall from previous chapters how often business firms ask for regulation, not because they wish to be restrained in the public interest, but because they prefer the noncompetitive life that "regulation" often secures.

All of this suggests a more general question, one that, surprisingly, almost never gets asked: What reasons do we have for believing that a regulatory commission will be willing and able to make a public utility behave more in the public interest than it would have behaved in the absence of regulation? The managers of privately owned utilities always claim that they know what the public interest requires and would pursue it even in the absence of regulation. We would be wise to entertain doubts about that claim. But would we not also be wise to entertain some doubts about the ability of regulatory commissions to ensure a better performance? The most effective constraint on the behavior of privately owned utilities may not be the detailed interference of regulatory commissions, but the knowledge that the utility must keep its customers happy if it hopes to avoid such interference.

The fact that government regulation will probably fail to secure an ideal performance from public utilities does not imply that regulation should be abandoned. Ideal outcomes are rare, and most of life is a matter of choosing the least unacceptable among imperfect alternatives. But by the same argument, an imperfect performance in the absence of regulation does not imply that regulation should be instituted. The market fails to secure wholly satisfactory results under a wide range of circumstances, and public utilities present one such circumstance. The question, however, is whether regulation is likely to improve performance. In answering that question we must look at the actual rather than the ideal results of regulation. And the costs to the taxpayer of hiring regulatory commissions along with their supporting staffs must be included in our calculation of relative costs and benefits.

Public Schools and Private Incentives

In Chapter 14 we used education as an example of an activity creating positive externalities, spillover benefits for which the beneficiaries do not pay. The consequence of such a situation is an inadequate demand. People will purchase education only up to the point where its marginal benefit to them equals its marginal cost. They will ignore the benefits that their educated status confers upon others and the total quantity of education produced will therefore be less than the optimal amount. In such a situation a case can be made for government subsidies, either to education suppliers or to education demanders. A properly established subsidy could adjust private marginal costs and benefits to conform with overall social costs and benefits.

But has government involvement in education corrected a free-market tendency to produce too little by creating far too much? The quantity of schooling (as distinct from education) is enormous in our society. But the quality of that schooling is quite another matter. How willing would you be to say that the government's total efforts on behalf of education have brought the marginal social benefits of education more closely into line with marginal social costs?

"Educators" insist, of course, that education is a profession, an art, a cultural adventure, a spiritual reality, and not a "business" that can be subjected to tests of economic efficiency or analyses based on marginal cost and benefit calculations. We should expect them to say that, perhaps even to believe it. But have you ever stopped to reflect on the significance of the fact that the "value" of educational services in government budgets is always measured by the cost of providing those services? As a result, anything which reduces the efficiency of school systems raises the "value" of education.

Government subsidies to education have been granted overwhelmingly to suppliers of the service: to schools rather than to students. That's one way to expand the quantity of an underproduced good. But it has some drawbacks. The competition that public schools face is seriously limited by the fact that those who opt for private schools must pay twice: once in private tuition charges and once again in taxes to support the public schools. That significantly reduces the attractiveness of the options available to consumers and makes it easier for the school to provide services that please the producers rather than the consumers. Are our schools operated for the benefit of students? Or for the benefit of teachers and educational administrators?

Students or their parents can in principle use the political process to control the quality of educational services provided by the public schools. But the political process contains substantial free-rider aspects of its own that reduce its effectiveness. The cost to any particular parents of fighting for improved elementary schools will be very high in relation to any benefits they can expect to obtain for their own children from their efforts. That's why so many people are "apathetic" when urged to join the PTA or attend the meetings of the local school board. They may be thoroughly unhappy with the schools; but they also sense that they couldn't bring about the changes they want. Only people who derive satisfaction from political activity itself are likely to expect a greater marginal benefit than cost from getting involved in the cause of school reform.

By requiring children to attend school for a certain number of years, the law compels parents to purchase for their children at least that quantity of education which confers significant spillover benefits on the community. If parents were allowed to select the school of their choice, competition might make schooling a more educational and enjoyable experience than it usually is now. But parents cannot easily choose between public and private schools if they are not allowed to allocate their education taxes to the schools of their choice. Many proposals have been made in recent years along these lines. The most prominent call for government-financed vouchers that could be spent at the school of one's choice. But these proposals have run into questions of church-state relations, fears of racial and class segregation, and the political power of professional educators who are like everyone else in not caring much for the effects of increased competition. Any significant reforms in the American system of elementary and secondary education will have to take account of the fact that the public schools do far more than teach (or not teach) the three R's. But the theory of externalities at least does not demonstrate that resources will be better allocated when all schools are owned and operated by government.

Pollution and Government Action

The possibility of reducing environmental damage through voluntary exchange is rarely considered seriously outside economic circles. Noneconomists are usually quite sure that a problem requires a prohibition: "If it's bad, forbid it!" And so most environmentalists want to ban pollution by law.

But will that really provide a solution? It's a fact of political life that pollution gets more rhetoric than effective action from our legislators. Before we impale those legislators on an ecology button, let's remember how important it is to balance marginal costs and marginal benefits, and how difficult this is to do in the absence of detailed information. Do our legislatures have adequate information with which to write pollution-prohibiting regulations? So many legislative mistakes have already become obvious, in just the first few years of environmental enthusiasm, that a certain skepticism seems in order.

Sometimes pollution control will require no government action at all. That happens, for example, when restaurants or theaters create sections for smokers and nonsmokers because they want the patronage of both. The fumes hovering over the smokers' heads do not become pollution until they assault the senses of nonsmokers.

People who hate the noise and dirt of the city move to outlying areas; people who detest the culture of suburbia live in small towns; people who despise the idiocy of rural life choose to live in the city.

The hard-of-hearing get residential real estate bargains under airport approach lanes; surfboard riders seek out companions and thereby voluntarily segregate themselves from swimmers who hate to dodge surfboards; the afternoon naptaker pays $1.59 for a box of wax earstoppers and thereafter lives in peace with the neighboring teen-ager's mufflerless motorcycle.

Not everyone is perfectly happy even in the best of all possible worlds. But voluntary exchange does reduce the total of costs imposed upon reluctant bystanders and does enable people to capture some of the spillover benefits that life in society creates. We don't live in the worst of all possible worlds, either.

But what do we do about that factory which is still spewing smoke and soot? Or the many other major examples of external costs that are reducing social welfare in our urbanized industrialized society and which private negotiation cannot effectively handle? The economist tends to recommend taxes rather than outright prohibitions and so often gets accused of recommending that people be granted "licenses to pollute."

A tax on industrial smoke is not a "license to pollute" if the tax adequately measures the marginal cost to society of additional smoke. For pollution is a cost imposed on others *without their consent*. If the firm pays the cost, presumably it gains the consent. We must assume, of course, that the government speaks on behalf of the whole society and that it can adequately assess the marginal cost of smoke. But we make the first assumption in urging any government action against pollution. And physical-quantity restrictions on pollution implicitly assume that the marginal cost is known. A total prohibition under any and all circumstances on pain of execution, for example, implies an infinite marginal social cost. We don't avoid the necessity of calculating social costs when we use physical-quantity restrictions; we just conceal from ourselves the fact that we have made a calculation.

The chief advantage of a properly set tax is that it internalizes externalities. It puts the costs of action on the actors and says to each, "Make your best adjustment in the light of your special circumstances." Firms then hunt for the lowest cost response, which may lead to new production techniques or simply to payment of the tax. If the level of emissions remains too high, the tax can be raised a little, as legislators search for rather than blindly postulate the optimum amount of environmental damage. The fact that firms never have identical production processes and that the managers of a firm will have better knowledge of their own costs and processes than any legislative body is an additional reason for attacking pollution through taxation.

The tax approach also reduces the inevitable political problems associated with efforts to eliminate pollution. A flat ceiling tends to present firms with immediate all-or-nothing choices and to arouse intense political opposition. The firm's managers will claim that they can't meet the standards, that they will have to shut down, throw X number of people out of work, reduce the community's tax revenues, and inflict a long parade of horrible secondary consequences on the region in which they operate. The typical response of agencies charged with administering the new regulations is then to grant a delay, during which the firm does little except lobby for another delay.

Perhaps nothing could make a larger contribution to the formulation of effective environmental policy than agreement on the fundamental proposition: Pollution is a cost generated by activities that produce benefits for those who undertake them, but a cost not borne by those who engage in the activities. This definition gets simultaneously at the nature of the problem and the condition of its resolution. The problem is that some people must bear costs to which they have not consented. The challenge to government is to impose those costs on the people for whose benefit they are generated.

A Look Ahead

We haven't said anything at all about one very prominent responsibility that many citizens today assign to the federal government: responsibility for the prevention, cure, or control of inflation and unemployment. It hasn't been overlooked. The difficult and important issue of economic fluctuations and stabilization policy will be our principal concern in the remainder of the book.

Once Over Lightly

The differences between "free enterprise" and government are not adequately described in such contrasts as competitive or noncompetitive, individual or social, private interest or public interest. The principles that guide decision making in the "free enterprise" sector are for the most part the same principles that guide the decisions of the individuals who act in governmental capacities.

The criterion of marginal cost-marginal benefit can be used to evaluate the efficiency of government actions. The assumption that people in government will, in making decisions, pay attention to the marginal costs and benefits *that accrue to them* helps us predict the consequences of government activity.

There is very little which is humanly possible that could not be achieved through voluntary cooperation. But voluntary cooperation, especially on a large scale, often entails substantial transaction costs. Government can usefully be viewed as an institutional arrangement for accomplishing people's goals under circumstances where the costs of arranging, concluding, and enforcing voluntary exchanges are too high.

The advantage of government in securing social cooperation is its power to coerce. This power is especially effective in reducing the substantial social costs that may be associated with the "free rider" problem.

Private economic decisions do not automatically conform to the public interest merely because they have been put under government regulation. Government regulators do not have complete information and often operate within contexts that systematically encourage decisions whose consequences are contrary to the intent of regulation.

If voluntary exchange leads to insufficient production of a good because of positive externalities, the government can expand production through subsidies to suppliers or to demanders. Subsidies to demanders are less likely to result in quality deterioration. The policy of huge government subsidies to education suppliers may be largely responsible for the low ratio of learning to schooling in our educational system.

If voluntary exchange leads to excessive production of a good or its byproducts because of negative externalities, a tax on the activity to be diminished has many advantages over alternative procedures as a way of promoting more efficient resource use.

QUESTIONS FOR DISCUSSION

1. Is competition more widely found in capitalist than in socialist societies?

2. When business firms lobby in the legislature on opposite sides of an issue that will affect their profits, are they competing with each other? How is this different from the activities that we usually have in mind when we think of business competition?

3. You pay your barber or stylist money to persuade him to cut your hair. Is this a bribe? What is the essential difference between this kind of payment and what we ordinarily mean by a bribe?

4. a. A legislator accepts a $5000 campaign contribution from the owner of a textile mill in his district.
   b. A legislator accepts a $5000 personal gift from the owner of a textile mill in his district.
   c. A candidate for Congress promises the textile workers in her district that, if elected, she will work for government restrictions on textile imports.

   Is anyone taking or giving a bribe?

5. Is it inefficient and wasteful to have more than one dairy deliver milk to the people living on a single block? Should dairies be assigned exclusive franchises for particular areas? Who benefits from having more than one dairy delivering milk to an area?

6. Why does the telephone company advertise despite the fact that it has exclusive franchises in the areas it services?

7. Is commercial airline service a "natural monopoly"? Why is it extensively regulated? Some people say that regulation of airlines is essential to prevent competitive practices that might reduce the safety of air travel. Would an airline be insufficiently concerned about safety if it were not regulated?

8. Visualize a city composed entirely of green (one-half) and purple (one-half) citizens. No one objects to living next door to someone of the opposite color. But they all object to having neighbors of the opposite color *on both sides* and will move if they find themselves in that position. Will a segregated or integrated housing pattern emerge under a system of voluntary exchange? Why? If integrated housing is considered a good thing, how could it be achieved under these circumstances?

   Suppose the people in a neighborhood band together in an association that tries to enforce racial quotas. They attempt to prevent black families from purchasing homes in areas where the black-white ratio is above the citywide average. Are they promoting segregation or integration?

9. If positive externalities create free-rider problems to the extent suggested by the text in its analysis of charitable programs, why do United Way compaigns work as well as they do in so many American cities? Are there elements of coercion in United Way fund drives, either in obtaining peo-

ple to work on the campaign or in inducing people to contribute? What might be the advantages and disadvantages of having local government assume the welfare functions currently performed through the United Way?

10. a. A common argument in support of government-produced goods is that they are vital to social welfare and therefore their provision cannot safely be left to the "whims" of the marketplace. Does this explain why parks and libraries are usually municipal services while food and medical care are usually secured through the market?

b. Why is the business of selling books usually handled through the market while the business of lending books is generally handled by government (public libraries)? Should libraries be provided by government because "there's no profit to be made from lending books"?

11. The court system is a good "produced" by government. Could a judicial system exist if it were not produced by government? If the judge and jury in civil suits had to be paid by the contending parties, would decisions tend more often to favor the wealthier party? Do wealthier people currently have an advantage in judicial proceedings under the government-produced court system?

12. Who benefits from government subsidies to colleges and the consequent sale of higher education at prices below marginal cost? Do you think that the subsidies which states grant indirectly to students through systems of tax-supported higher education provide greater benefits to high- or to low-income people?

13. The second annual report of the President's Council on Environmental Quality recommended the use of charges to industry based on the type and amount of pollutants discharged into waterways. How would the adoption of such a system constitute a redefinition of property rights? Is it correct to call this a system of "licenses to pollute"? Why might such a system move us closer to what the text calls an optimal amount of pollution?

14. Trace out the sequence of probable consequences from the imposition of taxes on the pollutants that steel mills emit into the atmosphere. How might such taxes affect the distribution of wealth and the allocation of resources?

15. "Taxes can't control pollution. They'll just drive the little firms out of business while the big firms, who can afford to pay, go right on polluting." Do you agree?

16. What's the difference between a tax on noise emitted by cars without mufflers and a fine for not having a proper muffler?

Aggregate Fluctuations and Economic Data

In 1970 the United States economy slid into a mild recession. The total output of new goods produced in that year declined slightly from the output of 1969, and unemployment rose. What made this somewhat surprising and politically disturbing was the fact that the average level of prices paid by consumers in 1970 rose 6 percent over 1969. In 1971 total production increased, but unemployment did, too. And 1971 consumer prices were an additional 4 percent above 1970 prices. The word began to spread that an unprecedented malady, one that even economists could not explain, had seized the economy: recession coupled with inflation.

The word that spread was incorrect. Inflation joined to rising unemployment had occurred before, most recently in the recessions of 1958 and 1960, though the inflation in those years had been considerably less rapid. And economists were not at a total loss for an explanation. But some oversimplified notions about the causes and interrelations of recession and inflation, notions that economists had probably helped create, were very definitely called into question by the experiences of these years. And when an even more severe recession came along in 1974, while prices were increasing at a rate greater than 10 percent per year, these oversimplified notions had to be abandoned. It was abundantly clear that recession and inflation were not "opposites."

Economic analysis has come in for heavy criticism in recent years because it can offer no simple diagnosis and prescription in the face of recession with rapid inflation. And insofar as economists have oversold their ability to understand and control these problems, they must accept some of the criticism. A decade ago many economists believed that they were in possession of *the* theory of inflations and recessions. But events have undermined this certainty.

While there is still much that economists know about these problems and even more that they are learning to understand, the reader must be cautioned as we move into the final chapters of this book. The principles are much less settled in the area we're now approaching. Or perhaps the principles are well enough established but the appropriate ways to apply them are unclear. And that could just be a consequence of the fact that the goals for knowledge in the areas we're about to study are far more ambitious than the goals in previous chapters.

Up until now we've been studying important but small and

relatively manageable problems, problems created by the way
in which particular prices and production decisions interact.
The study of inflation and recession, however, involves an examination of the general price level, total output, and employment
in the economy as a whole. We might compare the problems
studied so far to problems of how to stay warm, dry, and safe under
various weather conditions; the problems we'll encounter now are
more on the order of how to control the weather. That's clearly a
more ambitious undertaking, and one that may require us to adopt
some heroic simplifications if we are not to bog down in endless
details. But the more heroic the simplification, the greater the risk
of oversimplification and error.

So you're invited to come along now for what will be, even more
than in the preceding chapters of this book, a venture of inquiry.

Recessions and Unemployment

The fear that our society or any society may run out of jobs was
criticized in Chapter 13. We argued there that jobs represent
obstacles to be overcome, and that a society without jobs for
people to perform would have come close to abolishing scarcity.
Such a situation would be an occasion for rejoicing. Neither the
United States nor any other contemporary society is in such a
happy position.

Throughout the discussion in Chapter 13, however, we left out
of account a phenomenon that has puzzled and disturbed students
of economic systems for more than two centuries. It used to be
called the *trade cycle*, and later on the *business cycle*. Those terms
began to disappear from use as economists came to have increasing
doubts about the regularity of such fluctuations. The word *cycle*
has connotations of predictable recurrence, connotations that may
be misleading and can be avoided by substituting a more neutral
phrase, such as "fluctuations in the aggregate level of economic
activity."[1]

Whatever the fluctuations are called, there can be no doubt
about their existence and importance. If those who work for wages
entertain some irrational anxieties about the disappearance of job
opportunities, they may also have substantial grounds for completely rational fears. Our insistence that there is no overall
scarcity of jobs seems to be flatly contradicted by the experience of
every industrialized nation with recessions and depressions.

---

1. The study of such fluctuations, their causes and their cures, came to be called
macroeconomics in the 1930s—from the Greek word *makros*, meaning "large." The
remainder of economics was then referred to as microeconomics, from *mikros*,
meaning "small." There are serious ambiguities in this use of terms, and some
dangers. The beginning student ought to know that many economists would call
Chapters 2-15 microeconomics, and Chapters 16-21 macroeconomics. You won't
go far wrong if you understand macroeconomics to mean the study of fluctuations
in the aggregate level of economic activity, or the study of recessions and depressions, inflation, and aggregate economic growth or decline.

The Bureau of Labor Statistics in the United States Department of Labor maintains a statistical series on unemployment in our economy going back to 1929. The data are based on household interviews conducted in accordance with accepted sampling procedures. They recount a disturbing history.

The civilian labor force is defined to include everyone over the age of sixteen (over fourteen until 1947) not an inmate of an institution or in the armed forces, and either employed, actively seeking employment, or waiting to be recalled to employment. Table 16A shows the total number of people in the civilian labor force classified as unemployed in each year from 1929 to 1975, and the same figure expressed as a percentage of the civilian labor force. The figures are annual averages based on monthly survey data, and are given to the nearest thousand.

How can anyone looking at the data for 1931–1940 still say that scarcity of jobs is a fiction? In 1949, 1954, 1958, 1961, 1970–71, and 1974–75, unemployment jumped sharply. While we have not had a repetition of anything even approaching the decade of the 1930s, it seems obvious that we have had and continue to have periods in which many people cannot find employment. Our concern in this and subsequent chapters is to analyze this significant phenomenon, not to explain it away. But caution must be exercised in interpreting these figures. The problem is real, but not all statements of the problem are equally helpful.

EMPLOYED
+ ACTIVELY SEEKING
EMPLOYMENT
+ WAITING TO BE
RECALLED TO
EMPLOYMENT
⎫ UNEMPLOYED
⎬
⎭

= LABOR FORCE

Those not in the labor force are not counted as unemployed.

The Concept of Unemployment

When is a person involuntarily unemployed? When he wants to be working but isn't because he can't find a job. That seems straightforward and clear enough, but it contains some serious ambiguities.

Look at the data for 1942–1945, the years of World War II. No one claims that the United States had an unemployment problem during those years. Yet even in 1944, when people were being urged to leave school and take a job, to come out of retirement, to work six- and seven-day weeks, 1.2 percent of the labor force was classified as unemployed. Anyone who lived through those years would have trouble believing that 670,000 people could not find jobs in 1944. What was happening?

The trouble lies in the concept of involuntary unemployment. Involuntary implies "no choice" like the involuntary muscle contractions that occur in the body without any conscious decision and sometimes even against the person's will. Unemployment is never involuntary in that sense, for people in the labor force do make choices that affect their employment status. If that were not the case, the economic way of thinking could shed little light on unemployment problems; the basic premise of the economist's analysis is that people choose those options from which they expect the largest net advantage. And those who are unemployed have, in an important sense, chosen that status.

TABLE 16A   Unemployment in Civilian Labor Force

Year	Unemployed (thousands)	Percentage of Civilian Labor Force
1929	1,550	3.2
1930	4,340	8.7
1931	8,020	15.9
1932	12,060	23.6
1933	12,830	24.9
1934	11,340	21.7
1935	10,610	20.1
1936	9,030	16.9
1937	7,700	14.3
1938	10,390	19.0
1939	9,480	17.2
1940	8,120	14.6
1941	5,560	9.9
1942	2,660	4.7
1943	1,070	1.9
1944	670	1.2
1945	1,040	1.9
1946	2,270	3.9
1947	2,311	3.9
1948	2,276	3.8
1949	3,637	5.9
1950	3,288	5.3
1951	2,055	3.3
1952	1,883	3.0
1953	1,834	2.9
1954	3,532	5.5
1955	2,852	4.4
1956	2,750	4.1
1957	2,859	4.3
1958	4,602	6.8
1959	3,740	5.5
1960	3,852	5.5
1961	4,714	6.7
1962	3,911	5.5
1963	4,070	5.7
1964	3,786	5.2
1965	3,366	4.5
1966	2,875	3.8
1967	2,975	3.8
1968	2,817	3.6
1969	2,831	3.5
1970	4,088	4.9
1971	4,993	5.9
1972	4,840	5.6
1973	4,304	4.9
1974	5,076	5.6
1975	7,830	8.5

Source: Bureau of Labor Statistics

Don't jump to the wrong conclusion. We aren't supporting the notion that unemployment is due to laziness, or that everyone could find a satisfactory job if only he resolved to do so. We are rather suggesting that unemployment be considered a consequence of choice: something that is chosen because it is the best available opportunity. Strange as it may sound on first hearing, that does make sense when properly understood, and it provides a way of thinking about unemployment that helps us understand some otherwise inexplicable situations.

Consider the engineers to whom we have several times referred. When an airplane manufacturer tells an engineer in his employ that he is being laid off at the end of the week, the engineer will make plans. Because there are work opportunities available, he could begin a new job the next day. But it is not probable that he could the very next day go to work at another job with net advantages equal, or even very close, to the one from which he has been laid off. The condition of his finding a new job immediately might be a willingness to work for a small fraction of his previous wage or in some occupation that he intensely dislikes. If an engineer laid off on Friday refused to go to work on Monday as a restaurant dishwasher for $2.25 an hour (which we are now assuming to be the best option available to him for Monday), he would become officially unemployed. But he would be voluntarily unemployed inasmuch as he chose not to take the dishwashing job.

At the same time we should probably all agree that he would be foolish not to become officially unemployed. There are almost certainly better opportunities not yet available because they are not yet known to him. If he takes a job that pays $4500 a year in order to avoid being counted as unemployed, he reduces his opportunities to search for a better job. The value to him of time spent searching may well be greater than $2.25 an hour. He may even value just fishing for a few weeks at more than $2.25 an hour. If he has some savings accumulated, or his wife has a good job, or he is fairly certain that another engineering position will become available shortly, voluntary unemployment could be a very sensible choice for him.

Why stress the voluntary nature of unemployment? What's the point? The primary point is the fundamental ambiguity, bordering on meaninglessness, of the concept of involuntary unemployment. As long as useful work remains to be done—and that covers every place and time with which we are familiar—employment opportunities exist, including opportunities for self-employment. (Notice that the official definition misleadingly counts as unemployed those persons who are working around the house while looking for more attractive opportunities elsewhere.) Of course, available opportunities may be far below the individual's expectations; they may not yield an income on which he could begin to support himself adequately; and they may—a crucial point—promise a lower marginal benefit than he anticipates from continued job searching. The possibilities are many. Choice is therefore crucial.

But the concept of involuntary unemployment covers over the important factor of choice.

Employment versus Unemployment

Even the size of the labor force itself, used to calculate unemployment rates, is a product of choice. People choose to enter it and to withdraw from it, presumably on the basis of the value they place on available opportunities. This fact is sometimes used to argue that official unemployment rates minimize the actual problem in a recession because they ignore workers who become discouraged by the scarcity of jobs and stop looking for work, thereby dropping out of the labor force and consequently the ranks of the measured unemployed. That's a valid critical point. But it also cuts in the other direction. People enter the labor force because another family member has become unemployed, and that swells both the size of the labor force and the number of unemployed persons. From 1973 to 1975 the unemployment rate increased from 4.9 to 8.5 percent while the percentage of the noninstitutional population in the labor force also increased, from 61.4 percent, an historical record outside of World War II, to a new record high of 61.8 percent. When the unemployment rate peaked at 8.9 percent in May of 1975, the labor force participation rate was 62 percent.

It's worth noting that the 1974–75 *employment* rates consequently present a far less dismal and frightening picture than the unemployment rates. In 1975 average unemployment was 8.5 percent of the civilian labor force. That has been widely contrasted with the lower 6.8 percent unemployment rate in the recession year 1958 as well as with the less than 4 percent unemployment rates from 1966 through 1969. But if we calculate employment rates, we get a different picture. In 1958 total employment was 54.2 percent of the noninstitutional population. In 1966 it was 55.6 percent. In 1975 it was a relatively healthy 55.3 percent, much better than 1958 and not too far from 1966. The relatively high unemployment rates of the 1970s are associated with, and are in part the effect of, an exceptionally high rate of participation in the labor force. That's clearly a product of choice.

Moreover, by thinking of unemployment as involuntary, we rule out any way of distinguishing among the vast range of options that different unemployed people face. But there are significant differences between, for example, the situation of an unemployed head of household who is the sole income earner in the family and an unemployed teen-ager living with parents; a person who is and who is not receiving unemployment insurance; or a third family income earner leisurely trying to choose between several attractive employment opportunities and someone looking desperately for a job that will provide an adequate family income. Some unemployed people clearly have far poorer options than others. Surely we would not want to deny all that by lumping the unemployed into the single category of "people with no choice except to be unemployed."

It follows, then, that 670,000 persons were unemployed on an average throughout 1944 because this number of people preferred unemployment. Why? For the most part they were out of work in order to obtain a better job. They were looking or waiting. That obviously does not make them lazy or foolish. It doesn't even make them unpatriotic. Wartime demands called for numerous reallocations of labor among jobs. The individual who was looking for a higher-paying job in 1944 can also be viewed as someone trying to move from a socially less-valued to a socially more-valued task, with the competitively determined wage reflecting social priorities.

But what of 1933? Were 13 million people voluntarily unemployed? One in every four members of the labor force? Yes, strange as that answer may sound at first. They were for the most part unhappy, frustrated, and often desperate. Something had gone radically wrong with the economic system. The value of available job opportunities had diminished spectacularly and rapidly after 1929. This was the crux of the unemployment problem. Opportunities for gainful employment were so unattractive that almost 13 million people eager for job income had no better option than to be unemployed, despite the personal distress it entailed.

Once again, with all the emphasis we can muster: in defining unemployment as a consequence of choice, we are not assigning moral fault or minimizing the often tragic consequences of depressions. We are rather incorporating this problem, too, within the general analytical framework of economics, where action is assumed to result from choice of the best available opportunity.

So the BLS statistics on unemployment require considerable dissection and interpretation before they can serve as a guide to policy. No one has ever suggested that government policy should aim at a zero unemployment rate, a target that wasn't even reached at the height of World War II. Some unemployment is universally accepted as necessary if workers are to be allowed freedom of choice and if the labor market is to function as a system for reassigning workers in an economy characterized by continual change, both in technology and in the composition of demand for products. How much unemployment ought to be accepted, not as a problem but as a condition of freedom and fluidity? The answer can't simply be stated as a percentage. The tolerable or desirable minimum level of unemployment should and will increase as the opportunity cost to workers of being unemployed goes down. But unless we treat employment and unemployment as the results of choice, we cannot even talk about the opportunity cost of unemployment.

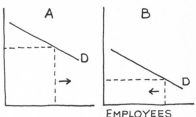

Higher wage rates draw employees into more highly valued tasks

Measuring Total Output

The experience of the Great Depression lent added impetus to private efforts that had begun in the United States around 1920 to compile reliable information on the overall performance of the economy. The best-known statistical series evolving out of these efforts is the national income and product accounts compiled by the Bureau of Economic Analysis (called the Office of Business Economics until 1972) in the United States Department of Commerce. If you read only the front page of the daily newspaper, you will have heard about gross national product. This is the most comprehensive item in the Department of Commerce accounts and the one most frequently quoted. Some people watch the behavior of GNP, as it is familiarly known, with the intensity of small boys on the morning of a picnic listening to the weather report.

What is the *gross national product*? It is *the market value of all the final goods produced in the entire economy over a given period, usually taken to be one year.* What does the GNP purport to measure, how is it related to other items in the income and product accounts, and how has it behaved over time? We shall necessarily simplify. If you don't trust simplifications, you may consult the annual National Income Issue of the *Survey of Current Business*, where you will find enough numbers to keep you thoroughly occupied for days.

Total Output Is Total Income

As the phrase *income and product* suggests, there are two ways to look at the major summary statistics in the system of accounts. Calculated in one way, they measure *the value of what is produced*. On the other side of the coin, they measure the *income earned* by the producers. The value created in one year by all the productive resources of the nation will be equal to the income made available to the owners of those resources, after appropriate adjustments. The reason, of course, is that in the long run income can come only from output and that every output constitutes income for someone. This necessary link between income and output (or product) provides part of the logical foundation for a method of analyzing aggregate fluctuations that we'll be examining in subsequent chapters.

Gross national product in 1975 was calculated at $1,498.8 billion. The income made available to individuals and households in 1975, for them to spend or save, was $1,076.7 billion. This latter figure is labeled *disposable personal income*. The difference between the two arises from deductions that governments and businesses make from the total value of output before it becomes available as disposable personal income. Business firms retain some of the income (output) produced in order to cover wear and tear on capital equipment associated with the year's production; in addition, corporations characteristically retain a portion of their net earnings rather than pay it all out to owners. Governments levy taxes of various sorts, a very large deduction from gross income as everyone knows. But governments and, to a much lesser extent, private firms, also pay out some income to persons in the form of what are called *transfer payments*. In the income and product accounts, these are income payments to persons that are deemed *not* made in return for productive services being currently rendered; pensions, social security benefits, and welfare payments are examples. The sum of these deductions, net of the additions, roughly makes up the difference between gross national product and disposable personal income.

The magnitude of the difference—$1,498.8 versus $1,076.7 billion in 1975—may prompt you to look skeptically at our previous assertion that output equals income "after appropriate adjustments." An elephant is just like a rabbit, too, after appropriate adjustments. But the deductions are income. Taxes are income claimed by government, and the deductions made by business firms are their attempt to hang on to some income rather than pay it all out to the owners of the firms.

Where Did the Output Go?

Income is desired because it permits the purchase of commodities and services. Who finally purchased the 1.5 trillion dollars worth of goods produced in 1975? The domestic purchasers of goods may be divided into consumers, government, and investors. Personal consumption expenditures in 1975 came to $963.8 billion. Government purchases of goods totaled $331.2 billion. What happened to the remainder? Most of it went into domestic investment.

Investment is defined as the purchase of capital; and capital means goods that will be employed in the production of future commodities or services. The distinction between an *investment expenditure* and a *consumption expenditure* will inevitably be somewhat arbitrary. An amateur tennis player purchases a racket for the sake of the future services he expects it to provide. Is the racket a consumption or an investment good? Family automobiles are also purchased for the sake of future services. A kitchen blender is an investment inasmuch as it is obtained for the sake of the goods it will produce in the future. But, nevertheless, the income and product accounts classify all these purchases as consumption expenditures except when they are made by business firms. If you buy a water cooler for your patio, that's a consumption expenditure. If one is purchased for the office where you work, that's an investment expenditure. The only such purchase by households that qualifies as investment in these accounts is the purchase of new housing. Here the stream of services extends so far into the future that it seems unduly misleading to count the purchase of a new residence as consumption. But the difference between automobiles and residences is one of degree. Customers, of course, usually don't worry about these fine accounting distinctions, and consider the purchase of a durable household good an investment.

Thus people say, quite correctly, that they "invested" in a clothes dryer, or a dining-room set, or new carpeting. That is completely consistent with our definition of investment. But accountants must make distinctions even if they seem to be arbitrary.

The components of investment, then, are (a) residential construction, (b) purchases of new business structures (offices, factories, stores), (c) purchases of new durable equipment (machinery), and (d) net additions to business inventories. The last item makes sure that everything produced is counted as purchased by someone. If a business firm finds itself unable to sell all the output it had hoped to sell, it is considered to have purchased that output itself and added it, reluctantly, to inventory.

In 1975 these components of investment were calculated as follows:

Residential construction	$ 48.7 billion
Nonresidential construction	52.7
Producers durable equipment	95.8
Addition to business inventories	−14.6
	$182.6

Notice that the net addition to business inventories was negative, suggesting that business firms entered 1975 with inventories larger than they preferred to carry.

One other component remains to be mentioned, a component whose significance may vastly exceed its relative size. We shall go into that question in Chapter 20. For now we shall only mention that the United States exported in 1975 $147.7 billion of commodities and services. When we offset this with the $126.5 billion of U.S. imports, we are left with $21.2 billion in what are called *net exports*.

The sum of consumer, government, investor and net foreign purchases of new goods in 1975 was $1,498.8 billion—the exact amount calculated as the gross national product. To be perfectly honest, the totals will never match exactly because there are bound to be errors and omissions in the measurement of such vast and variegated quantities as total national output and total purchases of new goods and services. But since they are equal by definition, the Bureau of Economic Analysis inserts a fudge factor and calls it Statistical Discrepancy.

The Historical Record

The history of gross national product and some of its components since 1929 is summarized in Table 16B. All figures represent billions of dollars, and are rounded to the nearest tenth of a billion.

As we noted earlier, recessions and depressions are marked by an increase in measured unemployment. They are also marked, as we would expect, by a decline in the rate of growth of gross national product. Pick out from Table 16A the years since World War II in which unemployment rose sharply. They are years in which gross national product either declined from the previous year (1949), remained basically unchanged (1954), or rose by a substantially smaller percentage than in the immediately preceding years (1958, 1960–61). The years 1970 and 1974–75 only appear to be an exception: the decline in GNP in these years is simply concealed by a rapid rise in prices (of which we'll say more a bit later). The decade of the 1930s is a whole sad history of its own.

Measuring Inflation

One more system of scorekeeping will now be introduced. All our talk about prices in preceding chapters has been about *relative prices*, or the ratios at which goods exchange for one another. Though we expressed these ratios in terms of money, we were not really interested in how much money, but rather in how much of other goods, had to be sacrificed to obtain some good in question. Thus we have so far said nothing about inflation. But inflation is an important problem and a major issue in the study of aggregate fluctuations and the struggle for economic stability.

Three Price Indices

The Bureau of Labor Statistics accumulates data on the average behavior of prices and publishes these in the form of price indices. The best known such index is the Consumer Price Index, which hits the front page of the newspapers every month whenever there is substantial public concern about inflation. Another BLS index, and one more useful for some purposes, is the Wholesale Price Index. This is not, as the name might suggest, an index of wholesale prices, that is, the prices paid by retailers. It is simply a measure of changes in the market prices of a long list of basic agricultural and industrial commodities, such as processed foods and feeds, textile products, hides, fuels, chemicals, lumber, metals, machinery, and so on.

A third widely used index of prices is the Implicit Price Deflator for gross national product, a measuring rod constructed by the Bureau of Economic Analysis. It reflects changes in the average prices of all new production of final goods, or all the items that contribute to the total of GNP. Table 16C summarizes all three indices from 1929 through 1975. (Note that the base year is different for the Implicit GNP Deflator.)

You can see clearly that prices fell sharply at the onset of the Great Depression. They fell slightly in the 1949 recession. But in 1954, 1958, and 1961, the Consumer Price Index and the GNP Deflator violated expectations by moving upward as employment moved downward. Inflation mixed with unemployment, a major concern after 1970, first showed its head in the 1950s.

Wars seem to promote inflation. The year 1951 shows conse-

TABLE 16B   Gross National Product (and components) and Disposable
Personal Income (in billions of dollars)

Year	Gross National Product	Personal Consumption Expenditures	Gross Private Domestic Investment	Net Exports of Goods	Gov't Purchases of Goods	Disposable Personal Income
1929	103.1	77.2	16.2	1.1	8.5	83.3
1930	90.4	69.9	10.3	1.0	9.2	74.5
1931	75.8	60.5	5.6	.5	9.2	64.0
1932	58.0	48.6	1.0	.4	8.1	48.7
1933	55.6	45.8	1.4	.4	8.0	45.5
1934	65.1	51.3	3.3	.6	9.8	52.4
1935	72.2	55.7	6.4	.1	10.0	58.5
1936	82.5	61.9	8.5	.1	12.0	66.3
1937	90.4	66.5	11.8	.3	11.9	71.2
1938	84.7	63.9	6.5	1.3	13.0	65.5
1939	90.5	66.8	9.3	1.1	13.3	70.3
1940	99.7	70.8	13.1	1.7	14.0	75.7
1941	124.5	80.6	17.9	1.3	24.8	92.7
1942	157.9	88.5	9.8	.0	59.6	116.9
1943	191.6	99.3	5.7	−2.0	88.6	133.5
1944	210.1	108.3	7.1	−1.8	96.5	146.3
1945	211.9	119.7	10.6	−.6	82.3	150.2
1946	209.6	143.8	30.7	7.6	27.5	158.6
1947	232.8	161.7	34.0	11.6	25.5	168.4
1948	259.1	174.7	45.9	6.5	32.0	187.4
1949	258.0	178.1	35.3	6.2	38.4	187.1
1950	286.2	192.0	53.8	1.9	38.5	205.5
1951	330.2	207.1	59.2	3.8	60.1	224.8
1952	347.2	217.1	52.1	2.4	75.6	236.4
1953	366.1	229.7	53.3	.6	82.5	250.7
1954	366.3	235.8	52.7	2.0	75.8	255.7
1955	399.3	253.7	68.4	2.2	75.0	273.4
1956	420.7	266.0	71.0	4.3	79.4	291.3
1957	442.8	280.4	69.2	6.1	87.1	306.9
1958	448.9	289.5	61.9	2.5	95.0	317.1
1959	486.5	310.8	77.6	.6	97.6	336.1
1960	506.0	324.9	76.4	4.4	100.3	349.4
1961	523.3	335.0	74.3	5.8	108.2	362.9
1962	563.8	355.2	85.2	5.4	118.0	383.9
1963	594.7	374.6	90.2	6.3	123.7	402.8
1964	635.7	400.4	96.6	8.9	129.8	437.0
1965	688.1	430.2	112.0	7.6	138.4	472.2
1966	753.0	464.8	124.5	5.1	158.7	510.4
1967	796.3	490.4	120.8	4.9	180.2	544.5
1968	868.5	535.9	131.5	2.3	198.7	588.1
1969	935.5	579.7	146.2	1.8	207.9	630.4
1970	982.4	618.8	140.8	3.9	218.9	685.9
1971	1,063.4	668.2	160.0	1.6	233.7	742.8
1972	1,171.1	733.0	188.3	−3.3	253.1	801.3
1973	1,306.3	808.5	220.5	7.4	269.9	903.1
1974	1,406.9	885.9	212.2	7.7	301.1	983.6
1975	1,498.8	963.8	182.6	21.2	331.2	1,076.7

Source: Bureau of Economic Analysis. Data for 1946–1975 reflect the comprehensive re-
vision of the national income and product accounts completed in 1975 and published in
Survey of Current Business, January 1976 (National Income Issue, Parts I and II).

Year	Consumer Price Index (1967 = 100)	Wholesale Price Index (1967 = 100)	Implicit GNP Deflator (1972 = 100)
1929	51.3	49.1	33.5
1930	50.0	44.6	32.6
1931	45.6	37.6	29.6
1932	40.9	33.6	26.6
1933	38.8	34.0	26.0
1934	40.1	38.6	27.9
1935	41.1	41.3	28.1
1936	41.5	41.7	28.2
1937	43.0	44.5	29.4
1938	42.2	40.5	29.0
1939	41.6	39.8	28.6
1940	42.0	40.5	29.0
1941	44.1	45.1	31.2
1942	48.8	50.9	35.0
1943	51.8	53.3	37.5
1944	52.7	53.6	38.4
1945	53.9	54.6	39.4
1946	58.5	62.3	44.1
1947	66.9	76.5	49.7
1948	72.1	82.8	53.1
1949	71.4	78.7	52.6
1950	72.1	81.8	53.6
1951	77.8	91.1	57.3
1952	79.5	88.6	58.0
1953	80.1	87.4	58.9
1954	80.5	87.6	59.7
1955	80.2	87.8	61.0
1956	81.4	90.7	62.9
1957	84.3	93.3	65.0
1958	86.6	94.6	66.1
1959	87.3	94.8	67.5
1960	88.7	94.9	68.7
1961	89.6	94.5	69.3
1962	90.6	94.8	70.6
1963	91.7	94.5	71.6
1964	92.9	94.7	72.7
1965	94.5	96.6	74.3
1966	97.2	99.8	76.8
1967	100.0	100.0	79.0
1968	104.2	102.5	82.6
1969	109.8	106.5	86.7
1970	116.3	110.4	91.4
1971	121.3	113.9	96.0
1972	125.3	119.1	100.0
1973	133.1	134.7	105.9
1974	147.7	160.1	116.2
1975	161.2	174.9	126.4

TABLE 16C   **Three Price Indices**

Source: Bureau of Labor Statistics and Bureau of Economic Analysis

quences of the Korean war, and prices began rising in the 1960s concurrently with escalation of the war in Vietnam. While prices rose during World War II, they rose even more rapidly in the years right after the war.

The Wholesale Price Index seems to respond more vigorously to changing conditions than does the Consumer Price Index. It falls further and rises faster. But look at the remarkable stability of the WPI from 1958 to 1964, when the CPI was creeping persistently upward. Was the price level rising in this period? It has been argued that it was not, but that the CPI was rising because consumers were shifting from commodities to services whose output could not be expanded very rapidly and whose quality improvements are more difficult to measure.

Real and Apparent Change

If prices are rising over time, figures on gross national product and its components will overstate the actual increases in output of commodities and services from year to year. To obtain a truer picture of the expansion in the nation's output and income, GNP data must be deflated by an index of prices. The Implicit Price Deflators constructed by the Bureau of Economic Analysis are used to transform GNP data into dollars of constant purchasing power. Gross national product in 1972 prices from 1960 to 1975 is given in Table 16D.

That isn't nearly as impressive as the somewhat misleading picture in Table 16B (page 222). Gross national product actually fell in 1970, 1974 and 1975. The apparent increases shown in Table 16B were due to inflation; the real value of goods produced in those years declined from the preceding year. This is consistent with what we know about the rising level of unemployment in these years and the labeling of each as a recession year.

Words to the Wise

"You can't argue with the facts," we like to say, and numbers on unemployment, prices, or GNP look like hard facts. But facts are seldom as "hard" as they seem at first glance: they require interpretation to become meaningful. We have already warned at length about the problems inherent in determining the meaning of unemployment. Price indices contain different but important ambiguities of their own. As for gross national product, do not commit the error of identifying it with gross national welfare. Much that contributes to the expansion of welfare does not enter into the income and product accounts, and some of what enters may well create more ill-fare than well-fare. Two examples will suffice to teach you caution.

Among the services not counted by the Department of Commerce statisticians in the calculation of gross national product are the services of housewives. It is too difficult to evaluate them,

despite their enormous importance, so they are completely excluded from the accounts. But the value of housekeepers' services
can be measured by the payments made to obtain them; hence
they do enter into the accounts. As a result, gross national product
will tend to decline as a direct consequence of marriages and
increase with a rising divorce rate. It is doubtful that real welfare
moves in the same direction.

When a coal-burning station generates electricity, its output
enters GNP. When people are hired to clean and paint as a consequence of the sooty fallout from the generating plant, GNP rises
once more. Overcounting obviously occurs in this case: it would
make sense, if we were interested in welfare, to *deduct* the cost of
the cleaning from the value of the electricity generated. If
Chapter 14 did not put you sufficiently on guard, then be warned
once more: the consequences for human welfare of particular
economic decisions are not always what they seem at first glance.
Systems for keeping score are useful, but they inevitably harbor
deficiencies that must be kept in mind by those who use them. And
the good life is far more (or is it far less?) than the simple sum of the
values that enter into the national income and product accounts.

Almost everything in this chapter is prelude. Our primary aim
in Chapters 17–21 will be to acquire an understanding of fluctuations in the aggregate level of economic activity. What causes
recessions and widespread unemployment? What causes the average price level to creep—and sometimes to gallop—upward? Are
there ways of controlling recessions and inflations?

TABLE 16D   Adjusted Gross National Product

Year	Gross National Product in 1972 Prices	Percentage Change from Preceding Year
1960	$ 736.8 billion	2.3%
1961	755.3	2.5
1962	799.1	5.8
1963	830.7	4.0
1964	874.4	5.3
1965	925.9	5.9
1966	981.0	5.9
1967	1007.7	2.7
1968	1051.8	4.4
1969	1078.8	2.6
1970	1075.3	−0.3
1971	1107.5	3.0
1972	1171.1	5.7
1973	1233.4	5.3
1974	1210.7	−1.8
1975	1186.0	−2.0

Source: Bureau of Economic Analysis.

Even to begin answering these questions, we must first learn something about money. Money makes its formal debut as an economic concept in the next chapter.

Once Over Lightly

Learning to understand the causes of aggregate fluctuations in the level of economic activity is an ambitious undertaking. Learning how to prevent recessions and inflation is even more difficult.

Because the economic way of thinking interprets decisions as a response to expected opportunity costs, it views employment and unemployment as a product of people's evaluation of available opportunities.

The national income and product accounts compiled by the Bureau of Economic Analysis provide valuable information on changes in the level of aggregate output and income. But gross national product is seriously deficient as a measure of changes in national welfare.

In the income and product accounts, the value of income is by definition equal to the value of output. Moreover, the value of output is also by definition equal to the value of total expenditures—although a portion of measured expenditures may be an unintended addition to business inventories.

Recessions are generally characterized by a slowdown in the rate of increase in gross national product and a rise in the unemployment rate.

Inflation means an increase in the average cost of goods in terms of money, or a decrease in the overall purchasing power of money. The Consumer Price Index as calculated by the Bureau of Labor Statistics is the most widely cited measure of inflation. Other indices of changes in the price level are the Wholesale Price Index and the Implicit GNP Deflator.

Real, as distinct from nominal, output and income is measured by dividing the current dollar value of gross national product by the GNP Deflator. Changes in the unemployment rate are more closely correlated with changes in the rate of growth of real, rather than nominal, output.

QUESTIONS FOR DISCUSSION

1. "Full employment" of the labor force is often said to be an important goal for government economic policy.
   a. What is meant by full employment of the labor force? Would you favor policies to secure full employment at all times?
   b. Why do you think it is that economic commentators tend to define full employment as 96 to 97 percent employment of the labor force? (That is, we are deemed to have achieved full employment when the BLS data show that unemployment is down to 4 or at best 3 percent of the labor force.) How do they know that it should be 96 percent rather than 95 percent or even less?
   c. Are the people being counted as unemployed in a period of full employment (as defined above) voluntarily unemployed? Can you find evidence to support the claim that jobs are always available?
   d. If the BLS unemployment figure rises to 6 percent, are all the unemployed still to be thought of as voluntarily unemployed? Defend your answer.

2. Can there be "overfull" employment?
   a. Suppose that the vacancy rate on apartments in a large city is less than 1 percent. What undesirable consequences might be associated with such a full level of apartment employment? Would you enjoy moving to a city with such a low vacancy rate?
   b. If you are driving on only 80 percent of the automobile tires you own, is the spare tire unemployed? Would you like to be driving with your tires at "full employment"? Across the Great Salt Lake Desert?

3. Jones is a tool and die maker earning $8 an hour. He is suddenly laid off.
   a. He frequents employment agencies, reads want ads, and follows up leads on tool and die making jobs for two weeks. Is he involuntarily unemployed during this time?
   b. At the end of the two weeks he is offered a job driving a bread truck that pays $4.50 a hour. He turns it down. Is he involuntarily unemployed?
   c. He receives an offer of a job as a tool and die maker in a city 125 miles away. He turns it down because his teen-age children don't want to change high schools. Is he involuntarily unemployed?
   d. After three months of searching, Jones becomes discouraged and quits looking. Is he involuntarily unemployed? Or is he no longer in the labor force?

4. Which of the following situations does *not* result in voluntary unemployment?
   a. Smith quits his job because his employer requires him to start work at 4:00 A.M.
   b. Smith is fired when he refuses to do something that his employer orders him to do but which he considers unethical.
   c. Would your answer be different if the act ordered by Smith's employer were also illegal?
   d. Smith is told that he can continue in his job only if he accepts a 75 percent cut in wages; he quits.

5. A person who is laid off from his job goes to work for himself (becomes self-employed) "producing" information about alternative job opportunities. How long he will remain self-employed in this way depends on his "productivity" (is he generating what he considers valuable information?) and the opportunity cost of this self-employment. (He'll want to continue as long as his anticipated marginal revenue exceeds anticipated marginal cost.) How will the duration of measured unemployment be affected by

a. unemployment compensation?
b. food stamp programs?
c. persistent rumors that many large firms are beginning to hire?
d. a spirit of confidence and optimism?

6. Are the hypothetical individuals who made each of the statements below voluntarily or involuntarily unemployed? How would they be classified by most people? Why would you agree or disagree with the usual classification? It is important to notice that statements such as (h) and (i) may not express different situations at all. "I don't want to work (at any job I can find)" may mean "I can't find a job (at which I want to work)."
a. "I quit my job and I'm going to remain unemployed until I find a job that pays $1000 for ten hours' work a week."
b. "I was laid off last month. I had a great job as marketing consultant to a franchising chain. They paid me $1000 a week for about ten hours of work. I'm going to keep looking until I find another job like that one."
c. "I decided I could no longer be a part of the military-industrial complex; so I quit my job. I'm looking now for an engineer's position that doesn't require me to participate in murder, pollution, and mind-raping."
d. "When Boeing laid me off, I figured I could easily find another job in engineering. But now I don't care. I'll take any job at all that pays what I used to get."
e. "I've been out of work for six months and I'm pretty desperate. I'll do anything that's legal to get food for my family. But I have an invalid wife and five small children, so I can't take any job that pays less than $100 a week."
f. "I could get any one of a dozen jobs tomorrow. But I don't want to. I'm eligible for three more months of unemployment compensation, so I'm just going to take it easy until the checks run out. Oh, if something really good turned up, I'd take it, of course."
g. "I could get any one of a dozen jobs tomorrow. But I don't want to. I'm eligible for three more months of unemployment compensation, so I'm just going to spend my time really looking. I'm going to use those three months to find the very best job I can possibly get."
h. "I don't want to work."
i. "I can't find a job."

7. Why can't a society's output increase faster than its income? Could a society's income increase faster than its output?

8. If every American had a counterfeiting operation in the back room and added $40 per week to family income by printing four 10-dollar bills each week, wouldn't this increase national income without a corresponding increase in national output?

9. The Department of Commerce statisticians strive to avoid double counting in their calculations of gross national product. Why would there be double counting if the total output of new steel products and the total output of automobiles in a given year were both included in gross national product? Do you understand how double counting is avoided by *not* counting sales of intermediate products or by counting only the value *added* by producers?

10. List some ways in which increased *inefficiency* could cause gross national product to rise. Are there any goods contributing to the total of gross national product whose rising output clearly reflects *reduced* welfare?

11. Are government purchases of commodities and services consumption expenditures or investment expenditures? They must be one or the other. Why do you suppose the Bureau of Economic Analysis groups them separately?

12. Why must total expenditures for new goods and services, by consumers, investors,

government, and foreigners, necessarily equal gross national product? What if some of the year's output is not sold?

13. If it could be shown that a rising gross national product promotes a rising level of anxiety, tension, and conflict in the population, would you favor deducting these psychological costs to obtain the true value of gross national product? How would you do so?

14. Would you favor including the services of housewives in the calculation of gross national product? What arguments could be given for doing so? Are there any good reasons for continuing to exclude these services from the calculation of GNP?

15. As an economy industrializes, a larger percentage of its population tends to enter the labor force as conventionally measured. Fewer goods intended for use in the home are produced in the home, and a larger proportion of total product passes through the marketplace. What does this imply about the validity of GNP data in industrializing societies? Will estimates of per capita income derived from GNP data tend to overstate or understate improvement over time?

16. To be certain that you understand the relationship between nominal GNP, real GNP, and the price level, try deriving either the level of GNP in current dollars (Table 16B), the level of GNP in 1972 dollars (Table 16D), or the Implicit GNP Deflator (Table 16C) from the other two for any given year.

17. How much better off financially was a person in 1967 than in 1953 if his income increased over that period by 50 percent? Use the data of the Consumer Price Index to answer. Do you think your answer overestimates or underestimates the real improvement in the person's living level. Why?

18. What is the difference between holding down the price level and holding down the price index? What are some of the things you might do if you were in charge of constructing the CPI and wanted to conceal the extent to which the price level was rising?

The Supply of Money

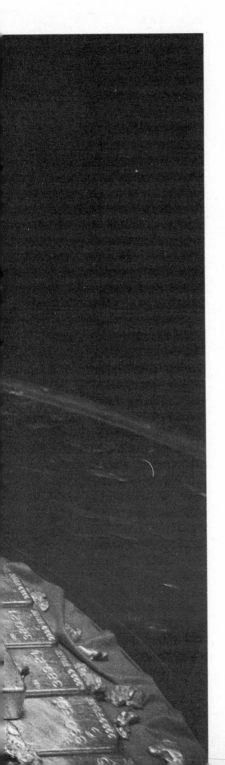

This chapter is going to discuss the supply of money in the United States. "At last," you may be thinking, "we come to something concrete. We won't have to puzzle over what the word really means, as we did with cost, efficiency, profit, or unemployment. Money is not a concept but an actual stuff, and everybody knows what the word means." Unfortunately, it just isn't so. Money is also a concept, and a rather fuzzy one at that. Let's take a look.

Money as a Unit of Accounting

You probably didn't even notice that we have come this far without discussing money. The previous chapters, after all, were replete with dollar signs, and dollars are money. But the dollars referred to so far were simply conventional units for discussing values, a common denominator that enabled us to compare and add apples and oranges, convenient transportation and unpolluted air, goods in the hand and goods in the bush, the services of engineers and the gains from exchange.

One important function of money in a social system is to provide such a unit for accounting. We might have used any other common denominator, such as bread or human labor. We could have stated the values of gasoline and sugar in terms of the number of standard loaves for which a gallon of one and a pound of the other will exchange. Or we could have expressed the gross national product as the equivalent of so many hours of "average" labor time. But we're all accustomed to thinking and talking about values in terms of dollars because we have had a lot of practice in translating the values of diverse commodities and services into dollar terms. Money functions effectively as a unit of accounting because of all the experience we've had with its more important function as a medium of exchange.

Money as a Medium of Exchange

A "medium of exchange" is just what the words say: a middle-thing used in the process of exchanging one good for another. The alternative to employing a medium of exchange is barter: exchanging the goods at our command directly for the goods we want to obtain. What do we use in the United States as our medium of exchange?

Most people who think about money think immediately of green pieces of paper, called Federal Reserve notes, and coins in various sizes and colors. Economists lump these all together and call it the currency component of the money supply. But what else do we use as a medium of exchange?

The most widely used medium of exchange is not currency but deposit credits in commercial banks, usually called checking accounts, but officially known as *demand deposits*. (Because they are deposits that can be withdrawn or transferred on demand. Savings accounts are called *time deposits* because banks may legally require advance notification of withdrawal.)

Students often have trouble at first seeing that demand deposits really are money. They themselves may handle all their transactions by means of currency, and when they receive a check, they cash it; that is, they obtain currency for the check and spend the currency. But student habits are in no way typical of the transaction procedures employed by business firms, government units, and households. The overwhelming majority of exchanges, measured in dollar value, employ demand deposits as the medium of exchange. Purchasers instruct their banks to transfer ownership of a portion of the purchasers' deposits to sellers: they write a check, in other words. Sellers typically deposit the checks rather than cash them, thereby instructing their own banks to collect the ownership whose transfer was ordered by the check writer. No currency at all will change hands. The bank in which the check is deposited will make an entry in its books; the bank on which the check is written will make an equal but opposite entry in its books.

It isn't hard to imagine a situation in which demand deposits are the only medium of exchange. As credit cards become more common, people will carry less currency and pay for more of their purchases with monthly checks. Couldn't all transactions be handled in this way? It would be possible, even though inconvenient in some cases. But currency could disappear from existence without any reduction in our use of money as a medium of exchange.

Currency plus demand deposits. Is that all? Suppose someone asks, "How much money do you have?" You would calculate the currency in your possession. Having read this far you would then add the balance in your checking account. Should you also add what you have in your savings account? You can get it out quickly or transfer it to your checking account. It's available for spending, even though savings accounts cannot be used directly as a medium of exchange. But then what of the deposit you have in a savings and loan institution? You could also convert that amount into "ready cash." And why not also the government bonds you own? They can be cashed too. How far shall we go in calculating how much money you have? Your automobile could also be converted into currency or a demand deposit. Is it therefore money?

Money as Liquidity

Notice what we've done now. We have shifted the definition of money from "the commonly employed medium of exchange" to "assets that can be exchanged in order to obtain other goods." But any asset at all, under the right circumstances, can be exchanged for other goods. Is every good therefore to be included in the money supply?

The distinguishing characteristic of money is its *liquidity*. Money is a liquid asset. The more liquid something is, the more moneylike it is. When an asset is completely liquid, it has attained the zenith of moneyness.

What do we mean by liquidity? *The liquidity of an asset refers to the cost of exchanging it for other assets.* An asset that can be exchanged for any other asset at a zero cost is a completely liquid asset. The Federal Reserve note in your wallet is an excellent example. It's an asset you can give in exchange for a great variety of other things you might want; sellers of every sort are willing to accept it without question *and without discounting it.* An asset that cannot be exchanged at all, because no one else would be willing to give anything in exchange for it, would be a completely illiquid asset. (Your toothbrush?) A Canadian dollar in Seattle may be as liquid an asset as a Federal Reserve note. Further south, away from the border, its liquidity declines, until merchants refuse to accept Canadian money altogether. If you own a government savings bond, you can exchange it for other assets; but first you'll have to incur the cost of a trip to the bank where you exchange the bond for currency. So government savings bonds are liquid assets, but they're not as liquid as Federal Reserve notes. Are they money? Just how liquid does an asset have to be to qualify as money? That turns out to be a difficult question on which competent people disagree. In this world of continuous variables and every shade of gray, assets will rarely hit either end of the liquid-illiquid continuum. Most assets are somewhat liquid. The point to remember is that an asset becomes more moneylike as it becomes more liquid, as the cost of exchanging it for other assets approaches zero.

The concept of liquidity is important in the economist's way of looking at the world. To possess liquid assets is to have a greater range of choices, better opportunities, and hence more wealth. Your wealth, by which we always mean the range of options available to you, will depend among other things upon the precise forms in which you're currently holding the goods you own, or in the useful jargon of finance, upon the *composition of your asset portfolio*. Suppose, for example, that you're in a strange city with a checkbook but no currency, and you're hungry. The restaurant signs "No Checks Accepted" establish that you are at the moment not as wealthy as you would be with $20 less in your checking account and a $20 bill in your wallet. You may also be driving an expensive sports car. But exchanging it for a meal (plus other assets) would almost certainly entail a substantial loss of wealth, because sports cars are not fully liquid assets.

We accept
Federal Reserve Notes
(eagerly)

No
Personal Toothbrushes
Accepted

How Money Creates Wealth

The advantages of using money rather than employing a barter system are enormous. The cost of exchanging would be far greater, and social wealth as a consequence far less, if there were no money to facilitate the process. In an economic system limited to barter, people would have to spend an inordinate amount of time searching for others with whom they could advantageously exchange. A violin maker would have to find a grocer, a haberdasher, an electrical utility, and a glue supplier, among many others, all willing to accept violins in return for the goods they sell. All that time devoted to searching would be time not available for violin making, and the production of violins would fall. Aware of the high costs of exchanging, people would increasingly try to produce goods for their own use, thus avoiding the necessity of searching out others from whom they can buy and to whom they can sell. Specialization would decline dramatically in a society confined to barter. And that means, of course, that people would lose the benefits that accrue from the systematic and widespread exploitation of comparative advantage. The evolution of some kind of money system in almost every known society, even when conditions were extremely unfavorable for it, is eloquent testimony to the advantages of having a generally accepted medium of exchange.

The violin maker turns his products over to those who want them without regard to the goods which these people produce for exchange. He sells the violins for money, a liquid asset that can subsequently be exchanged at no cost for whatever he wants. Everyone accepts money in exchange for other goods, at no discount, because . . . everyone accepts money in exchange for other goods at no discount! Circular reasoning? It doesn't matter. The fact is that what makes any asset acceptable in a society as a medium of exchange is the knowledge that it will be accepted by everyone else. An asset is liquid and therefore money because it can be exchanged for other goods at a negligible cost whenever the holder desires to do so.

The acceptability of money depends upon its acceptability to others.

Defining the Money Supply

So the moneyness of particular assets is a matter of degree. How then are we going to define the money supply in the United States? The answer is: somewhat arbitrarily. There just is no completely satisfactory way to decide what should be counted in the money supply and what should be excluded. A substantial number of economists believe that changes in the rate at which the money supply grows are the most important single factor causing recessions and inflations. Their contention is difficult to prove or disprove because they cannot agree on what counts as money. That isn't because they're a disputatious lot. The appropriate definition of money is a function of financial institutions and social practices that evolve over time, usually very slowly, but sometimes with dramatic suddenness.

If we adhered strictly to the definition of money as the common medium of exchange, we would want to define the money supply in the United States as the total of currency in circulation plus demand deposits at commercial banks. For that is what we use to pay for almost all our transactions. To avoid double counting we must include only the currency which is in circulation or outside the banking system. Thus when someone deposits a $20 bill in his checking account, the money supply does not change. The demand deposit component rises by $20, but currency in circulation falls by $20. If we continued to count as money the currency now in the bank's possession, we would come to the highly misleading conclusion that deposits or withdrawals of currency from checking accounts change the quantity of the exchange medium held by the community. But they obviously don't; they only change the *form* in which it is held. After you've written a check for "cash," you have exactly as much money as before, and so does everyone else.

But do we want to define money strictly as that which actually functions as the common medium of exchange? What we're really going to be after in these chapters is insight into the determinants of aggregate demand or total expenditures. That will partially depend, as we shall see, upon the amount of money people are holding relative to the quantities of other goods that they own or would like to acquire. The more money people possess, other things being equal, the more likely are they to surrender some portion of it in exchange for an alternate good when an attractive opportunity presents itself. Now it is quite clear that most people do not just look at their present stock of currency and demand deposits in deciding how much money they have. Savings held in commercial banks as time deposits and savings held in nonbank thrift institutions, such as savings and loan associations, would be regarded by most people as "available cash." So shouldn't we include these deposits in our working definition of the money supply?

The central bank of the United States, the Federal Reserve System, calculates the money supply in three principal ways and publishes each set of figures as M_1, M_2, and M_3.

M_1 is demand deposits plus currency in circulation.

M_2 is M_1 plus time deposits in commercial banks—those banks which provide checking-account service as well as accepting the deposits of savers, making loans, selling money orders, and so on.

M_3 is M_2 plus deposits in mutual savings banks and savings and loan associations—sometimes called nonbank thrift institutions.

The table below gives you some notion of the magnitude of each of these measures of the money stock. Since the money supply can and does fluctuate considerably from day to day, figures are usually expressed as averages over some period of time such as a month or a quarter. The numbers below are in billions of dollars and give the

TABLE 17A   Money Supply (in billions of dollars)

Year	M_1	M_2	M_3
1967	186.9	349.6	543.7
1970	221.4	425.3	657.0
1973	271.5	572.2	919.6

Source: Board of Governors, Federal Reserve System

averages of daily figures throughout the last month of three recent years.

The money supply (no matter which of the three ways we measure it) increased significantly between 1967 and 1973. Moreover, the percentage rates of increase varied considerably, both among the three measures of the money stock and from year to year within each measure. Why? How has this come about? Where did all this additional money come from?

Commercial Bank Lending and the Creation of Money

The basic answer is that it came about through a net expansion of commerical bank loans. *The money supply increases when commercial banks make loans to their customers and decreases when customers repay the loans obtained from commercial banks.* That's the short of the story. The long of it is a bit more complicated but not really difficult to grasp.

Suppose your application for a loan of $500 from the First National Bank is approved. The lending officer will make out a deposit slip in your name for $500, initial it, and hand it to a teller who will then credit your checking account with an additional $500. Demand deposits will have risen by $500. The money supply will be larger by that amount.

Where did the $500 come from? The bank *created* the $500 to lend you. Out of thin air? Not really. But the raw material isn't as important at this point as the fact that the bank really did create new money in making you a loan.

But suppose you don't have a checking account at First National? Then the bank can open one and start you off with a $500 balance. But suppose you don't want a demand deposit: you want the money? Slips! A demand deposit *is* money. You can use it to buy whatever it is you borrowed for. All right, but suppose you decide to withdraw your $500 right away in 20-dollar bills? Fine. The teller will accommodate you. The total of demand deposits will fall by $500, but the total of currency in circulation will increase by $500. The bank takes the currency from its vault, where it *is not* money, and gives it to you, whereupon it becomes currency held by the nonbank public or currency in circulation and hence *is* money.

Does it all seem too simple? Why don't banks keep on doing

COMMERCIAL BANK

ASSETS	LIABILITIES
+Your $500 IOU	+$500 Demand deposit

that indefinitely? It seems just like having your own money machine in the basement. We'll see in a moment that banks are
limited in their ability to make loans and thus add to the money
supply. But first let's see how the money supply is decreased.

One year later your note comes due. In the interim you've built
up your money balance to be able to pay off the loan on time. You
have $500 (plus the interest due, which we neglect for present
purposes) either in your checking account or your cookie jar. If it's
in the cookie jar, you turn it over to the bank on the due date and
money in circulation drops by $500. Note again that currency
counts as money when and only when it is held outside the banking
system.

If, as is more likely, you have the $500 in your checking account,
you write a check for that amount to the bank. The bank subtracts
$500 from your demand-deposit balance. The money supply goes
down by $500.

If you have grasped this simple process, you understand how
money, defined as M_1, is created and destroyed. Changes in the
size of M_2 and M_3 are the consequence of the public's preferences
regarding the form in which it wants to hold its stock of money
assets. But you must be wondering what has been left out. Surely
private, commercial bankers cannot create money without constraint. And you are right: they cannot. First of all, the bankers
must find people willing to borrow on the terms at which the banks
are willing to lend. Secondly, each bank must operate within the
constraint imposed by its reserves. That's the constraint which
government authorities use in their efforts to exercise control over
bank lending and hence over the process of money creation. Every
bank is legally required to hold reserves in forms specified by law. A
bank may make new loans, and thus create money, only when it has
free reserves, that is, reserves greater than the minimum amount it
is legally obligated to hold. And the Fed (the common name for
the Federal Reserve System) has the power to increase or decrease
the reserves of the banking system.

COMMERCIAL BANK	
ASSETS	LIABILITIES
− Your $500 IOU	
+ $500 curr-
ency from
your cookie
jar	

The Central Bank

The Federal Reserve System is the central bank of the United
States, created by an act of Congress in 1913. Although technically
owned by the commercial banks that are its members, the Fed is in
practical fact a government agency. Its board of governors in Washington is appointed by the president of the United States, with
the consent of the Senate. And the board effectively controls the
policies of the twelve banks that make up the system. We seem to
have twelve central banks, but this is only an appearance, a legacy
from the days when much of the country harbored a populist
suspicion of Easterners, Wall Streeters, and men in striped pants
with cutaway coats. These suspicions were allayed by scattering

banks around the country. But the Fed has actually been a single bank (with branches) at least since the legislative changes enacted by Congress in the 1930s. The power of any one of the twelve branch banks depends pretty much on the amount of influence it is able to exert on policy formation through its executive officers and research staff.

Many of the commercial banks in the United States are not subject to the rules of the Federal Reserve System. Banks holding charters from the federal government have the right to put the word "National" in their name and the obligation to join the Federal Reserve System. But many banks hold state government charters; they are permitted but not required to join the system. If they choose not to join, they operate in accordance with state definitions of reserves and state-established legal reserve minima. Although less than half of all the commercial banks in the United States belong to the Federal Reserve System, member banks have more than three-quarters of the total assets and liabilities of the entire commercial banking system. We're going to simplify this account by pretending that all banks are subject to the rules and regulations of the Fed. Since the Fed indirectly but powerfully influences the position of all banks and not just those subject to its direct regulation, this assumption won't yield a seriously misleading picture. We should note in passing, however, that the percentage of banks holding membership in the system has been decreasing in recent years, and that Fed officials believe this trend may be interfering with their ability to exercise a sufficiently precise control over the money supply.

Bank Reserves as Constraints on Money Creation

DEMAND DEPOSIT LIABILITIES:
$ 500 million

Required reserves:

8% of $2 million = $ .16m
$10\frac{1}{2}$% of $8 million = .84m
$12\frac{1}{2}$% of $90 million = 11.25m
$13\frac{1}{2}$% of $300 million = 40.5 m
$17\frac{1}{2}$% of $100 million = 17.5m

TOTAL: $ 70.25 million

Because of its power to fix legal reserve requirements for member banks (within wide limits set by Congress) and its power to expand or contract the dollar volume of reserves, the Fed controls the lending activities of the commercial banking system and thus the process of money creation. Reserve requirements differ for time deposits and demand deposits; moreover, the legal reserve requirement on demand deposits currently varies between 8 and 17.5 percent depending upon the size of a particular bank's demand deposit liabilities. Under Fed regulations that became effective in 1975, a bank with $500 million in demand deposits must hold reserves equal to 8% of the first 2 million, 10.5% of the next 8 million, 12.5% of the next 90 million, 13.5% of the next 300 million, and 17.5% of all demand deposit liabilities over 400 million dollars. (Note that demand deposits are bank *liabilities*: your bank owes you the amount in your checking account.) The Fed also decides what may count as legal reserves. Since 1960 it has been the banks' vault cash plus the deposits the commercial banks themselves have at the Federal Reserve Bank of their district. To see what all this has to do with changes in the money supply, we'll come in for a close-up look at the First National Bank of Anywhere.

Suppose that the First National Bank has demand deposit liabilities of $90 million and legal reserves of $12 million. (We ignore the complicating but for our purposes irrelevant calculations that would be necessary if we took account of other liabilities and the reserves held against them.) With a little pencil work you can quickly calculate that First has $1 million of free reserves. Against the first 2 million of those deposits it must hold an 8% reserve or $.16 million; against the next 8 million it must hold a 10.5% reserve or $.84 million; and against the remaining 80 million it must hold a 12.5% reserve or $10 million. With $12 million in actual reserves and only $11 million legally required, First National has free reserves of $1 million. The bank is therefore able to make new loans of $1 million if it can find acceptable borrowers. Let's assume it does so and watch what happens as a result.

First National extends the loans by creating new demand deposits for its borrowers. After the loans have been made, then, First has $91 million in demand-deposit liabilities and an unchanged $12 million of reserves. Since with a marginal reserve requirement of 12.5% only $.125 million of additional reserves must be held against the additional $1 million in liabilities, First will still have free reserves of $.875 million. But the bank cannot expect those new liabilities to remain on deposit. The loans were presumably taken out to finance expenditures. So the borrowers will write checks against the new deposits, payable to customers of other banks for the most part, and First National will lose reserves. To keep the example neat, we'll assume that the $1 million just borrowed is all paid out by the borrowers to depositors in other banks. Recipients of the checks deposit them in their own banks; these banks send the checks to the Fed for clearance; the Fed subtracts the amount of the checks from the reserve deposit of First National and adds it to the reserve deposits of the recipient banks; the checks are then forwarded to First National, which deducts the amount from the demand-deposit balance of the payers. At the end of this process, First National will again have $90 million in demand-deposit liabilities but now only $11 million in legal reserves.

By this process First National has converted its excess reserves into an addition to the stock of money. The new money has left First National and now exists as new demand deposits in other banks. But First National has acquired additional earning assets in the form of new loans, which was the purpose of the whole operation.

It should be clear from this brief account that excess reserves plus a demand for bank loans on the part of eligible borrowers are the two factors jointly controlling the expansion of the money supply. The Fed can therefore facilitate the growth of the money supply either by reducing the legal reserve requirements or by

FIRST NATIONAL BANK

ASSETS	LIABILITIES
+$1 mill. IOUs	+$1 mill. demand deposits

FIRST NATIONAL BANK

ASSETS	LIABILITIES
−$1 mill. reserves lost to other banks	−$1 mill. demand deposits lost to other banks

somehow increasing the dollar volume of reserves. The latter is in fact the Fed's regular operating lever in money management, through a process we'll describe in a moment. Postponing that question, however, we want to trace out what happens when reserves increase.

The Effect of Changes in Bank Reserves

Go back to the case of First National. We started the bank out with $1 million in free reserves. Suppose those reserves had just been created by the Fed because it wanted to expand the supply of money. We traced through the process by which the lending of the reserves added $1 million to the stock of money. But that won't be the end of the matter. A one-dollar change in reserves tends to cause an eventual change of *several* dollars in the money stock. That's why bank reserves are sometimes called "high power money."

To see why this is so, look at the new position of the banks in which that freshly created money was deposited. They jointly acquired $1 million in additional demand deposits plus $1 million in additional reserves. Remember that when the Fed cleared the checks, it transferred a corresponding volume of reserves from the account of First National to the accounts of the recipient banks. So those banks acquired, dollar for dollar, new reserves to match their new demand deposits.

Under a fractional reserve banking system (where reserves need only be some fraction of deposits), new deposits plus matching new reserves create free reserves. Just to keep matters simple, assume that all the deposits flow to banks in the $10–100 million category so that they are all subject to a 12.5 percent legal reserve requirement. These banks will consequently find themselves with $.875 million in free reserves. If they don't want to hold the reserves and can find acceptable borrowers, they can now make new loans in that amount, thereby creating an additional $.875 million of new money. But that still isn't the end, because the banks in which this newly created money is eventually deposited will acquire free reserves. There will now be $.875 million of new demand deposits plus $.875 million of new reserves, which amounts to a $765,625 addition to free reserves (if the applicable reserve requirement is still 12.5 percent). The whole process can thus repeat itself again.

The "Money Multiplier"

The essential point is a simple one which should not get lost in the arithmetic. When the Fed (or any other factor) adds one dollar to bank reserves, it enables the commercial banking system to create several dollars of additional money. Exactly how many additional dollars will depend upon the applicable reserve requirement and the extent to which the new money created is shifted out of demand deposits. Some portion of newly created demand deposits does tend to be withdrawn into circulating currency. Currency in circulation is no longer vault cash and hence it's a deduction from reserves. And that "leakage" of reserves will reduce the value of the "money multiplier."

To illustrate: If all banks were subject to a 12.5 percent marginal reserve requirement, if all free reserves were loaned out, and there were no leakage of currency into circulation (and no transfers from demand deposits into time deposits), then $1 of new reserves would lead to the creation of $8 in additional money. Why exactly $8? Because $1 + (.875) + (.875)(.875) + (.875)^3 \ldots$, the expansion path of the money creation process, ultimately approaches $1 \times 1/.125$, or 8.

The actual money multiplier for M_1 is much less than that, running in recent years between 2 and 3. A multiplier of 2.5 would result from some combination such as an average applicable reserve requirement of 15 percent and a 25 percent leakage of currency into circulation—which would occur if the public withdrew $1 in currency for every $4 added to the money stock. Of course, whether the money multiplier is 2 or 8 or anything in between, the expansion process depends upon the ability of banks to locate eligible borrowers. So it takes time; it doesn't occur instantaneously.

$$1 + .6 + .6^2 + .6^3 + \ldots + .6^n = 2.5$$

The discussion has been carried on in terms of reserve creation, additional loans, and more money. It also works in reverse, of course. When reserves are reduced by an action of the Fed, the power of banks to lend is contracted. When a bank's reserves fall below the legal minimum, it reduces its rate of new loans below the rate at which old loans are being repaid in order to acquire the additional required reserves. If the entire banking system is doing this, the result is a net contraction of loans and hence a reduction in the money supply. Eventually, through the acquisition by the commercial banks of additional currency and the reduction of demand deposits as the public repays loans, the legal minimum reserve-to-deposit ratio will be reached. The process of contraction will stop.

The Tools Used by the Fed

How does the Fed actually go at the job of expanding or contracting the money supply? The most powerful tool and the one that sets the stage for the rest is the authority to establish legal reserve requirements. Changes in reserve requirements are generally viewed by Fed officials as a blunt weapon, not suitable for the delicate surgery that monetary management usually requires. They prefer to take the reserve requirements as the framework and alter the volume of reserves.

How is that done? The briefest explanation is that the Fed creates and destroys reserves in the same way that commercial banks create and destroy money: by extending and contracting loans.

The Fed can extend a loan to a commercial bank directly. It does so by crediting the bank's reserve account and taking in return the bank's IOU or someone else's IOU (a government bond, for example) that happens to be in the bank's portfolio—just as a commercial bank lends to its customers by creating a deposit balance in return for an IOU. The interest rate at which such loans are made is called the *discount rate*. It's a financial-page celebrity because many people look upon it as a sign of current Fed policy. It probably is more of a symbol than a genuine rationing device since the Fed is selective about the banks to which it will loan. Official Fed policy is to accommodate special circumstances rather than loan to any bank willing to pay the rate, and to behave more like a Dutch uncle than a profit-seeking lender. But that's what most people look for from a central bank.

The principal technique that the Fed employs is the purchase and sale of United States government securities in what are called *open market operations*. The Fed currently holds a portfolio of government securities approaching a value of $100 billion. When it increases its holdings by purchasing securities through dealers in government bonds, it writes checks for the amount of the purchases on its own credit. These checks are deposited in commercial banks. When the banks forward the checks to their Federal Reserve Bank, they are credited with additions to their reserve balances.

In short, the acquisition by the Federal Reserve Banks of new earning assets, which is the same thing as the extension of credit to someone, whether the government or banks, tends to increase commercial bank reserves by that amount. And that, as we have seen, enables commercial banks to increase their own loans and thereby the money supply.

The entire process is reversible. The Fed can withdraw credit from member banks or sell some of the government securities already in its asset portfolio. This results in a reduction of commercial bank reserves. For example, when the Fed sells a $1000 government bond, the bond winds up in the hands of someone who pays the bond dealer with a check. But the dealer in turn pays the Fed with a check, and the amount of the check is deducted from the reserve account of the bank on which it is drawn. That wipes out a portion of the total reserves of the banking system.

FEDERAL RESERVE BANKS

ASSETS	LIABILITIES
+ Government bonds	+ Commercial bank reserves

COMMERCIAL BANKS

ASSETS	LIABILITIES
+ Reserve accounts	+ Demand deposits

Who Is Really in Charge?

Open market operations, as we said, are the principal working tool of monetary management. A special committee, made up of the seven members of the board of governors and five of the twelve Reserve Bank presidents, sits as the Open Market Committee and continuously determines the direction of monetary policy. The question of the effectiveness with which the Open Market Committee manages the money supply has long been debated by friends and critics of the Fed, both among economists and politicians.

There are two main questions. One is the determination of policy. Does the Fed set appropriate goals? Does it try to do what it ought to be doing? The other is the execution of policy. Does the Fed do an effective job of achieving the goals it sets for itself? The questions are related, of course, because intelligent policy formulation presupposes a realistic assessment of technical capabilities. The football coach who orders a passing strategy when his team is two touchdowns behind in the fourth quarter is making a poor policy decision if his quarterback has a rubber arm and all his receivers have butterfingers. Beware of textbook accounts which, like football plays on the blackboard, gloss over problems of execution and assume that the opposition isn't doing any planning of its own. It's a gross oversimplification to suppose that the Fed has a monetary brake and a monetary accelerator with which it adjusts the money supply as quickly and surely as you slow down and speed up your car in traffic. Monetary management may be more like driving a balky mule train which sometimes refuses to go and sometimes won't stop going even when firmly ordered to halt. To make matters worse, there are a bunch of bickering back seat drivers on the wagon and some of them aren't above shouting their own instructions or even trying to grab the reins. We'll return to these problems in later chapters when we examine monetary policy.

Why Should Banks Hold Reserves?

Throughout our description of money and the banking system we have treated reserves as constraints upon the power of banks to make loans and thus to expand the money supply. That seems to have little or nothing to do with the concept of a reserve fund, something that can be drawn upon in an emergency. But legal reserves do not in fact perform a significant reserve function. The reserve requirement is today primarily a control lever that enables the monetary authorities to adjust the stock of money in the hands of the public.

But isn't it necessary for the banks to hold reserves against the possibility of a "run" by depositors? If a lot of depositors suddenly lost confidence in a bank for some reason and tried to withdraw their deposits in currency, the bank would be unable to honor those withdrawals. And if that happened, the loss of confidence might spread to other banks and bring down a large part of the banking system.

There actually hasn't been a financial panic like that in the United States for over 40 years. The reason, however, has little to do with the level of bank reserves. Bank customers no longer rush to withdraw their deposits on every rumor of financial trouble because their deposits are now insured by the Federal Deposit Insurance Corporation. If a bank closes, for whatever reason, its depositors can expect reimbursement within a few days. Some critics argued when the FDIC was established in 1935 that the premiums it charged banks to insure their deposits were far too low, and that the FDIC would go broke trying to pay off depositors when banks closed their doors. But the very existence of the FDIC ended the phenomenon of bank runs; and in the absence of runs, banks no longer failed the way they formerly did. The FDIC premiums have thus proved more than adequate. And the institution of the FDIC has turned out to be probably the single most stabilizing reform of the 1930s.

Some credit must also go to improved Federal Reserve procedures since the 1930s. The Fed now understands clearly that it has the responsibility to provide short-term liquidity to the banking system, without regard to the amounts banks happen to be holding as reserves. Thus a bank today can meet any demand for currency, however large, by securing additional currency from the Fed. If the bank were to use up its entire reserve balance, the Federal Reserve Bank would simply loan the bank additional reserves, taking as collateral some of the IOU's in the asset portfolios of the borrowing bank. Banks are granted access to this "discount privilege" whenever they have a legitimate demand for additional reserves; and this has made the whole banking and monetary system more flexible in response to changing conditions as well as more resistant to crises and temporary dislocations.

What about Gold?

But hasn't something important still been left out of all this? If reserves aren't really reserves, what is it that provides backing for money? Doesn't money have to have some kind of backing? And where does gold fit into the picture?

The conviction that money must have "backing" if it is to have value raises an interesting question. What stands behind the backing to give it value? And behind the backing of the backing? But the whole set of questions is misdirected. In economics, value is the consequence of scarcity. And scarcity is the result of demand plus limited availability. It is clear enough why there exists a demand for money: it can be used to obtain all sorts of other things that people want, which is to say that it is accepted as a medium of exchange. The other part of the picture, limited availability, is taken care of, more or less effectively, by the monetary managers. No "backing" is required. If this makes you nervous or causes you to doubt the value of your currency or checking account, you can easily shore up your faith by "selling" your money to others. You will find that they are willing to take it and to give you other valuable assets in exchange.

Commercial Banks

Assets	Liabilities
− Vault cash	− Demand deposits
− IOUs	
+ Vault cash	

The critical factor in preserving the value of money is limited availability and confidence that the supply will continue to be limited. Nature has made gold relatively rare. It's up to the Fed to keep Federal Reserve notes and demand deposits relatively rare. But some people have more confidence in the reliability of nature than in the reliability of central bankers and governments. That is why some intelligent and well-informed people would like to see us return to a genuine gold standard, under which currency could be exchanged for gold at some fixed ratio. It is not because they think that money must have backing, but because they distrust governmental money managers. If the government were required to maintain the convertibility of demand deposits into currency, and currency into gold at predetermined exchange ratios, the limited availability of gold would severely restrict the government's power to increase the money supply.

As a matter of fact, governments are often tempted, especially in wartime, to create additional money as a way of financing expenditures without the painful necessity of openly levying taxes. And they haven't always resisted the temptation. The consequence has usually been inflation, a more concealed but hardly a more equitable way for the government to finance its expenditures. Urging a return to the gold standard would seem to be a counsel of despair, however. A government so irresponsible that it must be reined in by gold would be most unlikely to adopt a gold standard, and even more unlikely to respond to the pressure of such a rein. The problem of irresponsible government is a weighty one; but we cannot believe that the problem could be solved through a return to the gold standard.

Consideration of that issue does, however, raise the question of government spending, taxation, and deficits. The canons of financial orthodoxy long decreed that a government must *balance its budget*. The failure to do so was regarded as a clear sign of irresponsibility, and persistence in such a course as a guarantee of eventual economic disaster. That view was challenged head-on in the 1930s by the argument that government deficits, under the proper circumstances, were a powerful tool for the creation of prosperity. A new way of thinking about the interrelations between income, expenditure, deficits, money, and interest rates evolved, a way of thinking often referred to as "the Keynesian revolution." That's the subject to which we turn next.

Once Over Lightly

Money is a social institution that increases wealth by lowering costs of exchange, thereby enabling people to specialize more fully in accordance with their comparative advantages.

The moneyness of any asset is a matter of degree. An asset is money insofar as it is liquid. An asset is completely liquid when it can be exchanged for other goods at no cost. Whatever assets everyone freely accepts as a medium of exchange make up a society's stock of money.

In the United States today the stock of money is primarily the total of currency held outside the banking system plus the demand-deposit liabilities of commercial banks. But other assets, such as time deposits, which can be converted into currency or demand deposits at negligible cost, also contribute to overall liquidity and ought to be included in more comprehensive measurements of the money stock.

The money supply increases or decreases primarily as commercial banks expand or contract their lending.

The managers of the Federal Reserve System have the responsibility for regulating the size of the money stock. The Fed does so by controlling bank lending through its power to set the legal ratio between commercial bank liabilities and reserves and to expand or contract those reserves through loans to commercial banks and through open market operations.

The idea that money must have "backing" to have value is not correct. Money must only be acceptable as a medium of exchange to have value. The Fed maintains its acceptability by restricting the total supply.

QUESTIONS FOR DISCUSSION

1. Would your existence be more or less secure if we had a barter economy rather than one employing money? Why would we all be poorer if we had to rely exclusively on barter? Is a very poor person subject to 5 percent fluctuations in his income more or less secure than a wealthy person subject to 50 percent fluctuations in his income?

2. Can you think of any ways in which concentration on money obscures the real working and effects of economic events? What about an argument that the government of India could attack poverty by printing more rupees and distributing them to the poorest people?

3. Shares of common stock listed on a major exchange can be sold quickly—that is, exchanged for other assets. Is stock as liquid as money? Why might a person hold part of his wealth in common stocks and part in money? Why might he shift the composition of his portfolio in order to hold more of one asset and less of the other?

4. If you were to ask someone how much money he has in the bank, he might not distinguish in answering between his checking-account and his savings-account balance. Why would economists want to distinguish between the two?

5. At any moment in time some already printed Federal Reserve notes will be in (a) the wallets of the public, (b) the vaults and tills of commercial banks, (c) the vaults of Federal Reserve Banks. How does each enter into or otherwise affect the total money supply?

6. If money is created by bank lending, is it also created by the lending of savings and loan associations, credit unions, and consumer credit companies?

7. How does a withdrawal of currency from checking accounts affect the money supply? How does it affect a bank's reserves? How does it affect free reserves? What effect might this withdrawal subsequently have on the money supply?

8. People cannot spend the deposits they hold in commercial bank savings accounts or savings and loan institutions without first withdrawing the funds, that is, converting them into currency or demand deposits. But since they are able to do that at almost no cost, these deposits are assets almost as liquid as checking-account balances.

   a. Does it follow that total spending ought to be more closely correlated with M_3 than with M_1?

   b. What does a faster rate of increase in M_3 than in M_1 suggest about the public's spending *intentions*?

9. If bankers can create money, why can't you? Is it against the law for you to create an accepted medium of exchange? Can you think of a situation in which you might succeed in creating a little money? (HINT: Demand deposits, which serve as money, are liabilities of commercial banks; suppose your promissory notes were considered in the community "as good as gold"?)

10. Use the information provided in the text to test your understanding of the relationship between bank reserves and money creation.

    a. Fog National Bank has $1 billion in demand-deposit liabilities. How many dollars must it legally hold as reserves against these deposits? Do you get an answer of $157.75 million?

    b. Suppose Fog Bank has $160 million in reserves. If we ignore time deposits and the reserves which they require, how large are the bank's free reserves?

    c. If the managers of Fog Bank prefer to maintain $2 million of reserves in addition to the minimum legal requirement, how large are Fog Bank's *excess* reserves?

    d. Fog Bank loans its excess reserve of $250,000 to the Lovers Lanes Company for the purchase of new pin-setting equipment. When the equipment supplier deposits the $250,000 check in the River National Bank, which has total demand-deposit liabilities of $200 million, what effect does this have on the River Bank's free reserves?

    e. River Bank extends a new loan of $216,250 to a silver processor, who uses it to purchase silver from a mine in Two Cushion, Montana. The Two Cushion Bank, where the check is deposited, has total demand-deposit liabilities of $7 million. How much will the deposit add to the bank's free reserves?

    f. The silver mine in Two Cushion uses all the money received to pay its employees. None of the miners maintains a bank account. They all cash their weekly checks and use currency to handle their purchases. What will happen to the Two Cushion Bank's free reserves right after payday?

    g. If all the merchants in Two Cushion use the local bank, what will happen to the bank's liabilities and reserves over the course of the week?

11. Money gets a lot of attention but tends to have a bad press. Are the authors of the following statements talking about money as we have defined it? Or are they using money as a synonym or symbol for something else? What is that "something else" in each case where you conclude that money is not really the subject of discussion?

    a. "The love of money is the root of all evil." (Often misquoted as "Money is the root of all evil.")

    b. "Health is . . . a blessing that money cannot buy."

    c. "If this be not love, it is madness, and then it is pardonable. Nay, yet a more certain sign that all this: I give thee my money."

    d. "Wine maketh merry; but money answereth all things."

    e. "Words are the tokens current and accepted for conceits, as moneys are for values."

f. "Money speaks sense in a language all nations understand."

12. To an employee, a bank is a place, people, and activities. But to an economist banks are often nothing but assets and liabilities in motion. Simplified asset and liability statements are given below for the Federal Reserve Banks and the Commercial Banking System, each viewed as a single composite bank.

Federal Reserve Banks

assets	liabilities
_____	_____
_____	_____
_____	_____
_____	_____

Commercial Bank System

assets	liabilities
_____	_____
_____	_____
_____	_____
_____	_____

a. Insert each of the following dollar amounts (in billions) into the appropriate place or places above. Don't worry if the assets aren't equal to liabilities; these are only partial statements of bank positions.)

   $80 U.S. government securities owned by the Fed
   55 U.S. government securities owned by commercial banks
   3 U.S. Treasury deposits with the Fed
   215 Demand deposits owned by the public
   8 Federal Reserve notes in commercial bank vaults
   200 IOU's of customers who have borrowed from commercial banks
   2 Member bank borrowings from the Fed
   30 Member bank reserves on deposit with the Fed
   65 Currency in circulation outside the banking system
   4 Treasury tax and loan account at commercial banks

b. How large is M_1?
c. The public decides to increase its holding of currency to $70 billion by reducing demand deposits to $210 billion. How might this additional currency be supplied and how would that affect the asset and liability components above?
d. What would be the effects of a Fed purchase of $2 billion in government securities from the commercial banks? What would be the effects of a purchase from the nonbanking public?
e. Trace the effects on various assets and liabilities if the Treasury borrows an additional $5 billion from the Fed and subsequently spends that amount for goods purchased from the public? What difference would it make if the Treasury borrowed from the commercial banks?
f. What would be the effect if the Treasury borrowed from the Fed and just kept the borrowed funds idle in its account at the Fed? Suppose it kept the borrowed funds idle in its tax and loan accounts with the commercial banks?
g. Where else could the Treasury go to borrow? What effects would you expect on the bank asset and liability statements if the Treasury spent money after borrowing it from the nonbank public?

13. If the Treasury were to sell bonds to the Fed and then purchase goods and services with the proceeds, the money supply would increase. If resources in the economy were

already fully employed, where would the goods and services purchased by the government come from? What would happen to prices? Do you agree that "inflation is a tax"?

14. Many people worry about the size of the national debt. (We'll examine that concern in Chapter 19.) The marketable debt of the United States government (the savings bonds that many individuals own are not marketable, because they cannot be bought and sold on the open market) currently stands at around $300 billion. Suppose the Fed, a government agency, bought up all outstanding marketable securities, so that—in a sense—the government only owed the debt to itself. How could this be done? What would happen as a result?

15. You're the manager of a commercial bank and you want to increase your bank's free reserves. Perhaps you currently have *negative* free reserves—in which case your bank is borrowing from the Fed and the Fed may be putting pressure on you to remove that debt. Or you may simply believe that your bank would be in a more advantageous position with a somewhat higher level of free reserves. What policies could you pursue to reach your objective? What effects would these policies have on the banking and monetary system?

16. Why does the Fed use open market operations as its principal tool of monetary management rather than changes in legal reserve requirements?

17. Why might the Fed find it significantly easier to expand the money supply in a period of prosperity than in a period of falling output and rising unemployment?

18. There were 14,338 commercial banks in the United States as of June 30, 1974. One-third of these, or 4695, were national banks and therefore required to maintain membership in the Federal Reserve System. Only 1068, one-ninth of all state banks, chose membership in the system, down from one-sixth of all state banks ten years earlier. Do you think membership should be required for all banks? How would you assess the political chances for such a proposal?

19. If it is *not* essential that money have "backing" of some kind, why do so many people believe otherwise?

20. "Nature has made gold rare but people have made it scarce." Explain.

Income-Expenditures
Analysis

John Maynard Keynes was born in 1883 and died in 1946. In between he made a modest fortune in the stock market, married a prima ballerina, edited the official journal of the Royal Economic Society, composed brilliant biographical sketches, served as a Treasury representative at the Versailles peace conference, resigned that position to write a scathing attack on the Treaty and its architects, was raised to the peerage to become Lord Keynes, and helped design the international monetary system that was put into effect after World War II. He did a great deal more, for he was a brilliant, versatile, and energetic man. But he achieved enduring fame because he wrote two books about money: the first was published in 1930, and the second was written out of dissatisfaction with the first immediately after its publication. The second and far more famous book was *The General Theory of Employment, Interest and Money.*

Origins of the General Theory

The *General Theory* is by common agreement an obscure and badly organized book. "What the *General Theory* Means" was a topic for numerous essays and symposia, evidence both that its meaning was deemed important and that few were certain just what the meaning was. Books and articles on what Keynes *really* meant are still appearing four decades after the publication of the *General Theory.* All commentators agree on this, however: Keynes was convinced that the economic analysis in which he had been trained could not diagnose and prescribe a cure for depressions, because its approach to the question actually assumed the problem away.

What do we observe in a period of depression or recession? Workers unable to find jobs because employers are not hiring because products cannot be sold. An imbalance, it would appear, between quantities demanded and quantities supplied. A surplus, or in the language of the nineteenth-century economists, an excess of supply.

The economist's solution to a surplus is a lower price. If workers cannot find jobs, it's because they're holding out for a wage that's above their marginal productivity; at some lower wage all those who want work will be able to find it. If producers cannot sell their entire output, it's again because they're asking too high a price; useful goods can always be sold at a sufficiently low price. It's a matter of supply and demand. A recession is simply a temporary disequilibrium. It will come to an end when prices and wages move to their equilibrium or market-clearing levels.

Time and Uncertainty

But how long will this take? It only happens instantaneously on the supply and demand graphs of economists. In the real world, market clearing prices must be searched for, and that process may take weeks, months, or even longer. In the interim the world does not stand still. Unemployed workers reduce their spending because they are no longer receiving income, which further reduces the demand for goods. Producers who find themselves with unwanted additions to their inventories cut back production, laying off more workers and reducing the demand for the other goods they use as inputs. Might not an excess supply of labor and produced goods cause a downward spiral in income and demand before prices had fallen far enough to eliminate the surpluses? In that case prices would have to fall still farther to close the gap between supply and demand. Don't recessions in fact display just such a cumulative pattern of declining production, reduced income, further declines in production, and further reduced income?

The timeless equilibrium analysis of traditional economics does not examine the groping process by which new equilibrium positions are found. It assumes, in effect, an instantaneous leap to a new equilibrium whenever an old equilibrium is disturbed. But if the causes of recessions are to be found in what happens while the economy is out of equilibrium, then the traditional analysis has indeed assumed the problem away.

The importance of expectations in shaping economic decisions in a monetary, as distinct from a barter, economy impressed Keynes very strongly. An emphasis on expectations meant an emphasis on the uncertainty of decision making, the frequency of mistakes, the need for time in which to adjust to unanticipated events, and the disorder of economic systems. None of this was captured in the timeless, orderly, errorless world of traditional equilibrium analysis. In the *General Theory* Keynes sought to explain the phenomenon of recession by taking into account the consequences of uncertainty and the processes of adjustment over time. This was the origin of income-expenditures analysis.

A Simple Keynesian Model

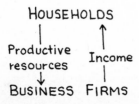

In order to present the logic of income-expenditures analysis, we're going to construct a very simplified economic system in which the relationships between key variables are clearly specified. (Economists refer to such systems as *models*.) We shall postulate an economy with no government and no foreign trade. There are only households and business firms. The households supply productive resources to the business firms which produce all goods, and the business firms in return pay out all income to the households. The goods produced will either be purchased by the households for consumption or purchased by business firms themselves for investment. (Thus we're abstracting from any investment expenditures by households.) The income paid out to households will either be consumed or saved.

The production decisions of business firms are made in anticipation of demand, both from the households as consumers and from other business firms as investors. Suppose that business produces $450 billion of consumption goods and $100 billion of investment goods. By definition, since the value of income is identical to the value of output, $550 billion of income is paid out to households. If the households save $100 billion of this amount and spend the other $450 billion on the consumption goods that were produced, and if business firms borrow that $100 billion of saving and spend it on the investment goods that were produced, all will be well. Everything produced for sale was purchased. There was no excess supply or excess demand at the end of the "period."

But now suppose that business firms had failed to anticipate demand correctly. Let's assume that business firms only want to purchase $80 billion of investment goods. (Firms for the most part purchase investment goods from other firms.) Twenty billion dollars of the total $550 billion in output will consequently not be sold as planned. It will become an unintended addition to the inventories of the producing firms. Because additions to inventory are investment, actual as distinct from intended investment will still be $100 billion. But now all will not be well. Some business firms clearly made mistakes. There was an excess supply of goods that showed up in undesired additions to business inventories.

The Response to Unintended Investment

What is likely to happen? The firms whose inventories are now excessive will want to cut back production in the next period. How far they cut it back will depend upon their new estimates of future demand. Suppose they decide that the unexpectedly low demand in the previous period was due to unique conditions that won't be repeated and so they again plan to offer $450 billion of consumption goods and $100 billion of investment goods. They will nonetheless *produce* only $80 billion of investment goods (plus $450 billion of consumption goods) and plan to make up the difference out of the inventories reluctantly accumulated during the previous period.

This could work out as planned. Total income will be $530 billion with output reduced to that level. If households purchase $450 billion of consumption goods and save $80 billion, while business firms purchase the expected $100 billion of investment goods, producer expectations will be fulfilled. There will be no

HOUSEHOLDS

Consumption expenditures — Consumer goods

BUSINESS FIRMS

Investment expenditures — Investment goods

INCOME ≡ Consumption + Saving

OUTPUT ≡ Consumption + Investment

OUTPUT: 550

CONSUMPTION: 450
INTENDED
INVESTMENT: 80
UNINTENDED
INVESTMENT: 20
____
550

SAVING: 100

OUTPUT: 530

CONSUMPTION: 450
INVESTMENT
PURCHASES: 100
INVENTORIES: −20
____
530

SAVING: 80

excess supply or demand. Note that total investment will be only $80 billion, matching total saving, because the $20 billion reduction in inventories is negative investment.

The Consumption Function

But is such an outcome at all likely? In particular, with household income reduced by $20 billion as a result of reduced production, can we expect consumption to hold at $450 billion? Keynes asserted that we could not expect this because aggregate consumption spending in any period will depend primarily upon the aggregate income of that period. Consumption spending will change in the same direction as income changes, though by a somewhat smaller amount than the change in income. He called this relationship the *propensity to consume* or *consumption function*. It is the key to the income-expenditures model.

Suppose that for every $100 change in aggregate income, aggregate consumption expenditure changes by $75. The *marginal propensity to consume* (the change in consumption divided by the change in income) is then .75. With a marginal propensity to consume of .75, aggregate consumption will be only $435 billion rather than the $450 billion anticipated by the firms selling consumption goods. And so there will again be some unintended investment. Total business inventories will not be reduced to the desired level.

Let's summarize the outcome during this period in two columns, the first showing what business firms planned for and the second showing what actually occurred.

marginal propensity to consume:

$$\frac{change\ in\ consumption}{change\ in\ income}$$

Intended output:	$530 billion	Actual income:	$530 billion
Planned sales of consumption goods:	450	Actual sales of consumption goods:	435
Intended investment:	80	Actual investment:	95

The *intended* investment total is made up of $100 billion in expenditures for new investment goods minus a $20 billion reduction in inventories from the preceding period. The *actual* investment total results from a net reduction of inventories by only $5 billion, as a result of the decline in consumption spending caused by the decline in income that resulted from the reduced output that was a response to an excess output of investment goods in the preceding period.

Note once again that actual investment is equal to actual saving: $530 billion in income minus $435 billion in consumption expenditures equals $95 billion of saving. Business firms implicitly expected households to reduce their aggregate saving by $20 billion in response to that $20 billion fall in income, for that is the only way in which consumption could have held at the hoped for level of $450 billion. But that assumes a marginal propensity to consume of zero: a change in income leading to no change in consumption. With an actual marginal propensity to consume of .75, the marginal propensity to save is .25 rather than 1.0. Saving falls by only $5 billion when income falls by $20 billion, and so $15 billion of expected sales to consumers fails to materialize, and business inventories at the end of the period are consequently $15 billion larger than intended.

As a result the economy is still out of equilibrium. What will happen next under the assumptions we're using? Business firms will again curtail production in an effort to reduce inventories to desired levels. But that will further reduce income, which will induce a further fall in consumption, which will again frustrate the sales expectations of business firms.

The income-expenditures model which we have just described in a very summary form presents a variant type of supply and demand analysis in which supply and demand are allowed to influence one another. A change in demand does not encounter an unchanged supply curve to bring about a new equilibrium. Rather the change in demand changes supply, the changed supply affects income and hence demand, the further change in demand once again changes supply, and equilibrium is finally reached through a series of mutual accommodations. The model describes a process of mounting frustration for participants in the economic system rather than the rapid accommodation to changed circumstances, largely through price changes, that would occur if decision makers had perfect information. It explains how output can fall and unemployment can rise contrary to anyone's intentions.

A Graphical Exposition

The model lends itself readily to a graphical exposition which will highlight the basic logic of the process we're trying to describe. Output and income are measured along the horizontal axis and represented by the letter Y (in accordance with a custom Keynes introduced in the *General Theory*). Consumption, saving, and investment (C, S, and I, respectively) are measured on the vertical axis.

By our assumptions, consumption is $450 billion when income is $550 billion, and it changes by .75 of any change in income. We therefore draw the consumption function to pass through the point measuring $450 billion on the vertical and $550 billion on the horizontal axis, and we give it a slope of .75 to show the marginal propensity to consume. (The slope is the vertical change divided by the horizontal change, or the change in consumption

vertical change

horizontal change

divided by the change in income—the definition of the marginal propensity to consume.)

Since income minus consumption is by definition saving, we can plot the saving function on the basis of the consumption function. The 45-degree line extending up from the origin marks off all positions of equality in the graph space between what is being measured on the horizontal and on the vertical axes. The vertical distance between that line and the consumption function therefore represents saving at any level of income. When income is $550 billion, saving is $100 billion. With a marginal propensity to consume of .75, the marginal propensity to save must be .25; the saving function consequently has a slope of .25.

Notice that the consumption and saving functions show the *intentions* of households with respect to consumption expenditure and saving. The actual level of each will depend upon income. Producers originally expected to sell $450 billion of consumption goods and $100 billion of investment goods. So they produced $550 billion in output and generated $550 billion of income. But unknown to producers, investors only intended to spend $80 billion. Intended investment is shown on the graph as a horizontal line at $80 billion.

The actual outcome was therefore $450 billion of consumption expenditures, $80 billion of *intended* investment expenditures, and $20 billion of *unintended* investment expenditures in the form of unwanted additions to inventory. The economy was in "disequilibrium."

Producers tried to reduce their inventories in the next period by curtailing production of investment goods to $80 billion. They anticipated $100 billion of investment purchases, and we have assumed it materialized in the next period. But, nevertheless, equilibrium was not achieved. For the $20 billion reduction in output reduced income by $20 billion, and consumption fell as a result, by $15 billion, to $435 billion. The total intended investment by business firms was $100 billion minus the $20 billion planned reduction in inventories. But inventories of consumer goods unexpectedly rose by $15 billion, and actual investment turned out to be $95 billion.

So producers collectively reduce output once more, this time by $15 billion, in order to sell off their unwanted inventories of consumer goods. But that reduces income by $15 billion and hence consumption falls again, this time by $11.25 billion ($15 billion × .75). Disequilibrium persists and production is reduced once more.

Where will it stop? It will stop when actual results match intended results. (That's the meaning of equilibrium in economic analysis.) But this will not occur until output and income have fallen from $550 to $470 billion, consumption has fallen from $450 to $390 billion, and saving has fallen from $100 to $80 billion. With actual saving reduced to $80 billion by declining income, intended saving and intended investment will be equal. And this is

Income falls by 20
then by (.75) 20
then by (.75)² 20
then by (.75)³ 20
* * *
―――――――――
until it has fallen by 80

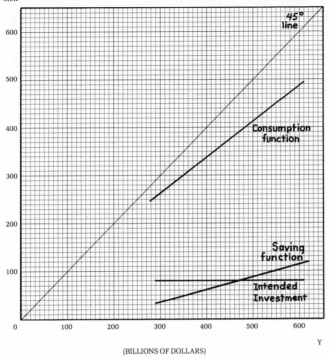

Figure 18A   A graphical exposition of income-expenditures analysis

the necessary condition for an aggregate equilibrium in our simple income-expenditures model.

Some Implications of the Model

The equilibrium values of income, consumption, investment, and saving can be read off the graph. Intended saving equals intended investment of $80 billion only when income is $470 billion. Consumption at that level of income is $390 billion. But the graph is merely a visual device to help you hold the picture together. What is important is the process of adjustment postulated by income-expenditures analysis and its implications for an understanding of fluctuations in the aggregate level of economic activity. The process has been described already. Let's think through some of the implications.

Relatively small changes in expenditures can cause substantial changes in output and income through the cumulative interaction of income and expenditures. Keynes called this *the multiplier process.* An initial change of $20 billion in intended investment had a multiplier effect of $80 billion on income in our model because the marginal propensity to consume was .75. The mechanics are unimportant. But if you're interested, you can note that the process is the same as it was with the so-called money multiplier introduced in Chapter 17 to describe the way in which additions to bank reserves can expand the money supply. A $20 billion reduction in income plus a reduction of (.75) $20 billion plus (.75)^2 $20 billion, and so on, sums ultimately to $20 billion × $\frac{1}{1-.75}$.

The adjustments of producers to changed circumstances do not necessarily lead toward an "equilibrium" *at high levels of employment*. "Equilibrium" can exist with the economy in a deep depression.

Saving is not the unmixed blessing that economists have traditionally assumed it to be. If intended investment falls, the attempt by savers to continue their current rate of saving will prevent consumption expenditure from picking up the slack. The result will be unsold goods, reduced output, and reduced incomes—until savers have been compelled by falling income to scale down their rate of saving to what investors want to spend. This comes close to reversing the traditional argument that high rates of saving are necessary to permit high rates of investment.

It has long been a fundamental tenet of economics that a nation's income and wealth grow roughly in proportion to the growth in its stock of capital. Investment is the process that adds to the capital stock. A higher rate of investment therefore means a faster rate of economic growth, a more rapid rise in national income, and a speedier improvement in living levels. But what determines the rate of investment? The classical answer was: the rate of saving. There is no way for a society to produce capital goods except by withdrawing some of its resources from the production of consumer goods. Those who save abstain from current consumption and either purchase capital goods themselves or turn over their income to others who purchase capital goods. Without saving there can be no investment. (If investment is financed by borrowing from abroad, foreigners must do the saving.) The incentive to save must therefore be preserved and extended, according to the classical argument; for it is the root cause of social progress.

Keynes's theory cast doubt upon the relevance of this line of reasoning by suggesting that the desire to save might be antithetical to investment and economic growth. In industrially developed societies, where the best investment opportunities had already been exploited and low prospective profit rates were discouraging to investors, additional saving might find no investors interested in putting it to work. In that case, an increase in "thrift" might so reduce aggregate demand as to lower the actual rate of investment and hence the rate of economic growth. This argument came to be known as the *paradox of thrift*.

Suppose that the investment plans of business firms are sensitive to changes in aggregate consumption. That's certainly a reasonable assumption. If investors use current developments as a guide to the future, they may become discouraged about future profit pros-

OUTPUT
OR
INCOME

C   S

I

LARGER
OUTPUT

pects as income and consumption levels fall and so retrench on investment plans. The curve of intended investment in Figure 18A would consequently slope upward to the right. If households then determined to increase their saving at current income levels (that is, shift the saving function upward) actual investment at equilibrium would be lower than it was before. The attempt to increase saving, instead of providing additional resources wanted for investment purposes, would trigger a recession. And as aggregate income fell, intended investment would also fall, pulling income down still further. You can check the mechanics for yourself by drawing a positively sloping investment curve in Figure 18A and noting the effect at "equilibrium" of any upward shift in the saving function.

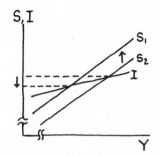

Saving, Investment, and Money

The income-expenditures model presented above abstracts from the phenomenon of money. The dollars used in the explanation are again only an accounting device, a common denominator enabling us to combine goods into such aggregates as consumption and investment. Did we spend all that effort in Chapter 17 on the concept of money only to ignore the subject in Chapter 18? That would be especially odd in view of the fact that Keynes included money in the very title of the *General Theory*, and that he suspected his economist predecessors of paying insufficient attention to the differences between a barter economy and a monetary economy. It is the existence of money which makes extensive specialization possible, which enables firms to produce without knowing to whom they will sell, and which consequently introduces into economic decision making the uncertainties that Keynes wished to stress.

The *General Theory* is in fact studded with observations on money and partially developed theories of the way money functions in aggravating the problem of aggregate fluctuations. But whatever Keynes himself intended, the income-expenditures model that his followers extracted from the book tended to become the theory that money was not particularly important.

Keynes used the supply of money in his analysis as a variable which helped to determine the rate of interest. The rate of interest, in turn, was allowed to exert an effect on the level of intended investment. Since intended investment, in conjunction with the saving function, determines the "equilibrium" level of income, money does play a role. But Keynes thought changes in the rate of interest would probably not be very effective in combating depressions. Users of his income-expenditures analysis, perhaps more Keynesian than Keynes, consequently tended to pay little attention to the functioning of money except to acknowledge the argument just outlined.

Let's clarify that argument. The rate of interest, Keynes main-

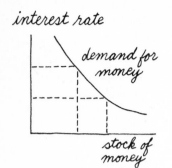

interest rate

demand for money

stock of money

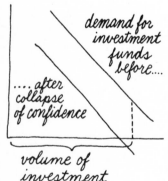

interest rate

demand for investment funds

investment

interest rate

demand for investment funds before....

....after collapse of confidence

volume of investment required for "full" employment

tained, was primarily a monetary phenomenon. This runs counter to the argument of Chapter 12 and represents a distinct heresy in the history of economic analysis. (Heretics haven't always been wrong, of course.) Keynes thought that interest rates reflected primarily the price of sacrificing liquidity. The quantity of money or liquidity that people want to hold will be less when interest rates are high because by holding money one sacrifices the opportunity to earn the prevailing rate of interest. At lower interest rates this opportunity cost of holding money will be less, and so the quantity demanded will be greater. The monetary authorities set the rate of interest by adjusting the stock of money along this downward sloping demand curve for money. By increasing the supply of money they can, within certain limits, lower interest rates.

The second stage of the argument asserts that intended investment depends, among other things, on the rate of interest. The prospect of a particular rate of return from a potential investment project is obviously more attractive when the rate at which investment funds can be borrowed is low. So whatever the opportunities investors discern, more investment will be undertaken at lower interest rates and less at higher interest rates.

The third stage of the argument turned all this into a somewhat peripheral concern, however, and encouraged Keynesians to neglect the study of money in their search for the causes and cures of recession. In a recession, Keynes contended, the confidence of investors tends to collapse. Investment projects that formerly seemed attractive now appear to hold out little probability of a positive return. Losses are feared more than profits are sought. Retrenchment becomes the order of the day. In such a situation, even reducing the interest rate to zero would probably not be enough to revive investment spending and so restore prosperity.

Loanable Funds and the Interest Rate

This line of argument also closed the door against a possible objection to Keynes's theory of the saving-investment-income relationship. The theory asserts that if intended investment falls short of intended saving, income will fall. It will keep falling until it has squeezed savers into reducing their rate of saving to the level that investors are willing to match.

But won't something else be at work? Saving generates a supply of loanable funds. Investment plans represent a demand for such funds. If planned investment is less than planned saving, there is a surplus of loanable funds, and the price at which they can be borrowed should fall. But if the return for loaning funds falls, won't savers decide to save less? And won't investors decide to borrow and spend more? And won't this tend to bring the intentions of savers and investors into balance without a recession?

Keynes undermined this line of argument by denying that saving or the supply of loanable funds was in fact significantly dependent on the rate of interest. The level of actual saving was dominated, he held, by income. Long before an excess supply of loanable funds had discouraged further saving and stimulated further investment, falling income levels would have dried up these funds at their source.

In short, changes in the rate of interest do not prevent the occurrence of recessions by bringing the intentions of savers into balance with the intentions of investors. On the contrary, it is the recession itself and the reduced incomes it causes that reconcile saving plans with investment plans.

A Glance Ahead

Income-expenditures analysis would not have caught on with economists as rapidly as it did after 1936 if this were all it had to say. It also seemed to show a way out of the impasse through the use of fiscal policy. But that's a topic for Chapter 19, where we shall also return to the question of money and the potential of monetary policy as a tool for economic stabilization.

Once Over Lightly

Economic theory is primarily a theory of order, showing how independent decisions are coordinated through market interrelationships. An adequate theory of recessions may have to be a theory of disorder, showing how uncertainty and imperfect coordination interfere with the achievement of high employment levels and the efficient use of resources.

Income-expenditures analysis offers a theory of aggregate supply and aggregate demand in which surpluses lead to declining demand rather than to the reduced prices upon which economic theory usually depends for a solution to problems of excess supply.

In income-expenditures analysis the cumulative effects of a "disequilibrium" are transmitted through the consumption function. Consumption is assumed to change as income changes, and in the same direction, but by a smaller amount. When producers reduce output because their sales failed to reach expected levels, they also reduce incomes. Lower incomes mean less consumption and therefore a further decline in sales.

Aggregate "equilibrium" is achieved in income-expenditures analysis when the level of income is consistent with the intentions of savers and the intentions of investors. Income will fall as long as savers try to withhold from consumption more income than investors want to spend. Eventually income will fall far enough so that savers will no longer want to save more than investors intend to invest.

A strong desire to save may lead to recessions rather than economic growth in an economy where the incentive to invest is weak.

Income-expenditures analysis has historically tended to minimize the importance of money. The job of the monetary

interest rate

demand from investors / supply from savers

loanable funds

managers was primarily seen as the control of interest rates. Interest rates were thought to be important primarily because lower interest rates could provide a minor inducement to additional investment.

The notion that interest rates could be an important factor in reconciling saving and investment intentions has been largely rejected by income-expenditures analysis on the grounds that changes in expectations and income swamp any effects that interest rate changes might have.

QUESTIONS FOR DISCUSSION

1. Can an economy be at equilibrium if much of its industrial capacity is standing idle and a large percentage of its labor force is unemployed? Is that a question about fact or a disguised argument about the proper way to use the concept of equilibrium?

2. Suppose that consumer demand for the following goods turns out to be less than producers anticipated, so that the goods already produced cannot all be sold at current prices. What consequences would you predict in the case of each good? Would prices or production levels be likely to fall first? How long will the sequence of adjustments take?
   a. automobiles
   b. beef cattle
   c. secondary school teachers

3. Is it true, as Keynes assumed in describing the consumption function, that people increase their consumption as their income increases but not by as much as the increase in their income? Does consumption in one period (a month, for example) depend upon income in that particular period? Would you expect a salesman receiving a highly variable monthly income to vary his consumption as his income varies?

4. Explain in your own words what is meant by the "multiplier." How does the multiplier depend upon the consumption function? If every increase in spending increases income, and every increase in income increases spending, wouldn't the ultimate effect of any initial change in spending be infinitely large? Why not?

5. The text presents two theories of the interest rate. One explains the interest rate as a product of the supply of, and demand for, loanable funds; the other as a product of the supply and demand for money.
   a. What is the difference between loanable funds and money?
   b. Do the two theories have significantly different implications?

6. If saving suddenly and unexpectedly increases, unintended investment will rise by enough to keep actual saving and investment equal.
   a. What form does this unintended investment take?
   b. What further consequences will this unintended investment have?
   c. Suppose that saving suddenly and unexpectedly decreased. Would such an occurrence be capable of creating a temporary inequality between saving and investment? Explain what might happen.

7. a. How are the marginal propensity to consume and the marginal propensity to save related?
   b. How is each related to the multiplier in income-expenditures analysis?

8. Does investment depend upon saving? Can investment occur if there has been no saving? What are the real differences between the older view that investment could only be maintained by maintaining saving and Keynes's view that a high rate of investment was a precondition for a high rate of saving?

9. Does the "paradox of thrift" imply that saving is an antisocial act and consumption an act that benefits society?

10. Why are producers more likely to forecast demand correctly in a barter economy than in an economy where goods are exchanged for money? Does this imply significantly less uncertainty in a barter economy? Evaluate the claim that uncertainty is one price we pay for affluence.

11. Would we all be better off if buyers had to commit themselves in advance to purchase goods and pay a substantial deposit before production begins? Do you know of any cases where this is done? If so, why do you think it is done?

12. a. How do interest rates affect investment spending?
    b. How do higher interest rates affect residential construction?
    c. "Shall we maintain production and allow our inventories of unsold goods to rise or should we shut down production until we've managed to sell off most of the finished goods now in the warehouses?" How might the level of interest rates enter into this decision?

    d. An electric utility postpones construction of a new generating plant because the market price of its bonds is disappointingly low. How does this illustrate the relationship between investment and interest rate?
    e. A corporation plans to begin a huge capital expansion program, using proceeds from a sale of new stock. But common stock prices decline and the firm postpones the stock sale and the investment program it was intended to finance. Does that have anything to do with interest rates?
    f. "Higher interest rates don't deter any business firm that has a profitable use for the money. If we can make 30 percent on an investment, we're going to invest whether we can borrow at 3 percent or have to pay 12 percent." Evaluate.
    g. "The higher the interest rate I can get, the more I'm going to invest. Investment increases as interest rates rise." Is that right? Reconcile those sentences with the text's analysis of the interest rate-investment relationship.

13. The condition for equilibrium in the simple Keynesian model is that intended investment equal intended saving.
    a. Would it be equivalent to state the equilibrium condition in this form: Intended consumption plus intended investment equals output? Explain why or why not.
    b. Can you represent this version of the model on the graph in Figure 18A?

Fiscal and
Monetary Policy

In March of 1975, Congress passed and President Ford signed a bill reducing federal taxes despite the fact that projected deficits for the current and succeeding fiscal years would be the largest peacetime deficits in our history. There was no outcry of disbelief or indignation: the economy was in a recession in 1975, and tax cuts were widely considered a proper remedy, regardless of the state of the federal budget.

Shifting Public Opinion

The United States economy was in a far deeper and more prolonged recession in 1932 when Franklin D. Roosevelt campaigned for the presidency on a promise to balance the federal budget if elected. The deficit at which Roosevelt was looking, even when adjusted for changes in the value of the dollar, was less than one-fifth the size of the smallest deficit being projected at the time of the 1975 tax cut.

Public thinking about deficits and recessions has obviously changed. Prior to the 1930s, the orthodox view was that government should actually retrench in a recession, cutting its expenditures and increasing tax rates if necessary to preserve a balanced budget. A balanced budget, in turn, was viewed as the test of responsible government and the surest indicator to the business community of the government's determination to maintain or restore "confidence." And confidence was seen as the key to recovery.

As for creating additional money to stimulate recovery— that was considered the very depth of irresponsibility. Downturns were supposedly the inevitable consequence of previous actions based on overly optimistic expectations; they had to be suffered because they were the appropriate penance for previous excesses, the means by which mistakes were cleared away so that solid foundations could be laid for subsequent advance. Once the mistakes had been corrected—through bankruptcies, forced sales, writing down of assets, readjustments of expectations—confidence would return and a new advance could begin. We are not saying that everyone held these positions, for the historical record shows that there were many who disputed the wisdom of such counsel. It was, nonetheless, the viewpoint that pretty much controlled the policy thinking of governments in the industrialized nations of the Western world prior to the 1930s.

The dominant view today is that government has a responsibility for the management of aggregate demand, and that the federal budget and the supply of money are tools which the government may use to fulfill those responsibilities. The question now is not *whether* but *how*. How can the government use its control over expenditures and tax receipts to stabilize the aggregate level of economic activity? That is the question of *fiscal policy*. How can the government, and primarily the central bank, use its control over the money supply to stabilize the economy? That is the question of *monetary policy*.

Income-Expenditures Analysis and Fiscal Policy

The rise of fiscal policy is closely associated with the development of income-expenditures analysis. If recessions occur because investors are unwilling to spend as much as everyone is trying to save, why can't the government take steps to correct the imbalance? Why allow an insufficient demand to reduce production and raise unemployment? The government is not bound by the narrow considerations that guide private spending and saving decisions. It can engage in compensatory finance, either by expanding its own purchases of goods or by stimulating private spending through tax cuts or increases in transfer payments. If we know what amount of total spending, by consumers, investors, and government, would generate a level of gross national product consistent with "full" employment, is there any excuse for allowing the economy to operate below capacity?

Beginning students of economics are sometimes too easily impressed by the simple mechanics of income-expenditures analysis. "If current demand is inadequate, the government has the power to raise aggregate demand to the appropriate level." That sounds straightforward and sensible. But it is, in reality, an extremely abstract assertion. As we tried to show in Chapter 15, government is not really like Aladdin's marvelous genie, always obedient to command and always able to accomplish its assignments. The agencies of government, for all their power and importance, are still made up of people, managed by people, run for people. And people here does not mean The People, another potentially misleading abstraction. It means people like us, who are neither omniscient nor omnipotent and are sometimes even guilty of defining the public interest in suspiciously self-serving ways.

The people in government do not have knowledge or capabilities beyond the knowledge and capabilities of mere mortals. "Raise aggregate demand to the appropriate level." That's excellent counsel. But who knows the current level of aggregate demand, the appropriate level, and the actions that will move aggregate demand from the wrong to precisely the right level? Who knows all the unintended side effects of such actions, and how to prevent the undesirable ones while bringing about all those that are desired? And what good will it do to know, if one lacks the

power to compel action? Especially in a democracy, power is
shared by many people with different perspectives and ideals and
what sometimes even look like conflicting interests. Among those
human beings who are neither omniscient nor omnipotent, we
must regrettably include Federal Reserve officials, congressmen,
members of the administration up to and including the chief
executive, and even the professional economists who serve on their
research staffs or function as their council of advisers (or as their
critics!).

A substantial part of what we're asserting here, though only
a part, can be described as *the problem of lags*. Time will
inevitably lapse between the appearance of a problem and its
recognition, between recognition and analysis, between analysis and decision, between decision and action, and between
action and its ultimate consequences. When we add to all this
the effects of ignorance and uncertainty, the prospects for
steering the economy neatly onto the full employment track
through fiscal policy or monetary policy no longer look as
bright as they do when we're considering hypothetical cases
where all the data are known.

The Federal Budget as a Policy Tool

There is at least a touch of humor in the belief that the federal
government can use its budget as a stabilization tool when almost
all observers agree that Congress no longer has effective control
over the budget. The spending programs of the federal government are so many and so complex that no one can even begin to
evaluate all of them for the purpose of determining annual appropriations. As a result, next year's budget begins by taking this
year's budget for granted and adding on. Once a program gets in, it
is almost impossible to dislodge, because its beneficiaries form a
knowledgeable and determined lobby for its continuance, and no
one on Capitol Hill has the time, energy, and interest to accumulate the evidence that could justify its removal.

Fiscal policy is not something under the control of the Council
of Economic Advisers. A change in government expenditures or in
federal taxes requires action by the House of Representatives and
then the Senate, with committee meetings before and often after,
and a presidential signature at the end. That takes time and timing
may be crucial. The discussions will be complicated and prolonged
by the fact that, even if Congress were to agree quickly on the
desirability of a change in expenditures or taxes of a particular
amount, it would still have to decide whose taxes will be changed
and which expenditures. Conflicting interests will be involved and
alternative theories about the expansionary or contractionary
effects of particular actions. Is it better to cut the taxes of low-
income people or to give tax credits for investment? Which will
have a greater impact on employment? And are we talking about

the long run or the short run? Meanwhile some members of Congress will certainly decide that an important tax or expenditure bill provides an opportunity to eliminate the depletion allowance for oil producers, give a bonus to retired people on social security, prop up the housing industry through a special subsidy, or take a slap at multinational corporations—to mention only some of the concerns that managed to achieve expression in the March 1975 "antirecessionary" tax bill.

The more in a hurry Congress and the president are, the more likely they are to produce fiscal policy actions that few competent and impartial observers will be able to defend. The imperative of haste tends to enhance the power of those who are willing to enforce their demands by threatening to block any action at all. But due deliberation, the careful assessment of alternatives, and the weighing of probable short- and long-term outcomes may require so much time that the moment for action passes before any action is taken. The 1974–75 recession probably began late in 1973. Congress passed an antirecessionary tax-cut bill at the end of March in 1975; even at that late date, the bill contained evidence of undue haste. Only six months prior to the tax cut, the official word was still WIN (Whip Inflation Now), evidence of the sometimes lengthy lag between the appearance and the recognition of a problem.

Advocates of stabilization through fiscal policy who are not mesmerized by the genie conception of government have long been aware of these difficulties. They know that the protracted discussions which precede any congressional action on taxes and expenditures could easily make fiscal policy unworkable: action might not be possible until the time for it has passed. They have consequently looked around for ways to speed up the process. One proposal recommended by some economists and urged by President Kennedy was that Congress authorize unilateral action by the president. Appropriations for particular projects could be approved by Congress and then put on the shelf, to be taken off whenever the president and his advisers decided that the stimulus of increased government expenditures was called for. Congress could also authorize the president to increase or decrease tax rates within narrow limits when aggregate demand seemed excessive or inadequate.

This proposal doesn't exactly assume a genie: it attempts to create one. If you're wondering why Congress never acted on such a "sensible" recommendation, think for a moment about the political power that a president would command if he could unilaterally determine the timing of tax decreases and the placement of expenditure projects. Do you recall the furor that erupted in the early 1970s when a president tried to "impound" appropriations on the grounds that they would add to the deficit and increase the rate of inflation? We are not likely soon to sanction such actions by even the most trusted of leaders. And that means fiscal policy will continue to be at best a rather clumsy tool for stabilizing total spending.

The Revival of Monetary Policy

What about monetary policy? We introduced it in Chapter 17, then ignored it in Chapter 18. It has only been within the last decade that monetary policy has achieved anything like equal status with fiscal policy in the thinking of economists. The impotence of monetary policy as a means of restoring prosperity seemed to many to have been adequately demonstrated in the Great Depression, when the Fed pursued an "easy money" policy but could not stir a revival of bank lending and private spending. The power of fiscal policy had seemingly been just as clearly demonstrated by the "fiscal experiment" of 1940–1944. When the urgencies of war finally overcame concern for a balanced budget and the federal government began spending profusely, private spending also revived. And once restored by a massive injection of federal spending, private consumption and investment were able to take up the slack when government expenditures fell sharply after the war.

Monetary policy inched its way back into esteem through a concurrence of events. One was the unexpected mildness of recessions in the postwar period and the persistence of inflation. Inflation was a problem against which monetary policy might be more effective because, in the metaphor widely used, one could pull a balloon down with a string even though pushing on the string would not make it *rise*. So the monetary managers were able to practice their stabilization skills to some extent by trying to control inflation. These experiments in turn persuaded many observers that monetary policy, though perhaps impotent at the depth of a severe depression, might well be effective as an expansionary tool in mild recessions. One further reason for the revival of monetary policy was the research done during this period by economists who were convinced that changes in the money supply had a more predictable impact on total spending than the advocates of fiscal policy believed.

How does monetary policy affect total spending? Income-expenditures analysis divides total spending into the three major components of consumption, investment, and government expenditures, and asserts that they jointly determine the level of total output and income. In summary:

$$C + I + G = GNP \text{ (gross national product)}$$

Monetary policy supposedly affects GNP through its impact on interest rates; lower interest rates stimulate investment spending and, to a lesser extent, consumption spending.

Not all economists believe that this is the best way of looking at the question. They prefer an older analytical framework often

Pushing on the string won't make the balloon rise. But relaxing the pull will allow it to rise.

Question: Is the monetary balloon filled with a lighter-than-air gas?

called the *equation of exchange*. The easiest way to get at the equation of exchange is through some data on the behavior of total spending and the money supply. (We'll state the equation after we have presented all the variables.)

Table 19A shows how M_1, M_2, and M_3 have grown since 1960. The data on the money stock, in billions of dollars, are actually the average during December of the preceding year. Thus money supply data for December 1959 are presented for 1960, on the assumption that the stock of money most likely to influence 1960 spending is the stock at the beginning of the year.

The second column in each section of the table was obtained by dividing the money stock into the dollar value of gross national product. The assumption here is that GNP is a good proxy for total spending. There are, as you know from Chapter 16, many expenditures that do not enter into the calculation of gross national product. But GNP is the best measure we have, and it is reasonable to suppose that total spending from year to year will vary proportionately with GNP.

TABLE 19A

Year	M_1		M_2		M_3	
	Money stock	GNP ÷ money stock	Money stock	GNP ÷ money stock	Money stock	GNP ÷ money stock
1960	$143.4	3.53	$210.9	2.40	$303.8	1.67
1961	144.2	3.63	217.1	2.41	319.3	1.64
1962	148.7	3.79	228.6	2.47	342.1	1.65
1963	150.9	3.94	242.9	2.45	369.2	1.61
1964	156.5	4.06	258.9	2.46	400.3	1.59
1965	163.7	4.20	277.1	2.48	434.4	1.58
1966	171.3	4.40	301.3	2.50	471.2	1.60
1967	175.4	4.54	317.8	2.51	495.1	1.61
1968	186.9	4.65	349.6	2.48	543.7	1.60
1969	201.7	4.64	382.3	2.45	589.0	1.59
1970	208.7	4.71	392.2	2.50	607.2	1.62
1971	219.6	4.84	423.5	2.51	656.2	1.62
1972	233.8	5.01	471.7	2.48	745.1	1.57
1973	255.3	5.12	525.3	2.49	844.9	1.55
1974	270.5	5.20	571.4	2.46	919.5	1.53
1975	283.1	5.29	612.4	2.45	981.6	1.53

Sources: Board of Governors of the Federal Reserve System and Bureau of Economic Analysis.

What do the data show? The relationship between the stock of money and total expenditures is reasonably stable from year to year no matter which concept of money we use. The ratio of GNP to M_1 has been rising over time, but it has been rising fairly steadily. The ratio of GNP to M_3 and especially to M_2 has been remarkably stable. In the 1970s, through recessions and recoveries, through energy crises and "double digit" inflation, when the total quantity of currency, demand deposits, and time deposits was increasing by as much as 11 percent per year, the ratio of GNP to M_2 remained within the narrow range of 2.45 to 2.50.

The Velocity of Money Circulation

It will be easier to talk about that ratio if we give it a name. Fortunately, it already has a name: those who study the relationship between the money supply and aggregate spending call it the *velocity of money circulation*, or just *velocity*.[1] It is the average number of times each unit of money had to change hands in order to accommodate total spending on GNP.

The economic meaning of the velocity numbers becomes clearer if you look at them in a slightly different way. In 1970, for example, the public held currency, demand deposits, and time deposits equal in total to 40 percent of total expenditures on GNP. In 1975, when M_2 was $220 billion greater, it was still less than 41 percent of GNP. And in none of the intervening years did the ratio move outside those narrow boundaries. It certainly would appear that the public prefers to hold currency plus demand and time deposits equal to 40 or 41 percent of expenditures on GNP.

Does it follow from all this that the Fed can control the rate at which gross national product grows by controlling the rate of growth in M_2? Have we perhaps found a key to stabilization policy in this stable relationship between M_2 and GNP? Matters unfortunately are not that simple.

GNP is the product of real output and the price level. In other words, an increase in GNP could come about through a decline in the level of production and an increase in prices. That's exactly what did occur from 1973 to 1974: Gross national product rose by 8 percent, but it did so because a 10.3 percent increase in prices more than made up for a 2.2 percent decline in real output. Inflation is hardly compensation for recession. The ability to control the rate of growth in GNP will only be socially useful if it entails the ability to affect separately the rate of real growth and the rate of change in the price level.

The Equation of Exchange

Another question we must ask is whether the money stock and GNP would continue to be so closely correlated if the Fed set out consciously to use one as a means of controlling the other. Perhaps we could have more confidence in the *future* stability of that relationship and hence its usefulness for policy purposes if we had a

1. It is sometimes called the *income velocity*, because it is actually the velocity with which money circulates relative to expenditures for goods included in the calculation of the national income.

satisfactory theoretical explanation for it. Here is where we can put the equation of exchange to work.

The equation asserts that

$$MV = PQ$$

where M is the stock of money, V is the velocity of circulation, P is the price level, and Q is *real* output or gross national product measured in dollars of constant purchasing power. If you think about it for a moment, the equation of exchange is a translation of the basic income-expenditures equation: C + I + G = GNP. MV and C + I + G both define total spending. And PQ simply divides GNP into its two components, the price level and real output. But the equations are competitive as well as equivalent. One ignores the money supply, the other ignores the distinctions between consumption, investment, and government expenditures.

It should be clear simply from looking at the equation of exchange that the effectiveness of monetary policy as a stabilization tool will depend upon the predictability of V as well as the separate responses of P and Q to any change in MV. Do we have adequate theoretical reasons for believing that V will be stable or at least will behave predictably when monetary policy manipulates M?

Let's get at that question by rewriting the equation of exchange:

$$M = \left(\frac{1}{V}\right)PQ$$

While the equations are mathematical equivalents, the form above makes more behavioral sense. People don't think about the velocity with which they want to circulate money and then take steps to reach their preferred velocity. But people do think about their money balances; they think about them in relation to their anticipated expenditures; and they take actions designed to move their money balances toward the levels they prefer. 1/V is the public's total stock of money balances expressed as a fraction of PQ, which is the volume of current expenditures. It follows that V will be stable if the public does not quickly or easily change its demand for money, or, more specifically, its preferred ratio between money balances and current expenditures.

Actual and Preferred Money Balances

The public as a whole must hold the entire money supply, because it isn't counted as money unless it is being held by the public. So total money balances will always be identical to M (regardless of which measure of M we use). But *actual* money balances may not be equal to *preferred* money balances. If the monetary authorities were to increase the money supply at a time when the public was satisfied with its current money holdings, some people would have to find themselves holding larger money balances than they pre-

M is the quantity of money supplied and the quantity being held.

Quantity actually held must equal M. Quantity public would prefer to hold may be greater or less than M.

ferred to hold. And so they would take steps to reduce their money balances back to the preferred level. And if the Fed were to reduce the money supply when people were holding their preferred amounts of money, they would try to raise their balances back up to the previous level.

Be sure that you don't confuse the concepts of money and income. Money is a stock. Income is a flow. When we talk about people's preferences for money balances, we are not talking about their attitude toward income. The preference for money balances is the same thing as the demand for money. And the demand for money is the demand for liquidity, not for more income. When someone says that Local 13 of the United Federation of Dingleworkers is "demanding more money," that translates in our terminology into a demand for more income (in the form of higher wages). People can increase their money holdings even in the face of a decreasing income if they are willing to reduce their expenditures for some period by more than the fall in their incomes. An increase in the demand for money always means an increased desire to hold money balances *in preference to alternative assets.* Thus a person who increases his money balances is simply holding more wealth than before in the form of money—rather than refrigerators, corporate bonds, and so on.

Nominal and Real Money Balances

It is the connection between actual money balances and preferred balances that explains how changes in the money supply affect the economy. But to see how it works you must distinguish between nominal and real money balances. A person's *real money balance* is the command over other goods that those dollars provide. You might feel secure with $200 in your checking account. But if the price level doubled, that money balance wouldn't be as comfortable. You would have to be holding $400 in *nominal balances* to maintain the level of your real balance. People's preferences are presumably for real balances; they're concerned, in other words, about the value or purchasing power of those balances. It's true that people may be fooled for a while into supposing that their real balances haven't declined when the price level rises; but they tend to discover the truth and make adjustments. A rising price level, by reducing the purchasing power of money, lowers real balances even though nominal balances haven't changed. A falling price level, other things remaining equal, raises real balances.

Effects of Changes in the Supply of Money

What will happen if the Fed increases the money stock at a time when the public is holding the amount of money it prefers to hold? People will find themselves holding more money than they want to hold. So they will spend some. They will shift the composition of

Meat eaten per year is a flow. Meat in the freezer is a stock.

The stock can be increased by purchasing more than is eaten for a time.

The desire to hold more meat in the freezer does not necessarily imply a desire to eat more meat per year.

Is Marcello holding a large money balance if he is holding 10,000 lire?

(That's less than $15.)

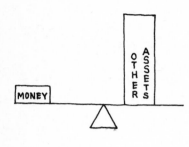

The attempt to exchange money for other goods increases P×Q.

The quantity of nominal money the public prefers to hold increases when P×Q increases.

P×Q stops increasing when the public is satisfied with its level of money balances.

their asset portfolios by exchanging money for other goods. The public as a whole cannot get rid of money in this way, because one person's surrender of money for an alternative good must be some other person's acquisition of precisely that amount of money. But the attempt on the part of people to reduce their money balances has effects that will finally bring actual balances into equality with preferred balances.

One effect will be on the prices of goods. With people more eager than before to acquire goods for money, the price of goods will be bid up. That's inflation: an increase in P.

If the enhanced bidding for goods does not raise their price, it must mean that the supply of goods has increased. That's an expansion of production: an increase in Q.

Now if the demand for money balances is a demand for *real* balances, then the rise in P or Q, or both, should eventually cause the quantity of nominal money balances demanded to increase. It will continue increasing as long as PQ is increasing; PQ will keep increasing as long as the public keeps increasing its demand for goods; and the public will keep increasing its demand for goods as long as its actual money balances are greater than its preferred balances.

Does that seem much too complicated to remember? Don't try to remember it! Think it through. The average amount of money you want to hold over some period of time will depend on your anticipated expenditures during that time. If the dollar amount of your anticipated expenditures goes up because prices have risen, you will probably want to hold more money on average, or to maintain the size of your *real* balances by increasing your *nominal* balances. The point of this whole account is that when the Fed forces more money onto the whole public than it wants to hold at the time, the attempt to reduce those now excessive balances leads to an increased demand for goods and hence either higher prices or expanded output or both. That's an increase in PQ. If you're a representative member of that public, your "share" of PQ will rise, and so you'll want to hold more money than you did before. It's all quite logical. PQ rises in response to the increased supply of money until the quantity demanded is equal to the larger quantity now being supplied.

It follows, then, that if the public's demand for money is stable, changes in the stock of money (M) will lead to proportionate changes in nominal gross national product (PQ). But two qualifications to this analysis must be mentioned.

Hyperinflation and Velocity

If the monetary authorities were to increase the money stock so rapidly that almost everyone came to expect large increases in the price level, the demand for money would almost certainly fall. Money would then be an asset whose future value relative to other assets was expected to decline rapidly. People would therefore want to exchange money for other goods before this happened. Money would become like the Old Maid card that all players try to pass on the moment it enters their hands, and the velocity of circulation would rise. That's what occurred in the German hyperinflation of the 1920s.

A continuing rapid rate of growth in the money supply caused prices to rise, the continuing inflation created expectations of further inflation, these expectations prompted an increase in V and an even more rapid inflation, the falling real value of money induced the monetary authorities to make even more nominal money available, inflationary expectations increased still further prompting an ever greater reluctance to hold money, until finally people quit work early in the day to spend their money income before it had become almost worthless. In such a situation, where no one wants to hold money, money is useless; the monetary system disintegrates and exchange must occur through the cumbersome processes of barter.

The demand for money depends upon its expected purchasing power.

When no one is willing to hold any money, the velocity of circulation approaches infinity.

Interest Rates and Velocity

That is one qualification to the generalization that changes in M will induce proportionate changes in PQ. The second qualification is less drastic. Suppose we ask why the public would want to hold money balances equal to 1/5 of anticipated expenditures rather than, say, 1/4 or 1/6. The general answer is that the public is balancing the marginal benefits against the marginal costs of holding additional money. The benefits are the expanded opportunities that liquidity offers. One of the costs is the income forgone by keeping assets in the form of currency or checking-account deposits rather than assets that yield interest. It follows, then, that at higher interest rates the quantity of money demanded for any volume of anticipated expenditures will be less than it is when interest rates are low.

This suggests our second qualification to the assertion that changes in M will induce proportionate changes in PQ. If the Fed increases the money supply when the public is satisfied with its level of money balances, people will begin exchanging money for other assets. But those other assets don't have to be refrigerators and porterhouse steaks, goods included in the gross national product. They could also be financial assets like government bonds or corporate securities.

An increased demand for financial assets will bid up their price and thereby reduce their percentage yield. (A security whose ownership yields $10 per year is returning 8 percent when its price is $125, but only 6 percent if its price rises to $167.) Declining rates of return on securities mean declining interest rates and hence a lower opportunity cost of holding money. As a result, the public might now be willing to hold money balances equal to some larger per-

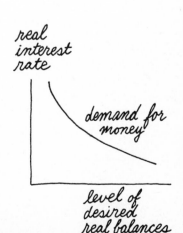

real interest rate

demand for money

level of desired real balances

centage of anticipated expenditures. In short, the effect of changes in M on PQ will be reduced somewhat insofar as the change in M alters interest rates and hence the quantity of money the public prefers to hold.

Uncertainties of Monetary Policy

This discussion should not leave you with the impression that there are any rigid links between M and PQ. The responses we have tried to describe take place only over time, at varying rates of speed, and to a different extent for different people. The danger in using the equation of exchange is similar to the danger in using income-expenditures analysis: both theories are highly aggregative. They consequently conceal changes in the *composition* of spending flows that may be quite as important as the changes in such aggregates and averages as C, I, Q, or P.

The velocity of circulation has proved to be broadly stable within the range of United States experiences since World War II. But we cannot jump from here to the conclusion that monetary policy is the solution to our quest for tools by which the government can stabilize the level of economic activity.

In the first place, the Fed does not directly control the money supply but only holds it on an elastic leash. That should have been clear from Chapter 17, even though we passed over most of the technical problems involved in managing the money supply.

Second, and more important, Federal Reserve officials face many of the same timing problems that Congress and the president encounter when trying to use fiscal policy. Federal Reserve policy making is much more insulated from political pressures than is government budget making, so the Fed can act more quickly once it spots a problem. But the Fed cannot avoid the difficulties presented by the time lags between the origin of a problem and its recognition or, even more important, between action and consequences. How long will it take for an increase in the rate of growth in the money stock to cause an increase in spending? Estimates vary anywhere from a few months to several years, and diligent research efforts designed to nail down the time distribution of monetary policy effects have not yet produced a workable consensus. These time lags may even turn out to vary in some way we can't predict, in which case economists would be trying to measure something that actually has no standard length.

Interrelations between Fiscal and Monetary Policy

Most economists today prefer to think of themselves as eclectics, willing to use fiscal or monetary policy rather than debate their respective merits. This may be evidence of an admirable open-mindedness. Or it may be simple prudence in the face of the difficulties encountered when one tries to measure their effects.

These difficulties are compounded by the fact that fiscal policies will usually have monetary repercussions whether or not they're intended. A fan of fiscal policy can then credit his preferred tools while the fan of monetary policy attributes the effects to the changes that the fiscal action induced in monetary conditions.

Why does fiscal policy inevitably have an impact on the monetary sector? Consider the case of the government decision in 1975 to provide a fiscal stimulus by cutting taxes while maintaining or even increasing expenditures. The Treasury must obtain money in order to spend. There are basically two ways to get it. The Treasury can either have new money created or it can borrow from the stock of already existing money. Whichever course is chosen, the fiscal actions will have monetary effects. Let's try to sort out the possibilities.

The Treasury does not ordinarily create new money on its own. As we saw in Chapter 17, the creation of additional money comes about through credit expansion by commercial banks and the Federal Reserve. We can therefore set the problem up in terms of the three sources from which the Treasury may borrow: the Fed, commercial banks, or the nonbank public.

Suppose the Treasury borrows from the Fed in order to secure the funds to finance expenditures not covered by taxes. The Fed in effect gives the Treasury additional deposits in exchange for government securities. When the Treasury then spends these deposits, they flow into the bank accounts or currency holdings of defense contractors, welfare recipients, military personnel, or whoever is on the receiving end of the expenditures. The money supply consequently increases.

These new deposits are also new reserves for the commercial banking system. Banks will therefore find their lending power increased. If they can locate eligible borrowers, the commercial banks will, by expanding their loans, create a further addition to the money supply.

It follows that the money supply could increase by the entire amount of the deficit even though the Fed directly financed only a portion of the deficit. A $50 billion deficit, for example, could be handled through some combination like a Fed purchase of $15 billion in new government securities and commercial bank purchases of $35 billion. The Fed purchase, by supplying new reserves to the banking system, enables the commercial banks to acquire additional government securities by creating new demand deposits.

Now suppose that the Fed wants to prevent any growth of the money supply due to increased Treasury borrowing. Insofar as the Fed is successful, the Treasury will be forced to compete with other borrowers for use of the existing money stock. Unless there are idle funds around, interest rates will consequently rise until the higher cost of borrowing squeezes out the excess demand. The net effect, then, will be an expansion of government spending and a

FEDERAL RESERVE SYSTEM

ASSETS	LIABILITIES
+ Government bonds	+ Treasury demand deposits

COMMERCIAL BANKS

ASSETS	LIABILITIES
+ Reserve accounts	+ Demand deposits

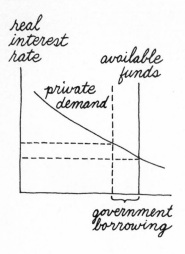

compensating reduction of private spending. But this defeats the original purpose of the government's policy; an increase in government spending that is exactly matched by a decrease in private spending provides no stimulus to total expenditures.

There's one other possibility. Suppose the public is holding large money balances simply because consumers and investors are fearful of the future and don't trust available financial assets. People might be persuaded to exchange those balances for government securities. That would give the Treasury the money it wants without an increase in the measured money stock. More spending would then occur with no increase in M because the government would be spending previously idle balances that the public had been persuaded to exchange for government bonds. In effect, V would have increased. But is that very likely outside a period of deep depression? Perhaps in the 1930s public confidence was so low that deficit spending could tap large idle money balances. But that doesn't seem to describe the situation at any time in the past three decades.

The conclusion is a simple one. Deficit spending by the government affects the monetary sector. It results in some combination of an enlarged money stock and higher interest rates. Insofar as the Fed tries to prevent public expenditures from crowding out private expenditures by making more credit available when the Treasury is borrowing, it causes a growth in the money supply. If the Fed tries to prevent an increase in the money supply, it will force private borrowers to bid against the Treasury for the limited supply of credit. Fiscal policy is inseparable from monetary policy.

Monetary policy, on the other hand, could be conducted independently of fiscal policy. Government spending uses money, but more money can be created and spent independently of any changes in the government budget. It doesn't follow, however, that fiscal policy cannot be a useful aid to monetary policy. Remember that the Fed does not directly control the size of the money stock. It can increase the available reserves of the banking system, but it cannot force anyone to borrow and thereby convert free reserves into money. Government borrowing and expenditure is one way to increase the money supply and to increase it rapidly. And in a period of low confidence, when consumers and investors don't want to borrow, fiscal policy might be the only way to make monetary policy effective.

All of this has one very practical implication. The sometimes vehement debates in recent years over the respective roles of fiscal and monetary policy in causing inflation were largely debates over a nonissue. The federal government ran very large deficits in the 1968, 1971, 1972, and 1973 fiscal years—about $85 billion altogether. To ask whether this would have caused inflation if the Fed had not simultaneously allowed a rapid expansion in the money supply is a somewhat pointless question; an expansion of the money supply was inevitable given the size of the deficits and the unwillingness of both the Fed and the Treasury to let mounting federal expenditures crowd out private spending.

The National Debt

The discussion in this chapter has been concerned with the broad effects of fiscal and monetary policy on total spending and some of the more obvious limitations on our ability to manage aggregate demand for policy purposes. We'll try to put all this into the larger context of current policy thinking in Chapter 21, after we have introduced an important but so far neglected factor: the United States' economic relations with other countries. Before ending this chapter, however, we ought to consider a related question that disturbs many people.

Conversations about deficit spending always come around eventually to the question of the national debt. This looms so large (if rather vaguely) in the public mind as a serious problem that Congress has placed a legal ceiling on the debt. It's an odd sort of ceiling, because the president periodically asks that it be raised and Congress always cooperates. But the existence of a statutory ceiling, even a flexible one, at least persuades people that someone has an eye on the problem.

What kind of problem is it? How large can the debt grow before we encounter disaster? Surely the government can't go on indefinitely living beyond its means, can it? When will the debt have to be repaid? And how?

Direct answers for direct questions. Very few knowledgeable people worry about the national debt or consider it much of a problem. It could probably grow to several times its present size without presenting any unmanageable difficulties. The federal government can, if it chooses, live beyond its means indefinitely. The debt doesn't ever have to be repaid. The question of how to retire the debt is academic in view of the fact that it will probably never be retired.

Nothing in that paragraph should alarm you or arouse the suspicion that the government is a welsher. No debtor has to pay back his creditors as long as the creditors don't demand repayment. And the individuals or institutions to whom the federal government is indebted are not holding government bonds out of either patriotism or necessity, but out of concern for their own financial welfare. They purchased the bonds because they decided the best thing they could do with their money was loan it to the government. Moreover, should they change their minds, they would find that the government cheerfully redeems certain bonds on demand and others at maturity, and that there exists an active market for the latter through which some other party can easily be found to take the bond and return the original purchaser's principal.

Refinancing the Debt

Despite the fact that bonds regularly fall due, requiring the federal government to repay the principal, the debt is never retired. The government secures the funds to repay the principal basically by selling more bonds. As long as it can find purchasers, the government faces no problems. And finding purchasers isn't difficult. If a particular issue of new bonds doesn't sell out, that means the Treasury Department has been stingy in setting the yield. A slightly lower price for the bonds, which comes to the same thing as a slightly higher interest rate, will bring a surge of additional offers to purchase.

You could do the same thing if you enjoyed an adequate credit rating, and many private firms and individuals do. They borrow for a set term, then extend the loan when it falls due. In effect they are paying the interest and borrowing the funds to repay the principal. Lenders are glad to cooperate because they earn their income by lending; the repayment of principal is a nuisance requiring the lender to find a new borrower, especially if the borrower is considered a good risk and the lender has little fear of default on the loan.

The federal government enjoys a uniquely high credit rating among lenders. Lenders do not request an audit of the government's books, demand collateral, raise embarrassing questions about the efficiency with which the government manages its business, or insist upon evidence that the government plans soon to begin living within its means. For they know that the federal government has the power to collect revenue by coercion and, even more importantly, that it enjoys a constitutional monopoly of the right to print currency. State and local governments can and do default on their obligations at times, as do some of the largest corporations, when their revenues fall short of expectations. But the federal government in such a fix could simply create the money with which to pay its debts. In a pinch it can always count on the cooperation of the Federal Reserve Banks. This power makes the bonds of the federal government uniquely safe and guarantees that buyers can be found at the right price.

Are we to conclude, then, that the national debt is neither a problem nor a burden? That would be going too far.

Dangers in the Debt

In the first place, increases in the debt mean that the government is either expanding the money supply or competing with private borrowers for available credit. If the economy is operating close to capacity, deficit financing may be inflationary. Of course, if the economy is in a depression, an increase in the debt may be the stimulus to demand that restores prosperity. It is thus not the absolute size of the debt so much as the direction in which it is changing that ought to be carefully watched.

Second, government borrowing pulls resources away from private into public uses. Taxation has the same effect. But taxes have a greater political impact, and expenditures undertaken out of tax revenues therefore tend to be scrutinized more critically than expenditures financed through borrowing. Whether this is a point for or against government borrowing depends upon how one evaluates the relative importance of public and private spending. Some students of American society maintain that we spend far too much on goods for private consumption (automobiles, houses, filet mignon) and far too little on the goods whose provision is largely left to government (education, public parks, national defense). But there are others who maintain just as insistently that government expenditure promotes social welfare less efficiently than does private expenditure. However you stand on that issue, the ability to increase expenditures without increasing taxes almost certainly enables governments to spend more than they otherwise would.

The Burden of the Debt

The often heard argument that deficit financing pushes the burden of present expenditures onto our descendants is almost wholly mistaken. The debt which passes on to future generations is for the most part matched by the bonds that we bequeath them. We leave them assets as well as liabilities, and hence no net burden of indebtedness.

When you stop to think about it, you realize that current expenditures, however they are financed, require the use of current real resources. Wars, for example, can be financed by borrowing, but they must be fought by drawing upon the current population and using the productive capabilities of the current economy. Highways, schools, and dams all require for their construction the use of current resources, resources that are consequently not available to provide other goods for the current generation—regardless of how these projects are financed. In fact, deficit financing may well make future generations better off. If the borrowed funds are wisely used in the construction of projects that will yield large future services, the current generation is sacrificing the present enjoyment of real resources in order to provide a larger real income to later generations. We are benefiting right now from past government expenditures on schools, roads, public buildings, parks, dams, irrigation projects, and other public investments, just as we are currently enjoying the fruits of past private investment in the form of a larger output of privately produced commodities and services.

There is one partial exception to all this. If a government borrows from foreigners to finance current expenditures, then it is attempting to use the current resources of foreigners rather than of its own citizens. And future generations will be left with the obligation to repay that borrowing by giving up some of their resources to foreign bondholders. Of course, if the projects for which the government borrows are good investments, they will augment the real income of future generations by more than enough to repay the resources originally borrowed from abroad. We see again that the wisdom of the project for which the borrowing is undertaken is more important than the mere fact that the expenditure is financed by borrowing. And this agrees with everything we know about private spending and borrowing. A business firm or a household will gain from going into debt whenever the project financed by borrowing increases the flow of future goods (income) by more than it increases the stream of future payments on principal and interest.

Numbers and Alarums

This discussion of the national debt has stayed away from actual numbers because the principles are more important than the numbers, however dramatic the latter can sometimes be made to appear. Some people are apparently thrilled in a terrifying sort of way by the news that if Alexander the Great had started to spend money after the Battle of Issus at the rate of $400 a minute, he would not yet today have spent a sum equal to the total of the national debt. But what does that mean? Do we gain a relevant sense of proportion from such numbers? Or are they like estimating the relative importance of mosquitoes and elephants by figuring out how many mosquitoes would have to be put on a scale to balance one elephant?

The interest paid by the federal government annually on the national debt may be a more meaningful measure of its significance, since the interest is rather like the "carrying charge" on the debt. It's currently close to 2 percent of the gross national product. That's a substantial sum; but it hardly spells fiscal ruin. Another way to put the debt into perspective is to note that in 1945, at the end of World War II, it was approximately equal to the total national income. Thirty years later the debt was more than twice as large but was less than 40 percent of the value of our annual national output.

In short, the national debt is not a major problem. If you've been worrying about it in a vaguely fearful way, we encourage you to discard your anxieties or transfer them to some social problem more deserving of your concern.

Once Over Lightly

The belief that government ought to take an active role in countering recessions through fiscal or monetary policy has achieved general respectability among economists and the public only over the last forty years.

Fiscal policy means the attempt by government to use its own budget (disbursements and receipts) to stabilize the aggregate level of spending.

The case for fiscal policy developed out of income-expenditures analysis and the contention that private spending intentions might be compatible with private saving intentions only at low levels of income, output, and employment.

Fiscal policy is in practice subject to important political limitations as well as limitations imposed by uncertainty regarding its precise effects.

Monetary policy is less subject than fiscal policy to political constraints but does not escape the problem of uncertainty regarding the precise nature, strength, and timing of its effects.

Changes in the money supply affect total spending in a predictable way (predictable, that is, with respect to broad and long-run effects) insofar as the public maintains a stable velocity of money circulation by attempting to maintain a preferred level of real money balances.

Fiscal and monetary policy are not independent stabilization tools because government borrowing affects the monetary sector of the economy.

The size of the national debt is a less important question than the size and timing of changes in the debt and the purposes to which the borrowed funds are put.

QUESTIONS FOR DISCUSSION

1. When did the Great Depression end? Why did it end? How do you know?

2. Assume that Congress and the president want to cut taxes by $5 billion to stimulate the economy in a period of recession. Does it matter whether they cut personal income taxes or corporate income taxes? Whether the cuts in personal income taxes are concentrated among low-income groups or more widely distributed?

3. Suppose the unemployment rate is 8 percent and economic statisticians tell the government that 2 of those 8 percentage points are a direct result of sharply reduced purchases of new automobiles. Discuss the advantages and disadvantages in such a situation of offering a tax rebate to purchasers of new automobiles equal to 10 percent of the manufacturers' suggested retail price. Is a dollar of tax reduction offered in this way likely to reduce unemployment more than a dollar of personal income tax reduction? Are the long-run effects on unemployment likely to be different from the short-run effects?

4. During the depression of the 1930s, increases in federal government expenditures were often accompanied by promises (threats?) of future tax increases to hold down the size of the budget deficit. Do you think this policy had any effect on investment spending?

5. Would you favor the proposal, mentioned in the text, to give the president authority to change tax rates or authorize expenditures on his own (within congressionally designated limits) as a way of making fiscal policy more flexible? Why or why not?

6. In what sense is the assertion that MV equals PQ a tautology?

7. Will an increase in M be more likely to raise P or raise Q (if V is constant)? What are some of the factors that might determine the relative impact on P or Q? Would it make any difference whether the increase in M came about because of Treasury borrowing or because of private borrowing?

8. If P rises while M remains constant, what happens to real money balances? If people were holding their preferred level of real balances prior to the increase in the price level, what actions might they take to restore the level of their real balances? Can inflation occurring simultaneously with a zero rate of growth in the money supply cause a recession?

9. "We cannot predict the effect of a change in the rate of growth in the money stock on the velocity of circulation unless we know how it affects people's expectations regarding future changes in the price level." Evaluate that argument.

10. Suppose the Fed substantially increases the free reserves of commercial banks, and the banks use these additional reserves to add more government securities to their portfolio of earning assets. How will this affect the yield on government securities? Why will it tend also to affect the yield on corporate bonds and mortgages?

11. Suppose everyone came to believe that prices were going to rise sharply in the next month or so. How would this belief affect their demand for money balances? How would it affect their demand for goods other than money? What effect would this likely have on the prices of goods other than money? What effect would it likely have on the price of money? (The price of money is the rate at which it exchanges for goods, just as the price of other goods is the rate at which they exchange for money.)

12. How much money do you hold on average over the course of a typical month? What would induce you to increase that amount?

To decrease it? How would you go about doing so?

13. The only practicable way to calculate the velocity of money circulation is to divide a measure of the money stock into some measure of total expenditures.
    a. Test your understanding of the velocity concept by thinking up some way by which it could be measured more directly.
    b. Suppose you kept track for one year of your daily holdings of currency and demand deposits. How could you obtain from these data a measure of your own personal contribution to the velocity of money circulation?

14. "An increase or decrease in government spending will usually entail an offsetting decrease or increase in private spending." Under what circumstances would you expect that statement to be true? Why? Under what circumstances would you expect that statement to be false? Why?

15. Examine the thesis that the federal budget deficits for the 1976 and 1977 fiscal years did or did not significantly "crowd out" private expenditures.

16. Senator Hubert Humphrey said shortly after the March 1975 tax cuts that "common sense" told him federal borrowing would not raise interest rates and crowd out private borrowers. "To a large extent this credit market question takes care of itself," he said. "Private demands for credit go down when unemployment is high. This makes room in the credit market for government demand which goes up." Do you agree?

17. Can you think of any experiment by which we might test the proposition that fiscal policy affects total spending regardless of what is happening to the money supply?

18. Does monetary policy require assistance from fiscal policy to be effective?

19. "The size of the national debt is not as important as the size of changes in the debt." Evaluate that assertion.

20. What would be the consequences of a systematic effort by the federal government to retire the national debt over a period of 20 years?

21. When a corporation successfully sells additional bonds or a new issue of common stock, it goes more deeply into debt. Is this evidence that the corporation is failing or succeeding? How well do analogies from the area of business indebtedness apply to questions of government indebtedness? Where do such analogies present a misleading picture and why?

National Policies
and International Trade

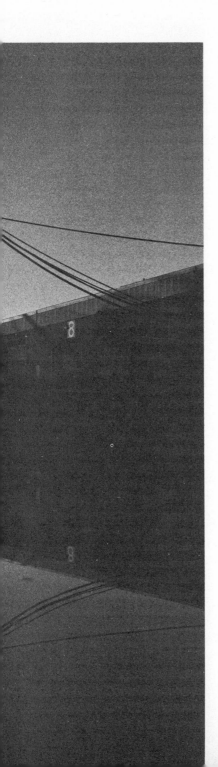

Why has a chapter on international trade been inserted between two chapters on national policy making? National economies exist within the international economy, but the position of this chapter implies just the opposite.

The implication was fully intended. International economic policies are constructed by national states, which frequently act as if other countries were enemies rather than participants in mutually advantageous exchange. We often hear today that nationalism is obsolete in the era of jet planes, rockets, space travel, satellite communication, and nuclear weapons. But that is not a description of reality so much as the statement of an ideal which much of the world is obviously determined to ignore.

A more important reason for discussing international trade before returning to domestic stabilization policies is that they are inextricably connected. And in two ways. The governments of national states attempt to bend the flow of international exchange to fit the pattern of domestic policy. But they are not altogether successful. International exchange often escapes from the channels to which national policies have tried to confine it and frustrates the intentions of domestic output, employment, and price policies.

Comparative Advantage and International Trade

The principle of comparative advantage received its first explicit statement in the early nineteenth century as an explanation of the gains to be obtained from international trade. But the principle has never fared well in the place where it originated. "Everyone knows" that imports replace domestically produced goods and destroy jobs, while exports earn income for domestic producers and create additional jobs. Policies aimed at restricting imports and subsidizing exports have consequently had a strong political appeal for centuries, and never more so than when a recession is cutting output and adding to the level of unemployment.

The argument that imports destroy jobs has the seductive appeal of a half-truth. When Americans buy Japanese radios they do not buy as many domestically made radios. An increase in radio imports can therefore lead to production cutbacks and layoffs in the domestic radio industry. So the owners and employees of radio manufacturing firms have an obvious interest in restricting imports. And when they go to Congress to request taxes or quotas on radio imports, they have a handy slogan with which to claim that such protection is good for the country: it protects American jobs. But the argument is misleading.

In the first place, jobs are created by the production of export goods as well as the production of goods that compete with imports. And American firms cannot continue to sell abroad if foreigners are not allowed to sell in the United States. Trade is a two-way street.

Second, jobs should not automatically be treated as goods. Some jobs no doubt are intrinsically satisfying and worth doing for themselves without regard to the commodities or services that result. But that's certainly rare. The justification for jobs generally is the income they provide for workers and the corresponding benefit to others in the form of useful goods. The "protect American jobs" argument ignores the gains in real income that come from specialization. If the Japanese can make better radios and sell them at lower prices than American manufacturers can, Americans ought to produce other products and buy their radios from Japan. The attempt to justify the protection of less efficient producers on the grounds that this will preserve jobs runs quickly into absurdity. Why not push the argument further and produce domestically all the coffee we consume? American soil, climate, and geography are not as well suited for the production of coffee trees as are large areas of Brazil and Colombia; but think of all the jobs we could create by building and operating huge greenhouses in which we try to duplicate the favorable growing conditions in those countries! And why stop with goods currently imported? Think of how many new jobs we could create by outlawing the use of automated equipment in the telephone industry!

Producer Interests and the National Interest

Economists have been arguing along these lines for two centuries against the proponents of restrictions on imports, but not with great success. A French pamphleteer-economist named Frederic Bastiat (1801–1850) wrote a witty satire in 1845 in the form of a petition by the French candlemakers for protection against the unfair competition of the sun. Their request to the Chamber of Deputies for legislation that would protect the jobs of candlemakers by prohibiting windows brilliantly exposes the absurdity of protectionist logic. Bastiat's satire has been reprinted numerous times; but the arguments he ridiculed do not disappear.

Part of the explanation must be found in the resistance of special interest groups to mere logic. People are readily persuaded by arguments in which they want to believe and have more difficulty understanding arguments that run counter to their interests. And the political process almost guarantees that those who stand to benefit from restrictions on international trade will have a louder voice in policy formation than will the larger group that stands to lose. Transaction costs prevent radio purchasers from organizing effectively to oppose domestic producers; and the foreign producers obviously have little influence on domestic policy.

A limited but legitimate argument for protection against imports can be constructed from the costs of change. The closing down of an industry unable to meet foreign competition entails losses for its owners and employees. The more narrowly specialized the displaced human and property resources, the greater the losses. There may be a case for protection in such circumstances. Notice, however, that the argument can be applied to the case of an industry hurt by domestic competition as well as foreign. Domestic competitors have political influence, of course, and are therefore harder to exclude by special legislation. Nonetheless, if resources were attracted into an industry because of government restrictions on imports, it may be unfair to jerk that protection away suddenly. So there is a case for the maintenance of prior and long continued restrictions on imports, or at least for their reduction (in the interest of efficiency) at a slow rate (in the interest of equity). Equity considerations along with political realities may also suggest a policy of transitional subsidies, designed to reduce the loss to workers and owners or to help them find new opportunities. But this argument cannot support the introduction of new or additional restrictions against imports.

There is no limit to the number of bad arguments that can be constructed in support of import restrictions, and it would be an exercise in futility to attempt to anticipate and refute each one. The fact that there is a kernel of validity in most such arguments complicates the task of their analysis: the valid reasoning must be winnowed from the chaff which surrounds it before the limitations of its applicability can be shown. Nothing would contribute more toward raising the quality of public discussion in this area than a firm grasp of the principle of comparative advantage.

The principle of comparative advantage shows why and how exchange creates wealth. It keeps insisting that the cost of a transaction is the value of what is given up and the benefit is the value of what is obtained, so that it is nonsense to claim that a country can grow wealthy by exporting more than it imports. The principle of comparative advantage undercuts the claim that one country may be more efficient than another in the production of everything: the logical impossibility of that is apparent from the very definition of efficiency as a ratio between the value of what is produced and what is consequently not produced, between the goods obtained and the goods that had to be sacrificed because their production entails genuine opportunity costs. By focusing on the real factors involved in production and trade, the principle of comparative advantage disperses the fog that creeps in when trade policy is discussed exclusively in monetary terms.

"But then we'd be losing dollars!" So? Dollars cost almost nothing to produce. If other countries want to trade transistor radios

A consumer who works against import restrictions cannot hope to receive more than a tiny fraction of the benefits. A producer lobbying for restrictions hopes for a very large benefit.

for dollars, that's a marvelous swap from our point of view, so marvelous, in fact, that other nations can be counted on not to do it for long. This becomes obvious as soon as one understands the concept of the balance of international payments. Unfortunately, the balance of payments is more often invoked to confuse than to clarify the issue.

The Balance of Payments

The balance of payments always and necessarily balances. You might be a bit surprised to hear that, since we are told so often that we must do this or cannot do that "because of the balance of payments." The implication is that its balance is precarious, and that we are in danger of disastrously losing our equilibrium. But if patriotism is the last refuge of a scoundrel, as Samuel Johnson suggested, the balance of payments is today very often the last refuge of Dr. Johnson's patriots. Special-interest groups looking for favors look also for a way to wrap themselves in the balance of payments. A little clarity on the meaning of the balance of payments can therefore go a long way toward locating the public interest amid the confusing claims of competing partial interests.

Balance-of-payments accounting is an attempt to keep track of international transactions by dividing them into transactions that earn foreign exchange, called credits, and transactions that use up foreign exchange, called debits. If you keep this basic definition in mind you should have no trouble deciding under which column to list a particular item.

Exports are credit items in the balance of payments. Foreigners who want to purchase our products must ultimately pay dollars to the American sellers. This results either in the reacquisition by Americans of dollars previously held by foreigners, in the acquisition of foreign currency used to purchase dollars, or in the acquisition of some other medium of international exchange that can be used to purchase dollars. U.S. imports simply reverse this flow. To purchase the products of some other country we must either turn over previously acquired holdings of that country's currency, obtain some by giving up dollars in exchange, or use up our stocks of some other accepted international exchange medium to obtain the required currency.

That's all there is to the balance of payments—if we define exports and imports broadly enough. Imports, for example, must include not only commodities like magnesium and tape recorders, but also services like the Geneva hotel room used by an American tourist or the entertainment provided in Fort Worth by an English rock group. Payment for these services entails the using up of foreign exchange, and so they are debit items in the U.S. balance of payments.

What about gold? Gold sales or exports are credit items, just like any other exports; gold purchases or imports are debit items. Gold sales are a way of acquiring foreign exchange just as are sales of wheat. Momentary confusion may arise from the fact that gold is itself considered a medium of international exchange. Treat it like any other commodity, however, and you'll get it in the correct column.

We must also include under imports the "purchase" of whatever it is we obtain when our government extends foreign aid or Americans send money to relatives in Europe. If it seems inappropriate to think of either activity as "importing," the fact remains that any payments made to foreigners by the United States government, private organizations, or individuals use up foreign exchange and must therefore be classified as debits. These payments may be used in turn to purchase American exports (sometimes that's a condition of the grant); if so, the export is a credit item; but the gift, grant, pension, or other remittance that made it possible goes under the debit column. Gifts to us by foreigners or payments made to Americans by Lloyds of London in settlement of insurance claims are correspondingly credit items in our balance of payments. And the sizeable income that we receive each year as a return on our overseas investment goes into the credit column, because it is a source of foreign exchange earnings for the United States.

What about the original acts of investing? Capital flows can be treated like commodities and services if attention is focused on the stock, bond, or other evidence of indebtedness that changes hands. Thus foreign investment by Americans amounts to importing securities. Investment by foreigners in the United States is a U.S. export of securities. If this way of describing the matter strikes you as strained, you can keep the effects of foreign investment clear by concentrating on the basic definition of credits and debits. Investment by Americans in the French economy is a debit item in our balance of payments because Americans must purchase French francs to buy an interest in French companies. And Britons buying shares of General Motors contribute to the credit side of our balance of payments because they must obtain dollars to complete the purchase.

To invest abroad is to import securities.

Why Credits Always Equal Debits

Suppose now that we sum the values of all the debits in the course of a year, then of all the credits, and find that they are not equal. We conclude in such a case that we made a mistake in record keeping! Errors and omissions are inevitable, of course, when one is trying to keep track of *all* international transactions. The value of some transactions can only be guessed at, as when the balance-of-payments accountants tacked on $40 million in the 1920s for imports of bootleg liquor. And the value of many perfectly legal transactions is estimated from incomplete records, inaccurate data, and partial samples. So measured credits and debits never

The balance of payments must balance because every international transaction is treated as an exchange: nothing is imported unless something of equal value is exported.

do turn out to be precisely equal in balance of payments statements. The keepers of the accounts rise to the occasion by adding the difference to the smaller of the two totals and labeling it Net Errors and Omissions.

"Aha!" says the voice from the rear. "It's all a trick. The balance of payments always balances because the Bureau of Economic Analysis puts in a fudge factor. Outside the artificial world of double-entry bookkeeping, however, it's perfectly possible for Americans to buy more from foreigners than they buy from us. Real world deficits can and do occur."

But the accounting conventions used to keep track of international exchanges are not arbitrary. They are based on the assumption that an exchange is in fact an exchange, so that every international transaction is properly entered on the ledger as simultaneously a "getting" and a "giving up." Credits are made to equal debits to reflect the fact that sales of goods are also receipts of payments. A Japanese radio imported into the United States means something was exported from the United States to Japan, whether commodities, services, dollars, yen, gold, or promises to pay later. And for accounting purposes, goods exchanged for each other have the same value.

The Ambiguity of "Disequilibrium"

But what do informed people mean, then, when they talk about deficits or surpluses in the balance of payments? And why are they ever concerned about disequilibrium in the balance of payments if in fact it always balances? The answer is that a deficit or a surplus is a discrepancy between what *actually* happened and what people *intended* to happen. That is always the meaning of a disequilibrium in the economic way of thinking and you've encountered it before.

A disequilibrium price for wheat does not show up as a difference between actual sales and purchases (which are necessarily identical) but as a difference between intended or desired sales and purchases. A disequilibrium in income-expenditures analysis does not mean that actual saving and investment are unequal (they cannot be) but that intended saving and investment are unequal. The implication of a disequilibrium is that matters will not continue in this way because intentions are not being realized and so adjustments are going to occur. It follows that we cannot use the concept of equilibrium or disequilibrium unless we have a clear notion of intended or desired results that we can contrast with actual results.

The concept of a balance-of-payments disequilibrium is so extraordinarily ambiguous that we would probably be better off if we discarded the notion altogether. There are just too many intentions of too many different kinds entering into the aggregate of international transactions for anyone to assert that intended credits are larger or smaller than intended debits—which is the meaning of a disequilibrium. In general, the larger the universe to which we try to apply the equilibrium concept, the more vague and uncertain is its

amount
actually
bought
and sold

amount
suppliers
intended
to sell

meaning and the more likely is it to obscure rather than clarify the problems at which we're looking.

A Dialogue about a Deficit

To claim that the U.S. balance of payments is in disequilibrium is to claim that something undesired is occurring. But from whose point of view is this claim made? Didn't the importers want to purchase whatever they purchased? Didn't banks want to loan whatever they loaned? Didn't the government, corporations, or individuals want to offer the gifts or grants they sent abroad? Who were the people for whom the results of international trade turned out to be inconsistent with what they had intended?

A simple little question should always be addressed to anyone who claims that the balance of payments is in deficit: "How do you know that?" The answer, if followed up properly, will tell you what it is that the speaker disapproves.

"We're losing gold." That was a common answer in the 1960s. But why call that a deficit? It was actually the way in which we paid for some of our purchases and so *avoided* a deficit.

"True," comes back the answer; "but a country cannot continue indefinitely to pay for its imports by drawing on its gold stock." And that's correct. But neither can a country continue indefinitely to pay for its imports by drawing down its stock of mineral resources. Nonetheless, no one regards Venezuelan oil exports or Rhodesian chrome exports as evidence of a deficit in those countries' balance of payments. Why single out gold for special treatment?

"Because if we lose all our monetary gold, we'll be forced to let the dollar depreciate." The United States government maintained the value of the dollar relative to gold up until the early 1970s by standing ready to exchange an ounce of gold for $35. If too many purchasers bought gold at that price, the U.S. would run out of gold and would have to allow the gold price of the dollar to fall. But why should we care if the price of gold rises to $40, $80, $200, or anything else?

"It isn't the price of gold we care about but the price of the dollar. We must maintain the dollar's value in terms of gold because the dollar is the major international medium of exchange. The whole world uses dollars because it has confidence in the value of the dollar. If we let the gold price of the dollar go down, we'll betray the world's confidence. Then what will there be to take the dollar's place as the medium of international exchange?" The argument is getting more complex, which is one of the points we've been trying to make: The assertion that the balance of payments is in disequilibrium is a way of saying that something undesirable is going to occur. The assertion is a deceptively simple way of making a very complex and uncertain argument without having to defend the steps in that argument or even acknowledge the actual goal. But now we can raise all sorts of critical questions. Foreigners were holding far more dollars in the late

By selling gold when its price rose above $35 an ounce, the US maintained the value of the dollar at 1/35 ounce of gold.

1960s than we could redeem in gold at $35 an ounce. They knew that; nevertheless they continued to accumulate and hold dollars. Is the real value of the dollar determined by the quantity of gold it will purchase or the quantity of useful goods and income-earning assets for which it exchanges? Foreigners want dollars for essentially the same reason as Americans: because they can be used to obtain Chevrolets, shares of IBM, and rib-eye steaks. The value of the dollar has not gone down unless its general purchasing power has decreased. Why the obsession with the amount of gold that a dollar will purchase?

"You've put your finger on the problem. The value of the dollar has been declining in the terms you've described. We must maintain its gold value as evidence that the United States intends to maintain the general purchasing power of the dollar. We cannot let the value of the dollar decline relative to other currencies. We must defend the dollar." But why?

"Because depreciation of the dollar is damaging to U.S. prestige. Because if the dollar depreciates Americans will pay higher prices for imports and get lower prices for exports. And because we are committed to a system of stable exchange rates and because we cannot allow the value of the dollar in terms of other currencies to bounce all around."

All three of those arguments were used in the 1960s to justify concern for the "deficit" in the U.S. balance of payments. We'll pass by the first and use the other two as an occasion for moving on to the important subject of exchange rates.

International Exchange Rates

Since the special problems of international economics are so closely bound up with the fact of different national currencies, it's important to understand what determines the rate at which one currency exchanges for another. We'll simplify the explanation by assuming that there are only two nations in the world, Germany and the United States. The United States uses dollars and Germany uses marks as the domestic medium of exchange. Americans who want to purchase German goods must therefore exchange dollars for marks, and Germans must exchange marks for dollars in order to purchase American goods. At what rate will they be exchanged for one another?

Suppose that one dollar can be exchanged for three marks. This exchange rate will determine the price to Americans of German goods and the price to Germans of American goods. A Volkswagen, for example, that carries a factory price tag of 7500 marks will also carry an implicit price of 2500 dollars. If the exchange rate were 1 dollar for 2.5 marks, a 7500-mark price would be a 3000-dollar price. Meanwhile, a factory price tag of 3000 dollars on a Chevrolet is read by Germans as 9000 marks when the exchange rate is one dollar for three marks. At a rate of 1 for 2.5, the Chevrolet, though its factory price remained unchanged, would seem to a German to have gone down in price to 7500 marks.

National Policies
and International Trade

It follows that the attractiveness of foreign goods will depend on the applicable exchange rate as well as the price levels in each country. A depreciation of the dollar, which is identical with an appreciation of the mark in our simplified case, causes German goods to look less attractive to Americans and American goods to look more attractive to Germans.[1] With a depreciation of the dollar against the mark, German imports (equals American exports) would tend to increase and American imports (equals German exports) would tend to decrease.

The exchange rate, in short, is a relative price that ties together two sets of relative prices. If the existing exchange rate does not accurately reflect the purchasing power of the two currencies and is not allowed to change, there will be the usual shortages or surpluses and consequently pressures toward change. Unless the exchange rate manages to bring the net attractiveness of American goods into balance with the net attractiveness of German goods, it will have trouble persisting. "Balance" here means that the quantity of dollars demanded by Germans is equal to the quantity of dollars supplied by Americans who want to buy marks. An equivalent way of stating it is that the quantity of marks demanded by Americans must be equal to the quantity of marks supplied by Germans who want to buy dollars. An inequality will mean either a shortage of dollars (equals a surplus of marks) or a surplus of dollars (equals a shortage of marks). Shortages and surpluses, as we saw in Chapter 4, can always be created by inappropriate prices. The price in this case is the exchange rate, or the price of one currency in terms of the other.

On the Manipulation of Exchange Rates

It is important to note what the preceding argument does not assert. It does not suggest that a country can increase its exports and decrease its imports simply by manipulating the rate at which its domestic currency exchanges for the currency of other countries. The argument actually runs in the other direction: a particular exchange rate must be consistent with underlying supply and demand conditions, or it cannot be maintained for long. We've already noted the frequent tendency for nations to push their exports while restricting imports. Devaluing their currency is a route they have often taken. But it isn't likely to succeed.

Suppose that an exchange rate of three marks for one dollar accurately reflects the relative purchasing power of marks in Germany and dollars in the United States. The U.S. government then

1. Students are often confused by the fact that a depreciation sometimes looks at first glance like an appreciation. You have to think about it for a moment to see that, when the mark goes from 35 to 40 cents this is a depreciation of the dollar—and an appreciation of the mark, of course. The British pound was devalued in 1967 when it was changed from $2.80 to $2.40. The value of the dollar increased, relative to the pound.

begins purchasing marks with dollars in order to drive up the price of the mark, from $33\frac{1}{3}$ cents to 40 cents (2.5 marks = 1 dollar). Using Volkswagens and Chevrolets again to represent all German and U.S. products, we note that this will at first make a 9000-mark VW seem more expensive to Americans than a 3000-dollar Chevrolet. To obtain a Volkswagen, Americans will now have to surrender 3600 dollars. Germans will simultaneously find Chevrolets cheaper; only 7500 marks will have to be paid to obtain 3000 dollars.

But all that is only the initial consequence. The quantity of U.S. goods demanded will now be greater than the quantity supplied, because both Germans and Americans will now be demanding only U.S. goods. And so domestic prices will start to increase in the United States. Assuming for the sake of simplicity that German domestic prices remain unchanged in the face of their concurrent excess supply of goods, the price of Chevrolets in the United States will rise to $3600. When domestic inflation in the United States has compensated for the devaluation of the dollar, the new exchange rate of 2.5 marks for one dollar will again be consistent with underlying conditions of demand and supply.

The crucial point is that this manipulation of the exchange rate did not secure a permanent increase in U.S. exports and decrease in U.S. imports. Instead it secured a 20 percent inflation to compensate for the 20 percent devaluation.

If most prices in industrialized countries are "sticky" in the downward direction so that relative price adjustments are usually adjustments upward, the attempt by governments to manipulate their exchange rates in this fashion is a recipe for international inflation. Suppose that during the period of adjustment between the dollar devaluation and the full U.S. inflation, when the domestic and foreign demand for German goods had temporarily dried up, German producers lobbied vigorously for a devaluation of the mark. Suppose further that their efforts were successful, and the German government began buying dollars to drive up the mark price of the dollar at about the time that the U.S. price level was approaching its 20 percent higher level. The whole process would begin again. German goods would now be in excess demand, and Germany would experience domestic inflation until rising prices had eliminated the excess demand for German goods.

The thrust of the argument in this section is that exchange rates cannot be set arbitrarily: they must be consistent with overall patterns of supply and demand. If for reasons of their own governments nonetheless insist upon "manipulating" exchange rates, they will either fail in the attempt or compel an alteration of the underlying conditions—like the inflation described above. A tailor cannot cut the cloth arbitrarily if he wants the suit to fit the customer. Of course, that does not logically exclude the possibility of cutting the cloth arbitrarily, and then slicing up and resewing the customer to fit the suit.

It was largely in order to prevent this kind of "competitive devaluation" that the Western nations established the International Monetary Fund after World War II. The IMF was supposed to assist any member nation whose currency was tending to depreciate and to advise on devaluation when it appeared that existing exchange rates seriously overstated the currency's value. With varying rates of economic growth from country to country and different rates of domestic inflation, exchange rates might have to be altered occasionally. But the objective of the Bretton Woods system (named after the town in New Hampshire where the international monetary agreements were negotiated in 1944) was *fixed* exchange rates. Each nation was supposed to buy and sell its currency in order to keep it pegged at the officially established rate of exchange. (Other currencies were pegged to the dollar, and the dollar was pegged to gold.) Out of all this, it was hoped, would develop an expansion of international trade.

The system was not a failure. International trade did expand under the Bretton Woods system, at roughly twice the rate of increase in domestic production. And the advantages of international specialization contributed substantially to rising levels of real income. But an international monetary system is difficult to maintain among governments pursuing divergent domestic policies. To see why this is so, try to imagine what would happen if Illinois decided to increase total spending within the state in order to raise the employment level.

Suppose it employs both fiscal and monetary policy. The state government increases expenditures from borrowed funds, while state banking authorities relax the reserve restrictions on banks within their jurisdiction. What will happen as a result is going to depend heavily on interstate economic transactions. If the easier credit availability in Illinois attracts borrowers from other states, the intended addition to the Illinois money supply will be diluted through a much larger territory. So Illinois might impose restrictions on "foreign" borrowing. But if the money supply does increase relative to neighboring states, Illinois prices will tend to rise relative to prices in other states. This will encourage Illinois citizens who can conveniently do so to purchase more from outside the state. So Illinois might levy special taxes on goods brought into the state. Meanwhile the increased government expenditures on highways and public buildings will be attracting bids from out-of-state contractors. They can be prohibited from bidding on state contracts. But construction workers would still come over from Hammond to Chicago and from St. Louis to East St. Louis in response to the more attractive job opportunities in Illinois. So the state government would have to prohibit foreigners from working in the state unless they held special permits; in other words they would have to adopt immigration quotas. But you have the idea by now. The states of the United States have a smoothly functioning and highly integrated "international" economic system primarily because the Constitution prohibits state interference with interstate commerce.

The world as a whole does not enjoy a constitutional prohibition of provincialism. And so producer interests in protection continued to express themselves in restrictions on imports. Governments that gave priority to the maintenance of high employment levels found their exports falling and their currencies depreciating relative to the currencies of nations that assigned more importance to price stability. The movement of capital between nations was sometimes encouraged, sometimes penalized, depending on the shifting objectives of national governments. The role of the dollar as the principal source of international liquidity came under attack as some nations objected that by agreeing to hold dollars they were in effect making loans to the United States, and that the United States was taking advantage of its privileged position to purchase valuable goods with cheaply produced dollars. Even in the United States there was objection to the arrangement on the grounds that domestic monetary authorities pursued high interest rate policies to make the holding of dollars more attractive and that this retarded investment and economic growth.

A notable irony of the Bretton Woods system was the frequency with which its stated objectives were deliberately frustrated in order to maintain the system itself. All sorts of restrictions on international exchange were adopted by national governments ostensibly to correct a "deficit" in the balance of payments that threatened the exchange-rate stability which was supposedly so important in promoting free and expanding international exchange. The United States played this strange game, too. At one time or another we raised the cost to American tourists of bringing back foreign merchandise, placed a tax on money borrowed by foreign corporations from U.S. sources, restricted foreign lending by U.S. banks, imposed first voluntary and later mandatory controls on direct investment abroad by U.S. corporations, recalled the dependents of American servicemen stationed overseas, threatened to impose quotas unless particular countries "voluntarily" curtailed their exports to us, and in a variety of smaller ways tried to discourage imports and encourage exports. All this was done to "protect the dollar" against the balance of payments "deficits" that supposedly threatened the international monetary order.

Fixed versus Floating Exchange Rates

In 1971, when the United States suspended the convertibility of the dollar into gold and other countries more or less reluctantly gave up the effort to maintain an established rate of exchange between their currencies and the dollar, some experts announced the breakdown of the international monetary system and the appearance of a world monetary crisis. They called for emergency conferences to create a new system that would restore order before the flow of trade and exchange broke down in chaos.

But other experts rejoiced in the disappearance of the old system. The first group's crisis was the second group's solution. Some had long argued that the real problems in the international monetary system arose from that system itself, from the attempt to maintain fixed exchange rates rather than allowing rates to float with changing conditions of supply and demand. Outside of academic circles, however, and especially among the economists working for central banks, floating exchange rates were regarded as unworkable if desirable and undesirable if workable. They would increase uncertainty for foreign traders and investors, it was argued. But they would also create additional uncertainty for domestic producers and investors, because a change in exchange rates could quickly and radically change the potential profitability of industries producing import-competitive goods as well as goods that might be exported. Moreover, governments were not likely to remain passive when a sudden depreciation in the currency of a major trading country led to an unexpected surge of imports or threatened established export markets. Governments would far more likely retaliate with trade and exchange controls that could eventually lead to a breakdown of international exchange.

Advocates of floating exchange rates replied that government attempts to maintain fixed rates had demonstrably failed. Such attempts did not in fact make it easier for international traders and investors to predict the future. On the contrary, they led governments into all sorts of trade and exchange restrictions, as price controls of any sort inevitably do. And they did not subject domestic policy to any "balance of payments discipline" because countries were always willing to devalue anyway when attention to the balance of payments might threaten cherished domestic objectives. In short, fixed exchange rates offered the worst of all possible worlds: increased uncertainty in the name of greater stability, restrictions on trade for the sake of free trade, and a "discipline" that inhibited flexibility while allowing irresponsibility.

Some of the evidence is now in. Floating rates do work. On the other hand, the majority of the world's countries do not let their currencies float freely, but rather try to keep them more or less closely related to some other, major currency. The dollar is only one such currency; the pound sterling, the French franc, and the mark have their own set of satellite currencies. Even the major currencies are not always allowed to float freely, as governments intervene to practice what has come to be called a "dirty float" rather than keeping hands off and achieving a "clean float." Don't conclude that "dirty" necessarily means naughty. The new head of the International Monetary Fund, presumably a spokesman for virtue, told an IMF conference in Nairobi in September of 1973 that he welcomed central bank intervention in currency markets as a way of reducing "gyrations" and pushing currencies toward their true "underlying value."

What Kind of International Order?

Is it true, as some contend, that with the collapse of the fixed exchange-rate system there is no longer any international economic order? For those who equate order with legal systems and international order with negotiated treaties, the statement might be true. For those who see evidence of order in the simple continuation and extension of international exchange, the statement is clearly false. What criteria are we using when we ask about international order?

From some points of view the present system is excessively orderly, far too efficient in transmitting economic effects internationally. Take a look at Table 20A which compares rates of increase in the consumer price level in ten countries.

TABLE 20A	Increases in Consumer Prices (annual rates of change)	
	1958–64	1971–73
United States	1.2%	4.8%
Canada	1.3	6.2
United Kingdom	2.4	8.2
Germany	2.2	6.3
Japan	4.8	8.3
France	4.3	6.3
Italy	4.2	8.1
Switzerland	2.2	7.7
Netherlands	2.7	7.9
Belgium	1.7	6.2

Sources: Bureau of Labor Statistics, International Monetary Fund, Organization for Economic Cooperation and Development. Data compiled by Research Department, Federal Reserve Bank of St. Louis.

In each country, consumer prices rose significantly faster from 1971–73 than they had done from 1958–64. In every case but one, the annual rate of increase was between 3.5 and 5.8 percentage points greater in the latter period. Each country has its own central bank, its own government budget, its own institutional patterns for price and wage setting; yet consumer prices changed in a strikingly similar way. What a remarkable coincidence—unless we assume that these countries' economies are part of an international economic system.

The same "order" that enables American teen-agers to carry Japanese transistor radios and puts American engineers and machinery to work exploring for oil in the Persian Gulf also frustrates upon occasion the domestic policies of national governments or powerful groups within those nations. Perhaps the difficult questions are not really questions of the best institutional arrangements for ordering an international economic system. Those may be mere technical questions for which a wide variety of solutions can easily be found if national governments stop pursuing domestic policies that interfere with any international order. That statement doesn't necessarily imply that national governments are villainous. But the overriding fact is that international policies are developed in the context of national economic policies. Governments today have programs by means of which they try to control economic growth, fluctuations in production, unemployment, price levels, and the distribution of income. And the realities of democratic politics decree that those programs take precedence over the maintenance of a stable international economic system.

The Public Interest

Amid all the confusion of conflicting answers, the question sometimes gets lost: Should investors, borrowers, consumers, producers, government agencies, and anyone else interested in international transactions be allowed to choose the opportunities they prefer, subject only to the usual constraint of agreement on the part of the other party to the exchange? Or should governments impose special restrictions on international exchange? That is the fundamental question of international economic policy, and the answer that one gives to it will shape all his thinking about balance-of-payments equilibrium, fixed or fluctuating exchange rates, and special measures to discourage or encourage exports or imports, whether of merchandise, services, or securities.

It is certainly possible that the interests of the larger public might require some restrictions on international exchange. But a thoughtful person will wonder why the national interest seems so regularly to require that more be given away than is received in return; that jobs be preferred to goods; that efficient producers be hobbled to prevent them from using their advantage to the detriment of less efficient producers; and that in general people be prevented from increasing their wealth by exchanging freely. The skeptic should be pardoned for concluding that the public interest may be something quite different from the national interest, at least as the latter is often defined by those who shape international economic policy.

Once Over Lightly

The movement of goods and financial assets across international boundaries can either frustrate or promote the domestic policies of national governments. Government stabilization policies have particularly close interconnections with international trade policies.

The principle of comparative advantage has not fared well in the area of international trade against well-organized producer interests, economic nationalism, and the enduring belief that imports cause unemployment.

The total credits in the balance of international payments always equal the debits. Any discrepancy can only be due to errors in record keeping.

A disequilibrium in the balance of payments implies that *desired* credits and debits (desired by whom?) are not equal. To assert that the balance of payments is in deficit is to imply that some credit items were unintended, cannot be expected to continue, or should not have been allowed to occur. The concept of a balance-of-payments disequilibrium is usually a complex policy judgment disguised as a simple statement of obvious fact.

A common meaning for "balance of payments disequilibrium" under the Bretton Woods system after World War II was "a situation inconsistent with maintenance of the present fixed exchange rates."

Exchange rates between national currencies must reflect the underlying forces of supply and demand for the currencies if they are to persist.

Adjustments in exchange rates designed to reduce imports and increase exports promote inflation in the devaluing country.

Floating exchange rates eliminate a large class of balance-of-payments deficits or surpluses: all those that translate as "a situation inconsistent with the present fixed exchange rates."

QUESTIONS FOR DISCUSSION

1. In order to take advantage of lower production costs, a Massachusetts textile manufacturer builds a factory in North Carolina and a United States television manufacturing firm opens an assembly plant in Mexico.

    a. In what ways is the action by the television firm different from the action by the textile firm?

    b. Is either action contrary to the national interest?

    c. Is either action likely to encounter effective political opposition?

2. The table below shows consumer price indices for four countries from 1970 to 1974 (1970 = 100).

United States	Canada	France	Germany
100.0	100.0	100.0	100.0
104.3	102.9	105.5	105.3
107.7	107.8	111.7	111.1
114.4	116.0	119.9	118.8
127.0	127.9	135.5	126.8

Do you think the similar patterns between the United States and Canada and between France and Germany are mere coincidence?

3. What would be the consequence for Volkswagen sales in the United States of a depreciation in the mark relative to the dollar? How would this affect the profitability of sales to the United States by the

Volkswagen Company? Would you expect the long-term effects to differ from the short-run effects?

4. One step taken by the U.S. government in the 1960s to correct the "balance of payments problem" was to restrict foreign investment by U.S. firms and banks. How would such a program, if it had been effective, have influenced U.S. debits and credits? Would the long-term consequences be different from the short-run consequences?

5. What is meant by "a favorable balance of trade," a phrase that has been in common use for several centuries? What is favorable about it? To whom?

6. Can a country export more than it imports? Be clear in your definition of exports and imports (for example, are financial securities and gold included in exports and imports?).

7. Suppose that the dollar were "threatened" by depreciation with respect to a set of other major currencies. What effect would each of the following have? Would they create additional pressure or counter the pressure toward depreciation?
   a. Americans increase investment abroad.
   b. American income from previous foreign investment increases.
   c. The United States government extends military aid to a foreign government in the form of twenty jet fighter planes.
   d. It is announced that, over the last quarter, foreign central banks have significantly increased their holdings of dollar balances.
   e. It comes to be widely believed that the U.S. government is planning to increase substantially the official price of gold.

8. Do exporters care whether their currency depreciates or appreciates in international exchange? Explain why. How do importers feel about exchange-rate changes? Why?

9. What is the difference between exchange rates that are free to fluctuate in response to conditions of supply and demand, and exchange rates that are fixed but are periodically altered in accordance with changed conditions of supply and demand?

10. Suppose that the Japanese yen is significantly undervalued in international exchange, but that the Japanese government refuses to revalue it upward (that is, change the price at which it pegs the yen to other currencies). What effects will this have on Japanese exports and imports of merchandise? What effect will it have on the Japanese domestic price level? (Hint: As Japanese exporters acquire foreign currencies, they turn them in to the central bank for yen.) What if the central bank sold Japanese government bonds in the same amount? (This is called "sterilization.")

11. If the value of Iran's merchandise imports is 20 percent greater than the value of its merchandise exports, does Iran have a deficit in its balance of payments?
   a. If the difference is covered by 20-year loans?
   b. If the difference is covered by one-year loans?
   c. If the difference is covered by selling gold from the national treasury?
   d. If the difference is covered by selling newly mined gold?
   e. Suppose that merchandise imports are 400 percent greater than merchandise exports *excluding petroleum*, and the difference is made up by selling newly extracted black gold?

12. Why do so many Americans believe that this country would be endangered by Arab ownership of "essential" U.S. industries, but do not believe that U.S. ownership of foreign industries poses a threat to the national security of those countries? Why are U.S.-owned foreign enterprises thought to be at the mercy of foreign governments and the United States at the mercy of foreigners who own U.S. enterprises?

13. How can U.S. imports reduce the domestic money supply? How can the Fed prevent this from occurring? What would be the consequences of such "neutralization" actions by the monetary authorities?

14. Why cannot one country have a comparative advantage over another country in the production of everything if the first country has excellent natural resources, a huge capital stock, a highly skilled labor force, and ingenious technicians and managers while the second country is poor in all four areas?

15. What evidence exists to support the view that Japan has a comparative advantage over against the United States in the production of small automobiles? How would you account for this comparative advantage? How would you explain the fact that the United States in general seems to have a comparative advantage in the production of large automobiles but a comparative disadvantage in the production of smaller ones?

16. How does the theory of external benefits and "free riders" help explain the generally greater legislative influence of producers than of consumers?

17. In the late 1960s the Fed tried to keep short-term interest rates up in order to "protect the U.S. balance of payments." How would this affect the balance of payments? The Fed simultaneously tried to keep long-term interest rates low to encourage investment and economic growth.

Where is the line between the short term and the long term? Can the "line" be crossed?

18. How would you expect a recession to affect a country's imports of merchandise, services, and securities?

19. Explain what Charles DeGaulle meant when he rejected U.S. complaints about French purchases of gold in the 1960s by stating that France could not be expected to finance an American takeover of French industry.

20. "Floating exchange rates free a nation to pursue the domestic policies it prefers." Is that true?

21. Is it harmful to U.S. prestige when the dollar depreciates? Why do you suppose that governments usually express more official alarm over depreciation than over appreciation of their currencies?

22. Estimates published in 1972 predicted that the Concorde SST would not repay its development costs, would create environmental problems, and would not generate sufficient additional revenue to cover the associated costs for the airlines that purchase them. These were essentially the objections that led to cancellation of government financing for an American SST. A counterargument in both cases has been that these planes would provide many additional jobs, help the balance of payments, and prevent other countries from gaining an advantage. How would you evaluate the issue?

Inflation, Unemployment, and Political Economy

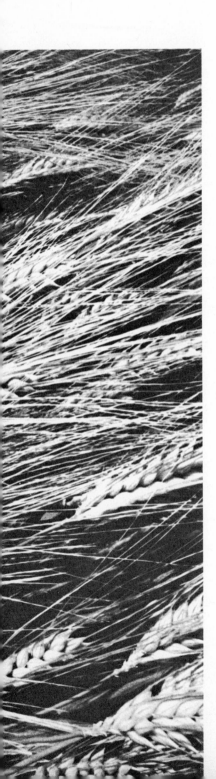

Nothing contributed more strongly to the public's sudden disillusionment with economists in the early 1970s than the appearance of rapid inflation combined with high and rising unemployment. That wasn't supposed to happen, according to the public's notion of what economists were teaching, because inflation and recession are opposites.

Inflation versus Unemployment

Inflation and recession are not actually opposites, of course. The opposite of inflation is deflation, a falling rather than a rising price level. There is no generally accepted term for the opposite of recession, but "boom" comes close: a period of increasing output and employment, mixed possibly but not necessarily with rising prices. But if inflation and recession aren't opposites in the strict sense, they have been considered opposites in the sense of sunshine and rain: the two are not expected to occur in the same place at the same time.

It's clear that the general public was surprised in 1970 when unemployment rose to 6.2 percent in the month of December despite the fact that the Consumer Price Index had been going up throughout the year at an average annual rate of 7 percent. The spectacular show was still to come, however. Unemployment rose during 1974 from 5.2 percent in January to 7.2 percent in December while the Consumer Price Index was adding the phrase "double digit inflation" to our vocabulary of jargon by jumping 11 percent.

Professional economists weren't as embarrassed by all this as some journalists and television commentators, perhaps too eager to proclaim a crisis, claimed they were. But it was true that the economics textbooks had for some years been analyzing inflation and recession as if they were the result of opposite forces and therefore could not occur simultaneously. They spoke of "gaps" between what aggregate demand was and what it ought to be. An inflationary gap meant that everyone together was trying to purchase more goods than the economic system could produce and bidding up the price level. A deflationary or recessionary gap meant that spending intentions were falling short of what producers wanted to supply, so that either prices were starting to fall, or, far more likely given the general sluggishness of prices under downward pressure, output and employment were declining.

This way of setting up the problem leaves the impression that inflation will not occur when a deflationary gap exists and recession cannot occur in the presence of an inflationary gap, so that inflation and unemployment are indeed opposites. If they are caused, respectively, by an excessive and inadequate level of aggregate demand, we should not expect to observe both at the same time. Moreover, the way to deal with inflation is clearly to "close" the inflationary gap by reducing spending. Recession calls for closing the deflationary gap by increasing spending. But then what does inflation *with* recession call for? It calls above all for some other way of looking at the problem.

The argument based on aggregate-demand gaps can easily be supplemented to allow for some inflation coexisting with high unemployment. Suppose the economy has been in a recession and is now recovering. We would not expect all prices and wages to stand still until rising aggregate demand had restored the entire economy to "full capacity" operation. Demand will expand faster in some areas than others, and sometimes more rapidly in sectors already operating close to capacity than in sectors where idle resources are especially large. And so some prices and wages will rise before unemployment has been reduced to the target level. In such a case policy makers might have to choose between less unemployment and less inflation; within a certain range, at least, one could not be reduced without increasing the other. This analysis is one source of the widely held view that high employment levels and price stability are *alternatives* between which we must choose by assessing the relative impact of each on social welfare.

We have paid little attention to the question of how much harm inflation or unemployment inflicts. But if they are alternatives, policy makers ought to have some sense of the costs involved in slighting one problem by choosing to focus on the other.

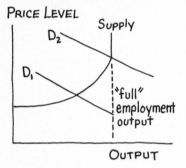

Increasing aggregate demand raises prices before "full" employment is reached.

PRICE LEVEL

OUTPUT

The Costs of Inflation

Why is inflation a social evil? It's hard to get people to take that question seriously in a period of fairly rapid inflation, when every pronouncement by politicians, union leaders, business executives, and television commentators begins with the assumption that it's a grave evil and asks only what must be done to stop it.

"In an inflation everything becomes more expensive. And that's obviously bad, isn't it?" It would indeed be bad if it were true; but it isn't true. If the price of everything increases in equal proportion, then nothing has really become more expensive. Money has simply become cheaper. Note carefully that "everything" includes the services of wage and salary workers as well as financial assets of every kind, from mortgages through bank deposits to the "entitlements" of people drawing pensions or social security benefits. Of course, all prices do not increase in equal proportion during an inflation, so that some goods do become more expensive in real terms. But it is a logical corollary that other goods then become less expensive in real terms. A large part of the social problem created by inflation is the tendency for goods to rise in price at different rates. But unless this has other effects, the losses must balance the gains. Insofar as inflation simply means a decrease in the purchasing power of money, it does not make the society as a whole worse off.

But inflation does tend to redistribute wealth and income. For all prices and wages will not increase in the same proportion and at the same time that the aggregate money demand increases. Some prices are set for only short periods of time and can move up quickly in response to increased demand: examples are the prices of farm products and many of the raw materials used in industrial production. Other prices, like those at a retail grocery chain, are revised less frequently and so respond less quickly to demand. Commercial and residential rents are usually set by contract and often cannot be changed for long periods; although there are ways for landlords to compel a reopening of the contract in order to negotiate a higher rental, these procedures entail additional costs to the landlord. Wages and salaries are typically established by agreements that are supposed to extend over longer periods of time; these agreements can also be renegotiated during the contract period, and some will even contain formal clauses calling for renegotiation if certain conditions change. Wages and salaries, however, tend to be less responsive to increased money demand than retail prices, though more responsive than rental prices. There are many prices that cannot be raised quickly because to do so requires the consent of a regulatory body that may move with glacial speed: railroads, airlines, gas and electric utilities, and telephone companies all complain of their inability to respond quickly enough to an increased money demand. Then there are creditors who have made long-term loans and cannot raise the payments they regularly receive for that service until the loan matures— which might be 25 years in the future. On the other hand, consider the happy position of the federal government, selling us national defense and a variety of social services and charging a price (the personal income tax) that not only increases but increases at a progressive rate as monetary demand increases. The net result of all this is that inflation redistributes income.

Prices that respond more slowly to increased demand don't necessarily increase less; they just take longer to get where they're going. But that still means income is redistributed during the transitional period so that some people will have lost out even after they have caught up. The redistributive effects of inflation depend heavily on how rapidly the inflation occurs, because this affects the ability of different people to anticipate and adjust to it. From 1967 to 1973, for example, the Consumer Price Index rose 41.4 percent while the mean hourly wage of production workers in private industry rose 46.5 percent. So wages more than kept pace. But when the price level spurted up 16.1 percent from January 1973 to July 1974, the mean hourly wage increased only 11.9 percent, so that the real hourly wage declined.

The strength of the popular pressure on government to control inflation (or at least seem to be controlling it) can only be appreciated if one understands why the beneficiaries of inflation so often join the victims in denouncing it. The principal reason is that they mistakenly think they are victims.

Someone who receives a 10 percent wage or salary increase almost inevitably regards the raise as completely merited, only just, perhaps long overdue. The fact that it reflects nothing but an increase or anticipated increase in the money demand for the worker's product is not something that can be readily observed. So it's overlooked. If prices then rise during the same period by 6 percent, owing to the same increase in aggregate demand that accounted for the worker's last raise, the worker will not rejoice in the fact that he gained from inflation. He will rather complain that inflation has eaten up 60 percent of his raise. We all tend to regard increases in our own money income as our just desert. Increases in the general price level, however, are bad and should be prevented. But prices are not only costs. Look at them from the other side and they're the components of income. We just don't tie the two together.

Effects on Production

Illusion thus plays a major role in making inflation unpopular and creating pressure on governments to do something about it. But the costs of inflation to a society as a whole are not completely illusory. Imagine a situation in which the various state governments controlled the standards for weights and measures. Suppose further that the officials in most states had come to the conclusion that the only way to effect a shift to the metric system was to be sneaky about it—to expand the inch gradually until it measured $\frac{1}{36}$ of a meter. So at periodic but unpredictable intervals over the next ten years, the officials of various states announced to their jurisdictions an official increase in the length of the inch—"never enough to notice," as they were fond of saying, but enough to increase the inch from its former length of .0254 meters to the desired length of .027 $\frac{7}{9}$ meters.

Where would the costs of such a procedure show up? In resources devoted to guessing the timing and rate of changes and ensuring against the consequences of mistakes; in resources spent on translating measurements when goods produced in one state are used in another; in resources employed to fit tools conforming to older specifications to products made to newer specifications; in resources wasted on the correction of mistakes arising from the increased uncertainty and the complexity of the coordinating task.

The real costs of inflation to a society are like the costs just described.

It is sometimes said that inflation is merely a change in the length of the measuring instrument. That may be true, but it doesn't follow that inflation has no real costs. An elastic measuring instrument is a serious problem whenever decisions have to be coordinated over space and time. A large real cost of inflation is the effort and other resources that people devote to "beating" it. As evidence, thumb through a few of the unbelievable number of paperback books published in the last few years telling people how to come out ahead or at least stay even during periods of inflation.

Is Indexing an Answer?

A number of economists have recently suggested *indexing* as a way of living with inflation. If all prices and wages could somehow be tied to a general price level index, so that everyone's nominal wealth and income moved up or down in automatic unison when the price level changed, most of the problems associated with inflation might disappear. We do some of that already with escalator clauses in wage contracts and with social security benefits that are now tied by law to the price index, and we could do far more. For example, the federal government could provide, for the unsophisticated saver of modest means, a simple, safe hedge against inflation by selling bonds whose value changes with the Consumer Price Index.

The indexing system adopted after 1964 in Brazil has been cited as evidence that a nation can survive with substantially higher inflation rates than the United States experienced even in 1974. But how well has Brazil survived? With the gradual extension of the system so that it compensates more fully and more quickly for all increases in the price level, Brazil may now be on the verge of building inflationary expectations so solidly into the economy that inflation will start feeding on itself. For example, an increase in the price level will call for higher wages, the money supply will have to be increased to pay the higher wages, and the larger money supply will pull prices up even faster. It's a way of living with inflation full of difficulties and dangers.

Moreover, contemporary Brazil is no one's model of a free and democratic society. How much did the political tensions generated by inflation contribute to the appearance of a military dictatorship in 1964? The annual rate of inflation in Brazil rose rapidly in the early sixties, from 40 to 55 to 80 percent per year in 1963 and on up to an annual rate of 150 percent in March of 1964. Then production collapsed and a military government seized power. And it was this military government that cut through the complexities and conflicting interests to establish an indexing system. Hitler, you may have heard, also achieved full employment without inflation and in addition managed to build the autobahns.

The Costs of Unemployment

What are the real costs of unemployment? Some economists calculate those costs as the difference between what real gross national product would be at some target rate of unemployment and what it is at higher unemployment levels. Serious criticisms have been directed against the assumptions employed in arriving at these estimates; but even more serious objections can probably be raised against their relevance.

The costs of unemployment are borne primarily by the unemployed, a fact that is not clearly illustrated by figures on aggregate real income losses. Moreover, unemployment costs are not entirely, and perhaps not even primarily, loss-of-income costs—unless we find a way to include increased anxiety, a reduced sense of personal worth, and heightened interpersonal tension in our estimates of real personal income.

But none of these costs falls with equal severity on each unemployed person. It is especially important in this context to view unemployment as a status which people *choose* because it presents the best option for given individuals in particular circumstances. The subjective value of that option varies enormously. We surely do not want a society in which everyone finds being in the labor force a better option than remaining outside it. Our goal is presumably to improve the quality of the options from which people can choose, and to improve especially the options available to those who are least advantageously placed. Enhancing the value of leisure may be a better way to lower the unemployment rate than getting more people to work.

An adequate discussion of these issues would carry us far beyond the area in which economists have any special insights to offer. But when we're tempted to pursue the goal of high employment in a single-minded way, we might profitably remember that employment would increase if we abolished all public assistance to the unemployed, if real incomes fell drastically, or if people could find no satisfactory uses for leisure time.

We have come to no revolutionary conclusions in our brief survey of the costs of inflation and unemployment, and we haven't even attempted the crucial task of weighing one against the other. Both are clearly social ills at the present time, and any choice between them will be difficult to defend rationally and perhaps impossible to defend politically. Public policy is in an uncomfortable corner if our only social choice is inflation or high levels of unemployment. But is that really the only choice we have?

The Phillips Curve: Use and Abuse

In 1958 a British economist named A. W. Phillips published a study on "The Relationship between Unemployment and the Rate of Change of Money Wage Rates in the United Kingdom,

1861–1957," and invented the "Phillips Curve." Phillips showed
that there was a stable relationship during the period he studied
between the unemployment rate and the rate at which the average
money wage increased. Unemployment was greater when money
wage rates were increasing more slowly, and fell in periods when
money wage rates were rising rapidly. That seems thoroughly
plausible. During periods of high demand for labor, employers will
tend to bid up wage rates to obtain and keep the employees they
want. In periods of high unemployment, employers will not have
to bid so energetically for labor, and wage rates will increase less.
But the argument was subsequently extended by others to suggest
that unemployment might be reduced by allowing an inflationary
rate of increase in money wages and, by extension, in the average of
all prices. The Phillips Curve of this latter argument purports to
show that there is a general tradeoff between inflation and unemployment, so that less of one can be obtained by accepting more of
the other. But the conclusion does not follow either from A. W.
Phillips' data or from reflection on the causes of inflation and
unemployment. And the notion that government policy makers
can reduce the rate of unemployment by deliberately causing
inflation is an extremely hazardous one.

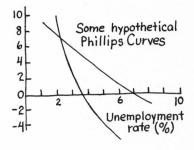

It is probably true that prices and wages will be more likely to
drift upward when the economy is close to "full" employment.
The economic system always contains a great deal of internal
movement: industries grow, others decline, firms rise and fall, new
production techniques are introduced, the composition of demand changes, people enter and exit from the labor force. Resources must therefore be attracted continuously into particular
employments through the offer of acceptable employment terms.
But employers and employees do not have perfect information.
They must search for what they want and incur the costs of that
search.

In a period of low unemployment, the cost of finding a new job
will, on the average, be lower for employees than during a period of
high unemployment; they will therefore be more ready to give up a
job when they think the wage is unsatisfactory and begin searching
for another. So employers will find it difficult to reduce wages.

Search costs for employers are higher in periods of full employment. And so employers will offer higher wages than they might
otherwise be willing to offer in order to avoid making an extensive
and costly search for the new employees they want and to reduce
the risk of losing present employees, who would be expensive to
replace.

The same argument applies to prices in product markets. When
the economy is operating close to capacity, excess supplies are
generally hard to find, and buyers will pay higher prices rather than
search for alternative sources of supply. In a period of high unemployment and substantial excess capacity, sellers will be shaving
prices because buyers are hard to find.

The identical conclusion emerges whichever way we look at it. "Full" employment fosters an upward creep in prices and wages; substantial unemployment and excess capacity encourages a downward drift in prices and wages.

The basic argument asserts that the direction of drift in price and wage movements is a response to tightness or slackness in markets. In other words, the level of employment is the cause and price-wage movement the effect. But we cannot assume that because full employment causes inflation, inflation will bring about full employment. When there is a big crowd at the basketball game, the gymnasium temperature rises because of body heat; but the athletic department cannot make a crowd come to watch a losing basketball team by overheating the gymnasium.

Nonetheless, the policy of deliberately stepping up inflation probably would lower the unemployment rate—temporarily. People are unemployed because they don't find the job opportunities of which they're aware sufficiently attractive. It follows that if the level of real wages could somehow be increased across the board, all employment opportunities would become more attractive and employment would increase—except for the fact that employers would then demand less labor at those higher real wage rates. The quantity supplied would increase, but the quantity demanded would fall. When money wages and prices advance together, however, as they do in a general inflation, real wages don't actually increase. But workers will think they have increased, and that will be enough to lower the unemployment rate.

A policy of deliberate inflation makes job opportunities seem more attractive by raising the money wage rate offers of employers. And this is how inflation reduces unemployment. But the higher wage rate offers are only seemingly more attractive. As long as potential employees don't realize that the job opportunities they're now accepting are in reality no better than the opportunities they previously rejected, employment will indeed rise. But it will subsequently fall back down to its previous level when employees discover what's happening: that inflation is creating the illusion of more attractive wage offers. No permanent reduction in unemployment will have occurred, but the economy will be undergoing more rapid inflation.

A deliberate policy of pursuing lower unemployment by accepting a higher rate of inflation calls, then, for continuously increasing the inflation rate so that workers always expect less than the actual rate of inflation. In that way they can be made to overestimate continuously the real value of the money wages they are being offered. Or else the policy assumes that employees pay exclusive attention to money wage rates, never to real wage rates. This is a superficially plausible assumption, since we know that few employees consult the most recent changes in the Consumer Price Index before deciding whether a wage offer is adequate. They look at *money* wage rates, in other words. But they also learn after a while that their wages buy less and adjust their perception of the wage rate's real value. An extreme example will make the point. In 1956 workers stood in line for jobs in manufacturing offering $2 an hour. In 1976 manufacturers can find almost no one who will accept employment at that wage. Employees do know, even if they've never heard of price indices, that $2 is a much lower hourly wage today than it was twenty years ago.

Policy cannot be constructed on the assumption that workers will be permanently fooled, for people learn from experience. And the simultaneous existence of high unemployment with very rapid inflation in the early 1970s ought to be sufficient evidence that people have learned. When they begin to assume continued inflation, they no longer suffer from the illusion that money wages and real wages are the same thing.

But suppose a government tried this approach to the unemployment problem, found that it couldn't actually lower unemployment, and decided to abandon the policy. It had been causing inflation by applying fiscal and monetary stimulus, and it now eases up. After a lag of some length, monetary demand will stop increasing so rapidly, and producers will be unable to sell at the prices they had anticipated, so inventories will mount, production will be curtailed, and unemployment will rise. Eventually sellers will learn not to expect such a rapid rise in prices, they will adjust downward the prices they ask and the prices they offer to pay for inputs, sales will revive, inventories will decline, production will start up again, and unemployment will fall. But that won't all happen within a week or even a month. The higher unemployment that will result from an attempt to slow down the rate of inflation will be temporary; but temporary can be a long time. The cost of letting inflation get out of hand may be very high indeed.

Conclusions and Implications

Let's try to summarize the conclusions that have emerged so far from our examination of the relationship between inflation and unemployment.

1. A movement from a situation of low employment to one of high or "full" employment will generally be accompanied by a rising price level. Increased demand will bid up some prices and wages even before "full" employment is achieved. Increases in aggregate demand when the economy is already operating in the vicinity of "full" employment will have their principal impact on the price-wage level.

2. An economy operating in the vicinity of "full" employment tends to experience creeping inflation. By lowering search costs for sellers, both of products and labor, and raising them for buyers, "full" employment promotes an upward drift in the terms of price and wage bargains.

3. The unemployment rate is affected by *changes* in the rate of inflation. An unanticipated increase in the inflation rate tends to reduce unemployment by making available job offers look more attractive than they actually are. An unanticipated decrease in the inflation rate tends to increase unemployment until sellers of products and labor services learn to adjust their expectations. But a constant rate of inflation, because it's presumably fully anticipated, probably has no effect on the unemployment rate.

There are some important policy lessons tucked away in those conclusions for anyone who dislikes both high unemployment rates and inflation.

1. Avoid recessions if you want to avoid inflation, because the process of recovery from a recession usually entails inflation.

2. Try not to let inflation get started if you want to prevent high unemployment, because slowing down the rate of inflation will ordinarily cause unemployment to increase.

3. Creeping inflation is probably the price that a society must pay for all the gains that accrue from continuous operation at or near the economy's capacity.

4. The Phillips Curve is a dangerous concept insofar as it encourages the illusion that a permanently lower unemployment rate can be "purchased" by accepting a higher rate of inflation.

Points 3 and 4 are not contradictory. Point 3 merely acknowledges the fact that upward price adjustments will dominate downward adjustments, leading to a slow upward drift in the price level, when an economic system is operating with very little slack. It warns, you might say, against the pursuit of perfection. Point 4 warns against confusing cause and effect by assuming that since high employment generates inflation, more inflation will generate higher employment.

Points 1 and 2 are lessons of doubtful value if we don't know how to avoid recessions or increases in the rate of inflation. A fiscal-monetary activist might extract from them a recommendation for fine-tuning. A fiscal-monetary passivist, on the other hand, will argue that the attempt to fine-tune is a principal cause of recessions and inflation, and will see in these lessons a case for restraint in the practice of demand management. It's time to face the much debated issue of fine-tuning and its equally debated opposite, automatic controls.

Fine-Tuning or Blindman's Bluff?

We have reminded you repeatedly that economic decisions are always made on the basis of expected and therefore uncertain costs and benefits that may turn out to be mistaken. That's also true for the makers of fiscal and monetary policy.

A successful program of aggregate demand management will require extensive information. Policy making today can take advantage of the vast strides we have made in recent years in the accumulation of statistical data on the economy's performance. But information of this sort will always be approximate as well as highly aggregative. Moreover, all the information available will be dated. It will summarize some situation in the past. But even very recent and reliable data aren't enough. Since any policy action will impinge on future situations the challenge is to obtain data on the future by extrapolating from the past. And that requires considerable theorizing to accompany the data.

What we really want to know is what will happen if various policy actions are taken. What will be the effects of the actions, direct and indirect, and how long will they take to make themselves felt? How long does it take for a purchase of government securities by the Fed to transform itself into an increased demand for consumption and investment goods? How much of the impact will come almost at once, perhaps as a reaction to the mere news of an easier monetary policy? How will the rest of the impact be distributed over time? Fiscal actions raise the same questions. The actual multiplier effect of a change in government expenditures or taxes can't be determined by arithmetic manipulations of various marginal propensities because we don't really know the future values of these propensities. Public attitudes toward tax and expenditure changes may bring about a shift in spending or saving plans so that the relevant multiplier changes when the policy action is announced. And the distribution of the multiplier effects over time is a crucial piece of information if stabilization policy is not to become destabilization policy.

Knowledge about the time lags between monetary or fiscal actions and their effects has been extremely hard to obtain, as we mentioned in Chapter 19. There is no way to deduce the distribution of lags from pure theory; we have to rely on empirical measurements. But how are we going to sort out the effects of a particular fiscal or monetary stimulus from the effects of all the other forces that will be impinging on the economy? There are good reasons for believing that the lags have no set length. To ask how long it will take for a particular fiscal or monetary stimulus to have 80 percent of its effects may be like asking how long it will take for 80 percent of the people to learn the news. Which news? Which people? Who already knows? Is it important news? To whom? What media of communication are available? Who has access to them? Who has an interest in spreading the news? Who might want to suppress or distort it?

Is It Better to Have Tried and Failed?

It has become increasingly obvious in recent years that we do not have the knowledge that would be required to steer the economy on a steady course of full employment with price stability. But are we better off than we would have been if we hadn't tried? Most economists now agree that fine-tuning, as it is called, has been somewhat oversold, that we have been too optimistic about our ability to reduce aggregate fluctuations through demand management. A smaller number go farther: they argue that the attempt to stabilize has increased both unemployment and inflation.

How could this occur? The key element in the argument is the relationship between unemployment and uncertainty. Unemployment occurs largely because mistakes are made and subsequently have to be accepted and corrected. It follows that anything which increases the probability of mistakes, of decisions based on a faulty anticipation of future events, will increase the average level of unemployment. The question then becomes: Has the behavior of the federal budget and of the money supply in recent years made the future more predictable? Or has it increased the uncertainties confronting economic decision makers?

Stabilizing Factors

We cannot jump from the fact that there have been no major recessions since the 1930s to the conclusion that the net effect of government stabilization efforts was greater stability. Other factors have been at work. We earlier discussed the importance of the Federal Deposit Insurance Corporation in eliminating the phenomenon of bank runs and the supporting role of the Fed as the guarantor of short-run liquidity to the banking system. Between them they have eliminated the panics that once swept regularly through the financial sector; and with financial panics a thing of the past, the economy has not again had to go through anything even remotely approaching the 25 percent contraction in the money supply experienced between 1929 and 1933.

Another stabilizing factor seems to have been the tendency for personal consumption expenditures after World War II to maintain their own steady rate of increase, with relative disregard for fluctuations in income. Some of this should probably be attributed to relatively high wealth levels, which enable people to maintain their spending during periods of temporarily reduced income. Some of it can also be credited to our system of progressive taxes on personal and corporate income that cushion disposable personal income against fluctuations in gross national product. The fact that government transfer payments move inversely to GNP has an added cushioning effect on aggregate consumption spending.

Destabilizing Factors

If personal consumption expenditures have been a steady and stabilizing component of aggregate demand, investment expenditures have not. You can go back to Table 16B (page 222) to see just how unstable private investment spending has been. But did fiscal and monetary policy compensate for this instability, or were they a major *cause* of the instability? The construction component of investment is sensitive to the interest rate and monetary policy does seem to have destabilized the building industry. What about the policy of shifting between tax surcharges to dampen inflation and special tax credits for investment spending to promote employment? Since there is usually considerable discretion about the timing of investment expenditures, couldn't government policy reversals be largely responsible for the large fluctuations from year to year in private investment? It's true that policy makers intended to reduce fluctuations through shifting tax policies; but it wouldn't be the only time a tax program hit something other than its target.

What have been the overall effects of government programs? Remember that an unanticipated change in the composition of spending will cause unemployment even though total spending does not change. When the government makes a decision to send men to the moon, to produce a particular military plane, to restrict oil imports, to subsidize a giant railroad system, to enforce high standards of job safety in industry, to become self-sufficient in energy by 1980, to encourage home ownership through government-subsidized loans, to enlarge steel-making capacity by granting special tax refunds for investment—when the government does any of these things, it signals labor and other resources to move in specific directions. It tells people to change their places of residence, to acquire particular knowledge and skills, to sink resources into specific projects. *Any subsequent slackening of government intentions or shift in emphases announces that these resource movements were partly mistaken and creates unemployment.* It may also trigger surges of investment spending by industries trying to make rapid adjustments to revised government policies. How sure can we be that private economic decisions are the unstable factor for which government decisions must compensate?

The Case for an Automatic Pilot

Increases in the unemployment rate are political signals, however, for an expansion of aggregate demand, an expansion that will be inflationary if the unemployment is due to something other than a deficiency of aggregate demand. We can at least imagine a scenario in which the government's actions, undertaken to fine-tune the economy, foster temporary unemployment, government reactions to this unemployment lead to inflation, and attempts to stop the inflation aggravate unemployment. Some economists today are persuaded that this has in fact been occurring and that the government could consequently make its most effective contribution toward the elimination of aggregate fluctuations by not trying so hard to eliminate all fluctuations. A graceful elephant could succeed in stabilizing a small boat on a rough sea by shifting its weight with delicacy and perfect timing. Some of the passengers might nonetheless prefer that the elephant sit as still as possible. Whether you decide it's consequence or coincidence, the fact remains that our most rapid inflation and highest unemployment rates since World War II appeared after both major political parties had committed themselves to fine-tuning of the economy through aggregate demand management.

"Automaticity" is the policy goal of economists who doubt the practicality of discretionary demand management. They want the Fed to maintain a steady hand on the money stock, either holding it constant or causing it to increase by some definite, known, and uniform rate. As for fiscal policy, they want only as much as comes about automatically, without the discretionary intervention of Congress or the Executive Branch. When an economic downturn begins, tax receipts will automatically fall because corporate and personal incomes are declining; government outlays will increase somewhat insofar as government transfer payments rise when the aggregate level of economic activity declines. These automatic stabilizers presumably function in the manner of mechanical governors, dampening oscillations in the economy. The proponents of automaticity argue that any additional discretionary policy actions are more likely to aggravate than reduce instability, because discretionary actions are hard to time appropriately and because anticipation of them creates additional uncertainty for private decision makers.

The contemporary case for an automatic pilot must be distinguished from the view which dominated economic thinking prior to the 1930s and the publication of Keynes's *General Theory*. The older view was that government should actually retrench in a recession, cutting its expenditures and increasing tax rates if necessary to preserve a balanced budget, while monetary authorities tightened credit conditions to discipline speculative tendencies. But such a policy, if adopted, would be a discretionary policy, not an automatic one. And it would be equally capable of aggravating instability because of faulty estimates, errors in timing, and the additional uncertainty it would create for decision makers.

There are automatic monetary stabilizers as well as automatic fiscal stabilizers in the economic system. A boom will eventually run against rising interest rates and credit rationing if the monetary managers don't feed the boom by pumping new reserves into the banking system. And during a period of economic decline, lending terms will tend to improve as the demand for credit slackens, thus encouraging some potential investors. But the monetary managers have in fact behaved perversely a good part of the time, according to the leading opponents of monetary fine-tuning. For one thing, they have paid too much attention to interest rates, and by attempting to stabilize interest rates they have caused the money supply to grow erratically. This in turn has fostered an irregular rate of growth in national income, higher unemployment, and an inflationary expansion of the money supply in response to the rise in unemployment.

The question of the proper target for monetary policy has been a controversial one for a long time. At one extreme is the view that the monetary managers should pay attention exclusively to monetary aggregates, whether that's some measure of the money stock or the supply of reserves to the banking system, which is the basis on which the money stock expands. At the other extreme is the view that the monetary managers should pay exclusive attention to interest rates, using some such measure as the federal funds rate, which is the rate of interest paid by commercial banks to borrow one another's reserves.

The disagreement is complicated by the apparently widespread belief that interest rates reflect the scarcity of money, so that rates can be made to fall by increasing the money supply fast enough. We must think carefully about the relationship between monetary policy and interest rates if we are to avoid the error that many financial commentators were committing in 1974 by using the high prime rate as conclusive evidence of tight money. When the Fed increases the supply of money, the demand remaining constant, elementary supply and demand analysis tells us that the price of money will fall. That's correct. *But interest is not the price of money!* Interest rates can be thought of as the price of credit; but the price of money is the value of money or its purchasing power. Just as the price of strawberries is measured by the amount of money for which strawberries exchange, so the price of money is measured by the amount of strawberries for which it will exchange—or the amount of pipe wrenches, baked beans, book ends, and so on.

When the Fed increases bank reserves as part of an easier money policy, banks are enabled to expand their lending. Credit becomes easier to obtain and interest rates consequently do tend to move downward. Easier money leads to lower interest rates—at least temporarily.

But we must push the analysis further. What happens to the new money created by the Fed when it adds to bank reserves and the banks make additional loans? The increase in M will tend to increase aggregate demand. If the demand for credit from consumers, investors, and government expands when aggregate demand grows, that will tend to pull interest rates back up. The net effect after a longer period of time cannot easily be predicted. More importantly, if the expansionary monetary policy leads to an excessive rate of increase in aggregate demand, prices will start to rise. And *the expectation of rising prices will cause interest rates to rise.* Why? Because if prices are expected to increase by 10 percent per year, lenders will demand an additional 10 percent in interest as compensation for the anticipated decrease in the value or purchasing power (the price) of money. And borrowers with the same expectations of inflation will consent to pay the additional 10 percent because they anticipate repaying the loan with depreciated dollars. The *nominal* interest rate will then exceed the *real* interest rate by 10 percent. And it is the nominal rate to which critics were pointing in 1974 when they complained about exorbitant interest rates.

From January 1973 to January 1974, consumer prices rose 9.9 percent and wholesale prices rose 17.4 percent. From January 1974 to July 1974, when the prime rate hit 12 percent, consumer prices continued to increase at an annual rate of approximately 10 percent and wholesale prices went up at almost 20 percent on an annual basis. What would you say were "reasonable" expectations in July of 1974 about the future behavior of prices and the value of money? A 12 percent prime rate was hardly surprising. But the real rate buried at the bottom of that nominal rate may have been as low as 2 percent.

The policy dilemma this poses for the Fed became exceptionally clear in early 1975 when interest rates were falling but some critics of the Fed complained that they were not falling rapidly enough and called for a faster rate of growth in the money supply to get interest rates down more quickly. The basic factual issues, the rate of growth in the money supply and the movement of interest rates, were not at issue. The federal funds rate had fallen from 13.5 to 6 percent between July 1974 and March 1975. The total of currency and demand deposits (M_1) had risen at an annual rate of about 2 percent over this same period. All parties agreed to those facts. Even more interestingly, there was a remarkable consensus among economists inside and outside the Fed that the 2 percent rate of growth was definitely too slow. But the commentators were offering two contradictory analyses in March of 1975. One group was saying that the Fed could and should push interest rates down more rapidly by accelerating the rate of growth in the money supply. The other group maintained that nominal interest rates might rise if the Fed increased the rate of growth in the money supply—even though this group also wanted a faster rate of money growth. In other words, one group was saying to the monetary managers: "Increase the money supply until interest rates go down far enough." And the other was saying: "Increase the money supply, but ignore interest rates which might well rise as you do so."

The published reports of the Open Market Committee's policy directives in recent years reveal continuing uncertainty about whether monetary aggregates or interest rates are the proper target at which to aim. As long as there is also uncertainty about the actual relationship between changes in one and changes in the other, as well as uncertainty about the impact of each upon spending decisions, the effectiveness of monetary policy in stabilizing economic activity will remain doubtful.

What Are the Unanswered Questions?

Disagreement among economists on the desirability of attempts to fine-tune the economy with the tools of demand management are evidence of the unsettled state of economic knowledge. While much has been learned since the 1930s, many fundamental questions are still unresolved.

How stable is the demand for money, both in the short run and the long run?

How stable is the relationship between consumption and disposable income?

How does monetary policy affect interest rates, both the nominal rate quoted by lenders and the real rate that results from subtracting expectations of future inflation?

How do interest rates affect consumption and investment spending?

How do increased government expenditures affect consumption and investment spending, both directly (by perhaps displacing them) and indirectly (by stimulating them)?

How long are the lags between policy actions and their effects on spending decisions?

One can hope that further empirical inquiry and theoretical discussion will eventually resolve these questions. But that would not necessarily end the controversy. Underneath all these questions, and indeed underneath most significant controversies in economics, lies a much broader question and one far more difficult to answer: *How effectively does the market function to allocate resources?* How flexible are prices and how quickly do resources move in response to a decrease in demand in one area and an increase in another? For if prices are inflexible, especially in a downward direction, and resources respond sluggishly to changes in demand conditions, or if powerful economic interests are more *controlling of* than *controlled by* supply and demand, then even the most adroit management of aggregate demand will have little chance of promoting full employment and price stability.

The Popularity of Direct Controls

The general public has never had much trouble believing that inflation is the result of irresponsible behavior on the part of sellers, whether of labor or products. The public looks for villains when things go wrong, and seems to find them in the business firms that announce price increases and the union leaders that call for wage hikes. An excessive rate of increase in demand is a force too abstract and impersonal to be a good candidate for villain, so that corporations and unions tend to be blamed for inflation even when wages and prices are clearly being pulled up by excess demand, not being pushed up by market power. That's why the imposition of wage and price controls during a period of inflation usually encounters an overwhelmingly favorable response from the public, at least initially. A case in point is the wage-price freeze announced in August of 1971.

The popularity of wage and price controls as a way of dealing with inflation makes it all the more urgent that the public under-

Note (margin): stability of the velocity of money; stability of the consumption function; determinants of real and nominal interest rates; effects of interest rate changes on spending; government expenditure: stimulus or "crowding out"?; time lags

stand the mechanisms of inflation. If wages and prices rise after the fiscal or monetary authorities have expanded aggregate demand faster than real output can keep up, or after some disaster (war, oil embargoes, crop failures) has reduced the level of real output, controls are worse than useless. For they suspend the rationing system through which scarce goods get allocated among competing claimants. This means that the goods will have to be allocated by other criteria; buyers will get in line early, cultivate contacts, try to negotiate special agreements, or offer illegal monetary inducements to get around the maximum price. The incentive to hoard goods will increase because goods are undervalued at their legal prices and because buyers cannot be sure of obtaining supplies in the future; this further aggravates the scarcity. Producers will have less incentive to expand output and maintain quality. Production will fall further as manufacturers find themselves unable to obtain particular inputs that have suddenly disappeared from suppliers' inventories; they may even have to suspend production and lay workers off. Export controls will be instituted to keep other countries from taking advantage of the controlled prices. Bartering will creep into the supply system, not only decreasing efficiency but also stirring up cries of inequity from those producers who have nothing of value to offer their suppliers. Items will unexpectedly disappear from retail shelves—paper bags, shoe heels, plastic syringes, lawn fertilizer—as shortages multiply and breed further shortages. Relative prices will not be able to change in response to changing relative scarcities, and so the structure of prices will start to give misleading signals to resource users. In short, suppression of the price system suspends the mechanism of economic coordination, leading to inequities, inefficiencies, and disruptions of production that only worsen the imbalance between demand and supply.

Imposing price controls in the face of an inflation caused by too many dollars chasing too few goods aggravates the problem by reducing the supply of goods and diminishing the incentive of demanders to economize in their use. And this is true whether the imbalance was caused by an excessive creation of dollars or a deficient creation of goods. Moreover, it diverts the attention of the public from the actual causes of the inflation and the proper remedies. Of course, a government whose fiscal and monetary policies have fueled an inflation will be only too happy to encourage the public's belief that private avarice is the root of the problem, that public-spirited self-restraint on the part of citizens is the ultimate answer, and that the rascals who have no public spirit must be controlled by law. Congress will rarely admit that its own spending habits are the cause of any ills.

What Can We Learn from Wartime Price and Wage Controls?

The wage and price controls of World War II are sometimes

brought forward as evidence that controls can in fact be effective in preventing excess demand from pulling up prices. But this argument ignores some important facts. For one, it overlooks the public's willingness to put up with shortages and tolerate inequities when they are viewed as temporary necessities. Above all, it overlooks the alternative rationing system created by the federal government during World War II to allocate scarce goods among competing claimants: the complex point system, the books of ration stamps, the special gasoline coupons, the priority allocations, and the army of controllers required to make the system work even as well as it did. It overlooks the role of wartime patriotism in securing the voluntary cooperation that kept the system functioning for several years, as well as the illegal and semilegal evasions that sometimes helped the system work by enabling people to circumvent it. And when the controls were removed, as they eventually had to be, the excess money demand dammed up behind them poured out to raise prices 33 percent between 1945 and 1948.

A Defensible Case for Price and Wage Controls

There is a defensible case that can be made for price and wage controls as a supplementary tool for dealing with unemployment and inflation. Arthur F. Burns, who became chairman of the board of governors of the Federal Reserve System in 1970, had long maintained in company with most economists that the key to a stable price level was monetary and fiscal restraint on the part of government, not wage or price controls. But when he found himself in charge of imposing an important part of that restraint, Burns reluctantly concluded that labor and product markets might not function well enough to let fiscal and monetary policy be effective. He argued that strong unions and business firms with substantial market power were able to raise wages and prices in the absence of any increases in demand. Confronted with this situation, monetary and fiscal authorities had to choose between causing unemployment by refusing to expand total demand or causing inflation by underwriting the wage and price increases.

Market Power, Unemployment, and Inflation

To understand Burns's reasoning, suppose that a significant number of wage rates are set by collective bargaining and that unions have the ability to obtain wage increases in excess of productivity increases. That would mean that unions (or some unions) can obtain for their members a wage that is above the value of labor's marginal productivity. Another way of putting it is to say that the unions can persuade some employers to pay workers a wage greater than the value of the marginal worker's net contribution to the firm's revenue.

Employers adjust to such a situation by reducing the number of

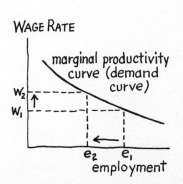

workers they hire. They may not actually lay anyone off; instead they will just refrain from replacing workers as they retire or quit. The result is a reduction in the number of jobs available and an increase in measured unemployment. It makes no difference if we assume that employers can raise their prices and recover the higher labor costs without reducing employment. At higher prices they won't be able to sell as much, and the reduced sales will eventually lead to employment cutbacks. Even if union members realize that higher wages will mean fewer jobs, a majority may vote for the wage increase in the belief that they themselves will be protected by seniority; they are risking the jobs of others.

Rising unemployment caused by this kind of market power puts the government under pressure to adopt an expansionary fiscal or monetary policy. When it does so, prices rise generally. The rise in the price of everything else reduces the relative price of the good whose sales had fallen, its sales expand once more, and employment in that industry is restored. If employers lack the market power to pass the wage increase along to buyers, the increase in the price of all goods does the job for them. The real wage is consequently reduced, and employment is restored to its initial level. The upshot of the matter is that the use of excessive market power creates unemployment problems, and that to deal with the unemployment problems the government is forced to cause inflation.

How did we get into such a bind? Is there a way out? Burns suggested three principal causes of the problem: strong unions, business firms selling in insufficiently competitive markets, and innumerable government regulations which tolerate, encourage, and even require practices that raise costs and reduce efficiency. In the last category Burns included subsidies to farmers, legal restrictions on entry into various trades or professions, import quotas and tariffs, the federal minimum wage law especially in its application to teen-agers, aspects of our welfare programs, price maintenance laws, and the failure to enforce antitrust legislation. The solution is structural reforms directed toward increasing competition and thereby making wages and prices more responsive to forces of supply and demand. (Keep in mind that union strength, corporate market power, and anticompetitive government regulations must be increasing if the problem to which Burns calls attention is growing worse.)

But reforms of that sort can't be implemented quickly. The active connivance of government in creation of the problems suggests that such reforms will only be possible, if they're possible at all, after a long campaign of public education. In the meantime, if Burns's analysis is correct, we shall have to make do with second-best policies. Some legal controls on prices and wages may be necessary if we are to avoid confronting the nation's fiscal-monetary managers with the unpleasant choice between accepting unemployment or causing inflation.

But even limited wage and price controls are going to pose major difficulties. On whom will they be imposed and how will this be determined? Who will decide when adjustments are called for and by what criteria? And whatever the economic rationale, will the political system be adequate to such a task? It is essential to note that Arthur Burns assigns much of the blame for the decline of competition to government policies. Is it realistic to expect the same government to undo its own work? Regulatory agencies like the Interstate Commerce Commission or the Civil Aeronautics Board that have long taken their function to be the prevention of competition will not suddenly revise their thinking and procedures. State legislators who bow to industry lobbies and create legal cartel arrangements aren't likely to acquire new wisdom or courage any time soon. Anticompetitive laws in the areas of agriculture, labor, and international trade continue to command a congressional majority. Who will mind the sheep when the shepherds have such a taste for mutton?

Incomes Policy

A phrase sometimes used in place of "wage and price controls" to describe the kind of approach recommended by Burns is *incomes policy*. It's an apt phrase because it calls attention to the origins of the problem and the inherent difficulty of resolving it. The problem is that people are collectively claiming for themselves more than 100 percent of the national income and that some groups may now have sufficient political or market power to create unemployment and inflation while pursuing their goal. But if the government tries to control the prices and wages that these groups set, it implicitly makes a decision on how income ought to be distributed. And that's precisely what is at issue. A democratic government will not be able to use incomes policy to rein in conflicting interests because *it is incomes policy over which the interests are conflicting*. A particular criterion of fairness cannot be used to settle a dispute over the appropriateness of that criterion. The genie conception of government conceals this dilemma.

We may be able to see that the economic system does not work as it should, and to outline government policies that would improve its performance. But won't the same forces responsible for the unsatisfactory performance of the economy block the adoption of the political policies recommended as solutions? It is painfully reminiscent of the fable about the mice who wanted to protect themselves against cats by putting a bell on each cat. If cats let themselves be belled by mice, however, mice would have no reason to want bells on cats.

Does that strike you as a woefully unsatisfactory conclusion after so many pages of wrestling with data, concepts, and hypotheses? Try looking at it as the beginning rather than the conclusion. Economics shows how a society can reduce the costs of obtaining the goods it wants. It does not guarantee that any costs can be brought down to zero and scarcity abolished. As long as price stability, high employment, rising real incomes, efficiency in resource allocation, equitable distribution, political and cultural freedom, and other such goods are *competing* goods, we shall have to choose and accept the costs of our choices. Economics can only suggest ways to reduce the cost of obtaining some set of those objectives.

Perhaps the conclusion really asserts that we must now begin discussing among ourselves the kind of economy, social structure, and political order within which we want to live.

Once Over Lightly

The notion that inflation is caused by excessive aggregate demand and recession by inadequate aggregate demand implies that inflation and recession won't occur together. The fact that they have occurred together in recent years is an argument against focusing exclusively on aggregate demand fluctuations as the cause of rising prices or rising unemployment levels.

Unemployment increases in response to disappointed expectations and can increase regardless of the current rate of inflation. Inflation creates an illusory optimism that will reduce unemployment only so long as people fail to anticipate it. Slowing down the rate of inflation will add to the level of unemployment until people learn to revise the expectations the inflation created.

The closer to its capacity an economic system is operating, the more likely is it that relative search costs for buyers and sellers will generate an upward drift in the nominal level of wages and prices.

Because inflation is not perfectly anticipated, it tends to redistribute income. The unpopularity of inflation arises in part from the fact that many who gain assume they have lost.

The costs of unemployment are seriously underestimated if we look only at lost income and output. But they are difficult to assess adequately without good information on the options available to those who are counted as unemployed and some who may not be counted because they have withdrawn in discouragement from the labor force.

There is no convincing evidence that government efforts to produce "full" employment and price stability have actually resulted in lower unemployment rates and less inflation than we would have experienced in the absence of such efforts.

There is evidence to suggest that federal government activities, including some of its stabilization efforts, have been seriously destabilizing in their consequences.

Economists disagree on whether economic fluctuations would increase or decrease if discretionary stabilization policy were abandoned in favor of exclusive reliance on automatic stabilizers.

Price and wage controls might be of some use in promoting high employment without inflation if they were used against groups whose growing political or market power enabled them to raise prices in the absence of any demand increases.

Imposing controls when prices are rising because total monetary demand has increased faster than real output is dealing with symptoms rather than causes, and is likely to aggravate the problems it's intended to solve.

Improved government policy with regard to unemployment and inflation will require better information about many economic relationships of which we are currently uncertain. It may also require that we create a political consensus with regard to the proper goals of economic policy.

QUESTIONS FOR DISCUSSION

1. a. Why is the price level likely to rise faster the lower the level of unemployment in the economy?
   b. Does raising the unemployment rate slow down inflation? How so? How long does it take?

2. a. Is aggregate demand inadequate if there is a shortage of automotive mechanics and a surplus of secondary school teachers?
   b. Can substantial unemployment exist at a time when listed job vacancies exceed total unemployment?

3. "There is no danger that a government deficit will cause inflation when unemployment stands at 8 percent of the civilian labor force." Do you agree?

4. How and why does the attempt to lower the permanent rate of unemployment by deliberately causing inflation depend upon an illusion?

5. Numerous public opinion surveys in 1974 and 1975 revealed that the majority of Americans regarded inflation as a more serious threat than unemployment.
   a. Does this imply that the majority of Americans would rather be unemployed in a period of stable prices than employed in a time of rising prices?
   b. If the management of a firm allowed employees to vote on whether the firm should lay off 10 percent of the employees or reduce wage rates by 5 per-

cent, how do you think they would vote? Do you think the outcome of the vote would depend on whether the employees knew in advance exactly who would be laid off?

6. If inflation redistributes income and wealth, there will be gainers as well as losers. Which classes and categories of people are most likely to gain and lose from an inflation? What difference does it make how well the inflation is anticipated?

7. Suppose we adopted a system under which the federal government made weekly payments to each unemployed member of the labor force for as long as the person remained unemployed. Evaluate the problems such a program would encounter and its probable effects.

8. Supply and demand conditions in the market for college professors have changed markedly from the 1960s to the 1970s. Is it easy for college administrators to lower salaries when supply increases and demand decreases? What reaction would you expect from professors who were told that market conditions call for a 7 percent reduction in their annual salary? What reaction would you expect from them if they were told that the budget will not allow for any salary increases this year —although the Consumer Price Index has risen 14 percent since last year? Does inflation ease the process of making relative price and wage adjustments?

9. Some people argue that the complexity of federal tax laws generates significant social waste. It encourages the extensive use of valuable resources (accountants, lawyers) in searching for loopholes and prompts people toward inefficient activities that are profitable because of tax-law quirks. Does inflation generate similar kinds of waste?

10. Secretary of the Treasury William Simon told the House Ways and Means Committee in 1975 that there was no subtler and surer means of overturning the existing basis of society than to "debauch the currency," that is, create continuing inflation. (Mr. Simon's statement cited Keynes and Lenin in support of this position.) Do you agree?

11. If the government decreased spending on highways by $5 billion and simultaneously increased spending on energy development by $5 billion, what effects, if any, would you predict on the level of unemployment?

12. "The basic cause of an excessively high unemployment rate is uncertainty." Explain whether you agree or disagree with that statement and why.

13. Would you expect a different effect on employment from the imposition of a temporary quota against imports than from the imposition of a quota that is expected to be permanent? Why?

14. Can discretionary monetary policy improve upon the automatic monetary stabilizers that would be operative if the Fed simply increased bank reserves at a steady rate? Under what circumstances would discretionary policy be destabilizing in its effects? Under what circumstances would it reenforce the operation of the automatic stabilizers?

15. Would you expect to find a relationship between an informed person's attitude toward attempts at fine-tuning and his reactions to the following judgments? Explain why.
    a. "Fiscal and monetary managers have better information than business decision makers because they have access to statistical data on the overall performance of the economy and don't have to concern themselves with details."
    b. "The government must establish procedures for national economic planning if we are to avoid the kinds of economic crises experienced in the early 1970s."
    c. "The market does not work as it used to. Competition no longer sets prices or allocates resources in the U.S. economy. Most of that is done by organized interest groups with substantial market power."
    d. "The U.S. economy displays an absurd social imbalance. Privately purchased goods are produced in abundance while public sector goods such as education must be content with the leavings."
    e. "Power tends to corrupt and absolute power corrupts absolutely."

16. Federal government expenditures for national defense, when expressed in dollars of 1975 purchasing power, have averaged just about $100 billion per year from 1966 through 1975. Suppose that world peace were somehow miraculously declared and the government abolished the national defense budget. What consequences would you predict for the economy? Do you think this would trigger a major depression? Why or why not? What fiscal policies would you recommend to accompany this disappearance of all national defense expenditures?

17. Suppose we knew that an increase in the budget deficit or in the growth rate of the money stock would have 95 percent of its impact by the end of two years, 55 percent of its impact within one year, and 20 percent within six months. Would that knowledge solve the timing problems associated with aggregate demand management?

18. "An easy money policy is good for the housing industry in the short run but bad in the long run." Evaluate that argument.

19. Can the monetary authorities raise or lower interest rates by decreasing or increasing the money supply? What limitations exist on their ability to do this?

20. Is a negative interest rate an absurd conception? Can you cite any negative (real!) interest rates in recent years? What was the real rate of interest earned on $100 in a 5 percent savings account during 1974 when the price level rose 12 percent? If you were a business executive able to borrow short-term money from the bank at 8 percent, would your decision on whether or not to go ahead with the loan be affected by your expectations regarding the behavior of prices in the coming year?

21. When are interest rates "too high"? Why is it difficult for the Fed to control the level of interest rates?

22. The text asserts that most economic commentators in the spring of 1975 were urging the Fed to increase the rate of growth in the money stock. As long as they agreed in this policy recommendation, why would it matter whether they disagreed over the effect this would have on interest rates?

23. If union-won wage increases add to unemployment and the Fed then expands the money supply to reduce the unemployment rate, who is the villain responsible for inflation?

24. If it is socially irresponsible for sellers to raise their prices in periods of inflation, why did the government raise the price of the annual *Economic Report of the President* from $3.05 in 1974 to $3.25 in 1975?

25. Is it socially responsible for the Civil Aeronautics Board to raise the prices of airline travel but socially irresponsible for food processors to raise the prices of frozen vegetables?

26. Make up two lists of prices and wages, one containing specific prices and wages that in your judgment are not adequately controlled by competition and the other containing specific wages and prices that you think are adequately controlled by competition. What criteria will you use? What evidence do you have to support your lists?

27. Is it unjust for money wage rates to rise less rapidly than prices? Is it unjust for some money wage rates to rise faster and others more slowly than prices? Can you think of some wage and salary rates that ought to rise less rapidly than prices? On what basis would you answer this question?

28. "A teacher of chemistry should not be paid more than a teacher of history simply because the demand for chemistry teachers is greater relative to the supply. Teachers are not commodities. They are professional persons with family responsibilities who are providing essential public services." Do you agree with that statement? Under what circumstances do you think its principles are most likely to find acceptance?

29. Is it possible to control inflation by having a panel of experts pass on all proposed wage or price increases? Should such panels include an equal number of business, labor, and consumer representatives?

Limitations of the Economic Way of Thinking

An answer presupposes a question, and the answers we discover are products of the questions we ask. A great deal therefore depends on where we begin, the point of view, what we assume before we start, and the concepts that we use to organize our thinking and questioning. Thomas Kuhn, an influential philosopher of science, has argued that all scientific activity is rooted in some *paradigm*, by which he means a set of working assumptions that guide inquiry by posing certain questions and ignoring others. Every scientific theory reveals something at the same time that it conceals something else. What does the economic way of thinking reveal? And what does it conceal?

What Economists Know

The economic way of thinking employs such concepts as demand, opportunity cost, marginal effects, and comparative advantage to order familiar phenomena. The economist knows very little about the real world that is not better known by businessmen, engineers, and others who make things happen. What he does know *is how things fit together*. The concepts of economics enable us to make better sense out of what we observe, to think more consistently and coherently about a wide range of interrelated phenomena.

This turns out in practice to be a largely negative kind of knowledge. Perhaps you detected, as you read through the chapters of this book, a greater emphasis on what *should not* be done than on what *should* be done. But negative conclusions are important, and they may be especially important in an area like economics. The economist Frank Knight used to defend the heavily negative character of economic reasoning with a quotation: "It ain't ignorance that does the most damage; it's knowin' so derned much that ain't so."

Too many people "know" how to solve pressing social problems. Their mental picture of the economic universe is a simple one, in which intentions can easily be realized and the only obstacle to a better society is therefore a lack of good intentions. How many times have we all encountered grand solutions to vexing social problems prefaced with the words "All we need to do is . . ."? But social actions have consequences that run far beyond those that can be easily predicted or foreseen. Restricting textile imports into the United States, for example, does, for the present at least, protect the jobs and income of textile producers; that's clear enough. But it takes a tutored eye to notice that this will shift even more income away from other Americans, by raising textile prices, reducing American export opportunities, and in general inhibiting the exploitation of comparative advantage. Again, it is easy to see that rent controls hold down the money payments that tenants must make to landlords. But how many advocates of such controls are aware of the alternative payments that tenants will have to make, of the new forms of discrimination that will replace discrimination on the basis of money price, and of the short- and long-run effects upon the supply of rental housing?

Nonetheless, people easily become impatient with those who warn against the inadvisability of actions that will make matters worse without proposing solutions of their own. And in a society such as ours, accustomed to the almost miraculous accomplishments of science and technology, the demand for "doing something" tends to exceed by a wide margin the supply of genuine solutions to social problems. We have probably erred in assuming that social problems can be handled in the same way that we manage technological problems. We know that conflicting interests create hard problems for social policy makers. We still underestimate the difficulties in the way of bringing about planned social change, largely because we underestimate the complexity of social systems, of the networks of interaction through which behavior is coordinated in a society and people are induced to cooperate in the achievement of their goals.

Economists and the Market System

This relates closely to the accusation that the economic way of thinking contains an implicit bias in favor of capitalism, competition, and free exchange. The accusation has substantial validity. Many economists have, of course, been socialists; many have had serious misgivings about the consequences of unrestricted competition; and economists are by no means unanimously in favor of completely free exchange. But the critics who accuse economics of this kind of ideological bias are really talking about a predisposition of thought; they are not denying any exceptions. And they have a point.

Economics developed in the late eighteenth and early nineteenth centuries largely out of efforts to understand the self-regulating aspects of economic systems. In the face of a widespread belief, amounting almost to a commonsense conviction, that political regulation was indispensable to an adequately functioning economy, economists assumed the task of expounding the alternative thesis. As they examined in ever greater detail and depth the interactions between the innumerable decisions that make up an economic system, they evolved a body of theory stressing the cooperative aspects of free exchange. The economist's way of thinking has tended to reveal the order, the coordination, that lies beneath the seeming chaos of an unplanned and unregulated economy. The elements of conflict, disorder, and disruption that are also found in every economic system have tended to be regarded by the economist more as disturbing factors than as objects of his primary interest.

On top of all this, economic theory often treats proposals for reform of the economic system rather unkindly. It is not that economists are themselves uninterested in reform, much less that they are the paid lackeys of the privileged classes. But economic theory, by revealing the interdependence of decisions, calls attention to the unexamined consequences of proposals for change. "It won't work out that way" is the economist's standard response to many well-intentioned policy proposals. Realism is not necessarily conservatism, but it often looks quite similar. And there is a sense in which knowledge promotes conservatism. Even physicists have been accused of hopeless conservatism by would-be inventors of perpetual-motion machines.

Individualism and Economic Analysis

But perhaps economics is unduly individualistic in its point of view. This is also an accusation sometimes leveled against the economic way of thinking: that it identifies the good with what individuals happen to want. And again, the charge has substantial merit. The fundamental concepts of economics refer to choice, the basis of any economizing activity. And the only choices about which we seem to be able to think and talk meaningfully are the subjective evaluations of individuals.

No one seriously believes that "the good" can be simply identified with "what individuals happen to prefer." But as a working assumption, this may be less dangerous than unexamined concepts of the social welfare, the national interest, or the good of society. The economist is occupationally conditioned to wonder about the composition of such aggregates as "social," "national," and "public." This may lead him to assign too much weight to what individuals happen to prefer; but what is the alternative?

Our choices as individuals are certainly conditioned by our socialization, and no one who has given serious attention to the processes of socialization will deny that our socialization sometimes serves us badly. But the implication we see in all of this is that *economics is not enough.*

Beyond Mere Economics

John Maynard Keynes once proposed a toast to economists, "the keepers of the possibility of civilization." The *possibility* of civilization—that is all. The efficient allocation of resources enlarges the realm of possibility; but it does not by itself guarantee the progress of civilization. A well-coordinated and smoothly functioning economic system gives individuals more opportunity to choose; it does not guarantee that they will choose well. The economic way of thinking, especially in a democracy, is an important preliminary.

Economists are for the most part prepared to admit that the concepts they employ sometimes distort the reality they study. And they are willing to submit their analyses and conclusions to the test of rational criticism. But some point of view is indispensable to any inquiry, in the physical sciences as well as the social sciences. A completely open mind is a completely empty mind, and empty minds learn nothing. If the economic way of thinking sometimes leads to distortions, to misplaced emphasis, or even to outright error, the appropriate corrective is rational criticism. The application of that corrective has frequently altered the conclusions of economic science in the past. It will probably continue to do so in the future.

Index

Sponsoring Editor: Bruce Caldwell
Project Editor: Sara Boyd
Designer: Michael Rogondino
Photographer: Nick Pavloff
Illustrator: Patricia Rogondino
Compositor: Dharma Press